ISBN 978-0-265-18870-5
PIBN 10185434

THE

BIBLICAL REPERTORY

AND

PRINCETON REVIEW.

INDEX VOLUME

FROM

1825 TO 1868.

PHILADELPHIA:

PETER WALKER, 1334 CHESTNUT STREET:

CHAS. SCRIBNER & CO., NEW YORK; REV. A. KENNEDY, LONDON, ONTARIO;
REV. WILLIAM ELDER, ST. JOHN, NEW BRUNSWICK;
REV. ROBERT MURRAY, HALIFAX, N.S.;
AND TRÜBNER & CO., LONDON.

1871.

Printed by ALFRED MARTIEN.

PREFACE.

———◆◆◆———

This volume has been called into existence by the earnest entreaties of the subscribers to the PRINCETON REVIEW, who needed some help to make available to them the valuable treasures in their possession.

Part I. is a RETROSPECT of the period in which the Review has been published, and of the share it has taken in the discussion of the various topics that have agitated the church and the world during the last fifty years. It is substantially a History of the Review, and is contributed by its venerable Editor.

Part II. is an INDEX TO AUTHORS. Like the other great Reviews of the period, the writers contributed to its pages anonymously, and for many years no one kept any account of their labours. Dr. Hope was the first who attempted to ascertain the names of the writers in the early volumes, and he was only partially successful. With the aid of his notes, and the assistance of Dr. John Hall of Trenton, Dr. John C. Backus of Baltimore, and Dr. Samuel D. Alexander of New York, the companions and friends of the Editor and his early coadjutors, the information on this head here collected is as complete as it is possible now to be given. A biographical notice is also given of the writers, as it was thought that many facts concerning them, if not now chronicled, would in a few years pass into oblivion.

Part III. is an ANALYTICAL INDEX to the First Series, by Dr. John Forsyth of Newburgh, N. Y.

This series of four volumes gave the impulse to the study of Biblical Interpretation both in America and in Great Britain. Many of its treatises have been repeatedly reprinted. No four volumes extant contain so much useful matter on the subject, and the Index will add to their usefulness.

Part IV. is an INDEX TO TOPICS discussed in the succeeding Forty volumes. To its preparation Dr. Forsyth has devoted much time and labour, and to it is appended an Index to the Short Notices prepared under his supervision.

It is believed that this volume will be useful to all who have any portion of the work; and will also be a ready guide to any who are seeking information upon the ecclesiastical, political, educational, and religious movements of the church, especially in the first half of this century, whether they possess the volumes of the Review or not.

PETER WALKER.

INDEX

TO THE

PRINCETON REVIEW.

PART I.

RETROSPECT OF THE HISTORY OF THE PRINCETON REVIEW.

THE Journal for many years known as the *Biblical Reper-tory and Princeton Review*, was commenced in 1825. 'The volume for that year bears the title, "Biblical Repertory; a Collection of Tracts in Biblical Literature. By Charles Hodge, Professor of Oriental and Biblical Literature in the Theological Seminary at Princeton, New Jersey." It did not aspire to originality. It purported to be, what the title imports, a repository for tracts on biblical subjects, selected from various sources. It was designed to render accessible to American readers some of the fruits of the mature learning of English and German scholars.

The first four volumes were conducted on this plan. In the fall of 1826 the editor went to Europe, where he remained until the fall of 1828. During his absence the work was under the direction of Professor Robert Patton, at that time con-nected with the College of New Jersey.

In 1829 the character of the work was changed. It was deemed expedient to give it a wider scope, and to include in its contents articles on all subjects suitable for a Theological Quarterly Review. The volume for that year has the title, "Biblical Repertory. A Journal of Biblical Literature and Theological Science; conducted by an Association of Gentle-men. Vol. V. New Series, Vol. I." The volume for 1830 was numbered as the second; thus four years were dropped, and the volume for the present year, instead of being noted as the 45th, is called the 41st.

The Association above mentioned was not defined within very strict limits; nor was it controlled by any special terms of agreement. It consisted of the more frequent contributors to the pages of the Journal, who were willing to assume the responsibility before the public of its character and contents. It included the Professors of the Theological Seminary, and some of the officers of the College. Although the labouring oar was still in one pair of hands, it was of importance that the work had the sanction of a number of gentlemen who had the confidence of the public; and it was a real advantage that all contributions touching delicate or difficult questions were read and canvassed by the Association before being committed to the press.

The work, as its title indicated, had special reference to the department of theology. It was not intended, however, to be limited to that department. Questions of science, philosophy, literature, and history, were considered as legitimately within its sphere. The articles on literary topics, education, and philosophy, from the pens of Dr. Archibald Alexander, and his sons, Dr. J. W. and Dr. J. A. Alexander, and the numerous contributions of Dr. L. H. Atwater on mental and moral science, served greatly to increase the reputation and extend the usefulness of the Journal. The same may be said of the papers on natural and social science contributed by the late Professor Dod, Hon. Chief Justice Lowrie, Hon. Stephen Colwell, of Pennsylvania, and Dr. J. H. McIlvaine, Dr. Stephen Alexander, and others. Another large class of contributions outside of the sphere of theology consists of papers on popular education, of which the late lamented Frederick A. Packard, Esq., of the American Sunday-School Union, was the principal contributor.

To no one are the pages of this *Review* more indebted than to the late Dr. James W. Alexander. His communications were numerous, varied, and always instructive. The articles furnished by him were, for the most part, devoted to historical, literary, and practical subjects; such as his papers on " Pascal's Provincial Letters," 1830; "Life and Times of John Livingston," 1832; "The Religious Condition of Holland," 1833; "Jansenius," 1834; "Monosyllabic Languages of Asia," 1834; "Civilization of India," 1835; "Life of Michael Servetus," and "Religion and Religious Literature of Europe," 1836; "Henry's Life of Calvin," and "Life of Savonarola," 1837; "Expository Preaching," and "Life of Wilberforce," 1838; "French Presbyterianism," and "Macaulay's Essays," 1840; and many others too numerous to mention. With these, however, were other articles, philosophical or theological in their character, as "Systems of Theology," 1832; "Transcendentalism," 1839; "Rauch's Psychology," 1840; "Emmons' Works," 1842; "Kant," 1863; "Metaphysical Theology of the Schoolmen," 1846; "Life of Hegel," 1848; "Immediate Perception," 1859; etc. No one of his associates at all approached him in the facility of production. Some of his most brilliant articles were thrown off almost at a single sitting. We have heard him say, that the only trouble he found in writing was turning the leaves.

The conductors of the *Princeton Review*, however, were Presbyterians. They firmly believed that the system of doctrine contained in the Westminster Confession of Faith, the system of the Reformed Church, and of Augustinians in all ages, is the truth of God revealed for his glory and the salvation of men. They believed that the upholding that system in its integrity, bearing witness to it as the truth of God, and its extension through the world, was the great duty of all those who had experienced its power. They believed, also, that the organization of the Presbyterian Church, its form of government and discipline, was more nearly conformed than any other to the scriptural model, and the best adapted for preserving the purity and developing the life of the Church. It was, therefore, the vindication of that system of truth, and of the principles of that ecclesiastical polity, the conductors of this Journal, from first to last, had constantly in view. In this world, life is a constant struggle against the causes of death. Liberty is maintained only by unsleeping vigilance against the aggressions of power; virtue is, of necessity, in constant antagonism to vice; and truth to error. That a

Journal consecrated to the support of truth should be controversial, is a matter of course; it is a law of its existence, the
condition of its usefulness. The Bible is the most controversial of books. It is a protest against sin and error from beginning to end. To object to controversy, therefore, is to object
to what is, in this world, the necessary condition of life. It
is, consequently, no just ground of reproach to this Journal,
that it has been engaged in controversy during the whole
course of its existence. If it has always contended for the
true and the right, and done this with due humility and
charity, it has fulfilled its destiny. That it has often failed—
at least in spirit and manner—may, and we fear must, be conceded. All such failures are to its surviving conductors matters of regret; but they can honestly say they have ever
laboured to support the truth of God and to promote the
interests of his kingdom to the best of their understanding
and ability.

Voluntary Societies and Church Boards.

The first controversy in which the *Repertory* took an active
part concerned the Education question. In 1829 the General
Assembly had reorganized the Board of Education, and called
upon the churches to sustain it in providing for the expenses
of candidates for the ministry in their preparatory studies.
At the same time the American Education Society, a voluntary association, having its origin in New England, and its
chief seat of operations in Boston, Massachusetts, offered to
grant its aid to all suitable candidates for the sacred office in
any part of the United States. Branch Societies were organized in different parts of the country, and a large number of
Presbyterian churches contributed to its funds in preference
to the treasury of our own Board. In the July number of the
volume for 1829, the late Dr. Carnahan, President of the College of New Jersey, published an article on "The General
Assembly's Board of Education and the American Education
Society," in which the objections to the plan of the American
Society were briefly and clearly stated. This called forth a
long communication from Professor Stuart of Andover, in
reply. Professor Stuart's article was printed at length in our

October number, with a rejoinder from the conductors of this Review. A separate edition of Professor Stuart's article, with a postscript of sixteen pages, being published, that postscript was reviewed in our number for January, 1830. This ended the discussion so far as this Journal was concerned.

In this controversy the general question of Ecclesiastical Boards and Voluntary Societies was not brought under discussion. The simple point was the wisdom, propriety, and safety of the plan adopted by the American Society. That Society not only required its beneficiaries to make a quarterly report, detailing how the amount they had received had been expended, and what each had received from other sources, but regarded its contributions as loans. All the candidates under their care were required to give their notes for the sums received, payable in one, two, and three years after the close of their preparatory studies, with interest after the same had become due. All the candidates for the ministry were thus placed in the relation of debtors to the Society, and must enter on their work burdened by this load of pecuniary obligation.

To this it was objected, 1. That the whole plan proceeded on a wrong principle. It assumed that the candidates had no right to the aid afforded; that it was a pure gratuity, which the donors, if they pleased, were authorized to demand should be refunded. This placed the candidates in the position of "charity scholars." Being so regarded by their patrons, they were so regarded by their associates and by themselves. This was an injustice and an injury. This Journal took the ground, "That whenever any man devotes his whole time and talents to the service of any community, *at its request*, it is obligatory on that community to provide for his support." The recognition of this principle changes the whole status of the candidate. He ceases to be regarded as an object of charity. All ground for the minute inspection into his receipts and expenditures is done away with. He is regarded as a man receiving no more than he is entitled to, and for which he renders a full return. This principle, it was contended, was scriptural, lying at the foundation of the institutions and commands of the Bible. It was, moreover, evidently just and reasonable; and was acted on by all civilized governments in the education of young men designed for the public service, especially in the navy and army.)

2. It was objected to the plan of the American Society that it was unjust to bring young men into the ministry burdened with debt. The salaries of young ministers are very seldom more than sufficient for their support, and in the majority of cases utterly inadequate for that end. If, in addition to providing for their necessities under these circumstances, they had to pay the money advanced for their education, they could not fail to be painfully embarrassed and harassed. To be in debt is to be in a state of depressing anxiety.

3. The Scriptures say, "The borrower is servant to the lender." If the plan of the American Society had been fully carried out, the great body of the younger ministry in the Congregational and Presbyterian Churches would have been in this state of bondage to that Society. Every one knows that virtually and effectively the power of such societies is in the hands of the executive committee. Thus, some half-dozen men, with no official relation to our church, would have this controlling power over our ministers. This was evidently intolerable. The objection was not that the power had been abused, but that it existed. The power in question "is a power of dictating to a large proportion of the pious youth of the country in what academy, college, or theological seminary they shall pursue their studies. It is the power of deciding under what theological influences our future ministers are to be formed. It is the power of holding and influencing these ministers as bondmen when they come out into the church."

4. This Society was in a great measure independent of public opinion; first, because it elected its own members; and, secondly, because its income, so far as derived from the payment of the notes given by its beneficiaries, was not derived from the churches.

The General Assembly's plan of operation was not subject to these objections. 1. Because the Assembly did not elect its own members, but was renewed every year by the Presbyteries. 2. Because its Board was not the creditor of those aided by its funds. 3. Because the candidates for the ministry were not under its control.

Much greater interest attached to the controversy respecting the conduct of the work of Missions, Foreign and Domestic. The General Assembly, in 1828, reorganized its Board of Domestic Missions. The American Home Missionary Society was at that time in operation, and rapidly increasing in influence. At first, it seemed to be hoped that the two organizations might operate harmoniously over the same field. The General Assembly, as did Dr. Green, Dr. Philips, and other leading friends of the Assembly's Board, expressed their cordial willingness that all Presbyterians should be left to their unbiassed choice as to which organization they should support. But it was soon found that in the existing state of the church harmonious action was impossible. There were so many interests at stake; so many causes of alienation between what became known as the Old and New-school parties, that the Assembly's Board under the control of the one, and the American Society under the control of the other, came into constant and painful collision. This of necessity gave rise to serious conflicts in the General Assembly. The friends of the American Society took the ground that the Assembly had no right to conduct the work of missions; that it was incompetent for that purpose; that voluntary associations were more trustworthy, more efficient, and more healthful; that two organizations for the same purpose were not only unnecessary, but injurious. They endeavoured, therefore, in every way to embarrass the Assembly's Board. In the Assembly of 1836 they nominated as members of that Board men known to be hostile to its very existence, and secured a hundred and twenty-five votes in their favour. In the same Assembly they succeeded in preventing the Assembly establishing a Board of Foreign Missions. One of the reasons most strenuously urged against the appointment of such a Board, was, that the Assembly had no right to conduct such operations. On this point Dr. James Hoge, one of the wisest and most moderate ministers of our church, said: "As the subject has been proposed in other forms, I have always objected. But the question is now brought before us in a new form, and is to be decided on the naked ground of the power and rights of the Assembly to conduct missions. And on this ground I cannot abandon it while I love the faith and order of the Presbyterian Church." He further said, that if the majority pursued the course which they did actually take, "it would convulse the church to its very centre." And so it did. The action of the Assembly of 1836 in reference to matters of doctrine and to the Boards of the church, was the proximate cause of the disruption which occurred in the following year.

The question of Voluntary Societies was not an isolated one. Its decision did not turn upon the point, which mode of conducting benevolent operations was in itself to be preferred. It was far more comprehensive. The friends of the Assembly's Board not only contended that the Assembly had the right to conduct the work of Missions, Foreign and Domestic, but that it was highly expedient that that work should be under the control of the constituted authorities of the church; that the selection, sending forth, and locating ministers, was properly an ecclesiastical function; and that it was to the last degree unreasonable and dangerous that that work should be committed to a society meeting annually for a few hours, composed of all who choose to subscribe to its funds (as was the fact with the American Home Missionary Society), and to a large degree controlled by Congregationalists, hostile on principle to our polity, if not to our doctrines. Besides the objections founded on principle, there were others not less cogent founded on the action of the American Home Society. It was regarded as a great party engine, devoting, apparently, its immense influence to revolutionizing the church. It sent out men educated in New England holding sentiments condemned not only by Old-school Presbyterians, but by the Woods, Tylers, Nettletons, of New England, and by such men as Drs. Richards, Fisher, and Griffin, of our own church. Its friends and beneficiaries voted *en masse* in the General Assembly against the condemnation of those sentiments, and in favour of allowing men never ordained as elders, sitting and voting in our highest judicatories. It is no wonder, therefore, that this controversy excited so much feeling. Throughout the struggle this Journal sided uniformly and earnestly with the friends of the Assembly's Boards. We refer especially to the numbers for July 1836, January 1837; and as to the controversy in another form, to those of July 1854, and July 1860.

Prelatical Controversy.

Attention from time to time was given to the prelatical controversy in various forms. Presbyterian principles were defended by Dr. Miller in his review of "Cooke on the Invalidity of Presbyterian Ordination," 1830; of "Brittan on Episcopacy," 1833; and of "Episcopacy Tested by Scripture," 1835. Also by Dr. J. Addison Alexander in numerous contributions, among which are the following: "Colton's Reasons for Preferring Episcopacy," 1836; "A Plea for Bishops," 1841; "Smyth's Lectures on Apostolical Succession," 1842; "Barnes on the Apostolic Church," and "Smyth on Presbytery and Prelacy," 1843; and the admirable papers on "The Eldership," "The Apostolic Succession," 1847; "The Official Powers of the Primitive Presbyters," "The Apostleship a Temporary Office," 1849; "The True Test of an Apostolical Ministry," 1851. Of these papers the least that can be said is, that they are unsurpassed in argument and style by any contributions to the pages of this Journal.

To the same head belong the articles on "The Oxford Tracts," 1838; "The Church of England and Presbyterian Orders," 1854; "The Church Review on the Permanency of the Apostolic Office," 1856, and the series of articles on the Church, viz., "Theories of the Church," a review of "The Unity of the Church, by Archdeacon Manning," 1846; "The Idea of the Church," "Visibility of the Church," 1853; "The Perpetuity of the Church," 1856.

Doctrines.

It is with unfeigned and humble gratitude to God that the conductors of the *Biblical Repertory and Princeton Review* can look over the comparatively long period of its existence with the conviction that from first to last it has been devoted to the vindication of that system of doctrine contained in our standards, and which, as all Presbyterians believe, is taught in the word of God. (No article opposed to that system has ever appeared on its pages.) Many of the distinctive doctrines

2

of the Reformed Churches have of late years been matters of discussion in different parts of the country, and especially within the bounds of our own denomination. As early in the history of this Journal as 1830, Dr. Archibald Alexander published two articles, one on "The Early History of Pelagianism," the other on "The Doctrine of the Church on Original Sin;" and, in 1832, another on "The Articles of the Synod of Dort." To the first of these the *Christian Spectator* for June 1830, published a critique, over the signature "A Protestant" (Prof. Stuart), which was reviewed in our October number for the same year. The discussion was continued in the *Spectator* in the number for March 1831, which contained two articles in reply to our review, one from "Protestant," and the other from the editors, continued and completed in the June number. Of these articles this Journal contained a review, published in October of the same year. See also the article entitled "Testimonies on the Doctrine of Imputation," 1839, of which twenty-four pages are filled with quotations from the Protestant Confessions and theologians in support of that doctrine. The same subject was discussed in the review of Prof. Stuart's Commentary on the Epistle to the Romans, 1833, and of Mr. Barnes' Commentary on the same epistle, 1835, and incidentally in several other communications in subsequent years.

At the same time the doctrine of Regeneration was under discussion. It was maintained, by some prominent theologians among us, that regeneration was the sinner's own act; that it consisted in his making for himself "a new heart." What that was, was differently explained. According to some, it was loving God; according to others, it was the purpose to seek happiness in God instead of in the world; according to others, it was the purpose to seek the happiness of the universe. According to all the new views, man was active in regeneration. The idea of passivity, as it was called, was held up to ridicule. The old doctrine, common to all Christian churches, that regeneration is the act of God; that man is the subject, and not the agent of the change; and that it consists in the quickening of the soul, or imparting to it a new principle of life, a new disposition, or, in the old scholastic language, "a new habit of grace," was vindicated in the article on "Regeneration, and the Manner of its Occurrence." To this article Dr. Samuel H. Cox replied at length in our number for October, 1831, which number contained our answer to his "Remarks."

The controversies which agitated our Church during the last thirty or forty years had, however, reference mainly to the nature of sin; the nature of Adam's sin; the effect of that sin on his posterity; the relation between him and his descendants; the nature of the hereditary depravity (or original sin); the inability of sinners; the work of the Holy Spirit in regeneration and sanctification of the soul. To the discussion of these subjects a large portion of the pages of this Journal, from first to last, has been devoted. And in reference to all of them it has been the honest endeavour of its conductors to exhibit and defend the doctrines of our standards, under the abiding conviction that they are the doctrines of the word of God. They have advanced no new theories, and have never aimed at originality. Whether it be a ground of reproach or of approbation, it is believed to be true, that an original idea in theology is not to be found on the pages of the *Biblical Repertory and Princeton Review* from the beginning until now. The phrase "Princeton Theology," therefore, is without distinctive meaning.

As the controversy concerning sin and grace assumed so many forms, and was so varied and long-continued, we cannot pretend to refer to the particular articles in which these doctrines are discussed. Besides the papers on the history of Pelagianism, on original sin, &c., above referred to, Dr. Archibald Alexander contributed an article in 1831, on "That Inability under which the sinner labours, and whether it furnishes any excuse for his neglect of duty;" another in 1833, entitled, "Melancthon on Sin," and in 1835, a review of an "Essay on Native Depravity, by Leonard Woods, D. D." On page 549 of that review Dr. Alexander says, "We are candidly of the opinion, that the integrity of the doctrine of original sin, as held by Augustine and the Reformers, is not affected by the peculiarities of the Andover school." This was said of the theology of that school as represented by Dr. Woods in 1835.

Again, Dr. Alexander says, "Even on the subject of imputation, Dr. Woods concedes so much, and expresses himself so modestly and candidly, that, although his views do not entirely come up to our standards, we should not have felt it necessary, in this review, to make a single remark. But the sentiments expressed in the eighth chapter are so foreign from our notions, that we cannot pass them by without a few remarks, which we hope to make in the same spirit of kindness in which Dr. Woods writes." In the eighth chapter of his Essay, Dr. Woods teaches that infants are not only born in a state of sin, but that they commit actual sins from the moment of birth. This Dr. Alexander considered impossible, as moral action implies the action of reason and conscience, a knowledge of law, and that certain acts are sinful. This Dr. Alexander affirms cannot be predicated of infants.

We quote these passages because they go to show not only the status of this *Review*, but also of our church generally, in relation to this subject. For more than sixty years certain differences of opinion had prevailed in our body on the nature of the relation between Adam and his posterity, the nature of original sin, of the sinner's inability, of the influence of the Holy Spirit in regeneration and sanctification. But so long as all parties held that men are born into the world, since the fall, in a state of sin and condemnation; that this fact was due to the sin of Adam; that men are dependent on the Holy Spirit for their regeneration; and that it is due to the sovereign and supernatural interposition of the Spirit that one man is converted and not another, the authority of the church in the exercise of discipline was not invoked. But when it was taught that all sin consists in the voluntary violation of known law; that men, since the fall, are not born in a state of sin; that they are not chargeable with guilt or moral pollution until, having arrived at the years of discretion, they deliberately violate the divine law; that all men have plenary ability to avoid all sin; and, having sinned, to return unto God and do all that he requires at their hands; that God cannot prevent sin, or the present amount of sin, in a moral system; that he cannot effectually control the acts of free agents without destroying their liberty; that in conversion it is man, and not God, who determines who do, and who do not, turn unto God; that election is founded on the foresight of this self-determined repentance on the part of the sinner;—when these doctrines came to be taught in our church, it was seen that the vital principles, not of the Reformed faith only, but even of Catholic Christianity, were involved.

It is to the discussion of these doctrines that a large class of articles in this *Review* for the last thirty years was devoted. It is unnecessary, and would be tedious, to refer particularly to these articles. Few only need be specified. The doctrinal articles contributed by Dr. Archibald Alexander already referred to, bring several of these topics under examination. The same is true of the articles on regeneration, above-mentioned, and of those entitled "The New Divinity tried," 1832, "Finney's Lectures on Theology," 1847; and the articles published in 1850 and 1851, on Professor Park's doctrine of the Theology of the Intellect as distinguished from the Theology of the Heart; the review of Dr. Edward Beecher's "Great Conflict," 1851, and of Dr. Samuel J. Baird's work on "The First and Second Adam," 1860. To these are to be added the numerous able articles from the pen of Dr. Atwater, philosophical and doctrinal, of which the following are a part: "The Power of Contrary Choice," 1840; "Doctrinal and Ecclesiastical Conflicts in Connecticut," 1853; "Modern Explanations of the Doctrine of Inability," 1854; "Old Orthodoxy, New Divinity, and Unitarianism," 1857; "Jonathan Edwards and the Successive Forms of New Divinity;" "Dr. Taylor's Lectures on the Moral Government of God," 1859; "Dr. George Duffield on the Doctrines of New-school Presbyterians;" 1867; "Prof. Fisher on the *Princeton Review* and Dr. Taylor's Theology," 1868.

The doctrine concerning the Person and Work of Christ has in different forms come up for discussion. To this head are to be referred the following papers from the pen of Dr. Archibald Alexander: "John Pye Smith's Discourses on the Priesthood and Sacrifice of Christ, and on Atonement and Redemption," 1829; "Symington on the Atonement," 1836; "Justification by Faith," 1840. To the same head belong, "The Review of Dr. Beman on the Atonement," 1845; "Bushnell's

Discourses on God in Christ," 1849; and "Bushnell on Vicarious Sacrifice," 1866; and numerous papers in which this subject is included in the discussion of the faith of the Reformed Churches.

As the modern German philosophy and theology have exerted great influence in America as well as in Europe, no Review in this country, devoted to theological literature, could fail of being called upon to discuss the principles which these new theories involved so far as they affected the integrity of Christian doctrine. The first article bearing on this subject in our pages was that on "Transcendentalism" in 1839. That article was a review of Cousin's Psychology translated from the French, with an Introduction and Notes, by Rev. C. S. Henry, D. D. The first twenty-four pages of that article, from the pen of Dr. James W. Alexander, presented a general view of the recent German philosophy; the remaining forty pages, by Prof. Dod, were devoted to an examination of Cousin's system. Few articles ever published in the *Princeton Review* have attracted such general public attention. It was reprinted both in this country and in Europe. Prof. C. S. Henry, in the preface to a subsequent edition of his work, animadverted with great severity on Prof. Dod's critique. It was in 1856, more than ten years after the death of Prof. Dod, that the most severe attack upon his article was made. This called forth a reply intended to vindicate his memory, by showing that the exhibition which he had made of Cousin's philosophy was perfectly correct. That reply fills fifty-four pages of the April number of the volume for 1856.

To the same class of articles belongs the review of Dr. J. W. Nevin's work on "The Mystical Presence," 1848. The first part of that review is devoted to an examination of the true doctrine of the Reformed Churches on the Lord's Supper; and the last twenty pages to an examination of Dr. Nevin's own doctrine, which we hold to be the application of the modern German philosophy to the explanation and subversion of Christian doctrines. The review of Dr. Schaff's Apostolic Church, 1854, is a discussion of the doctrine of "historical development," involving another phase of the German philosophy. The article in answer to the question, "What is

Christianity?" 1860, belongs to the same class. A certain class of modern theologians deny that Christianity either is, or involves a system of doctrine. It is a life; and that life is the theanthropic, but, at the same time, the purely human life of Christ, developed by a natural process in the church, as the life of Adam was devoloped in his race; so that redemption, (atonement and justification, as well as sanctification,) is purely subjective.

The articles on the Positive Philosophy, the one by Dr. Atwater, in 1856; the other by Dr. Shields, in 1858, were also designed to vindicate the fundamental principles of religion from the assaults of modern speculations.

Slavery.

The conductors of this *Review* have always endeavoured to adhere faithfully to the principle that the Scriptures are the only infallible rule of faith and practice. Therefore, when any matter, either of doctrine or morals, came under discussion, the question with them was, What saith the Lord? Nothing that the Bible pronounces true can be false; nothing that it declares to be false can be true; nothing is obligatory on the conscience but what it enjoins; nothing can be sin, but what it condemns. If, therefore, the Scriptures under the old dispensation permitted men to hold slaves, and if the New Testament nowhere condemns slaveholding, but prescribes the relative duties of masters and slaves, then to pronounce slaveholding to be in itself sinful, is contrary to the Scriptures. In like manner, if the Bible nowhere condemns the use of intoxicating liquors as a beverage, if our Lord himself drank wine, then to say that all use of intoxicating liquor as a beverage is sin, is only one of the many forms of the infidelity of benevolence. It is as much contrary to our allegiance to the Bible, to make our own notions of right and wrong the rule of duty, as to make our own reason the rule of faith.

It is well known that both slavery and intemperance were matters of national importance, and awakened earnest and continued controversy. As to slavery, so far as the North was concerned, it was universally regarded as an evil, which ought in some way to be brought to an end. The difference of opinion related to the means by which that end was to be accomplished. The Abolitionists, so called, maintained that all slavehood, as inconsistent with the inalienable rights of man, and with the law of love, is sinful; and, therefore, that immediate and universal emancipation was an imperative duty. Another necessary consequence of the assumption that "slaveholding is a heinous crime against God and man," is that no slaveholder could properly be admitted to Christian fellowship. As the people of God, under the old dispensation, were allowed by law to purchase slaves, and to hold those of heathen origin in perpetual bondage; as slavery existed among the Romans, Greeks, and Jews during the apostolic age; as neither Christ nor his apostles denounced slaveholding as a crime, nor taught that emancipation was an imperative and immediate duty; and as beyond doubt the apostles admitted slaveholders to the communion of the Christian church, the conductors of this *Review*, from first to last, maintained that the doctrine that slaveholding is in itself a crime, is anti-scriptural and subversive of the authority of the word of God. The articles specially devoted to this subject, are those on "Slavery," 1836; on "Abolitionism," 1844; on "Emancipation," 1849; besides incidental references in other articles, particularly in those published during the late war.

The principles maintained in those articles are, 1. That slavery is, as defined by Paley, "An obligation to labour for the benefit of the master, without the contract or consent of the servant." It involves the deprivation of personal liberty, obligation of service at the discretion of another, and the transferable character of the authority and claim of service of the master. 2. The slave, according to this definition, is the property of his master. But property is merely the right of possession and use. The rights therein involved differ according to the nature of the thing possessed. A man has the right of property in his wife, his children, in his houses and land, his cattle, his servants. Property in a horse does not involve the right to treat it as a log of wood; and property in man does not involve the right to use him as a brute. He can be used only as a rational, moral, and immortal creature can, according to the divine law, be rightfully used. All the rights conceded to him by the word of God must be faithfully regarded. 3. The master, therefore, is bound to provide for the intellectual and moral education of the slave. Every human being has the right to be taught to read the word of God, and learn the way of salvation for himself. Secondly, the master is bound to respect the conjugal rights of his slaves; and this forbids the separation of husbands and wives. Thirdly, he is bound to respect their parental rights, and this prevents the separation of parents and their minor children. Fourthly, he is bound to give them a fair compensation for their labour, which supposes the right, on the part of the slave, to hold property. Any laws inconsistent with these principles are unscriptural and unjust, and ought to be immediately abrogated. 4. The consequences of acting on these principles would be the speedy and peaceful abrogation of slavery, and the gradual elevation of the slaves to all the rights of free citizens. This is the ground taken in the article of 1836. In the conclusion of that article, it is said, "It may be objected that if the slaves are allowed so to improve as to become free men, the next step in their progress is that they will become citizens. We admit that it is so. The feudal serf first became a tenant, then a proprietor invested with political power. This is the natural progress of society, and it should be allowed freely to expand itself, or it will work its own destruction."

The great popular mistake on this subject—a mistake which produced incalculable evil—was confounding slaveholding with slave laws. Because a despotic monarch may make unjust and cruel laws, in order to keep his people in a state of degradation, that his power may be secured and rendered permanent, it does not follow that an absolute monarchy is "a heinous crime in the sight of God and man." In like manner, because the laws of a slaveholding state may be unscriptural and wicked, it does not follow that slaveholding is itself sinful.

Intemperance.

That drunkenness, or the excessive use of intoxicating liquors, is a soul-destroying sin, and one of the most prolific sources of misery and crime; and consequently, that it is the duty of every man to do everything, in itself right, which may

3

be in his power to counteract this great evil, is of course universally admitted. It is also generally conceded that voluntary
and total abstinence from the use of all intoxicating liquor, may
under some circumstances be expedient and obligatory. And
it is moreover generally admitted, that a public pledge of such
abstinence, and the formation of societies to secure such pledges
from all classes of the people, as a means of influencing the
public mind, are both allowable and useful. Against these
principles and measures no objection was made on the pages of
this *Review*. Almost all its conductors became members of
such societies. But when the friends of temperance took the
ground that all use of intoxicating liquor as a beverage is
sinful, and a just bar to Christian communion, they were constrained to enter their solemn protest against both of those
propositions, as unscriptural and fraught with great evils.

The ground taken in this *Review*, on this subject, was,

First. That the moderate use of intoxicating liquors as
a beverage is not sinful. 1st. Because such use is nowhere
forbidden in the word of God. 2d. Because such use is everywhere sanctioned in the Scriptures, not only by its being un-
censured, but by its being forbidden to the priests only when
engaged in the service of the altar, which implies that it was
lawful on other occasions, just as its prohibition to the Naza-
rites implies it was lawful for other men; by the increase of
corn and wine being pronounced a blessing; by the use of wine
being introduced in such sacred services as the Passover and
the Lord's Supper; and finally, because our Lord drank
and made wine.

Second. It was conceded that the use of a thing, lawful in
itself, may become wrong, when such use causes others to
offend. As Paul exhorts the Corinthians not to act unchari-
tably by such an use of meat as tended to lead their brethren
into sin; and avows his own purpose not to eat meat while the
world standeth, if meat make my brother to offend.

Third. The right to judge, whether the law of love, or expediency, renders a particular course of conduct obligatory, every
one must decide for himself. No one has the right to decide
for him. "Let not him that eateth despise him that eateth
not; and let not him which eateth not, judge him that eateth:

for God hath received him. ⸱ Who art thou that judgest another man's servant? to his own master he standeth or falleth." Rom. xiv. 3–4.

Fourth. Nothing which is matter of expediency; which is r ght or wrong according to circumstances, can be made 'a matter of universal or permanent obligation, or term of Christian fellowship. This common sense and the apostle Paul expressly forbid. He circumcised Timothy in Asia Minor, but positively refused to allow Titus to be circumcised in Jerusalem. (Dr. Archibald Alexander, as a general rule, never drank wine; but when the use of wine came to be pronounced sinful, he would sometimes, in company, take a glass for conscience' sake, and in so doing, we doubt not, he did nobly right.)

Fifth. For conventions or ecclesiastical bodies to pronounce that to be sin which the Bible does not condemn, or to make that a condition of Christian communion which Christ has not enjoined, is an usurpation, which every man, by his allegiance to God, is bound to resist.

The most elaborate discussion of this subject to be found in our pages, is the able review by the Rev. John Maclean, D. D., of two Essays, the one entitled Bacchus, the other, Anti-Bacchus, in the volume for 1841.

The Disruption of the Church in 1837—1838.

In all the controversies culminating in the division of the church in 1837—38, the conductors of this *Review* were in entire sympathy with the Old-school party. They sided with them as to the right, and, under existing circumstances, the duty, of the church, to conduct the work of education and foreign and domestic missions by ecclesiastical boards, instead of voluntary, independent societies. They agreed with that party on all doctrinal questions in dispute; and as to the obligation to enforce conformity to our Confession of Faith on the part of ministers and teachers of theology under our jurisdiction. They were so unfortunate, however, as to differ from many, and apparently, from a majority of their Old-school brethren, as to the wisdom of the measures adopted for securing a common object. In our number for January 1837, it is said, " Our position we feel to be difficult and delicate. On the one hand, we respect and love the great mass of our Old-school brethren; we believe them to constitute the bone and sinews of the Presbyterian Church; we agree with them in doctrine; we sympathize with them in their disapprobation and distrust of the spirit and conduct of the leaders of the opposite party; and we harmonize with them in all the great leading principles of ecclesiastical policy, though we differ from a portion of them, how large or how small that portion may be we cannot tell, as to the propriety and wisdom of some particular measures. They have the right to cherish and express their opinions, and to endeavour to enforce them on others by argument and persuasion; and so have we. They, we verily believe, have no selfish end in view. We are knowingly operating under stress of conscience, against all our own interests, so far as they are not involved in the interests of the church of God."

The first point of difference related to the Act and Testimony, and the measures therewith connected.   \

Such departures from the standards of the church in matters of doctrine and order; such diversity of opinion as to ecclesiastical Boards and voluntary Societies; such alienation of feeling and agitating controversy, had for years disturbed the peace and impaired the efficiency of the church, as to produce a state of things which on all sides was felt to be intolerable. With the view to reform these evils, and secure the peace and purity of the church, a meeting of ministers and elders was held in Philadelphia, May 26th, 1834. At that meeting it was determined to issue an Act and Testimony, setting forth the evils under which the church was labouring, and proposing means of redress. This document was originally signed by thirty-seven ministers and twenty-seven elders. It was sent forth among the churches, and all the friends of sound doctrine and of Presbyterian order were exhorted to sign it. "We recommend," say the original signers, "all ministers, elders, Church Sessions, Presbyteries, and Synods, who approve of this Act and Testimony, to give their public adherence thereto, in such manner as they shall prefer, and communicate their names, and when a church court, a copy of their adhering act." It was further recommended, that on the second Thursday of May 1835, a Convention be held in the city of Pittsburgh, (where the General Assembly was to meet), to be composed of two delegates, a minister and ruling elder from each Presbytery, or from the minority of any Presbytery, who may concur in the sentiments of this Act and Testimony, to deliberate and consult on the present state of the church, and to adopt such measures as may be best suited to restore her prostrated standards."

Many Old-school men, as zealous as any others, could not sign this document. They did not object to it as a testimony against false doctrine; nor as a means for arousing the attention of the church; nor as designed to concentrate the energies of its sounder members for the reform of existing evils, but, 1. Because it contained assertions as to matters of fact and expressions of opinion, (not however as to matters of doctrine), in which they could not conscientiously concur. 2. Because it operated as a new, unauthorized, and invidious test of orthodoxy and fidelity. Those who did not sign it were looked upon as timid and recreant. The editor of the *Presbyterian*, (Aug. 21, 1834), said, "We verily believe that every orthodox minister and elder, who refuses his signature under existing circumstances, will throw his weight into the opposite scale, and strengthen the hopes, and confirm the confidence of those who aim to revolutionize the church." 3. Because its obvious tendency, and, as the event proved, its actual effect, was to divide, instead of uniting, the friends of orthodoxy and order. The document was never signed by a moiety of the Old-school body. 4. Because the issuing a document of this kind, calling for the signatures of all sound men, who by their delegates were to meet in convention, and prepare for further action, was an extra-constitutional and revolutionary measure, which many good and true men could not approve. They believed that when evils exist in any organized community, civil or ecclesiastical, redress should be sought in the regular exercise of the constitution and laws, unless the evils be such as justify revolution. 5. Because, from the natural tendency of the measures adopted, and from the open avowal of some of the leaders in this movement, it was believed that if the party represented by the Act and Testimony did not gain ascendency in the church, the result would be secession and schism. There were, however, many who believed that secession, under the circumstances, would be a violation of principles and a breach of trust. They, therefore, stood aloof, and abstained from taking part in measures of which, as it seemed to them, schism was the natural consequence, if not the intention. They held that so long as the standards of the church were unaltered, and its ministers were not called upon to profess what they did not believe, or prevented preaching what they believed to be true, or required to do what their conscience condemned, to withdraw from the church was the crime of schism, which the Scriptures so expressly forbid. Moreover, they regarded the funds, the institutions, and influence of the church, as a trust committed to their care, which they were not authorized to throw up, or to leave in the hands of those whom they regarded as likely to abuse or pervert it. To abandon the church whenever an adverse majority gained ascendency for a time in its administration, would lead to never-ending divisions and incalculable evils. Many of the signers of the Act and Testimony disclaimed any intention to secede from the church; but others, among whom was the venerable Dr. Green, openly declared that such was their purpose. Happily the matter was not brought to that issue. The reform of the church was effected without that sacrifice. Candid men, we think, will admit that the above-mentioned reasons are sufficient to justify the course of those who dissented from the Act and Testimony movement. Their conduct, at least, can be accounted for on other grounds than those of faint-heartedness or unfaithfulness.

The second point on which Old-school men were divided, was, the proper grounds of ecclesiastical discipline. Our ministers and elders are required to adopt the Confession of Faith as containing the system of doctrine taught in the Holy Scriptures. No doctrine, therefore, consistent with the integrity of that system is the proper ground of discipline. It is not enough that a doctrine be erroneous, or that it be dangerous in its tendency; if it be not subversive of one or more of the constituent elements of the Reformed faith, it is not incompatible with the honest adoption of our Confession. It cannot be denied that ever since the Reformation, more or less diversity in the statement and explanation of the doctrines of Calvinism has prevailed in the Reformed Churches. It is equally notorious that for fifty or sixty years such diversities have existed and been tolerated in our own church; nay, that they still exist, and are avowed by Old-school men. If a man holds that all mankind, since the fall of Adam, and in consequence of his sin, are born in a state of condemnation and sin, whether he accounts for that fact on the ground of immediate or mediate imputation, or on the realistic theory, he was regarded as within the integrity of the system. In like manner, if he admitted the sinner's inability, it was not considered as a proper ground of discipline that he regarded that inability as moral, instead of natural as well as moral. If he taught that the work of Christ was a real satisfaction to the justice of God, it was not made a breaking point, whether he said it was designed exclusively for the elect, or for all mankind. If regeneration was referred to the supernatural and almighty power of the Holy Spirit, and election to eternal life to the sovereign grace of God, the integrity of that doctrine, as presented in our standards, was secured. If justification was regarded as a forensic or judicial act of God, declaring the sinner just, on the ground of the righteousness of Christ, and not because of anything done or experienced by the sinner himself, then the essentials of that cardinal doctrine were retained.

We do not say that the diversities above referred to are unimportant. We regard many of them as of great importance. All we say is, that they have existed, and been tolerated in the purest Calvinistic churches, our own among the rest.

But within the last forty years other doctrines came to be avowed. Men came to teach that mankind are not born in a state of sin and condemnation; that no man is chargeable with either guilt or sin until he deliberately violates the known law of God; that sinners have plenary ability to do all that God requires of them; that regeneration is the sinner's own act; that God cannot certainly control the acts of free agents so as to prevent all sin, or the present amount of sin in a moral system; that the work of Christ is no proper satisfaction to Divine justice, but simply symbolical or didactic, designed to produce a moral impression on intelligent agents; that justification is not judicial, but involves a setting aside of the law, as when the Executive remits the penalty incurred by a criminal. These latter class of doctrines were regarded as entirely inconsistent with the "system of doctrine" taught in our Confession of Faith. In the General Assembly of 1868 a protest was presented against the adoption of the plan of union then before the churches, urging, as an argument against the union, the alleged fact that such doctrines were tolerated in the other branch of the Presbyterian Church. The majority of the Assembly, in their answer to that protest, denied that allegation. They pronounced it to be incredible, on the ground that such doctrines were so obviously subversive of our whole system, that no church professing to be Calvinistic could tolerate them within their borders.

When, in 1830, and the years immediately following, church-discipline was invoked to arrest the progress of error, the Presbytery of Philadelphia included among the doctrines to be condemned, those included in the first, as well as those belonging to the second of the classes above mentioned. This was objected to by a large class of Old-school men, and by the conductors of this *Review* among the number: 1. Because, if the errors in question do not affect the integrity of the system, they were not the proper grounds of discipline. One of these doctrines was, that "faith is an act, and not a principle." But surely a man may hold that opinion, and yet be a Calvinist. When we are commanded to believe, we are commanded to act. Saving faith is the act "of receiving and resting on Christ alone for salvation, as he is offered to us in the gospel." It may be called a principle, as the abiding purpose of a man to serve his country, is, for him, a principle of action. Spiritual life, as imparted in the soul at regeneration, is a principle, manifesting itself in all holy acts and states; but we cannot see the necessity for assuming a separate principle for all holy exercises—a principle of repentance, a principle of faith, of hope, of love, and so on. However this may be, it must be admitted that this was not an adequate ground for ecclesiastical discipline.

The immediate imputation of Adam's sin we regard as a very important doctrine; not so much on its own account as on account of the principle of representative accountability on which it is founded, and which those who deny the doctrine are wont to reject. But that principle runs through the whole Bible, and is involved in the vital doctrines of atonement and justification. It is the ground on which God has administered his providence from the beginning. Nevertheless, it is notorious that the doctrine of immediate imputation has not been considered by our church as essential to the integrity of the Calvinistic system. This is plain, because it has been, and still is, openly denied with impunity by men of the highest standing in the church.

2. It was considered unreasonable and unfair to condemn one man for errors which had been, and continued to be, tolerated in others.

3. This course was deemed unwise, because it could not fail to embarrass the administration of discipline, and to divide the friends of truth and order in the church. It was impossible that they could be brought with unanimity to concur in sustaining charges so heterogeneous, embracing doctrinal statements with which only a small minority of the church could agree. We are constrained to say, with great respect for the Presbytery of Philadelphia, that the censure which that body pronounced in 1830, on the sermon entitled "The Way of Salvation," contains doctrinal principles which we do not know a single minister in the Presbyterian Church who is willing to adopt. It makes the penal character of the sufferings of Christ to depend on their nature and intensity, and not on the design for which they were inflicted. Any suffering inflicted for the satisfaction of law and justice, is punishment; and no suffering, no matter what its nature or intensity, is penal, unless inflicted for that purpose. Christ did not suffer the penalty of the law, because his sufferings were equal to the pains the redeemed would have endured throughout eternity, or even to what a single soul would thus endure; but because they were judicially inflicted in satisfaction of justice. He

4

bore our sins. You incarcerate a man to save him from a mob, and it is an act of kindness. You incarcerate him in execution of a legal sentence, and it is punishment. We think that any candid man will admit that those who disapproved of such a judicial judgment, did not deserve, on that account, to be deemed lacking in fidelity or zeal for the truth.

We do not wish to intimate that the books on which the Presbytery, and afterwards the Synod, of Philadelphia, founded their judicial action did not contain errors which called for the exercise of discipline. We believe they did contain propositions, which, according to the unanimous judgment of the Assembly of 1868, any minister should be required to retract, as the condition of his remaining in connection with the Presbyterian Church. The complaint is, that matters were included in the charges which even the friends of sound doctrine could not regard as proper grounds of discipline.

The third point about which Old-school men differed was the wisdom of some of the acts of the Assembly of 1837. When that Assembly met, it was found that the Old-school had a decided and determined majority. The opportunity had occurred to rectify some of the abuses which had so long and so justly been matters of complaint. It was not to be expected or desired that the opportunity should be lost. The abuse which was most immediately under the control of the Assembly, was the admission of Congregationalists as constituent members of our church courts. This was as obviously unreasonable and unconstitutional as the admission of British subjects to sit as members of our State or national legislature. To put an end to this abuse, the Assembly adopted the following report of their committee. "In regard to the relation between the Presbyterian and Congregational Churches, the committee recommend the adoption of the following resolutions:

"1. That between these two branches of the American Church, there ought, in the judgment of this Assembly, to be maintained sentiments of mutual respect and esteem, and for that purpose no reasonable effort should be omitted to preserve a perfectly good understanding between these two branches of the church of Christ.

' "2. That it is expedient to continue the plan of friendly intercourse between this Church and the Congregational Churches, as it now exists.

"3. But as the 'Plan of Union' adopted for the new settletlements in 1801, was originally an unconstitutional act on the part of that Assembly,—these important standing rules having never been submitted to the Presbyteries—and as they are totally destitute of authority, as proceeding from the General Association of Connecticut, which is invested with no power to legislate in such cases, and especially to enact laws to regulate churches not within its limits; and as much confusion and irregularity have arisen from this unnatural and unconstitutional system of union, therefore, it is resolved, that the Act of the Assembly of 1801, entitled a 'Plan of Union,' be, and the same is hereby abrogated."

These resolutions were carried by a vote of 143 yeas to 110 nays. Dr. Archibald Alexander, and all the other delegates from the Presbytery of New Brunswick, voted for their adoption.

The question then arose, How was the above resolution to be carried into effect? In other words, How was the Congregational element to be eliminated from our body? Three methods were proposed. First: To cite the judicatories charged with this and other irregularities to appear at the bar of the next Assembly. This was actually adopted, but afterwards abandoned, as likely to be cumbersome and interminable.

· The second method was that proposed by the Rev. Dr. Cuyler, who introduced a series of resolutions, the substance of which was a direction to the judicatories embracing Congregational churches, to require them to become Presbyterially organized, or to withdraw from our connection; and refusing to such judicatories the privilege of being represented in the General Assembly, until this elimination of Congregationalism had been effected.

The consideration of these resolutions was postponed to await the report of a committee consisting of five members from either side of the house, to consider the question of the amicable separation of the church. That committee reported that they unanimously agreed, 1st. That in the present state of the church such a separation was desirable; 2d. They agreed as to the terms on which it should be effected; but 3d. They disagreed as to the time when it should be accomplished, and as to the legal succession. The committee representing the majority, insisted that the separation should be accomplished at once, during the sessions of that Assembly; the committee on the part of the minority, insisted that it should be deferred for a year, by a reference of the matter to the presbyteries.

On the failure of this attempt, the Assembly, instead of taking up the resolutions of Dr. Cuyler, proceeded to effect the separation from Congregationalism by its own authority. This was done by what are called the "Abscinding Acts." It was resolved first, "That by the operation of the abrogation of the Plan of Union of 1801, the Synod of the Western Reserve is, and is hereby declared to be, no longer a part of the Presbyterian Church in the United States of America."

And subsequently it was resolved, "That in consequence of the abrogation by this Assembly, of the Plan of Union of 1801, between it and the General Association of Connecticut, as utterly unconstitutional, and therefore null and void from the beginning, the Synods of Utica, Geneva, and Genesee, which were formed and attached to this body, under and in execution of the said 'Plan of Union,' be, and are hereby declared to be, out of the ecclesiastical connection of the Presbyterian Church of the United States of America, and that they are not in form or in fact an integral portion of said church."

It was stated on the floor of the Assembly that less than one in four of the churches in the Synod of the Western Reserve was Presbyterian. We do not see how any one can censure the Assembly for refusing to recognize that Synod as a Presbyterian body, when three-fourths of the churches of which it was composed were Congregational. Dr. Alexander, who had voted for the abrogation of the Plan of Union, felt free, therefore, to vote for the disowning of the Synod of the Western Reserve as a constituent part of the Presbyterian Church. For the resolution disowning the three Synods in western New York, he could not vote.

It appears, from a minute made at the time, that the article on the General Assembly, in the *Princeton Review*, as first prepared, did not meet the views of its conductors. "The conductors of the *Repertory*," the minute states, "met a second time (July 19, 1837) to decide on the article on the Assembly. Dr. Miller and Dr. John Breckinridge approved of the action of the Assembly respecting the three Synods *in toto*. Professor John Maclean thought it might be justified, but would have preferred Dr. Cuyler's plan. Dr. Alexander disapproved of it on the ground on which it was placed by the Assembly. Professors J. W. Alexander, Dod, and Hodge, disapproved, and would have preferred Dr. Cuyler's plan. These three wished that idea to be expressed in the *Repertory*. It was decided to leave out the portion containing that expression— leaving it, as was supposed, undecided how the conductors viewed the matter. To this course all ultimately assented except Professor Hodge. He objected on the ground that the impression made by the article as it now stands, would be that the conductors decidedly sustained the measure in question." As his associates did not agree with him as to that point, he was, of course, overruled. The above details are of little interest to the church generally, but they are of interest so far as the history of this journal is concerned.

The grounds on which the majority of the conductors of this *Review* dissented from the act of the Assembly disowning the three Synods of Utica, Geneva, and Genesee, were: 1. That it was not a legitimate consequence of the abrogation of the Plan of Union that those Synods, with all their presbyteries and churches, were out of connection with the Presbyterian Church in the United States, and neither in form or fact an integral portion of that church. Even if originally formed on the Plan of Union, if they had become, and so far as they had become, Presbyterian in their organization, and had been duly recognized, they were entitled to be regarded and treated as Presbyterian churches and judicatories. This is all the constitution required. This the Assembly itself admitted, as it promised to recognize any of the constituent churches or judicatories of those Synods as soon as they reported themselves as constitutionally organized. But if presbyterial organization entitled them to recognition, it was a valid reason why they should not be disowned.

2. The presence of a few Congregationalists in a church court did not destroy its character, nor afford a reasonable ground for refusing to recognize it as in connection with the church. Committee-men (*i. e.* Congregationalists) have been allowed to sit as members of the General Assembly; and so were the delegates from the several Associations in New England. If their presence rendered the Assemblies in which they sat unconstitutional bodies, then all the acts of those bodies were null and void, and we have lost our legal succession.

It is to be remembered that the excision of the Synods in question was not an act of discipline; it was not founded on the prevalence of error in doctrine, or of "new measures." This the Assembly expressly disclaims. In the answer to the protest of the commissioners from those Synods, it is said, "There was no judicial process instituted." "Without impeaching the character or standing of the brethren composing those Synods, this Assembly, by a legislative act, merely declares them, in consequence of the abrogation of the Plan of Union of 1801, no longer a constituent part of the General Assembly of the Presbyterian Church in the United States." (*Digest*, 743). The objection to this action is, that the presence of a small minority of Congregationalists in a church court did not so vitiate its character as to justify its being disowned.

3. There were Presbyteries within the bounds of the Synods of Albany and New Jersey composed in part of Congregational churches; and yet the General Assembly did not disown either those Synods or the delinquent Presbyteries. This was an admission that the presence of Congregational members did not destroy the character of those bodies as Presbyterian organizations.

4. The action of the Assembly in disowning the Synods of Western New York was not necessary to secure the reform of the church. That end would have been attained by the due operation of the abrogation of the Plan of Union. The legitimate effects of that abrogation were: 1. To prevent the recep-

tion of any new churches formed upon that Plan. 2. To render it obligatory on all the Presbyteries to require the churches within their bounds to adopt an organization in accordance with our constitution, and to refuse to allow the representatives of Congregational churches to sit and act as elders. 3. To justify, and, it may be, to render it obligatory on future General Assemblies, to refuse to allow Presbyteries continuing their connection with Congregationalism, to be represented in those bodies. This would have effectually accomplished the reform contemplated by the abrogation of the Plan of Union of 1801. After having allowed for more than thirty years this union of Congregationalists and Presbyterians in our church courts, all that the Assembly had the right to do was to require that such union should forthwith and thenceforth cease. This was the ground taken by Dr. Alexander and the majority of the conductors of this *Review* in 1837, and on which the few of their number who still survive, still stand. What, however, was regarded as very lukewarm Old-schoolism in 1837, has now come to be looked upon as obsolete and narrow-minded. The Assembly of 1869, by a vote nearly unanimous, not only admitted (the abrogation of the Plan of Union notwithstanding) that Presbyteries do not forfeit their connection with the Presbyterian Church, although they include Congregational churches, but authorized, as far as it could do so, their being represented in the General Assembly for at least five years to come.

The Late War.

On the course pursued by the conductors of this *Review* in reference to the late war for the preservation of our National Union, little need be said. The first article having reference to our national difficulties was written before the secession of South Carolina, but did not appear in print until after that event, viz., January 1861. The article is entitled, "The State of the Country." It began by saying, "There are periods in the history of every nation when its destiny for ages may be determined by the events of an hour. There are occasions when political questions rise into the sphere of morals and religion; when the rule for political action is to be sought, not in considerations of state policy, but in the word of God. On such occasions the distinction between secular and religious journals is obliterated." It was on this ground that we, as conductors of a Theological Review, felt justified in entering upon the discussion of questions involving our national life. In taking this course we were sustained by the example of the whole religious press of the country, South as well as North.

The design of the article in question was, in the first place, to consider the complaints of the South against the North, which we endeavoured to show were either altogether unfounded, or did not furnish any justification for the dissolution of the national union; and, in the second place, to prove that secession was not a constitutional mode of redressing evils, whether real or imaginary. That article was received at the South, to our surprise, with universal condemnation, expressed in terms of unmeasured severity. At the North it was pronounced, "moderate, fair, and reasonable," except by the Abolitionists, who rivalled their Southern brethren in their denunciations.

In April of the same year (1861) appeared another article, on "The Church and the Country." Secession was then an accomplished fact, and the war with all its uncertainties was about to commence. The article was designed as a plea for the unity of the church, even in the event of the dissolution of the national union. The two great sources of apprehension that the political troubles of the country would lead to a division of the Presbyterian Church, were the alienation of feeling on the part of our Southern brethren, and the new, unscriptural, and anti-Christian sentiments which the leading men among them avowed on the subject of slavery. Instead of regarding it as merely allowable under certain circumstances, they had come to advocate it as a good; as the best organization of labour; as an institution to be conserved, extended, and perpetuated. They also maintained that slavery was founded on natural, and not on municipal law; that it did not depend on the *lex loci*, and therefore that slaveholders had the right to carry their slaves and to retain them as such, wherever they could carry any other kind of property, provided the holding of that kind of property was not specially forbidden by the sovereignty into which they went. On this ground it was claimed that slavery went of right into all the "territories" of the United States; that Congress had no authority to prohibit slaveholding in the "territories," but was bound to protect property in slaves as well as any other kind of property. The assertion of the right of Congress to prohibit slavery in a territory of which it was the local legislature, was declared to be "a thorough and radical revolution—it proposes new and extraordinary terms of union. The old government is as completely abolished as if the people of the United States had met in convention and repealed the Constitution."* How new this astounding doctrine was, is plain from the fact that the act of Congress prohibiting slavery north of latitude 36° 30' was, as Mr. Benton tells us, "the wish of the South, sustained by the united voice of Mr. Monroe's cabinet, (including John C. Calhoun and William H. Crawford), the united voices of the Southern senators, and a majority of the Southern representatives."†

It is to a discussion of the extreme views above-mentioned that the article in question is principally devoted.

In 1862 an article appeared, entitled, "England and America." The Christian public in this country were very slow to believe that England sided with the South in our recent struggle. This was so unexpected, so unreasonable, so contrary to the professed principles of both the government and people, that Americans could not believe it until the conviction was forced upon them. The whole secular press of that country, whether metropolitan, provincial, or colonial, with few exceptions, were as vituperative and denunciatory of the North, as the Southern papers themselves. The same is true, scarcely with the same number of exceptions, of the religious press, whether controlled by Episcopalians, Presbyterians, or Congregationalists. This is a fact for which we have never seen or heard any satisfactory explanation. The article in question was written as a protest against this unrighteous judgment. It was designed to show that the rebellion was made in the interest of slavery. This was proved from the fact that the grievances complained of had almost exclusive reference to

* Dr. Thornwell on the State of the Country, p. 26.
† Thirty Years in the Senate, vol. i. p. 8.

that institution. Those grievances were the denunciations of abolitionists; the obstructions thrown in the way of the restoration of fugitive slaves; the refusal to admit slaveholding in the free territories; the election of an anti-slavery president, and the like. It was proved by official declarations of public bodies; by the avowals of the leading politicians of the South; by the appeals of the Southern press to slaveholders to sustain a war made for their special interests. That English anti-slavery Christians should sustain a rebellion made to "conserve, perpetuate, and extend slavery," was a moral phenomenon that astonished the Christian world. In the second place, the article was designed to show that even with regard to slavery the South had no serious grounds of complaint; that the abolitionists, who denounced all slaveholders as criminal, were a small minority of the people of the North; that the general government, on which alone rested the obligation of executing the fugitive slave-law, so far from being remiss in the discharge of that duty, had erred in the opposite extreme ; and that in refusing to sanction slavery in the free territories, Congress had acted on the principles, not only of Jefferson, Madison, Monroe, Lowndes, and of all the great representative men of the South, but of the civilized world. Judge McLean, of the Supreme Court of the United States, said from the bench, that the great principle decided by Lords Mansfield and Stowell, against which *there is no dissenting authority*, was, "that a slave is not property beyond the operation of the territorial law which makes him such." He further said, the Supreme Court of the United States has decided that "slavery is a mere municipal regulation, founded on and limited to the range of the territorial law." Judge Curtis, of the same Court, said, "Slavery being contrary to natural right, is created only by municipal law. This is not only plain in itself, and agreed to by all writers on the subject, but it is inferable from the Constitution, and has been explicitly declared by this Court." He further said, "I am not acquainted with any case or any writer questioning the correctness of this doctrine." It was the practical assertion of this doctrine which men at the South said worked a repeal of the Constitution, and absolved them from all allegiance to the national government. That

England should desire the success of a rebellion having such an object, and sustained by such reasons, was a grief and a marvel to the Christian world.

The article on "The War," January 7, 1863, was written during the gloomiest period of the struggle. The South, although inferior in point of numbers, had many advantages. They operated near their resources; they were united; their labouring population being slaves were not combatants, who could carry on the work of production, while the whole white population were at liberty to take the field. The North laboured under the disadvantage of operating at a great distance from their resources, and over a territory a thousand miles in extent, and the people were far from being united. A large party was opposed to the war from the beginning. A still larger portion of the people was opposed to the administration, and did all they could to prevent its success. Many who at the commencement of the struggle sided heartily with the national government, had become alienated and hostile on account of the measures which had been adopted. The design of the article was to promote harmony among the people of the North. There could be no hope of such harmonious action unless the conscience of the people was on the side of the government. "There never was a time," the writer said, "when the public conscience was more disturbed, or when it was more necessary that moral principles in their bearing on national conduct should be clearly presented." It was then urged that the great principle that the moral law, or, the will of God, however revealed, binds nations as well as individuals, should be the rule of public action. The dictum of Coke, one of the greatest legal authorities, "That any act of Parliament which conflicts with the law of God, is null and void," should be written in letters of gold in every legislative hall and in every court of justice in the country.

On this principle the article urged that the legitimate and avowed object of the war, viz., the preservation of the union, should be religiously adhered to; and that the war itself should be conducted in strict observance of recognized military law. The two great subjects on which public sentiment was dangerously divided, were the right of the President to suspend the writ of *habeas corpus*, and his authority as commander-in-chief, and as a war measure, to decree the emancipation of the slaves. The article took the ground that both these rights belonged to the President during times of war, and for military ends, *i. e.*, for the preservation of the country and for the suppression of the rebellion.

While the conductors of this *Review* were thus earnest and constant in their support of the national government, they were so unfortunate as to differ from the majority of brethren as to the propriety of some of the acts of the General Assembly in reference to the war. The difference concerned the true limits of the authority of the church. The conductors of this journal took for their guidance in this matter the principle announced in a resolution adopted unanimously by the General Assembly of 1860. That resolution is in the following words, viz., "The General Assembly, on the one hand, disclaims all right to interfere in secular matters; and, on the other, asserts the right and duty of the church, as God's witness on earth, to bear testimony in favour of truth and holiness, and against all false doctrine and sin, wherever professed or committed." As Presbyterians, in common with all Protestants, hold that the word of God is the only infallible rule of truth and duty, it follows that the Scriptures are the standard according to which the church must form her judgments; and consequently that she cannot properly condemn as sinful anything which the Scriptures do not forbid; or declare anything to be obligatory as a matter of faith or duty which the Bible does not teach or enjoin. Nothing, therefore, which cannot be judged by the Scriptures as a standard, comes legitimately under the authority of the church. The church has no right to pronounce judgment on such questions as protection and free trade, internal improvements, banking, finance, or commerce. It cannot interpret the laws of the land, and adjudicate in questions of property. It cannot authoritatively expound the Constitution of the United States, and decide whether it does, or does not, recognize the right of secession, and, whether the paramount allegiance of the citizen be to his State or to the United States. Any act of the General Assembly violating these obvious principles; any act censuring Presbyterians for obeying their

States rather than the United States, or calling on them for a confession of sin and profession of repentance for obeying the former instead of the latter, as a condition of either Christian or ministerial communion, the conductors of this *Review* regard as wrong in itself and disastrous in its tendency. This, to the best of our knowledge and belief, is the only point connected with the war in which we had the misfortune to differ from our brethren.

Reunion of the Churches.

The course pursued by the conductors of this *Review* on this subject was determined by the following assumptions and principles: 1. That at the time of the disruption in 1837–1838, serious differences existed between the Old and New-schools. These differences related principally to matters of polity, and to the latitude allowable in the interpretation of our doctrinal standards.

2. That these differences were so great as to lead both parties to the conviction that an amicable separation was desirable.

3. They assumed, further, that reunion should not take place so long as these differences continued.

4. The Old-school, believing that their distinctive principles were right and obligatory, repeatedly declared that they had not, could not, and would not abandon them.

5. The New-school, with equal distinctness, declared that they had not, and would not change their ground. Under these circumstances it would seem that no party could wish a reunion of elements which had proved themselves so discordant as to render harmonious action impossible.

In fact, however, many Old-school men believed that the New-school had so far changed as to render reunion desirable. On the other hand, the majority of the New-school believed that the Old-school had so far changed that they were willing to be reunited with them.

The result is that the vast majority of both parties have come to the conclusion that both have so changed, that a wise regard to the interests of the cause of Christ demands that the reunion should be consummated. God grant that such may prove to be the case!

Some few, on both sides, do not believe in this change, and, therefore, do not approve of the union. To this small number the senior editor of this *Review* belongs. All, however, recognize it to be their duty to bow to the will of the majority constitutionally expressed, and to unite their prayers with those of their brethren that the blessing of God in rich abundance may rest on the reunited church.

Articles on the Assemblies.

Beginning with the year 1835, this *Review* has given annually, in its July number, an account of the proceedings of each successive General Assembly. The object of these articles was not merely to record the action of the Assembly, but to present a condensed outline of the discussions on all important points. No attempt was made to give the speeches of the several speakers, but a summary of the arguments on each side of disputed questions. As the period from 1835 to 1869 is one of the most important in our ecclesiastical history, these articles, it is believed, have an historical value, as they give information not elsewhere easily accessible.

Conclusion.

This *Review* has always laboured under one great disadvantage. It never had an editor devoted to its management. It has always been a by-business; taken up in intervals allowed by more imperative duties, and laid aside as soon as possible. Nevertheless it has cost a great deal of time and labour; yielding little compensation other than the hope of doing good.

The above retrospect of the history of this journal is due to its conductors, living and dead. It is due to them to vindicate their course during the past forty-five years of almost constant conflict. This vindication is the rather due because their course has been often misunderstood and misrepresented. That they have at times erred in judgment, may be taken for granted; that they have sometimes been unduly severe in their criticisms, we fear must also be acknowledged. For such severity the few who survive would be glad to make any possible atonement. Nevertheless we feel called upon to thank God that on no important question of doctrine or polity do our present convictions of truth and duty conflict with what we find recorded on the pages of this journal. Discarding all other claims, its conductors do claim credit for fidelity and consistency.

What is to be the future of the *Biblical Repertory and Princeton Review*, it is not for us to predict. If those whose views it has hitherto represented, wish it to live, they must sustain it. Our hope is, that now when the senior editor, who for forty-five years has borne the chief responsibility of its management, lays down the burden, the work will enter on a higher and more enlarged sphere of usefulness.

PART II.

———

ABBOTT, J. J., was born in Groton, Vermont, in July 1813. He received his preliminary education at Peacham, and graduated at Dartmouth College in 1839. After leaving college he taught a school two years in Mississippi, and then returned to Dartmouth, and served two more years as tutor in his *alma mater*. He then entered the Union Theological Seminary, and having completed his theological course in 1845, became pastor of the Congregational church at Bennington Centre, Vermont. At the end of two years he was compelled by ill health to resign his pastorate, and continued without charge till April 1850, when he was settled over the Congregational church at Uxbridge, Massachusetts, where he continned till December 1862. The next two years were chiefly passed at Washington, District of Columbia, where he acted as agent of the United States Christian Commission, and after the close of the war he accepted the charge of the Central Congregational church at Yarmouth, Maine, which he holds at the present time. Mr. Abbott is the author of a small work called "Home and Friendship," and of various contributions to periodical literature, among which may be mentioned a review of Boardman's "Higher Christian Life" in the *Bibliotheca Sacra*, and the article on "Millenarianism," which he contributed to this journal in 1852.

ADAMSON, JAMES, was born at Cupar-Fife, in Scotland, about the beginning of the present century. In 1829 he went out as a chaplain to the Cape of Good Hope in connection with the Church of Scotland, but left the established church at the disruption in 1843. In 1853 he appeared as a delegate from American missionaries at Natal to the General Assembly that met in Philadelphia that year, and addressed the Assembly. According to the report, after giving a history of the various evangelistic agencies in South Africa, he "made some very severe strictures on patronism as existing in the Scottish Church, and on the sectarian spirit of the British government, and declared his preference for the American field;" but after residing in the United States, chiefly at Philadelphia, over three years, he returned to Capetown, where we understand he still lives (1869). He contributed to this *Review* in July 1856, the article on the "Principles of the Philosophy of Language."

ADGER, JOHN BAILEY, was born in 1810, and is the eldest son of James Adger, who was a wealthy and pious merchant in Charleston, South Carolina. Young Adger received his classical education at Union College, New York, under Dr. Nott, and studied divinity at Princeton Seminary. At his first entering upon the ministry his mind was deeply impressed with the importance of giving the gospel to the coloured people in his own State; but finding no open door, he turned his eyes to the destitute and degraded of another land, and was sent out as a missionary to the Armenians in Asia Minor by the American Board of Commissioners for Foreign Missions. He laboured there nearly twelve years, but was compelled by impaired vision and failing health to resign. Soon after his return to his native State, viz., in 1847, he proposed to the Second Presbyterian church in Charleston to build a separate church for the benefit of the coloured people; which, in the face of bitter opposition from many citizens of Charleston, was done in 1849. This coloured congregation afterwards became the Zion church. In 1857 he accepted the appointment of Professor of Ecclesiastical History and Church Polity in the Seminary at Columbia, South Carolina, which he holds at the present time. While in the East, and since his return, he had collected a very rare and valuable library of over three thousand volumes, which was burned, after the occupation of Columbia, by the army under General Sherman. In 1833, while a student at Princeton Seminary, he contributed the article "Roman Catholicism" to this *Review*.

AIKEN, CHARLES A., is the son of the Hon. John and Mrs. H. R. (Adams) Aiken, and was born at Manchester, Vermont, October 30, 1827. He graduated at Dartmouth College, New Hampshire, in 1846; and after studying theology at Andover and in Germany, completed the course at Andover in 1853. On the 19th of October 1854, he was ordained and installed pastor of the Congregational church at Yarmouth, Maine, and continued in the charge till 1859, when he was elected Professor of the Latin Language and Literature in

6

Dartmouth College. In 1866 he was appointed professor in the same department in the College of New Jersey, which he held till 1869, when he was elected President of Union College, Schenectady, New York, his present position. He is the editor and translator of "Lange's Commentary on the Book of Proverbs." The articles contributed by him to this *Review* are,

1867. Epicureanism—Dr. Schaff's Church History.

1868. Whitney on Language.

ALDEN, JOSEPH, was born in Green county, New York, in the year 1807, and graduated at Union College in 1828, after which he studied theology in Princeton Seminary, and was two years a tutor in the college. He was then successively Professor of Rhetoric in Williams College, Massachusetts; Professor of Moral Philosophy in Lafayette College, Pennsylvania, and President of Jefferson College, Pennsylvania; and is now (1869) Principal of the State Normal School, Albany, New York. In 1838 he received the degree of D. D. from Union College, and in 1857 that of LL.D from Columbia College, New York. He is the author of several instructive works for the young, and has been a constant contributor to the periodical literature of the country. In the volume for 1830 he reviewed Payne's Elements of Mental and Moral Science, and Dugald Stewart's Works.

ALEXANDER, ARCHIBALD, the son of William Alexander and Ann Reid, was born April 17, 1772, in an old-fashioned log-house, about seven miles east from Lexington, in the romantic county of Rockbridge, Virginia. His father was an industrious farmer and storekeeper, and considered to be in very good circumstances, according to the notions of that period.

Archibald was the third of nine children, and at a very early age was taught his letters and to read the Testament. When he was about five years old his father went on a trading expedition to Baltimore, and there bought several convicts that had been transported from England for crime; among them was a youth of eighteen or twenty, called John Reardon, who had been for some time at a classical school in London, and could read Virgil and a little Greek. As he had not been accustomed to manual labour, Mr. Alexander concluded that Reardon might teach a school, in default of a better, and erected for him a log-house near a little spring, in his neighbourhood. "This place," says Dr. Alexander, in those delightful reminiscences which he has left of his early life, "was a mile from our house, and thither I trudged along every day, with my short legs and little feet, when not more than five years old. The master, as being my father's servant, lodged at our house, and often carried me in his arms part of the way. I had no fear of him, as at home I was accustomed to call him Jack, and often conveyed my father's commands to him." Before the year was out, the war of the Revolution commenced, the teacher became a soldier, and the school was broken up.

From this time, till he was ten years of age, Archibald attended various schools, but not regularly, and in the intervals assisted his father in the business of the store and the farm. Dr. Alexander used repeatedly to tell his children that his father gave him a rifle the day he was eleven years old; and how he would spend days in the mountains in search of cattle which were lost, able to catch and discriminate the bells of his father's herd at a distance which seems almost incredible. He was an expert swimmer, and grew up with that perfect knowledge of horsemanship which is still common to all young Virginians.

At this time the Rev. William Graham, a graduate of the College of New Jersey, opened an academy at Timber Ridge Meeting-house, and his father, having determined to give young Archibald a liberal education, sent him to this academy. Here Dr. Alexander began his classical education, and in afterlife to no man did he acknowledge himself so much indebted in regard to the direction of his studies and the moulding of his character as to Mr. Graham. Towards this instructor he ever felt an overwhelming debt of gratitude, and when, in old age, relieved of a portion of his former duties in the Seminary, he employed his leisure hours in writing a memoir of his early friend.

In his seventeenth year he had made such progress in his studies that he was engaged in reviewing his course, with the intention of graduating, when his father obtained an engagement for him as tutor in the family of General Posey of the Wilderness, a place twelve miles from Fredericksburg, now rendered memorable in the history of the United States. He was compelled instantly to leave the academy and enter upon his duties. Though at that time it was seemingly to him an adverse providence, yet he afterwards saw it to be one of the most blessed circumstances in his life. When he commenced his duties as a tutor, he found that his pupils had been carefully educated, and nearly as far advanced as himself, and he had to study at night the lesson for the next day. To these studies he attributed much of the accuracy he afterwards acquired in reading Latin; and his general knowledge was much increased by reading the works of Rollin, Rapin's History of England, the works of Flavel, and the Internal Evidences of Religion by Soame Jenyns, a work which made an indelible impression upon his mind. "This year, 1788—89," says he, "was in many respects the most important of my life. If I had not the beginnings of a work of grace, my mind was enlightened in the knowledge of truths of which I had lived in total ignorance. I began to love the truth, and to seek after it, as for hid treasure. To John Flavel I certainly owe more than to any uninspired author." At the close of his engagement, which seems to have been for one year, he returned to his home, with a determination to supply the defects of his intellectual training, and "we find him therefore retiring for days to the woods, and devoting himself to Euclid and Horace."

This is the period known in the Southern churches of America as the Great Revival, and young Alexander did not pass through it uninfluenced. Till recently he had no experience of religion as a personal concern, and no assurance of his salvation, or of his state before God. He heard of ecstasies and joys and hopes to which he was a stranger, but now he longed to know assuredly that he was among the number of God's people. He walked far into the dense woods, and in the caves of the mountains gave himself for days to the reading of the Scriptures and prayer, but found only a temporary relief, a momentary gleam of light, and relapsed into darkness and despair. He sought God in his ordinances, and for the first time approached the table of the Lord, but he only added to his other fears the harassing thought that he had drunk damnation to himself. In this state of mind he continued till his second communion, when the power of Christ to save was appropriated by his mind. On reviewing this period of his life, with the wisdom of experience, he says: "This shows how seldom believers can designate with exactness the time of their renewal. Now, at the age of seventy-seven, I am of opinion that my regeneration took place while I resided at General Posey's, in the year 1788."

Mr. Alexander was now at an age when it became necessary for him to choose some profession. The work of the ministry was clearly his choice, but he felt himself altogether unfit for it. By the persuasion of his friends and teacher, however, he was prevailed upon to offer himself as a candidate for the ministry, and was received by the Presbytery of Lexington on the 20th of October, 1790.

At this time there were no theological seminaries, and Mr. Alexander began the study of theology under the Rev. William Graham, who at first had only another student,—a number of young men who had been arrested in their academical course by the Revival were however soon added to the class. Mr. Graham was eminently qualified for training the youthful mind. He was a thoroughly educated man and a vigorous thinker, who had unweariedly studied the mysteries of his own mind, and knew how to impress the minds of others. He continually insisted upon independent research into all the subjects of study, and taught the students to depend upon their own resources rather than upon the opinions of authors. But with this he had no latitudinarian views, and a perfect consciousness of the correctness of his own opinions. The instructions of the school he also wished to reduce immediately to practice, and at the meeting of Presbytery at which he received his first pupils, he also obtained leave from the Presbytery for them to exhort in social meetings for religious worship. In a very short time Mr. Alexander was called upon to make his first public effort, and he thus describes it himself: "Although I did not know a single word which I was to utter, I began with a rapidity and fluency equal to any I have enjoyed to this day. From this time I exhorted at one place and another several times every week."

Mr. Graham was appointed a delegate to the Assembly of 1791, and conceived the very strange idea of taking Mr. Alexander with him as a ruling-elder. As he was small in stature and his whole appearance very boyish, he felt the ridiculous position he would occupy, and refused; but Mr. Graham would take no denial, and they set out on horseback together to Philadelphia. The Assembly that year comprised many notable men, and his sketches of what he saw and heard form a delightful fragment of the history of the church; but the circumstance which was most important in its results may be related in his own words. "While in Philadelphia I was frequently at the house of old Mrs. Hodge, the grandmother of Professor Hodge." He doubtless saw in this the first providential link in the chain that bound him to her grandson, and led him, when he entered the Seminary, to claim him as "his own son in the faith."

At this time there was a great need of more ministers in Virginia, and though Mr. Alexander had gone through the prescribed course of study, he was very reluctant to be licensed, on account of an abiding sense of unfitness, but the Presbytery and his preceptor had no idea that he would gain fitness by

inaction, and at their solicitation he submitted to be licensed
"as a probationer of the holy ministry" by the Presbytery of
Lexington, on October 1, 1791; but he says, "My feelings
were awful, and far from being comfortable."

It was his intention to return home after his licensure, and
prepare himself by study for his duties, but Providence had
for him a course of preparation of another kind. "After the
Synod adjourned (for Synod and Presbytery met at the same
place at this time) I went with Mr. Le Grand to an appointment which he had, some fifteen miles from Winchester. He
told me that I must preach, but I positively refused. He said
nothing at the time, but when the congregation was assembled
he arose and said, 'Mr. Alexander, please to come forward to
the table, and take the books and preach.' I knew not what
to do, but rather than make a disturbance I went forward and
preached my first sermon after licensure, from Galatians iii.
24, 'Wherefore the law was our schoolmaster to bring us unto
Christ.' My next sermon was preached at Charleston, from
the text, Acts xvi. 31, 'Believe in the Lord Jesus Christ, and
thou shalt be saved.' I had prepared a skeleton of the sermon,
and placed it before me; but the house being open, a puff of
wind carried it away into the midst of the congregation.
I then determined to take no more paper into the pulpit; and
this resolution I kept as long as I was a pastor," or, as he says
in another place, "for twenty years."

A religious awakening had begun in Jefferson county, and
the ministers there solicited him to come to their aid; so with
no other clothing than that he had taken with him for a few
days of absence, he obeyed the call, and in fifteen months
preached thirty-two sermons, and did not set his face homeward till March 1791. "I had no books," says he, "with me,
but my small pocket Bible, and found very little to read in the
houses where I stopped; I was therefore thrown entirely on
my own thoughts. I studied my sermons on horseback, and
in bed before I went to sleep, and some of the best sermons I
ever prepared were digested in this way and at this time."

"When I reached home," so he wrote almost half a century
after the event, "there was a great curiosity in men, women,
and children, to hear me preach. They had often heard me
speak in public, but preaching was another thing. Accordingly, on the next Lord's day, a great congregation filled the
court-house, which was then used for public worship, for at
that time there was no church in the place. My text was,
John ix. 25, 'One thing I know, that whereas I was blind,
now I see.' My delivery in those days was fluent and rapid.

I never appeared to hesitate or be·at a loss for words; my thoughts flowed too fast for me. I laboured under two great faults as a public speaker; the first was extreme rapidity of utterance, not so much from indistinct articulation as neglect of pauses. I ran on till I was perfectly out of breath, so that before I was done, my inhalations became audible; the other fault was looking steadily down upon the floor. This arose from a fear of losing the train of my thought; for my sermons were closely studied, though not written. My voice, though not sonorous, was uncommonly distinct and clear, so that without painful exertion I could be heard in the largest churches, or by a great assembly out of doors.

"As my health was now good, and I had no thought of taking a pastoral charge, I embraced an offer to travel as an itinerant missionary in Eastern Virginia. This mission was in pursuance of a plan adopted .by the Synod of Virginia," and Mr. Alexander and Mr. John Lyle having received the appointments, they were directed to proceed to Petersburg, and there separate. From thence Mr. Lyle was to go eastward, while Mr. Alexander was to turn westward along the North Carolina line. The incidents of this tour preserved by Mr. Alexander, are very interesting, and copious extracts from his manuscript are given in the Life by his son; but we can only state here that it occupied six months, at the end of which he reported to the Commission of Synod, and returned home, October 1792.

At this time there were several vacancies in Charlotte county and no ministers to fill them, and after consultation, it was determined that all the vacant churches should unite upon two ministers, who should serve them in rotation. The Rev. Drury Lacy and Mr. Alexander received a call to this charge, but the field covered an area of sixty miles by thirty, and the people were so much separated from their pastors, that it was soon found to be unsatisfactory, and a division of the diocese agreed upon. Mr. Alexander received for his share the churches of Briery and Cub Creek. Calls were put into his hands from these churches, and on November 8, 1793, he was received from the Presbytery of Lexington into the Presbytery of Hanover, and on June 7, 1794, was ordained to the pastoral office at Briery. In the retirement of his charge, he had more leisure to devote to systematic study than he had hitherto enjoyed; and in the short period of three years, he had so gained the affections of the people, that when they were no longer able to obtain his ministrations, they extended a call to his son, and afterwards to his grandson.

Hampden Sidney College, which had been founded in 1783, was now in a very low condition. Its president had resigned, and its trustees, after a vain endeavour to get the Rev. William Graham to accept the office, turned to Mr. Alexander. "I was," says he, "very averse to an undertaking of so little promise, but at length I was persuaded to make the trial, and the consideration had much weight with me, that if I did not succeed, I should leave matters no worse than they were, but that if I had success, I might be doing some public good. I accordingly consented in the autumn (1796) to go to the college in the following spring." He accordingly resigned the charge of the Cub Creek church on April 11, 1797, and took his seat as President of the college on May 31, 1797.

In the preceding winter he had looked out for colleagues to aid him in his work, and was successful in obtaining the services of John Holt Rice and Conrad Speece, men under whom the college in after years attained a high reputation, and who for many years were leading men in the church in Virginia. While Mr. Alexander was president of the college, he was diligent in accumulating knowledge, as well as in imparting it to others. "At the same time he was laborious in preaching the gospel, not only to his two congregations, but, according to the custom of the country, in many places on every side." These labours were too severe for his naturally feeble constitution, and he was compelled to resign the charge of the Briery church on November 16, 1798, and in the spring of 1801 the presidency of the college.

He had long had a desire to visit the New England States, and Providence seemed at this time to point to travel as a means of restoring his health. An expectation, however, prevailed among the people that he would soon return, and no effort was made, either by the trustees of the college or the elders of the churches, to supply the vacancy. Taking advantage of his going east, the Presbytery of Hanover elected him their delegate to the General Assembly, and putting his money and his clothes into his saddle-bags, he set out upon his journey. The first night after leaving home he was robbed of his money, and on the next day he was seized with so violent a fever that he was obliged to turn into a house, not far from the roadside, and ask for permission to lie down. After getting a little able to proceed, by an effort he reached the house of the celebrated blind preacher, Dr. Waddel, where he stayed several days to recruit his strength. Here we was struck with the beauty and accomplishments of Janetta Waddel, and determined to seek her hand. He was accepted, and proceeded on his journey under a pleasing obligation to return.

Dr. Alexander reached Philadelphia in time to meet with the Assembly, which this year comprised several eminent men, among whom were Dr. Jonathan Edwards, Dr. McMillan, Dr. Green, Dr. Woodhull, and Dr. McKnight. But more memorable to him, here, also, he first met with the Rev. Samuel Miller, now in the bloom of manly vigour, with whom he was destined to spend more than thirty-five years of harmonious labour.

As it was known that Mr. Alexander intended to go further north, the Assembly elected him a delegate to the General Association of Connecticut, and finding a companion in the Rev. Charles Coffin, they set out together on horseback. This year the Association met at Litchfield, which they reached early in the day of convocation. In his reminiscences, he says, "The appearance of the old country clergymen was to me novel and grotesque. They came into town on horseback or in chaises, wearing cocked hats, and sometimes queues dangling down the back. The opening sermon was preached by Dr. Perkins, of Hartford. The ministers all met at the house of the pastor, Mr. Huntington, and the first thing was a distribution of long pipes and papers of tobacco, so that the room was filled with smoke."

When the meeting of the Association closed, Mr. Alexander visited Boston, Newburyport, and other places in Massachusetts, going as far as Dartmouth College in New Hampshire. "In the retrospect of this tour he was accustomed to speak of it as one of the most agreeable and instructive portions of his life." He made the acquaintance of the most distinguished men in the New England States, and so favourable was the impression he had made upon some of them, that at the Annual Meeting of the Trustees of Dartmouth College, in August 1802, he was elected by them Phillips Professor of Theology. He had, however, other views, and in the fall returned to Virginia.

"His return to Prince Edward and the College was hailed with much cordiality, and the old president's house was put in repair in expectation of his new relations." On the 5th of April 1802 he was married, and in the month of May he resumed his charge of the College, with Mr. Rice as his principal coadjutor. Here, while we suppose he is enjoying the sweets of domestic happiness, we will insert the loving tribute of Dr. James Waddel Alexander to the memory of his mother. "It may be safely said that no man was ever more blessed in such a connection. If the uncommon beauty and artless grace of this lady were strong attractions in the days of youth, there were higher qualities that made the union inexpressibly felicitous during almost half a century. For domestic wisdom, self-sacrificing affection, humble piety, industry, inexhaustible stores of vivacious conversation, hospitality to his friends, sympathy with his cares, and love to his children, she was such a gift as God bestows only on the most favoured. While during a large part of middle life he was subject to a variety of maladies, she was preserved in unbroken health. When his spirits flagged, she was always prompt and skilful to cheer and comfort. And as his days were filled with spiritual and literary toils, she relieved him from the whole charge of domestic affairs. Without the show of any conjugal blandishments, there was, through life, a perfect coincidence of views, and a respectful affection, which may be recommended as a model. It pleased God to spare to him this faithful ministry of revering love to the very last, and when the earthly tie was broken, to make the separation short."

After his return from New England he received several invitations from churches to become their pastor, among these an invitation to visit the Third Church in Philadelphia. This was at first declined, but a second invitation was received in September; and coming at a time when the students had displeased him by their insubordination, he set off for Philadelphia, preached for them two Sabbaths as well as during the week, and received a unanimous call to the Pine Street church. On his return home, he procured a meeting of the Presbytery and of the Trustees of the College on the same day, and requested to be dismissed from both charges; and his friends seeing that he was perfectly decided in his purpose interposed no obstacle to his dismission.

On the 24th of November he began his journey from Virginia and reached Philadelphia on the 8th of December; and on the 21st of April 1807 he was received into the Presbytery of Philadelphia, and installed into the pastorate of the church on the 20th of May. Here he "enjoyed health, and had on the Sabbath large assemblies of attentive people; and the preaching did not seem altogether without saving effect." The vivacity and freedom of his discourses, always during this period pronounced without the aid of any manuscript, attracted very general admiration; and their solid contents and evangelical unction made them peculiarly welcome to experienced Christians. Being now brought nearer to libraries and learned men, and the means of acquiring books, he entered with great freshness of zeal into several interesting walks of clerical study." He took lessons in Hebrew from a learned Jew, perused the Septuagint, collating it with other versions, and pushed more deeply his researches into the original of the Old Testament, and filled his shelves with those folios and quartos of Latin theology which always continued to be characteristic of his library. He made himself also familiar with the Christian Fathers, both Greek and Latin, and studied the progress of doctrine in the church from the earliest periods to the writings of Hopkins and Emmons, which were now exerting a powerful influence upon the theology of New England. In this laborious study he seems only to have been searching for truth—gratifying his desire for knowledge—without any ulterior object in view, but God was preparing him for his life-work.

In 1807 Mr. Alexander was a commissioner to the General Assembly, and elected Moderator, and agreeably to custom he delivered the opening discourse at the Assembly of 1808. This sermon was published, and is upon the text, 1 Cor. xiv. 12, "Seek that you may excel to the edifying of the church." In 1810 he received from the College of New Jersey the honorary degree of Doctor of Divinity, and was elected President of the University of Georgia, but declined the appointment.

At this period the Presbyterian Church in America had no Theological Seminary, or "Divinity Hall." The training of young men for the ministry was entirely left to the pastors, many of whom were indifferent, or felt unwilling to take upon themselves so much often thankless labour; some, from a want of proper education themselves, were incapable of training others, and the necessity of having men specially set apart for the work was seen to be a necessity. Dr. Ashbel Green had addressed an overture to the Assembly on the subject in 1805, and Mr. Alexander, in his sermon before the Assembly in 1808, suggested that "every Presbytery, or at least every Synod, shall have under its direction a seminary established for that single purpose." Encouraged by this, Dr. Green, in 1809, introduced an overture from the Presbytery of Philadelphia, distinctly proposing the establishment of a theological school. This met with the approval of the Assembly, which decided upon having a seminary organized, with at least "three professors, who shall hold their office during the pleasure of the General Assembly." A board of directors was elected to carry this resolution into effect, and some preliminary preparations having been made in 1811, the Assembly of 1812 resolved to go into the election of one professor. "Silently and prayerfully these guardians of the church began to prepare their votes. They felt the solemnity of the occasion, the importance of their trust. Not a word was spoken, not a whisper heard, as the teller passed round to collect the result. The votes were counted, the result declared, and the Rev. Dr. Alexander was pronounced elected." Dr. Miller arose and said that he hoped the brother elected would not decline, however reluctant he might feel to accept; that if he had been selected by the voice of the church, however great the sacrifice, he would not dare to refuse. Little did he dream that on the following year he should be called by the same voice to give up the attractions of the city, to devote his life to the labours of an instructor."

It was a deep sense of duty that prompted Dr. Alexander to loose the bonds between himself and his charge, and accept this professorship. In many respects he felt his unfitness for the position, but who at that time could have been found that was more fit? He had by patient labour acquired an extensive acquaintance with Greek and Roman literature, but had not enjoyed that training in the niceties of language which was desirable in a teacher. He had a great volume of knowledge, but it had been acquired as it came within his reach, and to teach it, it needed to be digested and applied. But he loved learning, and felt that he was called of God to teach, and he set himself assiduously to perfect that which was wanting; and looking back upon his life and labours, it is the unanimous verdict of posterity, that no man in the church could have been found better fitted for the founder of the Seminary than him who was chosen by the Assembly.

On the 29th of July 1812, with his wife and four children, he set out for Princeton, New Jersey, and on the 12th of August he was inaugurated into his office. Being the only professor yet elected, the whole contemplated course of divinity, oriental and biblical literature, and ecclesiastical history and church government, demanded his attention. "As yet there were no buildings; the professor's house was at once library, chapel, and auditorium. The handful of pious young men gathered around their preceptor almost as members of his family; going freely in and out, sitting at his board, joining in his domestic worship, and, in a sense, not merely learning of him, but living with him. This continued to be the case for a number of years, for the Seminary began with three, and did not attain the number of thirty until the fifth year of its existence. In such a state of things, there is more freedom and frequency of intercourse than when more than a hundred are collected, when it would absorb all the time and strength of a professor to bestow the same personal attentions. In later years, it is but just, however, to observe, that Dr. Alexander gave as free access to his study as pupils ever enjoyed of a teacher. Few moments of the day passed without a knock at his door; and as his apartment was but a few steps from the principal edifice, it was resorted to by the young men with the greatest familiarity, and on every sort of errand, both temporal and spiritual."

Shortly after entering upon the duties of his professorship he was visited by a train of most distressing symptoms—chilliness, nervous perturbation and dyspepsia, with wakefulness, which often kept him the whole night without refreshing sleep. He became haggard and thin, and excepting in short intervals this was his condition for many years. This was no doubt the effect of intense application to study, but he never made it a reason for abstaining from duty, and continued to push forward his researches in every direction.

We will here take a glance at the inner life of the household of Dr. Alexander, as presented by his son. "He was now between forty and fifty, slender in person, clear in complexion, with a slight silvering of his abundant brown hair. His body was open to sudden impulses, seldom long at rest, and prone to motions and gestures, which were highly animated and expressive rather than graceful. Like most newcomers from a city, he for a time devoted himself to horticulture, but it never gained his heart, and he pursued it less than even his respected colleague, who likewise fell off in his zeal. He was always an early riser, and the older inhabitants of Princeton bear in mind his frequent long walks with his three elder sons, who were then little boys. He long retained his youthful fondness for a horse, and indulged moderately in riding and driving. Sometimes visiting the seaside, he used to vaunt that he could swim as boldly as when he was a boy. His delight was in his family. After being deeply absorbed in teaching, he would come in, full of animation, and ready to relax at the fireside. It was always his custom—a most delightful one for all about him—to pour out the fulness of his thoughts upon all that interested him, at the table and in the domestic group. Coming from his newspapers, his books, his class, from visits, church or journey, he gave forth a perpetual and vivacious flow of information. Nothing had escaped his eye, and nothing, even of details, seemed to be withheld in his narrative, yet without tedium or repetition. These daily conversations were the chief entertainment of his life, as they are the most delightful recollections of his household. Through his whole life his house was much frequented by guests, but at this period, though his quarters were never so strait, he was most visited from abroad.   Giving a hearty welcome, and most elated when his table was fullest, he gave himself little care as to display or fashion.   Many who may read these notices will recur with a melancholy pleasure to the days and weeks which they passed under his simple but hospitable roof.   He was addicted to sacred music, and as both he and Mrs. Alexander were gifted with clear and pleasing voices, the hours of family intercourse were enlivened by many a psalm and sacred song.   When such men as Dr. John H. Rice, or Dr. Finley, or Dr. Janeway, were added to the circle, the conversation took a higher flight, and we remember in his fireside discourses of that day, a vehemence and impressiveness which were wanting, except at some favoured moments, in his later years.   In all that regards the indulgence of the table he was frugal and plain in his tastes, and happily temperate, without anything like dietetic rigour.

"Nothing more characterized him than his fondness for communicating instruction on every subject, even the most elementary, within his reach.   It might be the alphabet, or Hebrew and Syriac grammar, or geometry and surveying, in which he was well versed, or metaphysics; he was unwearied and delighted, if only he had willing learners, and he had the art of making every learner willing.   Though he sent his boys to school, always giving his suffrage for the day-school method, he was constantly teaching his children.   Every one of them received from him, and commonly on his knee, the rudiments of spelling, arithmetic, geography, algebra, geometry, and the classic languages.   He would pass hours in a day giving lessons in the alphabet; breaking off a hundred times, as he observed the first symptom of weariness.   For in regard both to himself and others, he acted on Shakspeare's adage, 'No profit grows, where is no pleasure taken.'   Every corner of the house was occupied by bits of paper, flying like Sibylline leaves, and covered with spelling-lessons, executed by himself in printing characters, and decorated with bold but most unartistic drawings of beasts, birds, and houses.   As the little ones got on to the dead languages, which on his plan was very early, similar papers contained lists of Latin words to be committed to memory; and in the case of one son the number of such words amounted to thousands.   He quoted with approval the testimony of Dr. Witherspoon, who in presbyterial trials, used to examine the candidates on 'vocables' rather than on translation of books.   These avocations were confined to no hours. It might seem strange how he could endure the interruption; but it was his peculiarity that he seemed incapable of being interrupted. Except in hours of devotion his study was always free to his children, even the youngest; noise made no difference; their books and toys were on his floor ; and two or three would be clambering upon him, while he was handling a folio or had a pen in his hand. In times of health and spirits his manner of playing with his children was amusingly romping and even boisterous, and he threw them about with a sprightliness which often extorted a momentary cry of fear or pain. To this may be ascribed the unusual freedom which they always had in his presence, but which was checked in a moment when he grew suddenly sad or grave, as was often the case. Before dismissing the matter of family training, we ought to mention his constant and animated conversations with his children. It was his solace, at home and by the way. Without the slightest appearance of plan, but with an easy and spontaneous flow, he was, during some hours of every day, pouring forth a stream of useful information on all subjects, but chiefly on religion. The whole wealth of his extended reading and observation seemed at one time or another to be distilled in these familiar interviews. All the romantic and stirring events of his early mountain life, the tales of Indian massacres, to which his grandmother had fallen a victim, his journeys in new countries, and his school-boy days, came in for their share. He excelled in graphic narration, and attracted the attention of guests and strangers, even when directly addressing himself to babes. As soon as a child could comprehend the subject, he began with the beautiful stories of the Bible, and repeated them again and again, until the little ones were perfectly acquainted with them, long before they could make use of books. It was a common thing for his hearers to be melted to tears. This natural and extraordinary gift led him to indulge in biblical narrative in the pulpit, to a degree which we believe to be uncommon, and gave a singular attraction to certain discourses, especially on the parables and miracles of our Lord. For the same reason his addresses and sermons to children were incomparably winning, and his labours in this kind were sought for, far and near, much beyond his ability of supply. Without trying to speak in monosyllables, as if they were more intelligible than longer words, he always made himself perfectly intelligible to the humblest capacity."

When the number of the students of the Seminary became too great to be accommodated in the houses of the professors, they were permitted to meet in the lecture-room of the College, and the use of the College library was also granted to them. In 1817 they numbered over one hundred, and in 1818 they took possession of a building erected for their own use. "About the same time Dr. Alexander removed into the commodious dwelling in which he spent the remainder of his days. In the new circumstances, Dr. Alexander felt himself invigorated and advancing. With his colleague, Dr. Miller, he maintained the most pleasing and harmonious intimacy; and when an additional helper came, it was in the person of the Rev. Charles Hodge, whose talents he had early discerned, and whom he regarded more as a beloved son than even as a cherished pupil. He had by this time accumulated and digested much of what was to be the matter of his teachings; at least he had surveyed the entire field, and distinctly marked out its boundaries and divisions. His study-door was over against the Seminary entrance, and very near to it. These few steps he might be seen to take day by day, at the appointed hours, always in full time. And during many years of his life, this may be said to have been the only exercise he took; as he was now sliding into that habit which afterwards became inveterate. It is not believed that he seriously undervalued the importance of this means of health in others, but it is certain that in the last thirty years of his life, he used as little bodily motion as any man of his times, confining himself not only to one apartment, but to one chair. This was in striking contrast to the customs of Dr. Miller; and there was an amicable but incessant controversy between them on this point, often waged with as much ability as jocoseness. This proximity of the Seminary, and Dr. Alexander's habit of never denying himself to visitors, contributed very much to that frequency of intercourse with his pupils, which so many of them remember with pleasure. At all hours, and often in an unbroken succession for hours, he would receive visitors, and listen to them commonly with patience. He was certainly to be forgiven, if sometimes, in the presence of the more wearisome ones, he took up his pen, or gazed abstractedly upon that distant horizon marked by blue hills, which he loved to contemplate from his eastern window. Besides the perpetual work of preparation, in which he was now employed literally every day, his regular public services may be stated as follows: He gave one lecture, daily, which with the accompanying examination of his classes, occupied at least an hour. On Tuesday evening he attended an exercise of speaking, at which every student, at stated periods, pronounced a discourse of his own composition, on some religious subject. To this was added, during some years, the delivery of complete sermons by the students. All these were subject to the professors' criticism, and in these exercises the labours were shared by Dr. Miller. On Friday evening there was a debate, on some point in theology or allied subjects, in a theological society, comprising almost the whole Seminary. The utmost freedom was allowed, and the debate was concluded by the summing up of the professors, who were both always present. As this was a period of very active controversy in our church, on those points of theology which have since divided us, there was, as might have been expected, a peculiar animation in these discussions; and in our opinion he never shone more, or more displayed his stores of knowledge, his grasp of great subjects, or his acumen and dialectical force, than in some of these disputations, when, after being warmed by hearing the defence of specious error, he closed with the establishment of sound doctrine. The professors by turns attended evening prayers with the young men; the morning service being conducted by the senior students. At these exercises Dr. Alexander sometimes expounded a passage of Scripture, and sometimes made a brief but pointed exhortation. He was accustomed also to join his colleague in the meeting for prayer, known as the Monthly Concert. One day in each month was left vacant for the class prayer-meetings of the young men, and for their more solemn private devotions, to which many of them added fasting; and it was common for the professors to meet the whole body at a certain hour of the day. From this time forward, even before the erection of a separate chapel, there was a discourse to the students on the morning of the Lord's day, delivered alternately by Dr. Alexander and Dr. Miller.

" But there was no exercise which more impressed its character on the students of that day than the Conference of Sunday afternoon, which has been already mentioned. This meeting, it is believed, owed its origin entirely to the suggestion of Dr. Alexander, and was kept up as long as he lived. Indeed, there were some peculiarities in the manner of conducting it, which may be said to have grown out of his remarkable aptitude for free colloquial descant on religious topics. As the other exercises of the Seminary were intended to give fitness for the external work, this was directed solely to the cultivation of the heart, and there are not a few who bless God that they were ever brought under its sacred influence. Nothing could be more simple than the mode of managing this colloquy. After singing and prayer, a subject in experimental or practi-

8

cal religion, which had been named the week before, was discussed. The conversation was opened by one of the students,
whose turn it was; any others were allowed to express their
views, as they were called on in order, until a sufficient time
had been spent. The professors then closed with a familiar
discourse of from twenty to thirty minutes. As we have intimated, this was an occasion which more than any other Dr.
Alexander used for the outpouring of his profound personal
experience of Divine things. There was scarcely a topic in
regard to vital piety which did not come into discussion during the Seminary course. As he sat in his chair, he would
begin with a low voice and in the most ordinary tones of conversation, evidently relying upon the feeling of the moment, as
raised by foregoing remark, for all his animation. As he went
on and drew more largely on his recollections and his consciousness, he seldom failed to kindle, and sometimes at the
conclusion left all present in a state of high emotion. These
remarkable effusions sometimes almost took the form of soliloquy, as, losing sight of all around him, he uttered the serene
or enraptured feelings of a soul in communion with God. Singing and prayer closed the service, which commonly occupied
about an hour and a half. It is but just to add that Dr. Miller also delighted in this meeting, and contributed to it some
of his most valuable thoughts."

"During all this time he was preaching as much as many
pastors. Both to his own students and to those of the College
he was always welcome in the pulpit. For a time, he and
Dr. Miller, assisted afterwards by Mr. now Dr. Hodge, preached
on Sunday evenings in the village church. We have said
before, that during his whole life as a pastor, Dr. Alexander
used the free method, and carried no manuscript into the
pulpit. After his arrival at Princeton, he began to change his
method in a certain degree, making more experiment of written composition in sermons on important topics. And what
he wrote he also read; for he frequently declared his inability
to commit a discourse to memory. We are bound to say that
so far as manner and impression are concerned, these efforts
fell far below his ordinary discourses. The matter was always
equally valuable, and the train of thought was often close and
felicitous; but he was sometimes indescribably trammelled by
his paper, and was not a rhetorical reader; so that whole congregations used to brighten up as with a ray of sudden sun-
shine, when towards the close he would throw up his specta-
cles, cast about his penetrating glances, and, as if indignant at
his duresse, break forth in the liberty of his natural eloquence

No two preachers were more unlike than was he in the two portions of the same discourse. For this reason those who never listened to him at home, or were acquainted only with his discourses on great occasions, which were carefully written and read, have but the faintest idea of what he was as a preacher. And the period of which we are writing was that in which he condensed into his pulpit exercises the greatest amount of theological instruction, with the still unwasted vivacity of his earlier years. In two classes of sermons he especially excelled; first, in those which clearly and connectedly set forth the different parts of doctrine, in the way of definition and proof, so as to bring them within the scope of the humblest minds; and secondly, those in which he gave the history of a religious experience, in its origin, progress, and consummation, with minute dissection, graphic detail, and moving appeal to the heart. In the latter of these there were many who considered him unsurpassed."

It now becomes necessary to notice the commencement of his career as an author. Few men whose works fill so many volumes began to publish so late in life. In Philadelphia he had published his sermon at the opening of the General Assembly, and another called forth by the burning of the theatre in Richmond, Virginia, and had contributed several articles to various magazines, but he was more eager to acquire knowledge himself than to appear before the public as an author. To this, like the former part of his life-work, he was directed by an overruling Providence. In 1823 he was made aware that there was a knot of sceptics in the College, and as it was feared that their opinions might be diffusive, he was requested by one of the tutors to preach a sermon on the evidences of Christianity. He complied, and was requested to publish it, and having made some additions to it, it was brought out in an 18mo volume from the Princeton press, under the title of "Outlines of the Evidences of Christianity." This work has now been translated into several languages, and is the text-book in many schools and colleges. In 1826 he published "The Canon of the Old and New Testament Scriptures ascertained; or, the Bible Complete without the Apocrypha and written tradition," intended as a supplement to the above. This work has been republished in various forms both in this country and in Great Britain. In 1835 it was incorporated into the *Biblical Family Library*, published in Edinburgh, with notes by Dr. David Dickson, who characterizes it as "by far the most complete view of the whole subject that has hitherto been published."

In 1825 Professor Hodge began the publication of the *Biblical Repertory*, the original design of which was to bring within the reach of the English reader those stores of learning on biblical matters which were then only accessible to the readers of Latin and German. In 1829 its pages were opened for original matter, and from that time Dr. Alexander became a constant contributor.

In 1833 he published a "History of the Patriarchs," and in 1839 he contributed to a religious journal those "Thoughts on Religious Experience" which were in 1840 collected in a volume and published by the Presbyterian Board of Publication. This is perhaps the most original of his works. Much of it is his own experience, developed in the mental struggles of his youth, and subjected to the severe scrutiny of his riper years; the rest of it is the result of his daily contact with distressed souls, who by letter and personally resorted to him for counsel and relief. "As he advanced in life," says his son, "these confidential applications, both in person and by letter, were surprisingly increased, until the labour became almost burdensome. But it was by this very means, noiseless and unobtrusive as it was, rather than by formal teaching, by sermons, or by authorship, that he built up that character and attained that influence which were so universally recognized in the church. He lives now, in the memory of great numbers, especially of the clergy, as eminently a wise counsellor and a spiritual guide. In regard to such communications his reticency was almost extreme, and of his large correspondence on such topics he committed every vestige to the flames."

In 1841 he published "The Log College" and "The History of African Colonization," and during this period there was scarcely a week in which he did not contribute some paper to the religious journals.

"It has often been observed with justice," says his son, "that though Dr. Alexander had removed from his native State, he never lost influence there. Until his last breath he was intensely a Virginian; and nothing more kindled his restless eye, or animated his nervously mobile frame, or called out his colloquial fires, than any occasion for vindicating the honour of the 'old colony and dominion.' In return, his opinions continued to have much weight in the Virginia churches. More than once they sought to win him back to their bosom." In 1820 he was again elected President of Hampden Sidney College. The congregation of Cumberland simultaneously tendered to him a call to become their pastor, with the understanding that he was also to preach at the College church and at Briery. Immediately after this the Synod of Virginia chose him for their professor of theology; and these attempts to bring him back to his native State were renewed in 1831, when the Synod of Virginia urged him to accept the professorship of divinity in the Union Theological Seminary. He visited his old friends in Virginia frequently, preaching everywhere to · immense gatherings; and as it regards his judgments, feelings, and policy, he was decidedly a Southern man.

Though Dr. Alexander was the leading expositor of the old Calvinistic, or, as it is often called, "Princeton theology," he was always tolerant of those who differed from him. He also considered it unbecoming in a teacher of theology to be foremost in a field of strife, and while the contest between the Old and New-school raged in the church, in writing to Dr. Weed, he says: "We go on here upon our old moderate plan, teaching the old doctrines of Calvinism, but not disposed to consider every man a heretic who differs in some few points from us." He was opposed to all schemes that tended to the division of the church, and even as late as in 1837 he says: "I say, no division. Let us hold together as long as the foundation can be felt under our feet." He took no leading part in the division which took place in 1838, and never gave his assent to the Act and Testimony; but he never shrank from giving his opinion upon what he considered right, and all the influence of his judgment was thrown into the Old-school side.

When Dr. Alexander approached his seventieth year his mental vigour was not abated. He never had better health, and feeling little inclination to take out-door exercise, he prosceuted his literary and professional labours with untiring assiduity. The variety of his studies may be seen from the titles of the articles appended to this sketch; and he now completed his "Outlines of Moral Science," added several new lectures to his course, projected and wrote several hundred pages of a new work on Patristical Theology, composed a great number of biographical sketches and memoirs, and preached upon an average once every Sabbath.

"On the day of his entering his seventy-eighth year he visited the house of his eldest son, played gayly with the children, and seemed as alert and keen as in his best days. His attention to his grandchildren was remarkable. They clambered upon his knees as freely as their parents had done before them, were instructed by his drawings and his tales, and seemed to give him unmingled delight. He often prayed over them, laying on them his hands in benediction.

"It was almost a daily remark in the house, that these were

his best days, even in natural things, and that he never had so vivid an enjoyment of life. Such was his own delightful admission: 'Old age,' said he, 'is not an unpleasant part of life where health and piety are possessed.' A host of physical evils which had beset him in earlier days had now been mercifully removed. His simple nourishment was enjoyed without rule or scruple, and the morbid vigils which once distressed him gave place to balmy sleep. It was apparent to every one that he was in higher spirits, even if sometimes his alternations of depressed feeling would return. Occasionally he would break out in conversation with all the exuberance and glee of his youth; but the characteristic of his temper was a benignant serenity. From our earliest recollections he had been accustomed to sit and muse in the evening twilight, often prolonging these hours far beyond the time when lights are usually demanded. These moments, though solemn, appeared to be pleasurable. In these he pursued his most fruitful trains of thought. As he grew older, this solitary exercise was more frequent and protracted; and in no instance did it seem to merge into anything like slumber. It was a period to be gratefully remembered as one of singular peace."

From the general tone of his correspondence it may be gathered that he was habitually meditating on his approaching departure; but this gave no sombre colouring to his manners or his words. He saw beyond the grave "a heaven of joy and love," and in his family prayers, and especially in his sermons and addresses at the Lord's table, his countenance was often radiant with spiritual joy.

"Old age never seemed to occur to him as affording a motive to relax from labour. His principle was that the faculties were to be kept in vigour by perpetual use." Writing to Dr. Plumer, he says, "On this day week I expect to enter on my eightieth year; and of course I cannot expect to continue here much longer. I have no intention of resigning while my health is good and my mind sound. If I should be seized with paralysis, or some other disease which would disqualify me for performing the duties of my office, I might deem it expedient to resign; but it is my general purpose and hope to die in the harness." No one ever observed any appearance of decay in his mental powers. "At the stroke of the bell he might be seen, without fail, issuing from his study door, and going across the small space which divided the Seminary from his grounds; much bent, and with eyes turned to the ground, as he paced slowly on, wrapped in his cloak, and with his profuse silver locks waving in the wind; but often, as if at some sudden dash of thought, he would quicken his steps almost to running, and ascend the threshold with alacrity. This was a peculiarity of his motion all his life. His children always knew his whereabout by the vivacity of his changes, and used to say jocosely that he never closed or opened a door softly, and always ran up stairs. With his manuscript rolled up in his hand, he took the chair, and after a short and pertinent prayer, began his instructions. They were always such as kept his pupils in wakeful attention, and, so far as we know, were not less acceptable than those of his younger life."

The summer-heat of the year 1851 extended into the month of September, and had a debilitating effect upon his system. He was seized with a diarrhœa, which weakened him much; as it increased, it gave him no rest night nor day. With a clear perception of his approaching end, he sent for Dr. Hodge and committed to him his account book of the scholarships, and explained to him what he wished done in reference to them, and gave him some general directions as to his funeral. His son James at this time returned from a visit to Europe, and on the 17th of October, " taking him by the hand, he gave thanks to God for having preserved him, and for allowing this interview, which he had greatly desired. He then proceeded to give a number of directions and orders, with perfect composure and the deliberation of one who utters a series of charges from a memorandum. There was an air of unearthly authority which we remember with awe. He said that his end was approaching, and that all arrangements had been completed for the comfort and sustenance of his family. To his son he then gave the Hebrew Bible, which had been his daily companion for forty years. He designated for his eldest grandson the fine Clarendon Cicero, in ten quarto volumes, and caused us, for the second boy, to choose between Hesychius and Burmann's quarto Quintilian. He had previously pointed out for little William Alexander, one of his grandchildren, the walking-stick which he had long used. These things were done with all the calmness and cheerfulness of his most untroubled days. He proceeded to name two of his sons, who should have the entire control of his manuscripts, and of any notice that might be published of his life. He said that his treatise on *Moral Science* was in his judgment the most worthy of being edited. After having thus settled his last worldly affairs, he proceeded to talk freely about the work of God in the Reformed churches abroad, and when his strength was exhausted, dismissed his son. In all that he uttered he was clear, succinct, and decided, speaking with a mien which carried something of command."

On the same day Dr. Hodge saw him for the last time. To him he expressed his desire that Dr. John McDowell should preach his funeral sermon, but with the injunction that he should not utter one word of eulogy. He then, with a smile, handed him a white bone walking-stick, which had been presented to him by one of the chiefs of the Sandwich Islands, saying, "You must leave this to your successor in office, that it may be handed down as a kind of symbol of orthodoxy."

On the morning of the Thursday preceding Dr. Alexander's death, the Rev. William E. Schenck, then pastor of the First Church of Princeton, called to inquire after his health, when Dr. Alexander desired to see him, and, in an interesting interview, among other things said to him: "I feel confident that I am not mistaken. I shall not live long, nor have I any wish to stay longer. I have lived eighty years, which is more than the usual term of human life, and if I remain, I have little to look forward to but infirmity and suffering. If such be the Lord's will, I feel thoroughly satisfied, and even would prefer to go now. My work on earth, I feel, is done; and it seems to me (he added with great earnestness) as if my heavenly Father had in great mercy surrounded me with almost every circumstance which could remove anxiety, and make me feel that I can go without regret. My affairs have all been attended to, my arrangements are all completed, and I can think of nothing more to be done. I have greatly desired to see my son James before my departure, and sometimes feared I should not have that privilege, but the Lord has graciously brought him back in time to see me, having led him safely through much peril on the ocean. My children are all with me. The church of which you are pastor is prosperous and flourishing. The Seminary Faculty is again full, and the institution is in an excellent condition. The more I reflect upon the matter, the more all things seem to combine to make me perfectly willing to enter into my rest. The Lord has very graciously and tenderly led me (he added, closing his eyes and clasping his hands in a devotional manner) all the days of my life—yes, all the days of my life; and he is now with me still. *In Him I enjoy perfect peace.*"

In his illness his early days seemed to pass in review before him; and during one of those nights in which his devoted wife was watching by his side, he broke out into a soliloquy, rehearsing God's gracious dealings with his soul. On this occasion more than on any other, his emotions approached the form of holy rapture. "He was especially thankful," says his son, "that our dear mother was permitted to wait on him to the last; and when approaching his end, he said, with great tenderness, 'My dear, one of my last prayers will be that you may have as serene and painless a departure as mine.'"

"On Saturday, October the 18th, his weakness was extreme, and from this time he refused to take any anodyne. He said he knew that death could not be far off, and he wished his mind to be entirely free from the effects of stupefying drugs. During the night he suffered more pain than at any time previous, but in the intervals was perfectly calm and peaceful—more than peaceful—he seemed as happy as if he was already in heaven." In this state he continued, getting feebler every day, till Wednesday, the 22d of October 1851, when he entered into his rest.

By previous appointment, the Synod of New Jersey met this year at Princeton, on the 21st of October. Dr. Alexander had looked forward to this meeting with anticipated pleasure, and one day, a little before his death, had recalled by memory the names of one hundred and fifteen of the members who had formerly been his pupils. When the day came he was too sick to see them, but it was a dispensation of Providence grateful to their feelings, to permit so many of them to assemble around his bier. The Presbytery of New Brunswick, of which he had long been a member, claimed the honour of carrying him to the grave, and it was granted them. His sons, and one whom he always called his son, followed as mourners; then a long line of clergymen and others from the surrounding country swelled the melancholy train, for all felt "that a prince and a great man had fallen that day in Israel."

Janetta Waddel, the faithful partner of his life, and six sons and a daughter survived him.

Of American divines, the names of Edwards and Alexander take the first place; and between the lives of Brown of Haddington and Dr. Alexander there is a striking resemblance. They both in early life were educated under difficulties; with irrepressible desires for knowledge, they not only overcame their disadvantages, but became distinguished for their learning. Their studies and their works were to advance the practical and the useful. They both became the educators of numerous ministers, who treasured their instructions and revered their virtues. They were both happy in their domestic circumstances, and left behind them a numerous family of children and grandchildren, who, trained under happier auspices, built on the foundation they had laid, and made the

9

name more illustrious. They were respected by the men of their own time, and their names and their writings will descend as the heir-looms of the godly to all generations.

For further information concerning Dr. Alexander, we refer to "The Life of Archibald Alexander, D. D., LL.D., by his son James W. Alexander, D. D.," 1 vol. 8vo, or in a condensed form, one vol. 12mo. It is almost an autobiography, written in the later years of Dr. Alexander's life, and is exceedingly interesting. The passages above marked quoted are taken from this work. It was reviewed by Dr. Hodge in the *Princeton Review* for 1855. There is a short sketch in Sprague's *Annals of the American Presbyterian Pulpit*, with letters from Drs. Boardman, Hall, and Schenck. In the *Presbyterian Magazine* for 1852, there is a short memoir, with extracts from the *Minutes* of the Presbyteries of Lexington and Hanover, and in the *Home and Foreign Record* for 1851, there is an account of his funeral, by Dr. Van Rensselaer, and of his works issued by the Board of Publication, by Dr. Leyburn.

He contributed the following articles to this *Review:*—

1829. The Bible a Key to the Phenomena of the Natural World—Smith's Discourses on the Priesthood of Christ—Cause and Effect.

1830. Early History of Pelagianism—Dr. Daniel Wilson's Evidences of Christianity—Dr. Green's Lectures on the Shorter Catechism—The Doctrine of the Church on Original Sin.

1831. Dr. Woods on Inspiration—Dr. Matthews' Letters —On Inability of Sinners—Christian Baptism.

1832. Organization of the Presbyterian Church—Character of the Genuine Theologian—Articles of the Synod of Dort —The Formation of Opinions and Pursuit of Truth.

1833. German Works on Interpretation—Bishop McIlvaine's Lectures—The Racovian Catechism—Jay's Works—Life of Rev. George Burder—Becon the Reformer—Melanchthon on Sin.

1834. Catechism of the Council of Trent—English Dissenters—Evidences of a New Heart—The Church Establishment of England.

1835. Established Church of Scotland—The Present State and Prospects of the Presbyterian Church*—The Scottish Seceders—Wayland's Moral Science—Woods on Depravity.

1836. Abercrombie's Man of Faith—Symington on the

---

* This article is claimed to be the production of Dr. Alexander, in his Life, by Dr. James W. Alexander, p. 407. It is however attributed to Dr. Miller by others. See Life of Dr. Miller, by his Son, vol. ii. p. 271.

Atonement—Practical View of Regeneration—Letters on the Difficulties of Religion—Luther at Worms—Library of Christian Knowledge.

1837. Samuel Blair—Godwin on Atheism.

1838. Incidents of Travel in Egypt—General Assembly of 1638—Indian Affairs—Presbyterian Missions.

1839. Life of Joseph Brant—Memoir of Mrs. Hawkes—Auchterarder Case—Moral Machinery Simplified.

1840. History of the American Colony in Liberia—Justification by Faith.

1841. Pastoral Fidelity and Diligence—The works of Dr. Chalmers, (with J. W. A.)—Origin of the Aborigines of America.

1842. Independent Nestorians—Review of Gurley's Mission—Emmons's Works (with J. A. A.)

1843. Instruction of the Negro Slaves — Universalism Renounced.

1844. Mr. Kennedy's Report—Presbyterian Church in Ireland—Deistical Controversy in the West—Debate on Baptism.

1845. The Scotch India Mission—Life of Milner—Principle of Design, &c.

1846. Struthers's History of the Relief Church—Housman's Life—Works of Andrew Fuller.

1847. Horæ Apocalypticæ—Charles Simeon—Davidson's Presbyterian Church in Kentucky—Brown's Second Advent.

1848. Chalmers's Mental and Moral Philosophy.

1849. The Free Church Pulpit—The Calcutta Review.

1850. Robert Blair—President Wheelock—Close Communion.

ALEXANDER, JAMES WADDEL. Next to that of the founder, this name is the most prominent in the history of the *Biblical Repertory*. In September 1824, when he was a tutor in the College, he writes, "You have here another prospectus of another Princeton work which I trust will prove honourable to us, and useful to the cause." In the following December he writes again: "Mr. Hodge's new work will appear on the first of next month. I have been hard at work for some days, translating some German-Latin for him." And on January 11, 1825, "The first number of Mr. Hodge's new work is issued, and has a fine appearance." From that date until April 1859, when premonitions of the end were signified in his correspondence by such expressions as "the finger stutters in writing"—"writing, which was a solace, has become a very burdensome task"—he was a constant contributor. The number of his papers and the diversity of their topics, may be learned from the list appended to this article.

James Waddel Alexander was the eldest son of Archibald Alexander, D. D., and, on his mother's side, grandson of James Waddel, D. D. Both families belonged to Virginia, and James W. was born in Louisa county, in that State, in the house of his grandfather, whose name he received, on the thirteenth of March 1804.

At the time of his birth his father was President of Hampden Sidney College, in the county of Prince Edward; but in 1806, having accepted the call of the Third Church of Philadelphia, he removed his residence thither, and reached the city with his family early in December of that year. In the sixth year of that residence Dr. Alexander was · removed, by the unanimous election of the General Assembly, to Princeton, to open the first Theological Seminary of our church. "In the month of July 1812, Dr. Alexander arrived in Princeton, with his wife, then in the bloom and freshness of a health which endured to old age, and with four children, of whom the oldest was not nine years old." It was that oldest one who wrote this sentence in the life of his father in 1854. He had already begun the study of Latin in the school of James Ross, who was the author of the best Greek and Latin grammars of his day, and who could hardly ·be excelled at any time in the rigid accuracy with which he grounded his pupils in the rudiments of the classical languages. But it was only a beginning which he had time to make in Philadelphia, of that education which was to bear such good fruit in the future. In the Princeton "Academy," and successively under the Rev. Jared D. Fyler, Rev. (afterwards President) Carnahan, and Rev. Daniel Comfort as masters, his studies were pursued, and then, for a time, in the school of Mr. James Hamilton, subsequently a Professor in the University of Nashville. One or more of the theological students occasionally assisted him as tutors, and thus prepared he was admitted to the Freshman class in the College of New Jersey at the spring term of 1817, being no more than thirteen years of age. At the time of his matriculation, Dr. Ashbel Green was President of the College; the other chairs were filled by Dr. Philip Lindsley and Mr. Henry Vethake. The tutors were Robert W. Condit and Thomas J. Biggs. Among his classmates were several whose names have, like his own, become conspicuous in public life—such as Governor George W. Crawford, of Georgia; President Finley, of the College of South Carolina; Chief Justice and Chancellor Green, of New

Jersey; Governor and Judge Haines, of New Jersey; Rev. Dr. Kirk, of Albany and Boston; Professor Lindsley, of the Medical College, District of Columbia; President Talmage, of Oglethorpe University; Messrs. Gholson, Iverson, and Rodney, members of Congress; President Z. Butler, of Mississippi College.

In the second year of his College life Alexander began a correspondence with a friend in Philadelphia, somewhat his junior, and still a schoolboy, which was continued, with scarcely a pause, until within a few weeks of his death. His first letter bore the date May 5, 1819; the last, June 23, 1859. The whole number on his side was not less than eight hundred, and from them a copious selection has been published under this title: "Forty Years' Familiar Letters of James W. Alexander, D. D. Edited by the surviving correspondent, John Hall, D. D." In such a series of letters is to be found, besides the greatest accuracy of the facts which belong to a memoir, the best exhibition that is possible, of the developement of the writer's mind and character. It not only makes the writer the best biographer of himself, but *undesignedly* the best, and therefore the most unreserved, guileless, and complete. In this feature the Alexander "Familiar Letters" have scarcely a parallel in literature.

When he graduated, in September 1820, Alexander found no cause for congratulation upon his excellent opportunities; for he had not improved them as in his conscience he felt he should have done, to deserve the diploma he received. But about the same time his remorse was awakened for more serious than intellectual negligence. He had been living without the Christian principle. He had not honoured his church birthright. For a time, "he found no place of repentance, though he sought it carefully with tears." But at length he discovered that it was not to be found by tears. "On September 3, 1820, walking across the field, hardly daring to ask for faith or repentance, these words burst upon my mind—*'waiting for the moving of the waters.'* I saw myself the impotent man in a moment, and I thought that Christ had been saying to me, 'Wilt thou be made whole?' hundreds of times in my hearing, but now it seemed to be addressed particularly to me. From that moment I felt able to trust my whole hope and life upon the Lord." He went to his first communion April 1, 1821.

He immediately applied himself with the greatest diligence to the branches of study he had neglected in college, and found it an easy task to recover the lost ground, under the excitement of what now seemed to him newly-discovered treasures. As to his future life he felt as if there were no alternative to the ministry of the gospel, because he saw no other occupation in which he could so fully devote himself to his redeeming Lord, and use his influence for good. Accordingly, in November 1822, he placed himself in the Theological Seminary at Princeton, then under the instruction of Drs. Alexander and Miller, as professors, and the Rev. Mr. Hodge as assistant teacher. In his own class, numbering about forty, and in the two other more advanced classes, making nearly one hundred in all, and in the still larger accessions of the two following years, he found in the Seminary circle all that could be desired of fellowship and stimulus in preparation for the sacred calling. The catalognes of those years present many names that were then preparing for the distinction that has since surrounded them. Bush, Barnes, Woolsey, Pressley, Kirk, Waterbury (his roommate), Peers, Brinsmade, Bethune, Proudfit, and Nevin, are among them, and scores of others who, if less known in church and college, in authorship and leadership, were among the most laborious and useful of pastors and missionaries.

It was in the second year of his Seminary course that the trustees of the College, after two previous and unsuccessful efforts, again solicited him to take the office of Tutor in Mathematics. He was now prevailed upon to consent, as he saw the advantage it would afford him of improving his mind by general study, while it would only nominally separate him for a time from the Seminary. Accordingly, he transferred his residence to Nassau Hall in May 1824. A year afterwards he exchanged the mathematical for the classical tutorship. As his engagements in the College did not wholly intermit his theological reading; so he found time also for improving himself in German, French, mineralogy, geology, anatomy, music, and English literature, and began that practice of composition, in the shape of contributions to periodical works, which became the congenial habit of the remainder of his life. *The National Gazette and Literary Register*, a daily newspaper published in Philadelphia, with Mr. Robert Walsh as editor, was, as its name imported, and its editorship insured, a resource for scholarly men, both as readers and contributors. Young Alexander sent to its well-known "outer form" a number of classical and other communications—some of the most solid of them as "from the portfolio of a solitary student." To pass the censorship of a critic like Walsh, and to have an appearance in a journal which was then unique of its kind, implied, half a century ago, more than newspaper writing does at the present time. The successful trial of his hand upon the *Gazette* procured for Alexander a welcome from the same editor when he had established the *American Quarterly Review*. But, to use his own language, " I am willing deliberately to sacrifice the character of a man of science, of taste, of varied and elegant accomplishments, with all its ease, honours, and emoluments, for that of ' a man of God, thoroughly furnished unto all good works'—a character which is to be sought in the study of the sacred volume." He determined, therefore, to close his academical career, and to present himself to the Presbytery of New Brunswick as a candidate for licensure. After passing the requisite examinations, he was admitted to probation by that venerable body on the 4th of October 1825. His first sermon was preached, four days afterwards (Saturday) in the session-room of the Cedar-street church, New York. On the following Lord's day he preached in one of the churches of Brooklyn, and in the Cedar-street church. In the first week of December he left Princeton for a visit to his native State, a movement which resulted in making it his first home as a pastor. Having been heard in Baltimore, he was solicited to become the colleague of the aged Dr. Glendy in that city, and in Richmond he had the opportunity of receiving a call from the Shockoe-hill congregation; but he did not yield to either. Passing by such prominent positions, the young licentiate preferred the rural spot which his father had once occupied (and in which he himself was followed by his son), and was at the same time ordained to the full ministry, and installed pastor of the Charlotte Court-House church by the Hanover Presbytery, March 3, 1827. This happy settlement, however, was soon interrupted by an illness which kept the young pastor from his work from August 1827 to June 1828, by which time he had removed to Princeton, having been compelled by the condition of his health to abandon the Southern climate entirely.

The next position he occupied was that of pastor of what was then the only Presbyterian congregation in Trenton, New Jersey, where he continued from January 1829 to the close of 1832. He was very happy in this connection, especially as it included the time of his marriage (June 1830). " I should be unwilling to exchange Trenton for any pastoral charge which I have ever seen, excepting only Charlotte Court-House." Being the capital of the State, it was the residence of a number of prominent men of the bench and bar, and officers of the government and legislature. " Under the new circumstances I feel a greater stimulus to what may be called the external or literary part of preparation, than I ever experienced among my simple flock in Virginia." Outside of his theological reading, including daily study of the original Scriptures, he read largely in the Greek and Roman classics; added Italian and Dutch to his foreign languages; translated from the German hymnology; dipped into chemistry, physiology, and civil law, and indulged in a wide scope of miscellaneous literature. His pen was active on works which he projected and abandoned, and on some which, during these four years or subsequently, were published. It was then that he began to write for the press of the American Sunday-School Union, both for its periodicals and library—an employment he maintained till the last. His volumes, large and small, from that press, exceeded thirty in number. He had made some progress in preparing a Commentary on the Gospels for Sunday-schools, which he relinquished upon learning that the Rev. Albert Barnes was further advanced in a similar undertaking; but he completed for publication the volume of Sacred Geography which was begun by his brother Addison. The Union endeavoured to secure him as one of its permanent Secretaries in Philadelphia, but the proposal was declined, as were also overtures from churches in Lexington (Kentucky), and Baltimore, to become their pastor. He not only contributed largely to the quarterly numbers of the *Biblical Repertory*, but served for a time as its editor. It was at this period that the agitations in the church on questions of doctrine and polity were beginning to assume the serious aspect which ended in the division so lately healed by reunion. This sketch is not the place, even were it for other reasons now expedient, to state Mr. Alexander's position in the controversy. The ground taken by the *Repertory* is sufficiently well known; but the *spirit* in which he contemplated the strife is evinced in such exclamations as, "Oh for a corner where theological warfare is unknown!"—"The greatest heresy is want of love"—"What would I have? certainly peace; if possible, unity of doctrine; then unity of organization; if we cannot be 'like-minded,' we may at least be 'having the same love,' and the way to attain this seems to be 'let each esteem others better than themselves.'"

Although Mr. Alexander's pastoral work in Trenton was frequently diminished or interrupted by feeble health, his people would cheerfully have granted any amount of indulgence rather than part with him. But he was too sensitive and conscientious to retain his place under the circumstances, and having resolved to change his occupation for a time, he accepted an invitation of the proprietors of *The Presbyterian* to become its editor. He filled this post from November 1832 to the end of 1833, and then accepted the more congenial office of Professor of Rhetoric and Belles-Lettres in the College at Princeton, where he spent the next eleven years. His associates in the Faculty for more or less of his term of office were President Carnahan, Professors Maclean, Dod, Henry, Stephen Alexander, Hart, Torrey, Topping, Jaeger, Hargous, and De Sandrans. His father, and (from 1838) his brother, and his friend Dr. Hodge, were professors in the Theological Seminary; his relative, Dr. Benjamin H. Rice, was pastor of the village church. Here was a place eminently suited for his intellectual and social contentment; but, as he said in 1840, " I have always sat in my present chair with a feeling that it was right only as a refuge during ill health." He never rested from evangelical work. His preaching averaged sixty times for each year; and for seven years out of the eleven, he served regularly as the supply of the Witherspoon-street congregation, which is composed wholly of coloured people—a class in whose welfare his Virginia life had given him a particular interest. Besides his articles in the *Repertory*, he always had something in hand for the Sunday-school Union, or for the booksellers, or newspapers, aiming at the moral and social improvement of the young and of the labouring class. To this period belongs the publication of his works entitled, "The American Mechanic and Working Man;" also his "Good, Better, Best; or, the Three Ways of Making a Happy World," which was reprinted in London, with an introduction by Dr. Candlish; and "The Scripture Guide; a Familiar Introduction to the Study of the Bible." His literary reading kept up to the wide range which it had so long taken, and which his duties in the class-room required of one who was not satisfied to take his preparations at second-hand; for he contrived to subordinate every occupation to practical use: thus, he took lessons in drawing, that he might the better assist in the illustrations of his books for children, and pored over Greek tragedy in the hope of gaining a more accurate knowledge of New Testament grammar.

In the course of these years Mr. Alexander had several opportunities offered him of resuming the pastoral office, but he was waiting for strength to justify him in making a change towards which his heart was all the time inclined. The year 1844 brought the question before him with an urgency which seemed to open the way providentially for his return to the full work of the ministry. Duane-street church, in the city of New York, and Bowdoin-street church, (Congregational),

10

in Boston, simultaneously importuned him to become their pastor. After anxious deliberation he' believed it to be his duty to decide for New York, and he was accordingly installed there, October 3, 1844, just nineteen years after his licensure. It may be mentioned here that the honorary degree of Doctor of Divinity was bestowed on him, first by Lafayette College in 1843, and again by Harvard University in 1854.

In transferring his abode for the first time to a great city, and assuming the charge of a large congregation there, it was to be expected that a man of Dr. Alexander's piety, philanthropy, and conscientiousness would not only be surprised in the contrast with his secluded life hitherto, but that he would be more deeply affected at the new phases of misery, ungodliness, and disproportionate Christian zeal, than one who had become familiar with them all. It may be said without exaggeration, in view of the work to be done inside and outside of his parish, with his earnest desire to do good in every way, and with a nervous consciousness that it was impossible to fill the measure of his own convictions of duty, he was, throughout his life in New York, overwhelmed with labour and care. He could not confine his concern to a single congregation, steadily attending on the means of grace, and with few poor or uneducated persons in its connection, whilst tens of thousands lay around in poverty, degradation, and vice, unreached by the gospel. In every direction he saw opportunities of doing the work of Christ for the bodies, minds, and souls of a vast neglected population. Above the lowest strata of these, he saw enough in the condition of strangers, emigrants, young men, children, the respectable poor and aged, the sick and disabled, that called for more personal benevolence than the existing institutions could, or ought to be required to supply, independent of more strictly Christian effort. On the other hand, he believed that the church-system restricted itself too much to church-limits, leaned to conservatism rather than to aggression ; that the humbler classes were almost excluded from worship, and consequent access of the best of friends, by the worldly show of the houses of worship and the cost of sittings; and that there was a growing spirit of worldliness and "moderation" in the church itself, which suppressed the evangelical zeal and earnestness that constitute the life of practical religion. He thought that the times demanded a mode of preaching more plain, direct, and pungent than would please the prevailing taste, and which was surrendered only at the expense of the highest success. "When shall we come down from our stilts, and be in earnest with a perishing world?" His unvarying feelings to the end of life may be expressed in this language, used in 1851—"My mind works incessantly on such themes as these:—the abounding misery; the unreached masses; the waste of church-energy on the rich; its small operation on the poor; emigrant wretchedness; our boy-population; our hopeless prostitutes; our four thousand grog-shops; the absence of the poor from Presbyterian churches; the farce of our church-alms; confinement of our church-efforts to pewholders; the do-nothing life of our Christian professors, in regard to the masses; our copying the Priest and Levite in the parable; our need of a Christian Lord Bacon to produce a *Novum Organum* of philanthropy; our dread of innovation; our luxury and pride."

Having thus presented the state of his mind during the five years of his stay in the Duane-street congregation, it is only necessary to add that his time was occupied in doing what he could—probably more than he should have undertaken—to meet these causes of his lamentation. His new books were, " A Manual of Devotion for Soldiers and Sailors;" "Prayers and Hymns, &c. for the Blind;" " Frank Harper; or the Country-boy in town;" Thoughts on Family Worship." Among his multifarious subjects in the *Repertory* was, "Poverty and Crime in cities." He wrote for the American Tract Society, and the Presbyterian Board of Publication, as well as for the Sunday-school Union, and for the weekly religious papers. He prepared a report for the General Assembly on Parochial Schools (1846), and preached the Assembly's sermon on Missions (1847). For a time he was a regular monthly correspondent of the Dundee "Warder" in Scotland. He took special pleasure in his class on the catechism, in conversing with and in other ways benefitting young men, in the weekday services, in promoting through the agency of his congregation and otherwise, city missions, Sunday-schools, churches for the poor and for the coloured people, and in the duties of his position on the Executive Committee of Foreign Missions, Tract Society, and several organizations for evangelical efforts in the city alone. His visits and gifts to the poor and neglected, and the influence he exerted to procure help for them in every way, constituted an important department of his efficiency, not only as a pastor, but as a minister at large.

Those who knew his temperament saw how this would end. He himself admitted that his powers were tasked to a tension which must soon be fatal. In any other light the election by the General Assembly, which summoned him to the Theological Seminary at Princeton, would have met with serious objection;

but under the circumstances there could be no resistance. Dr. Miller, having, on account of age, resigned the chair of Ecclesiastical History and Church Government, which he had so reputably filled for thirty-six years, Dr. J. W. Alexander was chosen by the Assembly of that year as his successor. He removed to Princeton and soon opened his new course of instruction, but was not formally inaugurated until November 20, 1849.

The transition from the city to the village, from the active pastorate to the sedentary school, was too great and sudden to be entirely satisfactory. Besides, he was conscious that his aptitude lay in preaching rather than teaching. "I foresaw the evils I begin to feel; but they distress me more than I reckoned for. I miss my old women; and especially my weekly catechumens, my sick-rooms, my rapid walks, my nights of right-down fatigue." The preparation of lectures occupied many of the hours he had been accustomed to give to miscellaneous writing, but he contributed to every new number of the *Repertory*, and supplied an article for each of the twelve numbers of the "Princeton Magazine" published in 1850. In that year he gave one of the lectures, in the University of Virginia, of a course on the "Evidences of Christianity," which has been published in a volume with the rest of the series. His sermons averaged more than one a week.

Long before leaving New York, Dr. Alexander had foreseen that the tide of business would soon place the Duane-street church beyond convenient reach of the congregation. In 1851 that people were convinced of the necessity of removal, and as they were still without a pastor, they proposed to their late minister to build a church in a better situation, if he would consent to be recalled. He acceded to this proposal, and also to another which was made to him by the congregation on the most generous terms, that he should first recruit his health by a voyage. He served the Seminary to the close of April 1851. On the 24th of May he embarked for Liverpool, and reached Princeton in return on the fifteenth of the following October.

The late Rev. Dr. Hamilton, of London, remarked of the "Forty Years Letters" of Dr. Alexander, "no book gives me such a picture of American life and American religion." Many Americans will make a reciprocal acknowledgment of the effect on them of the letters in that collection which were written from Europe in 1851 and during the writer's second tour. Presupposing the general knowledge which educated persons have of Great Britain and the countries usually embraced in a rapid visit to the continent, the bird's-eye sketches of these notes bring the places, institutions, and people in a peculiarly vivid and fresh manner to the reader's mind.   Few travellers are so well prepared by previous information, taste, and good feeling, as this one for the appreciation and enjoyment of such a round as he took in 1851—from England to France, Switzerland, Germany, Holland, back to Scotland and Ireland: nor could he have desired more advantages of personal introduction and attention than he found in every quarter.

The November of 1851 found him at his new home in New York.   Duane-street was abandoned and the congregation worshipped in the chapel of the University while the church was in progress in Fifth Avenue.   A great change had passed over Princeton, for Dr. Archibald Alexander had lingered in his last illness for just a week after his son's arrival.   The history of the remaining years of his pastorate would be but a repetition of that of Duane-street as to the things that occupied the pastor's thoughts and filled his time.   From the day of its opening (December 19, 1852) everything in the secularities of the church was highly prosperous.   In less than a month the whole cost of the ground and building (more than one hundred thousand dollars) was paid, and all the pews (204) sold or rented.   In the same month the annual contribution for Foreign Missions amounted to $3,300; in the next month that for Domestic Missions to $3,750; in the next, for the Board of Education, $3,500.   Other objects—secular as well as ecclesiastical—were promoted with a corresponding liberality.   Outside of the church and its immediate adjuncts were sustained a large Mission Chapel, with a preacher and out-door assistants, Mission-schools, Industrial-schools, in addition to what was done through the many benevolent institutions of the city. The special interest of the pastor may be said to have been with these, for they came up more to his idea of church-work than the limited range of preaching to the same people in a church where the privilege of worship had to be bought. "Nothing tends to reconcile me more to pew-property."   He felt most apostolical in the plain expository line of the lecture-room, and with his classes of youth, and going from house to house among the poor, and preaching in the mission chapels. "I think if I could support myself, I would leave my charge any day, and begin down town."   Twice he declined an increase of salary, and was better satisfied to turn the liberality of the people into other channels.   The continued crowding of his pews, and the acceptance which his preaching found with his stationary congregation, seemed to have a contrary effect from that of making him contented with that as his place, and only to make him long the more for freedom to carry the gospel to the really destitute. The popular devices for effect through externals he despised, and one of his first successes in the Fifth Avenue church worship was to restore congregational singing under the lead of a single precentor, standing, as in old time, near the pulpit, and only *assisted* by the organ.

In the first six years of his ministry in the new church he took time for a few publications, in addition to his frequent appearance in the *Repertory*. "Plain words to a Young Communicant"—"The Merchant's Clerk cheered and counselled" —"The American Sunday-school and its adjuncts"—"Consolation: in discourses on select topics addressed to the suffering people of God"—indicate, as usual, the practical tenor of his writing. But the most elaborate occupation of his pen was upon the biography of his father, first published in 1854, in a volume of seven hundred pages.

Such large and various labours would seem to demand a condition of strong health to sustain them; but Dr. Alexander's life, at this stage, was frequently interrupted by indisposition, sometimes of the most painful and alarming kind; and his nervous system was never strong. In the spring of 1857, he was labouring with affections of the chest, that demanded an immediate cessation of labour, and this could be realized only by getting out of sight of New York. The generous acquiescence of his congregation enabled him to effect this object in the best manner for his comfort, by another trip to Europe, this time accompanied by his wife and youngest child. They reached Liverpool July 7, and were back by October 25, having spent the season in delightful excursions in Great Britain, France, Switzerland, Holland, Germany, and Belgium. The winter was spent with his usual activity, in and out of his particular church, and in the spring his heart rejoiced in a genuine religious awakening, that largely pervaded the city. His time was absorbed with visits to and from religious inquirers, and with the other duties required by the circumstances. He wrote sixteen tracts adapted to the occasion, most of which were afterwards collected into a volume, entitied, "The Revival and its Lessons," thousands of which were circulated in this country and in Scotland. Fifty-seven persons made their first profession in the April (1858) communion, and many subsequently; so that the year's report of the session in April 1859—the last one he lived to present to the General Assembly—gave a total of one hundred and twenty-five additions on examination. This number included some who worshipped stately in the Mission Chapel, which then was still under the care of the one session. The whole number of communicants at that time was 711, and how well the congregation was maintaining its work as well as its profession, is seen in the fact that its pecuniary contributions to public objects amounted in that year to forty-six thousand dollars, in addition to thirteen thousand paid for corporate expenses. And they have not lost the impulse; for in the tenth anniversary of the date referred to, (April 1869,) the aggregate sum is nearly double, ($109,500.)

In 1858 he published a volume of "Discourses on Common Topics of Christian Faith and Practice."

No recreations or vacations could permanently recruit the health of one who returned to such burdens of work, and who was so morbidly distressed by the inability to accomplish all that was in his heart. The spring of 1859 found Dr. Alexander so ill, that the session and trustees united in urging him to try a long recess. He was not well enough to take advantage of this until June 2d, on which day he left New York for Virginia. After passing some weeks at the University near Charlottesville, he proceeded to the Warm Springs, and thence to the Red Sweet Springs, where, in a childlike sleep, on the morning of the Sabbath, July 31, 1859, his spirit passed to its everlasting rest. Nothing now remained but to carry the body to its burial place in Princeton, by the side of his parents. The interment was made on the third of August, after services in the First church. Other commemorative services were held in the church in Fifth Avenue, on the ninth of October, which was as soon as the building could be used after completing some alterations which had been made, with a view to make it easier for the pastor's voice. The Memorial Sermons, preached on that day by Dr. Hodge, of Princeton, and Dr. Hall, of Trenton, were published, and contain the testimonials of two of the friends by whom he was longest and best known, to the excellence of his character, the usefulness of his life, and the value of his example.

The information more fully given, in other pages of this volume, as to Dr. Alexander's writings in the *Biblical Repertory*, will convey a better impression than anything that could be said, in this biographical sketch, of the extent of his knowledge, the versatility of his talents, his industrious use of books, and his facile use of the pen. But these were only intellectual gifts and literary accomplishments. When his writings in this journal, and in the other forms of their publication, are perused, it will be found that his prevailing object, from first to last, was to be useful, and useful in the highest and best of human concerns. Gifted as he was with a capacity to enjoy and create the pleasures of imagination, his whole aim was to be practical. Though wit and humour had their place in his nature, they had their time too, and it was short and infrequent, compared with what passed in seriousness, and often in deep sadness. It was the soul—in its Divine and immortal relations—that was the chief object of his care, both as he considered himself and the world at large. For these concerns he watched, prayed, laboured, and lived. None could know him without believing that he was eminently and habitually pious; and that the cultivation of piety in himself, and its promotion in all whom he could reach, infinitely transcended in his estimation and pursuit every other object of human existence. The Christian grace of love or charity seldom has a more consistent and constant exemplification than was shown in him; nor is one often found, who, with such firm opinions, unites such freedom from bigotry, and such a disposition to approve and enjoy whatever has the appearance of good, and can be used for good, wherever it is found. He could not make an enemy, or lose a friend. His heart was drawn most to the sorrowing, the despondent, the broken-hearted. He excelled in comforting and strengthening, more than in arousing or alarming. His talents enabled him to hold a high place in the best kind of popular esteem, and he could make his way in what considers itself the best society, but the sphere which he enjoyed most was that in which his Divine Master and Lord walked,—separated from the world, denying himself, seeking and saving the lost, and passing through great tribulation into glory.

We add a list of the articles contributed by him:

1830. Pascal's Provincial Letters—De Wette's Review of Luther's Letters—Last two paragraphs of Oberlin's Memoirs.

1831. Modern Judaism—Works of John Howe—Hengstenberg on the First Promise of Redemption.

1832. Book of the Soul—Systems of Theology—Academical Course of Candidates for the Ministry—Life and Times of John Livingston.

1833. The Religious Condition of Holland—Life of Farel—Parables of the New Testament.

1834. Monosyllabic Languages of Asia—Life of William Farel—Tholuck on the Sermon on the Mount—Dr. Sprague on the Internal Polity of Churches—Memoir of Rev. Rezeau Brown—Jansenius.

1835. Necessity of Popular Education—Jesus Christ the Example of the Minister—Civilization of India—Natural History of the Bible.

1836. Life of Michael Servetus—Sunday-school Books—Religion and Religious Literature of Europe—Modern Miracles and Wonders.

1837. Henry's Life of Calvin—Hungary and Transylvania—Life of Savonarola—True and False Religion.

1838. Expository Preaching—American Embassy to Asiatic Courts—Peale's Graphics—Gardiner's Music of Nature—Life of Wilberforce.

1839. Transcendentalism (with Prof. Dod)—Spring's Fragments—Continuation of Henry's Calvin—Anglo-Saxon Literature.

1840. The Sacrament of the Lord's Supper—French Presbyterianism—Predestinarian Controversy, &c.—Rauch's Psychology—Macaulay's Reviews—Alexander Henderson.

1841. The Works of Zwingle—Pantheism.

1842. History of the Reformation—Emmons's Works (with his father)—Chalmers on Education and Ecclesiastical Economy.

1843. The Evils of an Unsanctified Literature—Board of Publication—Foreign Missions—Classical Studies—Kant—Education for the Ministry.

1844. Hengstenberg on the Psalms—Neander's History of the Planting of the Church—Scottish Mission to the Jews—John Foster.

1845. Baird's Religion in America—Life of Arnold—Kidder's Brazil—Connection between Philosophy and Revelation—Calvin's Institutes—Religious Instruction of the Negroes—Poverty and Crime in Cities.

1846. Attraction of the Cross—Metaphysical Theology of the Schoolmen—Hopkins's Evidences of Christianity.

1847. Dewey's Controversial Discourses—Discoveries in the Region of Nineveh—Howison's History of Virginia—Davidson's Presbyterian Church in Kentucky.

1848. Teaching a Science: the Teacher an Artist—Turretin—Life of Hegel.

1849. The History of Catechising—Beecher and Wilson on Baptism—The Arnaulds—Autobiography of Dr. Green.

1850. Presbyterianism in Virginia—General Church History—Sears's Life of Luther—Close Communion—German Hymnology.

1852. Goold's edition of Owen.

11

1854. Curiosities of University Life—Preaching and Preachers.

1855. Remarks on the Studies and Discipline of the Preacher—Mrs. Sherwood and Henry Martyn.

1856. Quesnel and the Jansenists—Foote's Sketches of Virginia—Memoirs of John M. Mason, D. D.—Waldegrave on Millenarianism—Baird's Religion in America.

1857. Writings of Doddridge.

1858. Ancient Manuscript Sermons—Sprague's Annals of the Presbyterian Pulpit.

1859. Immediate Perception.

ALEXANDER, JOSEPH ADDISON. The senior Dr. Alexander was the father of eight children, all of whom survived both parents, excepting a daughter who died in infancy. His first son received the name of Mrs. Alexander's father—James Waddel; another was named for himself—Archibald: to his other sons he gave the names of men of the best kind of renown—Samuel Davies, the Virginia pastor and Princeton President; Henry Martyn, the missionary; William Cowper, the Christian poet; and Joseph Addison, the pure moralist and elegant scholar.

Addison, as he was always called, was the third son, and was born in Philadelphia, April 24, 1809; but in the summer of 1812 the family removed to Princeton, and that was his home to the last. In early childhood he began to show the love of reading and the capacity of acquiring languages, which laid the foundation of his future distinction; and at the age of ten he was using a miniature Hebrew grammar, having acquired the alphabet of that language almost as soon as he had the English. The rhymes that he wrote at that precocious period show how rapidly he was gaining command of the pen, and that he had acquired the rudiments of classical knowledge before he was sent regularly to school. His first teacher, out of the family, was Mr. James Hamilton; he then attended a school taught by Mr. Salmon Strong, under the general supervision of Dr. Lindsley, the Professor of languages in the College, and upon its discontinuance studied successively under Mr. Horace S. Pratt, and (1822—1824) Mr. Robert Baird, by which time he was prepared to enter college. Under the influence of his predilection for oriental languages, stimulated by his admiration of the character and pursuits of Sir William Jones, he had made sufficient progress in Arabic to begin to use the Koran.

The young linguist entered the Junior, or second in order of the four classes of the College of New Jersey, in the fall term of 1824. At that time the President was Dr. Carnahan; the other members of the Faculty were Dr. Philip Lindsley, Rev. Luther Halsey, Dr. John Maclean, and Mr. Robert B. Patton. At graduation his class numbered twenty-nine, and its catalogue has the names of men since known as Chief Justice Napton, of Missouri; Professors (in Medicine) Arnold, of Georgia, and Warner, of Virginia; Professor (in Law) McCall, of Pennsylvania; George W. Bolling, Esq., Rev. J. D. Condit, Ezra F. Dayton, James R. Talmage. At the Commencement, (September 1826) McCall, Napton, and Alexander, having shared the first honour, the latter took by lot the Valedictory, and his coequals the two Salutatories.

Being but seventeen years of age when he left College, Addison had time for maturing his studies before it was necessary to determine his profession; and declining a proffered tutorship in College, he gave three years to a wide circle of reading, but chiefly in his favourite department of Asiatic language and literature. At this early period he employed himself also in writing a large number of fugitive pieces for the periodical press, and for a time was co-editor, with one of his brothers, of the *New Jersey Patriot*, a newspaper published weekly in Princeton. He contributed several articles, in poetry as well as prose, to the *Philadelphia Monthly Magazine*. Some of these effusions show that he was competent to write on Persian literature, and the whole miscellany is characterized by the versatility of learning, wit and satire, gravity and levity, in each of which he always seemed to be equally at home. Through his familiarity with the Latin he, of course, easily acquired French, Italian, and Spanish, and he soon added German. It was his custom for many years to pursue his studies in all the languages that have been mentioned, *daily*. During his nineteenth year he read entire in the original languages the first eight books of the Bible, the Koran, Don Quixote, Gerusalemme Liberata, Luther's version of the Gospels, besides portions of other works. Among his English readings about this time were Coke upon Littleton, Vattel, Kent's and Blackstone's Commentaries, Chitty on Pleading, the Federalist, and Dugald Stewart's Philosophy.

Not satisfied with his College Greek he recommenced the study of that language from the grammar, and read afresh the poets and historians critically. He added the dialect of modern Athens to that of the classical ages. In the year 1829, in partnership with his brother James, he compiled "a Geography of the Bible" for the American Sunday-school Union.

It was as early as the third year of the first series of the *Repertory*, (1827), and when Addison was but eighteen, that he began to give his valuable assistance to our work. It was then done in a translation from the Latin of Turretin, and followed by another from the Greek of Justin Martyr. So soon as the *Repertory* was opened more fully for original articles, and especially for reviews, his writing became frequent, so that from the volume for 1833 to that of 1859, no year passed without some contribution from him. The list annexed to this notice will give the best information of their number, and the scope of the subjects treated. In 1830 he found time to prepare three papers for the *American Quarterly Review*, of which Mr. Robert Walsh was editor. These were on his most congenial topics—Mohammedan History, Sadi's Gulistan, and Anthon's edition of Horace. Mr. Walsh was also the editor of the *National Gazette and Literary Register*, a daily newspaper of Philadelphia, which was another of the receptacles for the lighter essays of both James and Addison.

In the third year after graduation young Alexander, for he was still in his minority, accepted a position as teacher in the High-school, opened in Princeton in November 1829, by Mr. Robert B. Patton, who had been a Professor both at Middlebury and Princeton. "Edgehill," where the school stood, was situated a little out of the village, and the main object of its establishment was to enable students to enter College with the best preparation. Alexander was with Professor Patton from the beginning, and resided with his family in the school-building, where also a number of students boarded. One of the means of self-improvement which he most appreciated whilst in this connection, was the assistance he gave to Professor Patton in preparing the American edition of Donnegan's Greek Lexicon: his principal work being the translation from the Greek-German Dictionary of Passow the definitions not found in Donnegan. He remained at the Edgehill school until his election, in July 1830, as Adjunct Professor of Ancient Languages and Literature in the College.

When it is considered how much the Scriptures of both Testaments had been the material of his critical study as a linguist, and necessarily therefore as an interpreter, for years, and how from childhood his associations in every way had been with the most decided class of Christians, it may seem remarkable that we have not till now reached the date of the effectual power of Divine truth on his heart. There can be no question of his intellectual faith and pure morals up to the time of his going to Edgehill; but it was not until the month of January 1830, that he could make record of having been "deeply engaged in a study new to me, and far more important than all others—the study of the Bible and my own heart." The passages copied by his nephew and biographer,* from his uncle's private journal for the first four months of 1830, prove that the awakening, conviction, and repenting of his soul toward God was no superficial, or merely mental operation. In the agitated and anxious experience that ensued, the human productions that were most useful to him were such as John Newton's Letters, Edwards on the Affections, Owen on Spiritual-mindedness, and the Life of Henry Martyn. At length, on the day he was twenty-one years old, he formally consecrated himself to God, solemnly renounced sin, and bound his conscience to watch against all temptation; at the same time avowing entire distrust of every reliance but that which he placed upon Divine grace, whether for mercy or a new life, and all through Christ.

In this new state of mind he took up his abode within the walls of the College, and there continued for nearly two years and a half. The duties of his post were easy, but a new field of employment was opened by the determination to direct his studies with a view to the ministry. Without interfering with the instruction of his classes, or attaching himself to the Seminary, he devoted his reading to the philological, theological, and practical study of the Scriptures, to metaphysics or mental philosophy, and church history. For relaxation he took up a survey of modern European literature as found in the periodical Reviews of the preceding century. A specimen of the habitual thoroughness of his studies is seen in his resolution to consult Gesenius's Lexicon for every principal Hebrew word and read the entire article—thus accomplishing the perusal of nearly the whole dictionary—a volume of more than two thousand columns. To all these he added the study of the Portuguese, Danish, and Turkish languages, as he found, or made, opportunity, and not omitting fresh excursions among the Greek and Roman classics. To exercise his memory he committed the whole book of Psalms, both in Hebrew and English, and the epistles of Romans and Hebrews in Greek and English. Then he mastered the Syriac and Chaldee grammars. His subjects in the *Repertory* through these few years, and his treatment of them, are conclusive evidence that there was nothing cursory or superficial in his more recondite studies, wide as was the range they took. This was not the only

---

* The Life of Joseph Addison Alexander, D. D. By Henry Carrington Alexander. 2 vols. Scribner, New York, 1870. 900 pages.

channel for his pen, and the rapidity and diversity with which
he could use it is exemplified in his throwing off forty paragraphs or papers for the weekly *Presbyterian* in the two
months from the end of November 1832.

When we hear of his resigning his professorship at the close
of the term mentioned above, it comes to us as a welcome an-
nouncement that the unceasing application of some fifteen
years is to have the intermission of a journey abroad. In
April 1833, Mr. Alexander embarked in a packet-ship at New
York, and passed a year in visiting the great points in England, Scotland, France, Germany, Switzerland, and Italy. At
Halle he found a congenial spirit in Professor Tholuck, and
heard several lectures from him, Professors Pott, Rediger,
Fuch, and Wegschneider. Dr. Barnas Sears, President of
Brown University, whom Alexander was so fortunate as to
meet in Halle, has written of this visit, "He was a great
favourite of Dr. Tholuck's—more so than any other American
or English visitor. After he left Halle for Berlin, Tholuck
often spoke to me of him in terms of the highest eulogy and
admiration. 'He is the only man,' said he, 'who could *always*
give me the right English word for one in German, apparently
untranslatable.' Indeed, these two men were, in several respects, very much alike. They were both fond of the languages, classical, ancient and modern, and were adepts in
them, being able to speak I know not how many of them. I
have heard them both speak at least six. Both were great
readers, and remembered every thing they read."

After passing more than two months in this interesting and
profitable society, our traveller proceeded to Berlin. There he
heard Strauss, Lisco, and Henry (Calvin's biographer) preach,
and Hengstenberg, Neander, Bopp, Schleiermacher, von Ger-
lach, and Ritter, lecture. Alexander gave two months to Berlin, studying in the intervals of lectures, and reading Rabbini-
cal Hebrew with Biesenthal. The principal professors showed
him every kind attention. Thence he went to Gottingen,
where he heard Ewald lecture once, and had an interview. In
Bonn, he met Professors Rheinwald, Augusti, and Nitzsch, and
attended a lecture by the last. Returning to Paris, (where he
found Cousin and de Sacy), he remained in France a short time,
and reached home from Havre, in May 1834.

He found a new situation awaiting him. Before his return
he had been appointed an assistant instructor in the department of Oriental learning in the Theological Seminary; and
although abundantly qualified for licensure for the pulpit, he
deferred that step in the belief that Providence had designated

a position for which his peculiar training had better fitted him. His special function in the Seminary was the teaching of Hebrew : but he formed of his own accord private classes, for such of the students as chose to undertake, in addition, the Arabic, Syriac, or Chaldee.   He set his mark of scholarship so high, that it required an amount of time and application, which put the earnestness of the young men to a strong test. For himself, among his new studies were the Ethiopic and Sanscrit grammars.   In 1834 he began to lecture on Isaiah, and thus to lay the foundation of the elaborate commentary, which he gave to the public twelve years afterwards.   We get a glimpse of the state of his spiritual mind at this time by such entries as the following in his journal of January 1835.   "Mercy and help, O Lord, my Sovereign Lord! Thou who lovest little children, make me a little child.   Make me humble, simple-hearted, tender, guileless, and confiding.   Kill my selfish pride. Shiver my hard heart.   Break my stubborn spirit.   Make me love my kind by making me to love Thee.   O soften me, my Saviour, by showing me thy own tender, bleeding, melting heart.   Purge envy from my heart by causing me to live and work for thee.   O that this foul fiend were wholly dispossessed!   I bless thee for trials : may they do me good.   Compel me to remember that I am not my own.   Save me from being the object of envy or ill-will.   Save me from the wickedness of trying to excite it.   Lord, I would give the world for true humility.   O make me—make me humble!"

The rank of assistant-teacher contented him, but the General Assembly of May–June 1835 wishing to give his position more prominence, elected him "Associate-Professor of Oriental and Biblical Literature."   The Board of Directors reported to the Assembly in 1836, and again in 1837, that while he had been engaged in giving instruction in that department, he had not yet accepted the appointment, but had it under consideration.   It was not until the session of 1838 that they were able to inform the Assembly that the Professor-elect had declared his acceptance.   The uncertainty of the issues of the church-controversy then prevailing were probably the chief reason for this delay.   While the matter was in suspense as to Princeton, an effort was made to induce him to accept the full Professorship of the same department in the Union Theological Seminary in the city of New York; but he preferred remaining where he was; and if the immediate demands of his classes did not take all his time he found extra-occupation in investigating the Polish, Malay, and Chinese languages, and in preparing several lads for college.   In December 1837 he writes of having "undertaken four distinct courses of exegetical instruction in the Seminary, all of which require attention, and two of them laborious study." He not only continued his contributions to the *Repertory*, but for a time served with Professor Dod as its editor.

When Mr. Alexander made up his mind to accept the professorship, a new motive arose for his entrance upon the ministry. Accordingly, in February 1838, he appeared before the Presbytery of New Brunswick, and was admitted as a candidate. In the following April he was duly examined, and licensed for probation. His trial-sermon was preached in the Lawrenceville church, where the Presbytery was convened, and his first sermon as a licentiate was delivered in the Princeton church. His preaching at once became attractive through the beauty, and often the eloquence, of the composition, though not accompanied with any of the arts of elocution, unless such as are found in a melodious voice and earnest manner. There was such variety and inequality, however, in the structure of his sermons, that they can hardly be described. They were sure to be original, evangelical, forcible, elegant, and tending to practical effect upon the conscience; sometimes transparently didactic, sometimes brilliant in imagination, but sometimes also too entirely devoted to instruction and careless of dress to meet the standard of popularity. Since his death forty-three of his discourses have been published in two volumes, and in them may be found a fair exhibition of his gifts for the pulpit, and the elements of his power as a preacher.

It was, in every way, a happy change in the monotony of his habits when it became requisite to prepare sermons, to preach in churches far and near, and to mingle in general society, from which he had a morbid shrinking that dated in his childhood. He could now be an example, as well as teacher, to candidates for the ministry, and found himself instructed as a Professor by his new experience, with its vicissitudes of failure and success. His inauguration, which took place on the 24th of September 1838, made no change in his course of instruction; neither did his ordination, a year after his licensure and by the same Presbytery, make any in his employments as a preacher. The latter ceremony took place at Lambertville on the day he was thirty years of age—April 24, 1839. Through the twenty years that remained to him he took pleasure in meeting the opportunities that opened for preaching, and as he was everywhere acceptable, these were not few—sometimes extending to the supplying of a pulpit for months in succession. Not the least profitable to himself and hearers were such services as he sometimes conducted every Sabbath afternoon for a whole season in a school-house in the suburbs of Princeton.

In 1853 Dr. Alexander (he had received the title from Rutgers' College) made another visit to Europe. He left New York—this time in a steamship—May 18th, and reached Boston on his return the last day of August. This was a tour of recreation, not of study. He heard many of the famous preachers of the day—McNeile, Candlish, Hamilton, Cumming, Binney, Melvill, A. Monod, Coquerel, Pressensé. In Westminster Hall he heard or saw Talfourd, Jervis, Pollock, Campbell, Shea, and other notables of the bench and bar.

Dr. James W. Alexander having resigned the chair of History in the Seminary, the General Assembly of 1851 transferred Dr. J. Addison Alexander to it, with the title of "Professor of Biblical and Ecclesiastical History." This continued to be his department until the Assembly of 1859 sanctioned another reconstruction of the Faculty, which gave him the Professorship of "Hellenistic and New Testament Literature." He had occupied this position but a few terms before his death, but a volume of his fragmentary "Notes on New Testament Literature and Ecclesiastical History" was posthumously published (Scribner: 1861). In 1851 appeared his "Psalms, translated and explained," in three volumes. In 1857 "The Acts of the Apostles explained," in two volumes; in 1858 "The Gospel according to Mark explained," in one volume. The Commentary on Matthew was unfinished at his death, but so much as he had prepared was published in 1861, as the last work on which his pen was engaged. His work on Isaiah, and in a measure that on the Psalms, were designed to set before critical students of the original, materials and helps for their investigations, rather than an explanatory commentary of his own; but the New Testament Explanations come fully up to their title as adapted to make intelligible every part and phrase of the three evangelical histories to which he put his hand.

It was in the summer of 1859 that Dr. J. A. Alexander's health began to show decided symptoms of failing. The death of his eldest brother in August of that year aggravated his depression. In November he had to abandon his lectures, but was still going about, even travelling as far as Philadelphia. The day before he died, though feeble, he took a drive, but after returning went to bed—in his study—and on the next afternoon, January 28, 1860, he gently expired. On the following Tuesday, the 31st, the funeral services took place in the

12

First Church of Princeton; Dr. Hall, of Trenton, preaching, Drs. Spring and Potts of New York, and Macdonald, pastor of the church, assisting in the solemnities, after which his body was laid beside those of his father, mother, and brother.

Enough has been expressed in this outline of Professor Alexander's life to indicate his most prominent qualities—such as those of a very learned man, indefatigable student, of brilliant and diversified talents, and constant culture, an able writer, eloquent preacher, and enthusiastic instructor. His propensity to the humorous was so characteristic, that it cannot be omitted in any enumeration of his traits; but, like his fondness for children and the great amount of amusement he afforded by writing for them and playing with them, what seems frivolous in comparison with the grave occupations of his life was but the incidental relaxation of an irrepressibly active and cheerful disposition. Of a character such as his, no mere biographical statements can convey an adequate impression. It must be seen in the many lights and particulars, such as those in which it has been placed by the copious memoir which his nephew has written, to be appreciated.

He is the contributor of the following articles.

1829. "Flatt's Dissertation on the Deity of Christ," and "Antitrinitarian Theories" were translated by J. A. A.—The Druses—Life of Erasmus.

1830. Life of August Hermann Francke—Madden's Travels.

1832. Arabic and Persian Lexicography—Historical Statements of the Koran—Gibbs's Manual Lexicon—De Sacy's Arabic Grammar—Hebrew Grammar.

1833. Murdock's Mosheim—Life of Farel—Theories of Education—Bush on the Millennium—Cyrillus Lucaris.

1834. German New Light—Rowland Hill—Guericke's Manual of Church History—Roger Williams—Antiquity of the Art of Writing.

1835. Commentary on the Book of Psalms—Stewart's Sketches of Great Britain—Barnes on the Gospels—Stuart's Greek Grammar—Bush's Hebrew Grammar—New Theory of Episcopacy.

1836. The late Professor Rosenmüller—Hengstenberg's Christologie—The English Bible—Colton's Reasons for preferring Episcopacy—Life of Augustine.

1837. Gleanings from the German Periodicals—Robinson's Gesenius—Isaiah vii. 8.

1838. Melanchthon's Letters—Henry's Christian Antiquities (with Dr. Miller)—Nordheimer's Hebrew Grammar—Hengstenberg on the Pentateuch.

1839. Critical Study of the English Bible.

1840. Kenrick's Theologia Dogmatica.

1841. A Plea for Bishops—New Works on Isaiah—Nordheimer's Hebrew Syntax—Bishop Doane and the Oxford Tracts (with Dr. Hodge)—Robinson's Biblical Researches.

1842. Smyth's Lectures on Apostolic Succession—Works on Genesis—Whately's Kingdom of Christ.

1843. Barnes on the Apostolic Church—Smyth on Presbytery and Prelacy.

1844. General Assembly of the Church of Scotland (with Dr. Hodge)—Junkin on the Prophecies—Bush on Ezekiel's Vision—Moderatism—The High Low Church.

1845. Sacerdotal Absolution (with Dr. Hodge)—New Edition of Pascal's Remains.

1846. Coit's Puritanism—Kitto's Cyclopedia of Biblical Literature.

1847. The Eldership—Historical Theology—University Education—Modern Jewish History—The Apostolical Succession.

1848. Bonar on Leviticus—Dr. Spring on the Power of the Pulpit (with Dr. Hodge)—The Gospel History.

1849. The Official Powers of the Primitive Presbyters—Davidson's Introduction to the New Testament—The Apostleship a Temporary Office.

1850. Grinfield's Apology for the Septuagint.

1851. The True Test of an Apostolical Ministry—Fairbairn's Typology—Free Church of Scotland—The Relation of the Old to the New Dispensation—Schaff's Church History.

1852. Hengstenberg on the Book of Revelation—Robert and James Haldane.

1853. Prophecy and History.

1854. Method of Church History—The Historical Scriptures.

1855. The Plan and Purpose of Patriarchal History—The World in the Middle Ages—The Coptic Language.

1856. Harmonies of the Gospels—Eli Smith's Arabic Bible.

1857. Giesler's Text Book of Church History.

1859. Praying and Preaching—Sawyer's New Testament—Trench on Revision—The Presbyterian Church in Ireland.

1860. Primeval Period of Sacred History.

1863. Micah's Prophecy of Christ. [One of his Lectures which it was thought desirable to print in the *Review* after his decease.]

ALEXANDER, SAMUEL DAVIES, the fifth son of Dr. Archibald Alexander, was born at Princeton, New Jersey, about the year 1819, and graduated at the College of New

Jersey in 1838. At first he studied civil engineering, but afterwards decided to devote himself to the ministry, and entered the Princeton Theological Seminary. He was licensed to preach in 1847, and in 1848 we find that he was pastor of the church at Port Richmond, Philadelphia. He accepted a call to the Village Church at Freehold, New Jersey, in 1850, and continued in that charge till 1855, when he removed to the city of New York, and became pastor of the Fifteenth-street church, now the Phillips Presbyterian church, his present charge. He received the honorary degree of D. D. from Washington College, Pa. He is the author of the article on the "Editions of the Pilgrim's Progress" in the volume for 1859.

ALEXANDER, STEPHEN, was born at Schenectady, New York, on the first of December 1806, and graduated at Union College in 1824. In 1833 he became a tutor in Princeton College, and in 1834 became adjunct Professor of Mathematics, which position he filled till 1840, when the Professorship of Astronomy was created and assigned to him. Upon the decease of Dr. Dod in 1845 he was appointed to the Chair of Mathematics, which he exchanged in 1851 for that of Mechanics and Astronomy, the branches of science which he now teaches. During these years he has made many valuable contributions to scientific knowledge, among which may be mentioned a paper on the "Physical Phenomena attendant on Solar Eclipses," read before the American Philosophical Society in 1843; and another "On the Origin of the Forms and the Present Condition of some of the Clusters of Stars and several of the Nebulæ," and also on the "Harmonies in the Arrangement of the Solar System, which seem to be confirmatory of the Nebular Hypothesis of La Place." These and other articles have given Dr. Alexander a prominent place among astronomers. In 1852, the degree of LL.D. was conferred upon him by Columbia College. The articles contributed by him to this *Review* were, in

1859. Hickok's Rational Cosmology (the physical portion.)
1867. A Philosophical Confession of Faith.

ALEXANDER, WILLIAM COWPER, the second son of Dr. Archibald Alexander, was that baby with which "Janetta wearied herself in carrying more than was necessary" on their journey from Virginia to Philadelphia. He was thus born in Virginia, but well entitled to be called one of New Jersey's most distinguished men. His preliminary education was both directed and in a great measure given by his father, and in

1824 he graduated at Princeton College. He chose the law as his profession and practised some years in Princeton; but during the great struggle between Mr. Adams and General Jackson for the Presidency he was led to take part in the political contest, and for many years was induced to represent the county of Middlesex, and afterwards that of Mercer, in the Assembly and Senate of New Jersey. In these positions, both in the Assembly and Senate, he was often chosen Speaker; for his dignified presence, perfect command of language, extensive information, and urbanity of manners, commanded the respect of all parties. In 1859, however, he withdrew from the political arena and accepted the Presidency of the "Equitable Life Assurance Society of the United States," but his reputation as an eloquent orator is so great that he is frequently called from the desk; and in 1860 he was sent by the State of New Jersey to the Peace Conference, which met in Washington before the commencement of the late war, and presided over its deliberations. He received the degree of LL.D. from Lafayette College, Pa. In 1852 he contributed the articles "Austria in 1848-9," and "Survey of the Great Salt Lake of Utah."

ANDERSON, SAMUEL McCULLOCH, D. D., was born December 18, 1823, in Butler county, Pennsylvania, and graduated at Washington College in 1846. He studied theology at the Western Theological Seminary, and was licensed to preach the gospel, April 8, 1851. In the same year he took charge of the church at Fredericksburg, Ohio, where he continued till compelled by ill-health to resign in April 1859. The summer of that year he spent on a farm, and feeling himself able to resume pastoral duty in the autumn, he accepted a call to the church of Davenport, Iowa. In this charge he continued till the winter of 1869, when he removed to Hamilton, Ohio, his present field of labour. In 1863 he communicated to this journal an essay on "Miracles."

ATKINSON, JOSEPH M., D. D., was born in Dinwiddie county, Virginia, on January 7, 1820; went first to Hampden Sidney College in that State, and afterwards to the College of New Jersey, where he graduated in 1841. He then entered upon his theological studies at Princeton Seminary, and was licensed to preach the gospel by the Presbytery of Winchester in 1843. His first pastorate was at Sheppardstown, Virginia, which he resigned in 1849, and accepted the pastorate of the church in Frederick, Maryland, which he held till 1855, in which year he removed to Raleigh, North Carolina, and has continued to be the pastor of the church in that city till the present time.

He contributed to this *Review* the following articles.

1852. Moral Æsthetics—National Literature the Exponent of National Character.

1853. Henry Martyn.

1855. The Zurich Letters.

ATWATER, LYMAN H., was born in New Haven, Connecticut, on February 23, 1813. He was prepared for College by Dr. H. P. Arms, now pastor of the Congregational church in Norwich, Connecticut; entered the Freshman Class of Yale College in 1827; and graduated with honour in 1831. As college students, Dr. Atwater and his life-long friend, Dr. Porter, now Professor of Metaphysics in Yale College, were noted for their devotion to the study of Intellectual Philosophy, both indicating at an early period a predilection for the sciences which it has become their life-work to teach. After leaving College, the next year was occupied in teaching the classics in Mount Hope Seminary, near Baltimore, and in the fall of 1832 he commenced the study of theology in the Yale Divinity School. In 1833 he was appointed a tutor in the College, but continued to prosecute his theological studies, and in May 1834 was licensed to preach the gospel by the New Haven West Association; and on July 29, 1835, was ordained and installed pastor of the First Congregational church of Fairfield, Connecticut. This is one of the oldest and most important churches in Connecticut, having been organized in 1650, and having had for its ministers a series of distinguished men. Mr. Atwater now became a member of Fairfield West Association, and in it, in conjunction with the late Dr. Nathaniel Hewit, Dr. Theophilus Smith, and Dr. Edwin Hall, distinguished himself as the advocate of orthodox opinions, in opposition to the errors of Drs. Taylor, Bushnell, and others. These errors had also insinuated themselves into the Presbyterian Church, and were one of the causes of the disruption of the church in 1837–8.

Dr. Atwater's first article in this *Review* was contributed in 1840, on "The Power of Contrary Choice," and since that time he has been a constant contributor. The mental power expressed in these articles, and the bold stand he had made for orthodox opinions in New England, brought him under the notice of the Faculty of the College at Princeton, who in 1851 conferred upon him the degree of D. D.; and in 1854 he was appointed Professor of Mental and Moral Philosophy in the College of New Jersey.

In 1863 the General Assembly elected him Professor of Theology in the Western Theological Seminary, but he did not accept the appointment; but for some years he has delivered a course of lectures to the students in the Princeton Theological Seminary on "The Connection between Revealed Religion and Metaphysical Science." In addition to his course on Mental Philosophy, Dr. Atwater in 1860 delivered a course of lectures in the College on Political Economy, and in the changes made since Dr. McCosh became Principal, his chair has been made to embrace Logic and Moral and Political Science. In 1867 he published a "Manual of Logic," which is now used as a text-book in several colleges. In 1869 he was associated with Dr. Hodge as editor of the *Princeton Review;* and had contributed the following articles to this series.

1840. The Power of Contrary Choice.

1842. Dr. Woodbridge on Revivals.

1843. Edwards's (the younger) Works.

1847. Inauguration of President Woolsey.

1848. Coleridge.

1851. The Method of the Divine Government.

1852. The True Progress of Society.

1853. The Ventilation of Churches—Doctrinal and Ecclesiastical Conflicts in Connecticut—The Bible in the Counting-house—Outlines of Moral Science, by Archibald Alexander, D. D.

1854. Modern Explanations of the Doctrine of Inability—The True Barrier against Ritualism and Rationalism.

1855. Recent Works on Mental Philosophy—Congregationalism—The Logic of Reason.

1856. Comte's Positive-Philosophy—Mill's System of Logic—Miracles and their Counterfeits—Lyall's Mental Philosophy—The Matter of Preaching.

1857. The Children of the Church and Sealing Ordinances—Ferrier's Demonstrative Idealism—Moral Insanity—Old Orthodoxy, New Divinity, and Unitarianism.

1858. Brownson's Exposition of himself—Butler's Lectures on Ancient Philosophy—Haven's Mental Philosophy—Jonathan Edwards and Successive Forms of New Divinity.

1859. Religion in Colleges—Transcendentalism in Political Ethics—Hickok's Rational Cosmology (with Prof. S. Alexander)—Dr. Taylor's Lectures on the Moral Government of God.

1860. Classification and Mutual Relation of the Mental Faculties—Reason and Faith.

1861. The New Oxford School, or Broad Church Liberalism—Liverpool Missionary Conference of 1860, or Results of

Missionary Experience—The Physical Training of Students—
Knowledge, Faith, and Feeling, in their Mutual Relations—
Some late Developments of American Rationalism.

1862. The Human Body as related to Sanctification—The
Nature and Effects of Money, and Credit as its Substitute—
Vindication of Hickok's Philosophy—A Plea for High Educa-
tion in Presbyterian Colleges.

1863. Hopkins's Moral Science—The Manner of Preaching
—Witherspoon's Theology—The Children of the Covenant, and
their Part in the Lord.

1864. Shedd's History of Christian Doctrine—The War and
National Wealth—Whedon and Hazard on the Will.

1865. Herbert Spencer's Philosophy, Atheism, Pantheism,
and Materialism—The late National Congregational Council.

1866. Imperfect Rights and Obligations as related to Church
Discipline—Dr. Spring's Reminiscences of his Life and Times
—Rationalism—McCosh on J. S. Mill and Fundamental Truth
—Ecce Homo.

1867. Drs. Hedge and Woolsey on College Studies and Government—Emanuel Swedenborg—Recent Discussions concerning Liberal Education—Dr. George Duffield on the Doctrines
of New-school Presbyterians.

1868. Truth, Charity, and Unity—Professor Fisher on the
Princeton Review and Dr. Taylor's Theology—The General
Assembly.

AXTELL, HENRY, was the second of three sons of the
Rev. Henry Axtell, D.D., of Geneva, New York, who all
became ministers of the gospel. He was born in Mendham,
New Jersey, in 1801, from which place his father removed to
Geneva a few years after. Henry graduated at Hanover
College, Clinton, New York, with the first honours of his class,
as his older brother had done before him, and, after his graduation, he received the appointment of tutor in the College,
which he held for some years. He subsequently studied
theology two and a half years at Andover, and one year at
Princeton, and was licensed to preach by the Presbytery of
New York on the 15th day of October 1829. His first pastoral charge was in Lawrenceville, New Jersey, to which he
was called in 1830; and on September 10th of that year he
was married to Miss Juliet Say, daughter of John Say, Esq.,
of Chuton, New York. From Lawrenceville Mr. Axtell
removed to Orange, New Jersey, in 1835, having been called to
the Second Presbyterian Church of that place. This charge
he resigned in 1838, in consequence of a bronchial affection,

which occasioned a loss of voice, and removed with his family
to St. Augustine, Florida, for the sake of the climate. Here
he lived for some years, in partial demission from ministerial
work. He became a member of the Presbytery of Georgia in
1840. While at St. Augustine, he officiated at the burial of
the remains of the soldiers who were killed in the Florida war,
which were brought there for interment, having been gathered
with great care from battle grounds. At the instance of
Colonel Belknap, commander at Fort Brooke, Tampa Bay,
that was created a chaplaincy post in 1843, and Mr. Axtell
received the appointment of chaplain, which he held until
1849, when he was transferred to New Orleans Barracks.
Here he remained as chaplain until the spring of 1853, when
he became disabled from duty through disease affecting his
mind. He was removed to Philadelphia for proper care, where
he died the following year. He had requested to be buried in
Orange, New Jersey, to which place his remains were removed
in July 1854, and were there interred with those of two of his
children, who had died during his ministry in that place; and
the people of his former pastoral charge then erected a monument to his memory. His widow and three daughters still
survive him.

Mr. Axtell was a man of great delicacy of taste and tenderness of feeling. He was cultivated in intellect and refined in
manners, and was gifted with exquisite perception of the bean-
tiful in nature and art, and loved the true in the works and
word of God. His contributions to this work were, in

1831. Biblical Eloquence and Poetry.
1834. Memorial of James Brainerd Taylor.

BAIRD, D. D., ROBERT, born in Fayette county, Pennsylvania, October 6th, 1798, studied at Washington and Jefferson Colleges, graduating from the latter in 1818. Entered
the Theological Seminary at Princeton 1819, and graduated in
1822. From 1821 to 1822, he was tutor in the College of New
Jersey. From 1822 to 1827, he taught an academy at Princeton with great success. Among his pupils here was the late Prof.
J. Addison Alexander. Meanwhile, in 1822, he was licensed to
preach the gospel. In 1827, he became engaged in the enterprise to supply the destitute in New Jersey with the Bible,
and with Prof. Maclean superintended the whole work until its
completion within the year 1828. In 1828, he was ordained
by the Presbytery of New Brunswick. Being providentially
prevented from going as a missionary of the American Bible
Society to Colombia, he next directed his attention to the cause

13

of education, in connection with the New Jersey Missionary Society, and by personal efforts secured the establishment of the present common-school system of New Jersey. Of this school system the Rev. J. W. Alexander, D. D. wrote : "It owes its passage to the zeal and labour of a single man, Rev. Robert Baird, who has been keeping the subject before the minds of the people, in newspaper essays for some months." From 1829 to 1834, he was general agent of the American Sunday-school Union, in whose service he travelled through almost every State and Territory of the United States. In 1835 he went to Europe, sent by the French Association, to explore the field for Christian operations, and returned in 1838. After the formation of the Foreign Evangelical Society, he again visited Europe, remaining there, with the exception of a few months, from 1839 until 1843, and making several briefer visits subsequently. His labours were chiefly in awakening among American Christians an interest in the conversion of the Roman Catholic population of Europe, and in organizing the means to assist the native Protestants in their efforts in this direction. But besides, he was deeply interested in the progress of other good causes. In Sweden, Norway, Denmark, and Finland, he was wonderfully successful in arousing an interest in Temperance, by his book on Temperance Societies in America; which was translated and published in Sweden at the expense of the king (Bernadotte). So striking were the results, that in his subsequent visits he was received with the most grateful and flattering attentions. In Russia he was instrumental in inducing the government, which had long refused to permit the existence of Bible Societies, itself to cause the Scriptures to be translated in modern Russ and published in a popular form. He became Secretary of the American and Foreign Christian Union, when the Foreign Evangelical Society was merged in it, in 1849, and was connected with the Union as secretary or director until his death, March 15, 1863. His scholarship, especially in the classics, was thorough and accurate; his memory wonderfully retentive; his acquaintance with the history of all nations so minute that he was at home in speaking or writing of any country, rarely forgetting a name or a date. His turn of mind was eminently practical, and his administrative ability was exhibited by the remarkable success of all the Christian organizations with which he became intimately connected. All his faculties were well balanced, and conveyed the impression of a full and healthy development. Added to this, personal manners gentle and courteous, a modesty that led him always to prefer others to himself; and, above all, a large-hearted, child-like, and engrossing Christian piety, secured him the love of thousands whom in his extensive travels he had occasion to meet.

His principal works were: "Religion in America," (London and New York, 1843, and new edition, New York, 1857,) reviewed in *Princeton Review*, by Dr. J. W. Alexander; "Visit to Northern Europe," 2 vols. 1841; "Protestantism in Italy," 1845 and 1847; "History of the Temperance Societies," 1836; "The Union of Church and State in New England," 1837, &c. Several of these works have been translated into French, German, Swedish, Danish, Finn, &c., and the last two were never published in English. His contributions to the periodical press —to quarterlies, &c., but especially to the daily and weekly journals—were extremely numerous. We think it probable that several of the articles on education in the early volumes of the *Review* were written by him, but can with certainty credit him with the following:

1830. American Sunday-school Union.
1832. Valley of the Mississippi.
1836. The Reformation at Genoa.

BAIRD, HENRY M., Ph. D., son of Dr. Robert Baird, was born in Philadelphia, January 17, 1832; after graduating from the University of the City of New York in June 1850, he spent the years 1851–3 in Greece and Italy, in the former country studying in the University of Athens. On his return to this country, studied theology in the Union and Princeton Theological Seminaries, graduating at the latter in 1856. From 1855 to 1859 he was tutor of Greek in the College of New Jersey. In 1859 he was elected Professor of the Greek Language and Literature in the University of the City of New York; this chair he continues to fill. He was ordained to the gospel ministry in April 1866. Besides a number of articles in the periodical press—the *New Englander, Methodist Quarterly*, etc.—he is the author of "Modern Greece: A Narrative of a Residence and Travels in that Country," etc., and of "The Life of Rev. Robert Baird, D. D." In 1863 he contributed to this *Review* the article on "The Liberties of the Gallican Church."

BAIRD, SAMUEL JOHN, was the son of the Rev. Thomas Dickson Baird, and was born at Newark, Ohio, in September 1817. His father having lost seven children by a former marriage, was at this time childless, and at the birth of this son, he received him as a gift of God in special prayer, and called him Samuel John—asked of God, given of God. His father devoted much care to his early education, and afterwards sent him to Jefferson College, Canonsburgh, Pennsylvania, but on account of feeble health he did not complete his collegiate course. On the death of his father in January 1839, he accepted an invitation to take charge of a school in the vicinity of Abbeville, South Carolina, and in 1840 he was united in marriage to Miss Jemima Jane Wilson, whose father and grandfather were ruling elders in the Upper Long Cane church. Immediately after his marriage Mr. Baird removed to Jeffersonville, Louisiana, where he opened a female seminary. Here he united with the Presbyterian church upon profession of faith, and shortly after, believing that he was called to preach the gospel, closed his school and entered the Theological Seminary of New Albany, as a candidate for the ministry. After an attendance of one year at New Albany, he concluded to perfect his literary training, and entered Centre College, Kentucky, where he graduated in the fall of 1843. A month previous to his graduation he was licensed to preach the gospel by the Presbytery of Transylvania, and devoted the next three years to missionary work in the Presbytery of Baltimore, in Kentucky, and in the southwest. His first pastorate was at Muscatine, Iowa; after three years he removed to Woodbury, New Jersey, and in 1865, by the advice of his physician he resigned the pastoral office there, in order to find some more active employment. Shortly after he received a joint commission from the American Bible Society and the Virginia Bible Society to labour as their agent in Virginia, to the duties of which agency he now devotes himself, with his residence at Staunton, Virginia.

In 1859 the degree of D. D. was conferred upon him by his *alma mater*, Centre College, and he is the author of the following works: 1. The Assembly's Digest, first published in 1855, and revised and republished in 1858. 2. The First Adam and the Second—The Elohim Revealed in the Creation and Redemption of Man. 3. The Socinian Apostasy of the English Presbyterian Church. An historical Discourse delivered before the General Assembly in 1856. 4. A Rejoinder to the Princeton Review upon the Elohim Revealed. 5. Southern Rights and Northern Duties in the present crisis. A plea for conciliation pending the Peace Convention of 1861. 6. The Church of Christ, its constitution and order. A manual for families, Sabbath-schools, and Bible-classes. 7. A History of the early Policy of the Presbyterian Church in the training of her Ministry; and of the first years of the Board of Education. 8. A

History of the New-school, and of the questions involved in the Disruption of the Presbyterian Church in 1838. Besides a number of articles contributed to the *Danville* and *Southern Reviews*, to this *Review* he contributed the following:

1858. The Providential Government of God.
1862. Slavery and the Slave Trade.
1863. Training of the Children.
1864. Water Baptism and that of the Spirit.
1865. Nature and Ends of Prayer.
1868. Dr. Gillett and Liberal Presbyterianism.

BAIRD, JAMES HENRY, a younger brother of Dr. Samuel John Baird, wrote the article on "Neglect of Infant Baptism" in the volume for 1857.

BARNES, ALBERT, was born at Rome, New York, on the 1st of December 1798. He received his preliminary education at the Fairfield Academy, New York, and graduated at Hamilton College in July 1820. It was at that time his intention to study law, but he was led by convictions of duty to devote his life to the Christian ministry, and soon after began the study of theology in Princeton Seminary. On the 23d of April, 1823, he was licensed to preach the gospel by the Presbytery of Elizabethtown, and after preaching at various places as a probationer, he accepted a call to the First Presbyterian church at Morristown, New Jersey. Among this people he laboured with much acceptance, and here he began those literary labours which have made his name famous in the world.

In the year 1830 he received a call to the First Presbyterian church in Philadelphia, and was installed its pastor on the 25th of June, and though now (in 1870) he does not attend to the active duties of the pastorate, as *emeritus* he holds a relation to that church which death alone can sever. We pass over the controversy that arose about his settlement in Philadelphia, as it was fully discussed in this *Review*, and will be found digested in the INDEX OF TOPICS. We think it sufficient here to state that he was no sooner settled in his new charge than he devoted himself with great assiduity to the completion of his series of "Notes on the books of the New Testament," which in process of time was followed by notes on Job, Psalms, Isaiah, and Daniel, of the Old. The "Notes" were intended chiefly for the use of Sabbath-school teachers, and in their form and manner of publication met a great popular want. They therefore soon attained a larger circulation, both in

Europe and America, than any similar work. Besides the "Notes," Mr. Barnes, in the thirty-five years of his ministry in Philadelphia, issued ten volumes of sermons and miscellaneous discourses, without ever allowing his literary labours to interfere with his pastoral duties. The morning was the time devoted to the composition of these works, and many of the inhabitants of Philadelphia relate that at an early hour they have seen him, through the gratings of his cellar window, sawing his wood for exercise, then with a lantern in the dark winter mornings wending his way to his study in the church, where he would often devote five hours to study, and return to his home before others were beginning the ordinary duties of the day. Such over-application could not be borne with impunity, and for some time he was nearly deprived of sight. He has now, however, partially recovered the use of his eyes, and is still engaged in literary work. We are happy in being able to add his own description of himself, given in a letter to a friend, on the anniversary of his birthday, December 1, 1868.

"I have a great desire to live. I am not tired of life, nor disgusted with the world, nor discouraged or disheartened in regard to the future. I believe that there are glorious things in prospect for our earth, and that it will be a greater thing to live for the next half century than it has been to live in the one that is past, and where we have had something to do. You have the advantage of me in another respect. You have the use of your eyes. I have not, and am obliged to write this letter by the aid of a machine, and this I can use but little. I preach a little, but have no charge, and am a practical farmer—with a farm of one acre. I remember the scenes of other years to which you refer. They are gone, and cannot be recalled. There are brighter scenes and even happier lands, and there will be prolonged and unbroken friendships beyond the grave—that grave which is but little before us."

In 1831 he contributed the article, "Memoirs and Sermons of Dr. Payson," to this *Review*.

BISHOP, GEORGE BROWN, was the son of the Rev. R. H. Bishop, D. D., and Ann Ireland, and was born in Fayette county, Kentucky, two miles south of Lexington, on the 30th of March, 1810. At the age of twelve years, he went to Paris, Kentucky, and studied Latin for six months, under Dr. William McGuffey. In 1824 Dr. Bishop removed to Oxford, Ohio, taking the Presidency of Miami University, and his son George entered the first Freshman class, being then in his fifteenth year. He graduated in 1828, and in November of the same year, united with the Presbyterian church of Oxford.

The time between this date and October 1829 was spent in a review of his studies. During this time he seldom left his room, except for his meals or a short walk, either before others had risen, or after the bustle of the day was over. This was a year not only of close application to study, but of soul-culture and growth in grace. He entered Princeton Theological Seminary on November 12, 1829, and during his stay there won the esteem and love of all who knew him.

He was licensed by the Presbytery of New Brunswick, New Jersey, April 28, 1832, and left the Seminary in October of the same year. Returning to Oxford, Ohio, he preached to vacant churches in the vicinity until April 1833, when he became stated supply to the church in that place. The following September he was chosen pastor, and in November was ordained and installed over them. In April 1834 he was married to Bethania L. Crocker; and in September 1834 he was elected to the Professorship of Biblical Criticism and Oriental Literature in the Indiana Theological Seminary, at Hanover, Indiana, (now the North-western Theological Seminary at Chicago,) and removed to his field of labour in October following. In this position he was permitted to labour about three years.

He ceased from his earthly labours on December 14th, 1837, aged 27 years, 8 months. He was in early childhood, as in after life, remarkable for his honesty, integrity, gentle, amiable disposition, quick perception, and studious habits. His mother and sisters often remarked that he was "all they could desire," and this seems to have been the estimate of all who were afterwards associated with him during his active and useful life. The secret of his eminent Christian character, and his great usefulness, may be found in the fact, that, from the time of his entering the Seminary at Princeton to the close of his life, he never failed to spend the greater portion of his early morning hours in devotional exercises and the study of the Scriptures. The Bible was his delight and constant companion, and his Greek Testament was always in his pocket, that he might have profitable employment for any leisure moment. He daily read from the Latin, Greek, Hebrew, and German versions. So thorough was his knowledge of the Scriptures that he seldom had occasion to use a Concordance, being able to refer to the chapter and verse of almost every passage. As a pastor, though so young and placed in trying circumstances, his humble, devout, and dignified bearing commanded the respect and affection of his people. He never selected a text, prepared a sermon, or entered the pulpit, without first earnestly invoking the Divine blessing. His prayers, exhortations, and sermons, were largely composed of Scripture language, and were pointed and discriminating. As a Professor, he was not only singularly earnest and faithful, but beloved by his classes. Every recitation was opened by prayer for Divine guidance and illumination, and the first day of every month was set apart for special religious exercises. The Sabbath was so precious to him that he always rose earlier than usual for his private devotions, and required a strict observance of the day from all the members of his household.

His contributions to religious purposes often exceeded twice the amount which, at the beginning of the year, he had set apart for benevolent objects. Few men have given so great promise of usefulness to the church, or have, in so short a time, accomplished so much for the honour of our Master. He left a copious Diary, from which his widow has prepared a Memoir which has not yet been published. The article on "The Wants of the West," in the volume for 1836, is a contribution from his pen.

BLACKBURN, WILLIAM MAXWELL, is a native of the State of Indiana, and the oldest son of an elder in the Presbyterian Church. In 1850, when about twenty-one years of age, he graduated at Hanover College; after which he studied theology at the Princeton Seminary. He began his ministry at Three Rivers, Michigan, but in 1856 he accepted a call to the newly organized Park church at Erie, Pennsylvania, in which he continued till 1863, when he undertook the pastorate of the Fourth church at Trenton, New Jersey. In all these charges, especially in the latter two, large accessions of members were made to the churches and heavy debts liquidated, while under his ministry.

While at Erie he wrote a series of Sabbath-school books, designed to elevate that class of literature, which were published by the Presbyterian Board of Publication; and in 1862 he spent a few months in Europe, visiting especially those places which were distinguished in the Great Reformation, and collecting all the rare books which illustrated that period. This fondness for Church History had been stimulated in him by the admirable lectures of Dr. Joseph Addison Alexander in the Seminary; and now having a mass of rare material in his possession, he issued in succession from the press of the Presbyterian Board, a series of monograms upon Aonio Paleario, Zuingle,˙ Farel, Calvin, Admiral Coligny, and St. Patrick, which have been received with much favour both in this country and in Great Britain.

In 1867 he was offered the Presidency of Hanover College, his *alma mater*, but declined the appointment. In 1868 he was elected to the chair of Biblical and Ecclesiastical History in the Theological Seminary of the Northwest, at Chicago, Illinois, and was installed in September. He engaged to become a special contributor to this *Review* in 1870, but his only contribution included in this Index is on the "Culdee Monasteries," in the volume for 1867.

BLEDSOE, ALBERT TAYLOR, is the eldest son of Moses O. Bledsoe, who, about the year 1816, founded and edited at Frankfort, Kentucky, the paper now called *The Commonwealth;* and the grandson of the Rev. William M. Bledsoe, a Baptist clergyman, who, during the persecution of the Baptists in Virginia, removed from Orange county to that wild region of the State which was afterwards known as Kentucky. His mother is Sophia C. Bledsoe, the daughter of Samuel Taylor, and the sister of the late Samuel Taylor, of Richmond, Virginia, and the niece of Creed Taylor, of Needham, who, for many years before his death, was one of the two Chancellors. of Virginia. He was born at Frankfort, Kentucky, November 9th, 1809, and graduated at West Point in 1830. He resigned from the army in 1832, and studied law under his uncle, Samuel Taylor,˙who was justly deemed, by all who knew him, both a great lawyer and a good man. After having studied ·law ·for one year, he accepted the position of tutor in Kenyon College, Ohio, and removed to that institution with the view to educate a younger brother, whose sudden death defeated his design. He then entered the Theological Seminary connected with Kenyon College, and studied theology under the Right Rev. C. P. McIlvaine and the Rev. William Sparrow, as well as Greek and Hebrew under the Rev. William Nast. After his graduation, he was admitted to orders, first as a deacon, and then as a presbyter, in the Protestant Episcopal Church of the United States. Finding ·it impossible, after a few years of close study, to continue, with a clear conscience, his connection with the Episcopal Church *as a minister,* he resigned his office as a presbyter. In announcing this fact, Bishop McIlvaine did not allude tọ the causes of his resignation, except in so far as to say it was for reasons "not affecting his moral character." In 1838 he removed to Springfield, Illinois, and entered on the practice of the law, in which he soon had great success. Not finding this noble profession, however, as congenial to his tastes

14

and habits as literary and scientific pursuits, he accepted, in 1848, the Chair of Mathematics and Natural Philosophy in the University of Mississippi. He occupied this chair from the fall of 1848 to the fall of 1854, when he entered upon the duties of the Chair of Mathematics in the University of Virginia, to which he had been elected. On quitting the University of Mississippi, the Trustees of that institution conferred on him the degree of LL.D., about the same time that the same degree was conferred on him by Kenyon College, Ohio. From his election in 1854, or rather from his acceptance of the office, he was Professor of Mathematics in the University of Virginia until 1865. When, in 1865, the Visitors appointed by Governor Pierpont vacated all the Chairs, and proceeded to a re-election, he was not one of the candidates. In 1845, while engaged in the practice of the law, he published "An Examination of President Edwards's Inquiry into the Freedom of the Will." In 1853, while at the University of Mississippi, he published, "A Theodicy; or Vindication of the Divine Glory as Manifested in the Constitution and Government of the Moral World." In 1856 he published "An Essay on Liberty and Slavery," and in 1866, he published, "Is Davis a Traitor; or Was Secession a Constitutional Right previous to the War of 1861?" In 1868, he published, "The Philosophy of Mathematics; with Special Reference to the Elements of Geometry, and the Infinitesimal Method."

We cannot enumerate the articles he has written for various periodicals. In 1867, he founded in the city of Baltimore *The Southern Review*, of which he is now the senior editor, and has been the principal contributor. In 1846, he contributed to this *Review* the article on the "Accountability of Men for their Faith."

BOARDMAN, HENRY AUGUSTUS, was born at Troy, New York, on the 9th of January 1808, and graduated at Yale College in 1829; after which he studied theology at the Princeton Seminary. On leaving the Seminary in 1833, he became the pastor of the "Tenth Presbyterian Church in Philadelphia," and has continued in that charge to the present time. During much of his life he has been subject to a severe bronchial affection, yet his labours both in the pulpit and from the press have been very abundant. Among his theological writings may be specified, "The Scripture Doctrine of Original Sin," first published in 1839; "The Great Question," in 1855; "The Society of Friends and the Two Sacraments," in 1857; all of which are now admitted to be standard works on the themes which they discuss. On controversial and ecclesiastical matters, in 1841 he published "Correspondence with Bishop Doane on the Oxford Tracts;" and 1844, "The Apostolical Succession;" in 1849, "The Doctrine of Election;" in 1855, "The Christian Ministry not a Priesthood;" and in 1866, "The State of the Church: being a review of the Proceedings of the General Assembly of 1866." With the warm interest he has always taken in the prosperity of the country, he has allowed few occurrences of great public interest to pass without directing the minds of the people to the moral lessons and duties arising from the occasion, and among his published addresses may be mentioned, "The American Union," 1850; "The Federal Judiciary," 1862. In 1865, "The Peace-Makers," and "The Peace we Need, and How to secure it." Of his very many publications on miscellaneous matters, the principal are, "The Importance of Religion to the Legal Profession," 1849; "A Discourse on the Life and Character of Samuel Miller," 1850; "The Bible in the Family," 1851; "The Bible in the Counting-house," 1853; "The Low Value set upon Human Life in the United States," 1853; "Moral Courage," 1857; "Christian Union," 1859; "The Life and Character of the Rev. Cortlandt Van Rensselaer, D. D.," 1860. The most of these works have gone through several editions in this country, have been reprinted with commendatory prefaces in Great Britain, and some have been translated into other languages. In 1853 he was elected by the General Assembly to the Chair of Pastoral Theology in the Seminary at Princeton, made vacant by the death of Dr. Archibald Alexander; but at the solicitation of his church and many of the most distinguished inhabitants of Philadelphia, he consented to abide with them, and declined the appointment. In the following year he was elected Moderator of the General Assembly. He received the honorary degree of D. D. from Marshall College, Pennsylvania. When a student at Princeton Seminary in 1833, he reviewed "Gall's Lesson System of Education" for this work.

BOCOCK, JOHN H., is a native of Buckingham county, Virginia. He received his classical education at Amherst College, Mass., when Dr. Heman Humphrey was president, and afterwards studied theology at Union Theological Seminary, Virginia, under Dr. Baxter. He was ordained to the ministry in 1839; and for the first five years was installed over a pastoral charge in Buckingham county, after which he removed to another country charge in Louisa county; and in 1853 he accepted the charge of the church at Harrisonburg, Virginia.

In 1856 he was honoured with the degree of D. D. by Washington College, Virginia, and installed pastor of the Bridge Street church, Georgetown, D. C. Here he was the beloved pastor of this people till 1861, when the war broke out, when he entered the Confederate army as chaplain. After the war he accepted a call to the church at Fincastle, Virginia, his present charge. He made some popular contributions to *The Presbyterian* newspaper in 1860, under the head of "The Twos," "The two Civilizations," "The Two Styles of Religion," "Coxiana," "The Response to Bishop Potter," &c. The articles contributed to this *Review* by him were,

1847. Relation of Romanism to the Religion of the Bible.

1848. Liberty and Loyalty.

BRECKINRIDGE, JOHN, the son of the Hon. John Breckinridge, Senator, and Attorney-General of the United States under the administration of President Jefferson, was born at Cabell's Dale, in Kentucky, on the 4th of July 1797. His family had been Presbyterian from the time of the Reformation, and during the protectorate of Oliver Cromwell removed from Scotland to the north of Ireland, whence they emigrated to Pennsylvania. They subsequently removed to Virginia, and finally to Kentucky. His father died when he was nine years old, and from that time he was placed under the care of his mother and an elder brother, who was appointed his guardian. He attended the best schools in Kentucky, and when no more could be done for him there, he was sent to the College of New Jersey, to perfect his education, in the hope that he might distinguish himself as a lawyer, as his father had done before him. He entered Princeton College in the autumn of 1814, and graduated with honour in September 1818. But while seeking merely scientific knowledge, he came to the true knowledge of himself, and the mercy of God to him as a sinner, and from that time he esteemed all other knowledge poor in comparison with it, and determined to devote his life to the ministry. After graduating at the College he acted as Tutor during the next two years, at the same time prosecuting his studies in theology at the Seminary, and on the 1st of August 1822, he was licensed to preach the gospel by the Presbytery of New Brunswick. The foreign field was chosen by him as his field of labour; but at this time an offer was made to him of the Chaplaincy to Congress, which he accepted, and fulfilled its duties in the session of 1822–3. It is probable that he accepted the Chaplaincy in the hope of making an acquaintance with public men, that would be of advantage to him in foreign countries, for he had not abandoned the idea; and on the 23d of January 1823, he married Miss Margaret Miller, the eldest daughter of Dr. Samuel Miller, who had pledged herself to go with him wherever the providence of God should direct. But events beyond his control frustrated this design, and the McChord church in Lexington, Kentucky, having kept its pulpit vacant about a year in the hope of obtaining him as their pastor, he was induced to accept the charge, and was ordained and installed on the 10th of September. He continued in this charge until the summer of 1826, when he became colleague to Dr. Glendy, the pastor of the Second Presbyterian Church in Baltimore, who was then in advanced years. He was installed on the 13th of October, and continued a member of the Presbytery of Baltimore till his death.

In our sketch of the life of Dr. Archibald Alexander, we saw how imperfectly the ministry were educated in his early days, before the institution of the Princeton Seminary; but after the machinery for educating was provided there was still a great want of labourers, both in the domestic and foreign field. To supply this want, in 1818, six years after the Seminary had been founded, the Presbyterian Church organized its Board of Education to assist young men in preparing for the ministry, but for twelve years its annual income was often under a thousand dollars, and seldom reached fifteen hundred. It did not meet the wants of the church, and the General Assembly of 1831 resolved upon the reorganization of the Board.

On the first meeting of the Board after its reorganization, Dr. William Neill, the Corresponding Secretary, resigned, and the next day (June 8) Mr. Breckinridge was elected his successor. For some years the destitutions of the church had pressed upon his mind. A thousand congregations had been represented as without a pastor, not to mention the wants of a world beyond; he therefore felt that he could not resist the call, which appeared to be the voice of God speaking through his church. With this voice sounding in his ears, and the sight of a perishing world before his eyes, with chivalric heroism he severed the most endearing ties, and rushed from State to State proclaiming the danger and calling for help. Such devotion to a cause could not be witnessed without touching a responding chord in the human breast, and wherever he went great crowds were attracted by his eloquence, and responded to his appeals. No preacher ever before or since had such a controlling influence upon the American people. The Board of Education was in a short time raised into a position of usefulness, and every depressed interest in the church now looked to him for aid.

At this time there occurred the most exciting event in his life. In 1832 he got involved in a controversy with the Rev. John Hughes, a Roman Catholic clergyman of great ability, who was afterwards created an archbishop, on the question whether the Roman Catholic or Presbyterian Church was most inimical to civil and religious liberty. This question was discussed by them both orally and through the press. It filled a great portion of the columns of *The Presbyterian* in 1832 and 1833, and was published in a condensed form, in an octavo volume, in 1836. In this controversy he distinguished himself as an able orator and controvertist, and by the variety and extent of his knowledge of the history of the church and its opinions.

In May 1835 the General Assembly elected him Professor of Pastoral Theology in Princeton College; and about the same time Union College conferred upon him the degree of D. D. He now resigned the office of Secretary of the Board of Education, but he had the satisfaction of knowing that he had achieved all that was possible, or needful for the cause. The number of candidates assisted by the Board had been increased from 123 to 608, and the annual receipts from $3998 (the largest sum received in the previous twelve years) to $46,680. So great a number of candidates has never since been attained; and an equal amount of funds, with a wider field and accumulated wealth, the Board has often found it difficult to reach. His administration gave stability and form to the Board, and the subsequent improvements have been merely in systematizing and economizing its workings.

On the 1st of May, to the great gratification of his family, he removed to Princeton, where kind friends had purchased for Mrs. Breckinridge a house for her home, and on the 5th of May he was inaugurated into the Professor's Chair. "Yet this new home which promised so much to earthly comfort and affection, promised but deceptively. Dr. Breckinridge's time was divided between the ordinary duties of his professorship, and an active agency in behalf of the funds of the Seminary, which took him very much away from his family. Then, after only eighteen months in Princeton, he was urged to undertake an agency for the new Board of Foreign Missions; and, though declining the proposal, consented to spend the winter of 1837–8 in the city of New York, labouring in this cause. Thither to a hotel the entire family removed," and did not return to Princeton till the spring.*

Mrs. Breckinridge's health was now very delicate, and in

* Life of Dr. Samuel Miller by his son.

the hope of restoration her husband accompanied her to Saratoga, and not receiving any benefit, concluded to try the Red Sulphur Springs of Virginia, but on the journey she became worse, and returned to her home in Princeton, where in a few days she died, June 16, 1838.* The chief bond of his attachment to Princeton being broken, the Foreign Board again urged upon him the acceptance of a General Agency, and he finally consented to act, and by his visits to the churches north and south gave a great impetus to the cause. In 1839 he received a call to the First Presbyterian Church in New Orleans, which he did not accept, but supplied their pulpit during the winter, and returned to the north. In the summer of 1840 he was married to Miss Mary Ann Babcock, of Stonington, Connecticut, and returned to New Orleans in the winter, where he again supplied the pulpit of the First Church. Towards spring he felt much prostrated, and leaving New Orleans in May, with considerable effort he reached the home where he was born, near Lexington, Kentucky. Here he received the devoted attentions of his mother and his other relations, and lingered till the 4th of August, 1841.

Dr. Breckinridge, though a very young man, exerted a great influence on all the questions that agitated the church in his day; and a romantic interest is now associated with his name. He is regarded as the personification of all that is noble and gentle in his humanity, and all that is fearless and self-sacrificing in the work of his Master. One who knew him well, a kindred spirit, when contemplating his character in 1839, said, "Dr. John Breckinridge is in Kentucky. It occurs to me to say of him, that I never saw him idle or lounging a moment, nor ever diverted to minor matters or levity; I never saw in him the slightest tendency to worldliness; I never saw him in any company, even of the most fashionable political grandee, where he did not take a high religious stand, and avow high Christian opinions, with an air of conscious superiority; and I never detected him in any sort of self-pleasing or shrinking from sacrifices or hard duty. I know no minister whose private intercourse is so purely and zealously religious."†

"The close of such a life is necessarily a matter of extreme interest and importance. We will therefore give some facts concerning it. He was endowed by nature with a degree of intrepidity of character—perhaps, more properly speaking,

* About a year after her death a "Memorial" of her was printed for private circulation.

† Familiar Letters of James W. Alexander, D. D., October 3, 1839.

hardihood of spirit—which made him, all his days, insensible to fear; and we suppose that at any moment during his life, this quality alone would have enabled him to die with perfect composure. He had besides, in the highest possible degree, that sense of propriety, and that perception of what is becoming, which constitute the highest charm of the behaviour of a gentleman, in all circumstances; and this ruling characteristic was so strong to the very last, that some hours before his departure he put his thin hand in ours,* as he feebly revived from a season of great bodily suffering, and with a voice nearly inaudible, but perfectly steady, said—'Do not permit me, in moments like these, to do anything unbecoming.' To say that such a man meets the king of terrors with all the dignity that could illustrate the names of heroes or philosophers, is to say nothing. And yet there was no insensibility to the solemnity of the occasion, or to the overwhelming importance of the event. For the same morning, when asked about his spiritual consolations, he replied, 'I have no fear, but I have not that rapture of which many have spoken. I never had much rapture in religion. My views of the depth of sin and of the awfulness of eternity have been such.'

"The principal seat of his disease was in the throat, and for several months before his death, that eloquent voice, which had filled so many hearts, and thrilled so many spirits with all high and tender emotions, was already hushed to the lowest whisper. At the same time his frame was reduced to the last degree of emaciation, (though he daily rose and dressed himself, almost to the last,) and his nervous and vital energy so much prostrated, that he could not endure the least excitement, whether physical or mental. While these circumstances rendered his great and enduring self-possession and composure the more remarkable, they explain also how it was that the last months of his life were essentially months of solitude and of silence. It was a continued season for divine meditation, for inward prayer, and for sweet communion with God.

"On one occasion, the day perhaps before his death, he called his only son, a youth of thirteen years, to his bedside, and with the tenderest admonitions, and the most fervent blessings, besought him to remember that he had consecrated him from the womb to the service of God—as a minister of his son Jesus Christ; and that, unless his whole heart and soul were in this great work, it would be an abomination in the sight of God if he should intrude into it. An hour before his death he became apparently entirely free from pain, and his

* Drs. Robert J. and W. L. Breckinridge.

poor frail body sunk into a posture of rest and quiet. He was, as he had constantly been, in the perfect exercise of all his senses and faculties. After a few moments he said, 'Nothing is impossible with God;' and a little after—'God is with me.' These were his last words."

His contributions to this journal were, in

1830. The Claims of Foreign Missions.

1832. Sprague on Revivals of Religion.

BRECKINRIDGE, ROBERT J., a younger brother of Dr. John Breckinridge, was born at Cabell's Dale, Kentucky, March 8, 1800. He pursued his studies successively in Princeton, Yale, and Union Colleges, at the last of which he graduated in 1819. He then commenced the study of law, and practised in Kentucky during eight years (from 1823), in which period he was several times a member of the State legislature. In 1829 he united with the Second Presbyterian church in Lexington upon profession of faith, and soon after commenced the study of theology, with the view of entering the gospel ministry, and, as a ruling elder, was a member of the General Assembly in 1831 and 1832. In October of 1832 he was ordained and installed pastor of the First Presbyterian church of Baltimore, (succeeding his brother, Dr. John Breckinridge, in the pastorate), in which charge he remained during thirteen years, and rose to eminence as an eloquent and successful preacher of the gospel. In 1845 he accepted the Presidency of Jefferson College, Pennsylvania, and together with the duties of this office supplied the pulpit of a church in a neighbouring village. In 1847 he returned to Kentucky and became pastor of the First Presbyterian church of Lexington, and accepted also the office of "Superintendent of Public Instruction" for the State. The duties of this latter office were at that time exceedingly onerous, requiring in their discharge the full amount of the wisdom and energy and resources of no ordinary mind; but he was enabled so to discharge its responsibilities as to establish the present common-school system of the State, and to leave but little for his successors therein to accomplish, except to carry out the plans and suggestions which his judgment had matured or pointed out. He resigned this charge, together with his pastorate in Lexington, in 1853, having been elected by the General Assembly Professor of Exegetic, Didactic, and Polemic Theology in the then newly established Seminary in Danville, Kentucky, an office which he retained until December 1, 1869, (the end of the Seminary term), when he

15

resigned in consequence of the action of the General Assembly of that year in relation to the Seminary.

Dr. Breckinridge has participated largely in the religious, moral, and philanthropic discussions of the last forty years and upwards. While in Baltimore he edited the *Literary and Religious Magazine*, and the *Spirit of the Nineteenth Century:* and having during his visit to Europe in 1835 purchased and transmitted to this country a large collection of rare and valuable literature, (patristical, ecclesiastical, exegetical, and theological), he was enabled to sustain with signal success the principles of the Protestant Reformation in his controversy with the Papists in Baltimore. In the General Assembly of the Church (of which he has been very frequently a member), he has always exerted a commanding influence. He took an active part in the controversies which resulted in the division of 1837–8, steadfastly maintaining the old theology against all attempts at innovation, though always aiming to base the discussion upon fundamental principles, and discarding all merely personal aspects of the case. It was mainly through his action that the Managers of the American Bible Society receded from their resolution to adopt the revised edition of the Bible as their standard. He likewise took an active part in the anti-slavery discussion which so long agitated the country, (and when in Scotland held a public discussion of the subject with Mr. George Thompson, which was published), but was very decided in his opposition to extreme views on either side. While in Baltimore he received, for his kind services to the free blacks of Maryland, a piece of gold plate, as a present from more than a thousand of them.

In 1838 he published two volumes of "Travels in Europe;" and in 1843, "Presbyterian Government not a Hierarchy, but a Commonwealth," and also, "Presbyterian Ordination not a Charm, but an Act of Government." In 1845, "The Christian Pastor One of the Ascension-Gifts of Christ." In 1851 he delivered his elaborate discourse on the "Internal Evidences of Christianity" before the University of Virginia, which presents the question in some respects in a new and very striking aspect; and in 1852 was issued his tract, "On the Use of Instrumental Music in Public Worship." And then, in 1857 and 1858 (for we omit a number of other tracts and essays), he published in two volumes, "Theology, Objectively and Subjectively considered," the system to be completed in a third volume, which will treat of "Theology Relatively considered." These volumes have had a very extensive sale; and the view which they present of the doctrine of the imputation of Adam's sin to his posterity, while it rejects utterly the Realistic or Placæan notion, varies somewhat from the views entertained by the conductors of this work.

In 1861 Dr. Breckinridge, along with several other clergymen, established the *Danville Review*, which strongly supported the Federal Government during the late war; and also the utterances of the General Assembly on the same subject. On January 4, 1861, (the day of National Humiliation), he delivered at Lexington, Kentucky, a discourse on the state of the country, and its duty in the then existing crisis, which produced a profound impression through the whole nation.   It was widely published by the newspaper press, both secular and religious, and was, besides, issued in immense numbers in pamphlet form, and simultaneously in the cities of Louisville, Cincinnati, and Baltimore.   The effect of this discourse was most marked and happy in dissipating utterly the figment of State-rights as entertained by the Secessionists; and the view of the subject which it presents became at once the acknowledged view of all the supporters of the Federal Government. This discourse was immediately followed by a series of articles in the *Danville Review*, sustaining the government, and which were in like manner republished by tens of thousands and scattered broadcast over the land.   And so important were they deemed to the true interests of the country, that in order to facilitate their dissemination the Adams Express Company gave orders to all their agents from Maine to California to transmit the publications of Dr. Breckinridge free of charge. . The writer of this sketch, when with the army at Little Rock, Arkansas, (1864), was informed by a highly respectable clergyman, (then on a visit from California), that the first two of those essays were really instrumental in saving California to the Union.   He, being a loyal man, was greatly distressed by the vacillating condition into which the emissaries of secession had brought the State, even till she seemed ready to unite with the South.   But on receiving the number of the *Review* containing the first of those articles, hope awoke within his soul, and he immediately made himself master of the argument, and went rapidly through the State delivering it to the masses, and so too when he received the second.   A gentleman of great political influence on hearing the argument, immediately united with him in presenting it, and the result was, secession was repudiated.

But of all the labours of Dr. Breckinridge that upon which his heart was most set was the Seminary in Danville, which the General Assembly had placed mainly under his charge, to establish and bring forward to usefulness and efficiency. He had succeeded in obtaining for it a noble endowment, all things considered; and never did parent entertain a fonder affection for a child than he for this institution. It was the child of his matured strength and manhood, and the fondest hope of his declining years. Its interests were as dear as life to him, and over them he watched with all the fondness of parental love and anxiety to subserve them every way in his power. He had originated the idea, had devised mainly its admirable "Plan;" and his happiness knew no limit as he saw it rise and prosper, and year after year send forth from its halls many able ministers of Christ to enter upon their great work in the Master's vineyard. And though this prosperity (with that of all the literary and theological schools in the Border States and in the South) was interrupted by the late war, he had, in view of the resuscitation of the Seminary, devised and adopted all the requisite measures to secure a return of that prosperity in preportion as the partisan feeling should pass away from the minds of our Southern brethren. He deemed it unwise to seek this return by compromising the position defined by the General Assembly in her utterances during the war, and in his own articles aforesaid. But at this stage, in consequence of a course of procedure referred to in his resignation itself, he has felt compelled to resign his professorship, as above stated.

Dr. Breckinridge is still in full possession of his faculties, and there are some years of hard work in him yet if his life be spared.

He received the degree of D. D. from Union College, New York, and that of LL.D. was conferred upon him first by Jefferson College, Pennsylvania, and afterwards by Harvard University, Massachusetts.

While in Baltimore he wrote two articles for this *Review*, one on "Colonization and Abolition," which contains on pp. 293, 294, that remarkable definition of American slavery, which has perhaps been oftener cited and referred to than any other utterance elicited during the discussion of the Slavery question in this country. The other a short "Treatise on the Scapular," containing a severe exposure of that frontless conglomerate of Papal superstition, blasphemy, and impiety. They are both in the volume for 1833.

BROWN, REZEAU, was the son of the Rev. Isaac V. Brown, D. D., and was born at Lawrenceville, New Jersey, on the 30th of September, 1808. In boyhood he was feeble in constitution, but distinguished by an early developement of his intellectual faculties. At the age of fifteen he was admitted into the Junior Class in the College of New Jersey, and at the close of the course of two years received its highest literary honours. It was his intention to study medicine, and during his college course he assisted his uncle, Dr. Van Cleve, in the manipulations illustrative of his lectures on Chemistry, which he delivered during the two successive winters; but though he always retained a great love for the study of chemistry, mathematics, and natural philosophy, another path was marked out for him by Providence. "There has no doubt happened a great change in my character," says he, "which I date from March 1827. I was before that a mere worldling, careless of eternity, thoughtless of my own eternal interests and of those around me, a profane swearer, Sabbath-breaker, and everything else that is wicked, though only to that degree which was consistent with a decent exterior, and what were considered quite regular and moral habits in a young man. At the time mentioned, I was led in a most sudden and surprising way, when I was alone one evening, to look upon myself as a deeply depraved and guilty sinner, and to experience, in a lively manner, the feeling of my desert of hell. But in the course of a few days, I was enabled, as I thought, to cast myself on the Lord Jesus Christ as my Redeemer, and I felt through him a sweet sense of forgiveness and reconciliation with God." In June he was admitted to the communion of the church in his native village, and he passed the winter in New Haven, attending the lectures of the Medical Faculty, and particularly the study of mineralogy and chemistry under Professor Silliman. At this time, however, his mind was turned towards the ministry, and all his spare time was devoted to the study of Hebrew, Syriac, and German. In the spring of 1828 he was appointed a Tutor in the College of New Jersey, and held the situation two years and a half, at the same time studying theology in the Seminary, and finding leisure hours to pursue the study of the Hebrew, Arabic, French, and German languages. It was with the view of devoting his life to the ministry in the foreign field as well as to indulge a natural taste, that he so arduously studied the modern languages. In 1831 he resigned his position in the College, in order to devote himself entirely to the work of the ministry. "His friends often told him that his feeble body was unfit to endure the labours of the sacred office. To this his uniform reply was, that he longed for the service, and could never be satisfied that he had done his duty till he had made the trial." In April 1831 he was licensed to preach the gospel by the Presbytery

of New Brunswick, and in the month of October he received
an appointment to a vacant field at Morgantown, Virginia,
from the Board of Domestic Missions. Here he preached
statedly at three different places, about fifteen miles apart, and
constant exercise on horseback seemed to be advantageous to
his health, or at least for a time suspended the morbid action
of his system. His services were highly acceptable and accompanied with the Divine blessing. But the rigours of winter in
this mountainous region were felt to be too severe for him, and
in June 1832 he returned to Princeton, and again sat down to
study with an intensity of application that could not be justified in his feeble state of body. In the autumn, after preaching a few weeks at Trenton, he was prevailed upon to join Dr.
James W. Alexander in Philadelphia as assistant editor of *The
Presbyterian;* and while there seldom a Sabbath passed in
which he did not preach in some of the churches.

Early in 1833 he made arrangements to visit Europe in
company with a friend, but towards the end of March he was
seized with catarrh so violent that he was compelled to hasten
home to his father's house. His body wasted away; every
means used for his restoration proved vain; and he departed
this life on the 10th of September, 1833.

His contributions to the religious and periodical press were
varied, and have not been collected. "The Memoirs of Augustus Hermann Francke," published by the American Sunday-
school Union, is a translation from the German by him. His
memory is lovingly embalmed in this work by an article from
the pen of his friend, Dr. James W. Alexander, from which
this is an abstract. He contributed to this *Review* one
article:

1833. Memoir of Rieu.

BURROWES, GEORGE, was born at Trenton, New Jersey, on the 3d of April, 1811. He received his classical education at the school of Mr. James Hamilton, afterwards Professor of Mathematics in the University of Nashville, Tennessee, and for three years took charge of an Academy at Allen-
town, New Jersey. In November 1830 he entered the Junior
Class in the College of New Jersey, and graduated in 1832. In
the fall of that year he commenced the study of theology in
the Princeton Seminary, but for some months he also acted as
a Tutor in the College, and completed his theological course in
the fall of 1835. In July 1836 he became pastor of the West
Nottingham church and what is now Port Deposit church, at
the same time taking charge of the West Nottingham Acade-

my. His pastorate here was greatly blessed by additions to the church, but in 1840 he was induced to accept the Chair of Latin and Greek in Lafayette College, which he held till March 1855. He was much broken down in health at that time, and for four years recruited his strength as a country pastor. In June 1859 he went to California with a commission from the Board of Education to lay the foundation of a Presbyterian College on the Pacific coast. In this he has been eminently successful, and as *The Founder of the University of San Francisco* will be long remembered there. In the October number of *The Record* for 1869, there is an account of the University as seen by Dr. Speer, in which he shows that from an humble beginning in 1859, with four boys, one of them not six years of age, in the dark basement of Calvary Presbyterian church, by his vigorous efforts, succeeded (when forced to desist from labour for a period of three years) by those of the Rev. P. V. Veeder, in ten years there has been raised an institution which is an honour to the Presbyterian Church, and the most prosperous of the kind on the Pacific coast, and which promises to be a blessing even to other lands. It has good buildings, a collection of superior scientific apparatus, an efficient corps of instructors, and nearly two hundred students, embracing some of European, Mexican, and Asiatic origin. Dr. Burrowes recently returned to San Francisco, in restored health, and has been put in charge of a new department of the University, located upon a fine property at present about three miles from the city, while Mr. Veeder presides over the City branch. It would, however, be unjust to ascribe all the merits of this enterprise to the instructors, as the institution owes much to the sagacity and good management of the Hon. H. H. Haight, Governor of the State, the Hon. H. P. Coon, late Mayor of the City, James B. Roberts, Esq., and the other Trustees.

Dr. Burrowes's principal literary work is his "Commentary on the Song of Solomon," which was published in 1853. He was also some months editor of the *Pacific Expositor*, and furnished two articles to this *Review:*

1849. The Song of Solomon.
1850. The Reformation in Spain.

BUSH, GEORGE, was born at Norwich, Vermont, on the 12th of June, 1796. His father was an educated man, who had studied for the law, but owing to ill-health had never practically pursued it. At nine years of age he lost his mother, and in after-life he often lamented his want of a mother's care. Neither of his parents were professors of religion; and he has been often heard to relate that "when about six years old, when out visiting one day, he saw a little child pray at its mother's knees, and it affected him so much that he thought he should like to pray too, and he accordingly then began. But his views of theology were at that time of course very simple. He had always thought the Lord was good, and would take care of him; but he believed in the devil also, and greatly feared him. So he used to have two prayers, one to the Lord and one to the devil."* While a boy he was very studious, and his companions do not recollect of "his joining them in so much as one play." At the age of fourteen his father put him into a printing-office to learn the trade, but the printer, after a trial of three months, found him so absent-minded that he "told his father it was of no use, he was fit for nothing but a scholar." He was then sent to an academy till he was about eighteen years of age, when he entered Dartmouth College, and taught school in the vacations to pay his college expenses. He graduated at Dartmouth College with the highest honours in 1818, and shortly after entered the Princeton Seminary to prepare himself for the ministry. In 1822-3 he was a Tutor in the College of New Jersey, and in 1824 he accepted the charge of a church at Indianapolis, Indiana, in which he continued four years. While there he married the daughter of the Hon. Lewis Condict, of Morristown, New Jersey, by whom he had one son, but in 1827 his wife died, and though very many inducements were offered to cause him to prolong his stay in the West, he would not consent. He had determined to consecrate his life to literature, and as the best field for his exertions made his residence in New York, and in 1831 he was elected Professor of Hebrew and Oriental Literature in its University. In 1832, his first work, "The Life of Mohammed," was published in Harper's Family Library ; and in 1834, he commenced the publication of a "Commentary on the Book of Psalms," embracing the Hebrew text, with a new literal version. Only three or four numbers of this were printed. In 1835 he published his Hebrew Grammar, of which a second edition appeared in 1838. In 1836 he published a compilation of valuable extracts from Oriental travellers, illustrative of the topography, manners, usages, and language of the Scriptures; and in 1840 he commenced the publication of his "Notes, critical and explanatory," on the Old Testament, of which eight volumes have been issued,

* Memoirs and Reminiscences of the late Professor George Bush. By Woodbury M. Fernald.

embracing Genesis, Exodus, Leviticus, Joshua, Judges, and Numbers.

In 1844 he commenced a monthly magazine called the "Hierophant," in which he discussed the nature of the prophetic symbols, and indicated a disposition to recede from the rules of interpretation and opinions commonly received in the Protestant churches. This was further manifested in 1845, when he published "Anastasis, or the Doctrine of the Resurrection of the Body, rationally and spiritually considered."* In 1844, Dr. James W. Alexander writes to his friend, Dr. Hall, "Bush is going fast over to the New Jerusalem. In the *Tribune* he challenges all the world to prove the resurrection. He has a book coming out on the Soul.† He practises Mesmerism. He told me of a lady who can read any one's character by feeling a paper on which he has written, and read me a copy of his own character thus deduced. His talk is mild, self-complacent, and fascinating. He has a man translating the German account of the famous Clairvoyante of Prevorst. You can imagine nothing of the sort too big for his swallow." What Dr. J. W. Alexander perceived in 1844 did not however take place till 1848, when he consented to receive the rite of ordination privately, and it was administered to him by Dr. Lewis Beers, an aged clergyman in the New [Jerusalem] Church, at Danby, New York.

"He was invited at this time to become the pastor and preacher of the New Church Society in the city of New York, which office he accepted, but resigned his pastorship after a few months, on account of his many literary labours, yet continued as a preacher to them for about four years. In 1854 he removed to Brooklyn, and preached to the New Church Society there for about seven years. He was not without troubles arising from the usual parish sources, from conflicting opinions, and from inferior and differing minds, but he endeared himself very greatly to his Society and church, and is remembered with much esteem and affection."

The most important labour of Prof. Bush, after his ordination in the New Church, was the editing of *The New Church Repository and Monthly Review;* devoted to the Exposition of the Philosophy and Theology taught in the Writings of Emanuel Swedenborg. It was commenced in 1848 and continued through eight years, but he was then compelled to discontinue it for want of patronage, its average number of subscribers being only from eight to nine hundred. His other works were

---

* This work was reviewed by Dr. Yeomans in the volume for 1845.
† This was reviewed by Samuel Tyler, Esq., in the volume for 1846.

16

" Statement of Reasons for embracing the Doctrines and Disclosures of Swedenborg," 1846; "Mesmer and Swedenborg," 1847; "Reply to Rev. Dr. Wood's Lectures on Swedenborgianism," 1847; "Life; its Origin, Gradations, Forms, and Issues," 1848; "Letters to a Trinitarian," 1850; "New Church Miscellanies," 1855; "Priesthood and Clergy unknown to Christianity," 1857. In this work he does not deny "a divine Priesthood in Christ, nor of a spiritual Priesthood as pertaining to all his true people. His object is in fact to deny the existence of any other Priesthood, in a just view of the Christian economy." "The Professor," says his biographer, "was an uncompromising opponent of the New Church Convention, claiming too greatly the prerogative of the Mother Church, and to dispense rules to associate churches." It is directed against what exists in the " New Church" and not against the old church he had left. All Protestants hold the opinion above stated. In 1858 he published his "Notes, Critical and Practical, on Numbers," resuming the series he had commenced while connected with the Presbyterian Church, but knowing that " if he introduced any of his New Church views into the work it would defeat its sale, he gave it the same character it bore in former days." Before he did this, however, he consulted with his friend, Asa Worthington, on the expediency and propriety of the step. "He had doubts whether it was right for him to do so—right to give a less lucid commentary upon the word than he had the ability to do by adopting the New Church rule of interpretation; but it was concluded that even the old method was a help to the understanding, and therefore better than nothing; while if the new rule was applied, prejudice would be so strong against the work that it would not be read, and both objects—the one to gain his bread and the other to aid the seeker after light—would be thereby defeated." This seems not to have been the only point on which he accommodated himself to the old theology, for Dr. James W. Alexander, in his letter of September 30, 1856, says, " Bush writes to me. He expatiates on the excellencies of Howe, Owen, and Burroughs, in precisely the same terms which he would have used thirty years ago."

In January 1849 Mr. Bush was again united in marriage, and by this marriage had three children. He continued to preach to the Society in Brooklyn till February 6, 1859. He was now suffering under a granular degeneration of the liver, and removed to a farm near Rochester, New York. " After reaching his rural home he never opened any book but the Bible, Thomas à Kempis, and the Village Hymns. It was his habit during his life, after family worship, to read the word in the original. This he continued till within six weeks of his departure." In the house there was a room in which an aunt and a cousin of his had died, and Mrs. Bush had arranged it for his study, from an undefined dread that if he slept in that fatal room he would be more likely to die there. But as he became too weak to climb up stairs she thought it best to place a sofa-bed in the study, and there he slept his last sleep. On the evening of the 19th of September 1859 his articulation became indistinct. Calling for "his eldest son, George, a youth of nine years, he kissed him, told him to be a good boy and kind to his mother, and requested him when he was old enough to read his New Church writings, for he said, they are true. He then requested his wife to kneel down and repeat the Lord's Prayer, and then placing her hands on his head to repeat the baptismal blessing, 'The Lord bless thee and keep thee; the Lord make his face to shine upon thee and be gracious unto thee; the Lord lift up his countenance upon thee and give thee peace!' He regretted during the day that there was no minister sufficiently near to administer the sacrament of the Lord's supper. About twenty minutes before his departure he wished all others but his wife to seek rest. He then motioned her to sit by him, and partly resting on her lap said, 'There, let it be so!' A moment after, he opened his eyes and looked at her. Then they became fixed, and he closed them himself, and after a feeble gasp passed away." A duodecimo volume of Memoirs and Reminiscences of Prof. Bush has been collected and published by the Rev. Woodbury M. Fernald, for the benefit of his family, from which this article is substantially taken. His contributions for this *Review* were:

1830. Fry on the Second Advent.
1832. Remarks on Galatians iv. 21–31.

CAMERON, HENRY CLAY, is a native of Shepherdstown, Virginia. He received his classical education in Georgetown, District of Columbia, from the Rev. James McVean; entered the Junior Class in Nassau Hall in 1845, and was graduated with honour at the Centennial Commencement of the College of New Jersey in 1847. The next three years he was engaged in teaching in Virginia, after which, in 1850, be entered Princeton Theological Seminary, but in 1851–52 became one of the Principals of the Edgehill School, and was not graduated till 1855. In 1852 he was made a Tutor in the College of New Jersey; in 1855, Adjunct Professor of Greek; in 1860, Associate Professor; and in 1861, Professor of the Greek

Language. He spent the years 1857–58 in Europe, in study and travel; was Instructor in French in the College from 1859 to 1869, and has been Librarian since 1865. In this capacity, and as the editor of the *Catalogus Collegii Neo-Cæsariensis*, having in his possession a record of the principal events in the lives of the Alumni, he has been of great service to us in the preparation of this INDEX, and several of the notices are entirely from his pen. In connection with Professor Arnold Guyot, LL.D., he has published large Classical Maps of Greece, Italy, and the Roman Empire. In October 1859 he was licensed to preach by the Presbytery of Philadelphia, and on February 1, 1863, ordained to the gospel ministry. His contributions to this work are,

1866. Forsyth's Life of Cicero.
1867. The Queen's English *vs.* The Dean's English.

CARNAHAN, JAMES, was born near Carlisle, Pennsylvania, on the 15th of November, 1775. In 1780 his father removed to the neighbourhood of Canonsburgh, where young Carnahan received his rudimentary education. In 1798 he entered the Junior Class in Princeton College and graduated in 1800, when about about twenty-five years of age. He then returned to Canonsburgh and studied theology under Dr. John McMillan one year. From 1801 to 1803 he was a Tutor in Princeton College, and continued his studies in theology under the direction of its President, Dr. Samuel Stanhope Smith. In April 1804 he was licensed to preach the gospel by the Presbytery of New Brunswick, and on the 5th of January, 1805, he was inducted into the pastorate of the Whitesborough and Utica churches in the State of New York. In this charge he continued nine years, when he removed to Georgetown, District of Columbia, and opened a classical academy. In 1823 he was chosen President of the College of New Jersey, and held the position over thirty years, with honour to himself, and for the prosperity of the College, but feeling the infirmities of age pressing upon him, in 1853 he tendered his resignation and in 1854 removed to the residence of his son-in-law, William K. McDonald, Esq., at Newark, New Jersey. Here he died on Friday the 3d of March, 1859, in the 84th year of his age; and his remains were borne to Princeton on the Tuesday following, and deposited beside those of the illustrious presidents of the College that had preceded him.

When Dr. Carnahan came into office in 1823, the Faculty consisted of five members: a president, vice-president, a professor of mathematics, and two tutors. When he resigned, it was composed of fifteen, a president, vice-president, six professors, two assistant professors, three tutors, a teacher of modern languages, and a lecturer on zoölogy. "He had the sagacity," says Dr. Leroy J. Halsey, "to surround himself at all times with a Faculty equal in ability and talents to any in the history of the institution. The names of Joseph Henry now of the Smithsonian Institute, of Stephen Alexander the eminent astronomer, of Dr. Torrey the botanist, of Professor Guyot, of Albert B. Dod, of J. W. Alexander, and Dr. John Maclean, who succeeded him in the presidency, will illustrate the character of the Princeton Faculty under Dr. Carnahan's administration. It was probably the period in which the College reached its greatest prosperity and its widest influence—great as had been the reputation and ability of the men who from its origin had been called successively to its headship. An excellent classical scholar, a sound teacher of philosophy and ethics, exemplary and consistent in all his conduct, he gave his whole time and talent to the College; and to his diligence, fidelity, and wisdom, much of this healthful growth of thirty years must be attributed. As a writer in the Cyclopedia of American Literature well remarks, 'He was less brilliant than his predecessors, but he brought to the service of education a balance and constancy of solid qualities, and an administrative talent in finance, which joined to proverbial truth and uprightness, made his green old age peculiarly honourable.'

"His distinguishing attribute of character was practical wisdom. In sound sense, unerring judgment, few men have excelled him. This made him a successful head in guiding the College, and governing the youth committed to his charge. He was so modest and unpretending a man in all his feelings and habits, that the public were little aware of the great work he accomplished at Princeton. The whole number of students graduated at Nassau Hall, from the beginning of the College to his resignation, in 1853, a period of one hundred and seven years, as stated by Dr. Van Rensselaer from the College records, was three thousand three hundred and ninety; and yet during his administration of thirty years more than half of these graduated. He thus conferred the first degree upon a larger number of alumni than all his predecessors had done. It is somewhat singular that a man with no great claims to popular eloquence, or preëminence as a preacher, should have done such a work as this, in a position, which for more than seventy years had been adorned with a succession of the greatest pulpit orators in our annals. Still Dr. Carnahan was not without his attractions in the pulpit, especially to cultivated minds. Though his manner was quiet, he always inspired the respect and confidence which the consciousness of accurate knowledge gives a man. Tall in person, neither lean nor corpulent, and preaching in the black gown which was then the fashion at Princeton, he was always heard with attention and interest, and his appearance at Commencements and other public occasions was dignified and commanding."

He had little desire to appear as an author while he lived, and he directed in his will that none of his manuscripts should be published. To this *Review* he contributed two articles:

1829. General Board of Education and the American Education Society.

1834. Review of John Sergeant's Address.

CHILDS, THOMAS S., was born in Springfield, Massachusetts, on January 19, 1825, graduated at the University of New York in 1847, and at the Theological Seminary at Princeton in 1850. He was licensed to preach the gospel by the Presbytery of New York, April 17, 1850, and ordained and installed pastor of the First Presbyterian church, Hartford, Connecticut, on the 30th of June, 1852. On November 1, 1865, he resigned this charge and was installed pastor of the First Congregational church, Norwalk, Connecticut, on the 7th of February, 1866, his present charge. He is the author of several tracts and sermons, and contributed to this *Review* in

1857. Theology of John Robinson.

1863. The Life of Edward Irving.

CLARK, JOSEPH, was born at Carlisle, Pennsylvania, on the 11th of October, 1825. His parents were Presbyterians of Scotch descent, who felt it their duty to train their child in the principles they themselves believed, and at the early age of sixteen he united with the Presbyterian church at Carlisle, then under the pastoral care of the Rev. T. V. Moore. Shortly afterwards he was sent to the Academy at New Bloomfield, where he declared his intention of devoting himself to the ministry. He pursued his collegiate course at Marshall College, then located at Mercersburg, where he graduated with the highest honours in 1848. He received his theological education at the Western Theological Seminary, and was licensed to preach the gospel by the Presbytery of Carlisle on the 11th of June, 1851. Soon after this he was invited to fill the pulpit of the Presbyterian church at Chambersburg, and so acceptable were his services to the congregation that a call was made to him to become their pastor, and he was ordained and installed on the 3d of June, 1852. He discharged the duties of his office with great acceptance till October 1859, when, in consequence of a disease of the throat, which made public speaking perilous, he was compelled to resign.

Mr. Clark then engaged as a partner in a planing-mill, in the hope of restoring his health by out-door exercise and a more active employment. In this he was not disappointed, and with improved health he often filled a vacant pulpit. The last act of his life was to prepare an address for the "Day of National Humiliation," which he was not spared to deliver. Though he was diligent and successful in the prosecution of his secular employment, yet he had no love for it; and he longed for the opportunity to employ his talents more entirely in the service of his Master. As it was a matter of doubt whether he would be long able to preach regularly, he conceived the idea of establishing a Theological and Scientific Review, and had so far committed himself to the undertaking that he had offered his establishment for sale, written three articles for the first number, and engaged the literary services of others, when, on Monday, the 3d of June, his arm was crushed by a falling log, and he died on the following Friday, June 7, 1865. He left a widow and four children.

Mr. Clark's aim as a pastor was to instruct from the pulpit, and by disseminating among the people the publications of the church; his time was therefore spent in pulpit preparation rather than in social visitation among them. He also thought it important that every minister in the Presbytery should read the *Princeton Review*, and regularly forwarded a list of subscribers. He was very methodical in the distribution of his time, and set apart a large proportion to reading and writing. He was a forcible writer and a bold investigator of truth, and pushed his researches into every province of physical and moral science, as well as into theology. The articles he contributed to this *Review* attracted considerable attention at the time of publication, and many inquiries were made in regard to their authorship. They were,

1862. The History and Theory of Revolutions.
1863. The Scepticism of Science.

CLARK, WILLIAM JAMES, was born in Philadelphia, on the 25th of August, 1812. His classical education was received partly at Bristol College, (now extinct), and subsequently under the best private teachers in his native city. His theological education was obtained in the Episcopal Theological Seminary of Virginia, from which he was graduated in 1837. He was ordained to the diaconate by the venerable Right Rev.

Clanning Moore of Virginia, in that year; and to the priest-hood in 1838 in Middletown, Delaware, by the Right Rev. Henry U. Onderdonk of Pennsylvania. His first parish was that of St. Andrew's, Wilmington, Delaware. Afterwards he was in Maryland and Pennsylvania, in the latter of which his labours were most richly blessed in Williamsport, where he saved the church building from the hands of the sheriff, and laid the foundation of a large and flourishing congregation. Much of his ministerial life has been employed successfully in teaching in Washington City and Georgetown, District of Columbia. After a short sojourn in Ohio, where the climate proved injurious to his health, he removed to Philadelphia. Here he was employed as agent for two local institutions, when he accepted the charge of the Episcopal church of Trinity parish, in Vineland, New Jersey. His labours there have been eminently successful, and bid fair to give an impetus to the cause of Christian truth in West Jersey. He is the author of two pamphlets, which have been extensively circulated and favourably noticed by the papers and reviews. The first of these was, "A Letter to the Committees of the Domestic and Foreign Boards" of the Episcopal Church. The second was entitled, "The National Foundry for the West: Where shall it be located? a letter to the Hon. John Sherman, United States Senator from Ohio." This letter was strongly endorsed by Senator Sherman, who gave it a very wide circulation. In addition to these he is the author of sketches entitled, "Lights and Shadows of a Country Parson's life;" "The Sponsor in Baptism," a treatise on the whole subject; and "Church Wardens and Vestry Men," defining their duties. He has a number of treatises now nearly ready for the press, which he has never found time to complete. Two of these are, "Baptism:—considered in its relation to the other parts of the Christian system;" and "Twelve Years in a School-room," relating his experience as a teacher.

He contributed to the *Princeton Review* in

1846. The Blasphemy against the Holy Ghost.

1848. The Doctrine of the Inward Light.

1849. Croly on Divine Providence—Prichard's Natural History of Man.

CLELAND, THOMAS, was born in Fairfax county, Virginia, on the 22d of May, 1778. About the third or fourth year of his age he removed with the family into Montgomery county, Maryland. "The principal object that drew my father into Maryland was to take charge of an old mill establishment, by lease, for eight years. It was on Seneca Creek, and owned by a widow Perry, and was much out of repair. Father being an excellent mechanic soon repaired it and gained a large custom, took his wheat to Ellicott's Mills, laid out the proceeds in goods at Baltimore, and established a small country store at home; and this acquired a mill property which enabled him to rise above poverty and advance a little in the world. During this time I went to school to different teachers, Timothy Sullivan, Alexander Penman, and George Dyson. The first two were Irish redemptioners, as they were called, compelled to serve for a limited time to pay the expense of their passage across the ocean. The latter was an Englishman. Besides the common reading, he made us memorize the Lord's Prayer, the Ten Commandments, and the Apostles' Creed. The Old and New Testaments were read as school-books; and here, I may say, I received my earliest impressions, though very feeble indeed, by this course at school.

"In the fall of 1798 father made his arrangements to remove to Kentucky, Washington county, where he had procured an entry of five hundred acres of forest land. My maternal grandmother resided near Redstone, on the Monongahela river, which we reached in nearly two months, and there remained until father built a flat-boat, in which to descend the Ohio river. We left on the last day of November; I was in my twelfth year, and on account of a recent illness had to be carried to the boat. The descent of the river in these times was perilous, frequent attacks were made by the Indians on the boats descending; but a kind Providence interposed in our behalf, being safely conducted until we reached a small stream called Goose Creek, a short distance above Louisville, Kentucky.

"We were compelled, for want of better accommodations, to remain in our boat two weeks. Afterward a small cabin about twelve feet square was obtained, a few miles out from the river, belonging to Col. Richard Taylor, father of the renowned hero of Monterey and Buena Vista. In the meantime my father had gone to look for his land, and, if possible, to have erected a hasty building for our accommodation. He reached the neighbourhood, examined the premises, selected the spot, engaged the workmen, and was then taken with a violent attack of pleurisy. He was absent more than six weeks without our knowing the cause. The Taylor family, old and young, were very hospitable and kind to us. William, Hancock, and "Little Zack," as General Taylor was then called, were my play-

17

mates. Mrs. Taylor conceived a great fondness for my mother, and treated her as a sister.

"At length father returned, very feeble indeed; we had well-nigh lost him. About the last of April we started for our new home, at which we arrived in safety. Everything was new, rough, and wild. Late in the season as it was, we made out to inclose and cultivate twelve acres of ground. Every blade, top, and ear were saved and carefully secured, which with pumpkins, and a cellar well-stored with potatoes, we made quite a flattering appearance for persons unaccustomed to the arts and toils of farming. Here commenced a new era in my juvenile life, everything to do to obtain a livelihood—the forest to clear away, buildings to erect, the hand-mill to push around to obtain bread. Sometimes I was mounted on a three-bushel bag of corn to take to the nearest mill, which was thirteen miles distant, three miles below where Springfield now stands, then an unbroken forest.

"My father having seven children to provide for, and being in moderate circumstances, not only from this consideration, but also from flattering representations made to him by several young lawyers of his acquaintance, that a fine harvest for that profession was in full prospect in Kentucky, was induced to select for me that profession. With this object in view, and having previously made the necessary arrangements for books, boarding, &c., I set out with him for Greensburg, county seat of Green county, on the first day of January 1795. I was now in my eighteenth year. I was first under the superintendence of James Allen, Esq., who was a young lawyer, and clerk of the county. With him I commenced Rudiman's Latin Grammar, and during my stay there, some eight or nine months, I read all the Latin authors commonly used in those days.

"The Kentucky Academy, recently established at Pisgah, Woodford county, was my next place of location. At this institution I spent eighteen months of the most interesting and important portion of my early life. During all the time of my sojourn here I pursued my literary studies with uncommon ardour and industry. Many nights I slept not more than four hours. Never did any one read with more avidity a novel or romance than I did the story of Dido and Æneas in Virgil. I sometimes got four hundred lines at a lesson. I read the Odes of Horace in nine days, including the revision. Passed rapidly through the Satires, Cicero's Orations, the Greek Testament, Lucian's Dialogues, and then was forwarded with the first class, which had just commenced the second book of Xenophon's

Cyropædia, which author is as far as I ever went in the dead languages."

Mr. Cleland seems never to have had any desire to be a lawyer. His early education could not be called a religious one. Neither his father nor his mother made any profession of religion, but from the books he had read and the people he had associated with, he had come to the conclusion that "no man could be safe that was not good." He thought, "I must somehow get to be a preacher, in order to make sure of the good man when I come to die. From that day, singular as it may be, I never wavered, never hesitated one moment as to what I would choose were I ever called into public life. Here I find the germ, perhaps the embryo-existence of my earliest thoughts and impressions, erroneous as they were, that first directed and fixed my determination towards the ministry. I was always, for some reason or other, shy and reserved in the company of my father, but not so with my mother. She knew all my mind, and communicated to my father my notions on the subject of the ministry. He was entirely acquiescent, left me to my own choice, had no objection to my becoming a preacher, provided I could make a good one."

Before going to Pisgah, "external morality without an interest in Christ was all the religion I knew anything about, but now I was as one newly waken up. I commenced a regular course of *seeking* religion; attended public worship on the Sabbath, prayed in secret, or rather attempted to do so every morning and evening without fail;" and, looking back upon this period after a long life, he says, "I am better satisfied now that I was under the gracious influence of the manuduction of the Spirit, silently and gradually drawing me along, than I had any idea at the time."

The severe course of study he pursued at Pisgah brought on sickness, and for some time he was compelled to return to the farm, where he recruited his health by labour and hunting in the woods. In the autumn of 1799, when in the twenty-second year of his age, he went to Lexington to finish his education at the University of Transylvania, but his studies were in a few weeks suddenly terminated by the death, first of his mother, and shortly afterwards of his father, and from the College walls, says he, "I was suddenly translated to take my position at the head of a destitute family. I considered my literary pursuits now at an end—all access to the pulpit completely barred, so that I unhesitatingly abandoned all hope or expectation of arriving at that holy calling. I had now in a measure to occupy the place of my father. I was head of the family; wrought on the farm day and night; and public inn-keeper, where many travellers resorted for entertainment, not knowing the death of their former favourite host and hostess. Considering the family now as my own, I thought it my duty to set up family worship. I commenced right away the same evening after my return. We needed God's assistance very much in our destitute condition, and it was proper we should ask it of him. In the discharge of this duty there were ap-palling difficulties enough to discourage a young practitioner; at night there would be from six to twelve travellers around the fireside, some of them infidels, with only now and then one of some Christian denomination. But amid all these outward difficulties, in addition to my own feebleness and youthful in-experience, I rejoice this day that God put it into my heart to begin, and that he enabled me to pray and not to faint. I believe now, though I did not know it then, that I was the only one who was in the habit of praying in the family in all the region round about; and soon it was noised about, to the great wonder and surprise of many, that so young a man and under such circumstances, should be found engaged in holding family worship. But this very circumstance was the introduc-tion to my further public usefulness.

"About the middle of June 1801 was the Cane Ridge meet-ing in Bourbon county; it was the time of the great revival, particularly in the southern and western portions of Kentucky. The *falling exercise,* as it was called, was in full operation. I was determined, if possible, to attend this meeting, respect-ing which great expectations were formed. Having made my arrangements, placing the family under suitable protection, I attended the meeting. A great and solemn one it was, sure enough. But to my great disappointment I felt unmoved, cold and hard as a stone. Thus I continued till the hour of preaching next day, which was the Sabbath. The preacher in the morning was my old favourite, the Rev. Robert Marshall. The text was Cant. ii. 10, 'Rise up, my love, my fair one, and come away.' The preacher, if I may so say, 'struck the trail' of my experience some distance back, and came on plainer and plainer, and at every step more sensibly, and with more effect. At length he came right up with me—my religious state and feeling were depicted better than I could have possibly done it myself. 'Rise up, my love,' was pressed upon me in the ten-derest and most affectionate manner. I thought indeed it was the heavenly Bridegroom calling and inviting his poor feeble and falling one to rise from my low condition, and come away and follow him more entirely. My heart was melted! My bosom throbbed! My eyes, for the first time, were a fountain of tears. I wept till my handkerchief was saturated with tears. I felt like giving way. I felt an indescribable sensation, as when one strikes his elbow against a hard substance. My position was discovered by a friend standing near me. He took hold on me, and gently drew me beside him, with my head in his lap. There I continued weeping, talking, praying, exhorting, &c., till the sun was no more than two hours high. As to the duration of my exercise, it appeared to me to have been not more than an hour—something like it had, all along, been so much desired that I seemed to covet its uninterrupted continuance. To say this was the time of my *change of heart*, I will not. I hope that had taken place before. I rather considered this a revival, an enlarged manifestation of that grace which had been communicated to me before; but which had undergone much obscurity and depression."

Shortly after this he attended a camp-meeting at Hite's Spring, and was involuntarily led to pray and exhort till exhaustion took place and he was compelled to desist. He was soon sent for to converse with distressed souls, all over the country, and the desire for him to preach and exhort was so strong that he consented to hold meetings at various places. Very many were converted, but having no official authority to do anything, they were induced to join the different denominations around, as there was no organized Presbyterian church in the neighbourhood.

On the 22d of October, a few weeks after the meeting of Hite's Spring, he was married to Miss Margaret Armstrong, who continued to be his faithful helpmeet till the 24th of April, 1854, and made him the father of ten children. "The marriage took place during the session of Presbytery in the New Providence church. The Presbytery, consisting of three ministers, adjourned to the place of marriage, and some time after supper they again constituted themselves into a Presbytery, and in spite of all the objections he could urge against his further prosecution of his studies for the ministry, before they permitted him to go home, regularly entered his name as a candidate, and gave him the text, 1 Cor. ix. 16, 'Wo is me, if I preach not the gospel,' as the subject for a sermon to be read at the spring meeting. During the fall and winter I held," says he, "religious meetings regularly every Sabbath, at one place and another, and nearly every other night in the week at different points, sometimes four or five miles distant. The labours and burdens of the day, which were neither few nor small, frequently disqualified me for the night-service. But so it was; the calls and invitations were pressing and numerous and almost irresistible."

We pass over the account of his trials before the Presbytery. He was licensed to preach the gospel on April 14, 1803, and in October 1804 he was ordained pastor of a newly gathered church in his neighbourhood, called Union, consisting of over a hundred members, all poor, and not able to invest in their call for his labours once a month more than one hundred dollars. He had two other preaching stations, Springfield, in which there was made a subscription of forty dollars, and Hardin's Creek of thirty, and "in the collecting thereof the amount fell short of those sums." Here he laboured as a messenger of the gospel to his own neighbours for the space of ten years, with great acceptance; and we will now give some examples of the way in which he laboured here for his own self-culture and the extension of the kingdom of God.

"In the year 1806 I commenced a correspondence with W. W. Woodward, a bookseller in Philadelphia, who was then publishing the best theological works the times afforded, and from him I received my first invoice of books, amounting to little upwards of nine dollars. It was indeed to me a little treasure. Here was Guise's Paraphrase on the New Testament, Brown's Dictionary of the Bible, Butterworth's Concordance, and Mason's Student and Pastor. This was the commencement of a growing select library, which for a number of years afterwards was pronounced to be the best minister's library in the whole connection. It was gathered gradually, read carefully, and digested thoroughly. I soon found that others wanted books all around me. I endeavoured to procure them at intervals, until in process of time the amount of invoices from that one man was upward of $3000.

"By my own suggestion the following plan was carried out at Union. A small box, with lock and key, was fixed under the pulpit board, with a hole above, like a money drawer, into which were dropped small strips of paper, with such inquiries as, What is the meaning of such and such a text? naming the chapter and verse. How do you reconcile such a passage with another that seems to contradict it? Sometimes a case of conscience was stated for inquiry and advice. These papers were to be anonymous, for reasons that are obvious. The benefit would accrue not only to the unknown individual, but others would become interested. The box was to be examined every day of preaching, the papers taken out and read publicly, and the answer was to be given after the close of the sermon the next day in course. This device I found to be of considerable service to myself. There were matters brought up in this way that I had never thought of, and which occasioned no little research and investigation in order to find out the solution.

"In these days there were no education societies, no theological seminaries; and moreover there were few young men anywhere to be found who appeared willing to set their faces toward the ministry. The General Assembly saw the great scarcity of ministers in her connection, and but little prospect of a sufficient number coming forward to supply the annual decrease occasioned by death, and having no other remedy to afford, recommended most urgently on each Presbytery to look out within their bounds for at least one poor and pious youth, who might be induced to turn his attention to the gospel ministry, to patronize him, induce the churches to help, and do anything they could to enlarge the number of the ministry. The number of young men, from first to last, that were under my supervision, as students of divinity, were some fourteen or fifteen. Some were with me six months, some twelve, and others two years. Some were in indigent circumstances and received their board gratuitously; some at half-price, or as suited their circumstances or convenience. My circumstances were by no means affluent; my salary, if it deserved the name, quite small and inadequate; my chief dependence being my own barn and store-house. My wife manufactured the most of our domestic wear for ordinary purposes; our family, too, was at an age to demand increased attention and expense. We were compelled to use the strictest economy, yet we had no lack. I never had an empty pocket entirely since I had commenced domestic life."

Having accepted a call to the New Providence and Cane Run churches, on the 31st of March, 1813, he came into Mercer county, where he had bought a farm contiguous to the New Providence church, and entered on his pastoral duties on the first Sabbath of April. He still, however, continued to preach every fourth Sabbath at Union, but after three years, as it was twenty miles distant from New Providence, with a considerable struggle he abandoned the field he had so long cultivated and a people near to his heart.

"After the old revival in 1800–1803 there had been an awful spiritual dearth in all the churches, many churches receiving very few, some no accessions at all for upwards of twenty years. About the year 1823 we may date the commencement of a noiseless, gentle, and gradual revival of religion in the New Providence church, which continued without any abatement for six or seven years, during which time there were added 240 members. There had been a small increase of 77 members the first ten years of my ministry. But ere long the good work commenced among the young people, and ceased not until not one young female in the whole congregation of New Providence was left out, and not more than a half-dozen of the youth of the other sex.

"About the year 1815, without any seeking of my own, commenced my literary controversy with Barton W. Stone. The manner in which I was drawn into it is explained in my introductory chapter to 'Unitarianism Unmasked,' which was the third and last book I published against the Arian and Socinian heresies. Though I never calculated on becoming a writer, yet almost unexpected and undesignedly I was called to .take up my pen on various occasions. I here insert a list of my principal publications, which may be found in various bound volumes, and the years in which they were published. A Familiar Dialogue between Calvinus and Arminius, 1805; The Heavenly Society, Rev. vii. 9. Funeral of Mrs. Jane Horton, 1808; The Socini-Arian Detected. · Series of Letters to Barton W. Stone, 1815; Letters to B. W. Stone on Trinity, Divinity, and Atonement of Christ, 1822; Reply to Right Reverend Bishop David, 1822; Brief History, &c., of Cumberland Presbyterians; by order of Synod, 1822; The Destructive Influence of Sinners, Eccl. ix. 18, 1823; Evangelical Hymns, (selected), 1825; Preservation and Perseverance of the Saints, Isa. xxvii. 3, 1827; A Wheel within a Wheel, (Sermon on Ezek. i. 16), 1829; Various articles for *Calvinistic Magazine*, 1829; Familiar Dialogue between Calvinus and Arminius on the Doctrines of Election and Predestination, 1830; Various articles for the *Presbyterian Advocate*, 1830; Difficulties of Arminianism, 1831; Strictures on Campbellism, 1833; Outward Rites and Inward Graces, not Identical and Inseparable, Rom. ii. 28, 29, 1833; Funeral Sermon of Mrs. Judge Underwood, 1835; Funeral Sermon of Mrs. Hickman, 1836; The Conservation and Preservation of the Saints, Ps. xxxvii. 28, 1836; Trial and Acquittal of John the Baptist, 1853. In addition to these an unpublished manuscript, 'Candid Reasons for not being an Anti-Pedo-Baptist.' I presume it was owing to my literary productions that the attention of Transylvania University was attracted, when, on the 10th of July, 1822, I received from that institution the honorary degree of D. D. This was as unexpected as it was undeserved or unmerited.

"Amid the multiplied calls and demands upon my time, both ministerial and domestic, in the kind providence of God, I have never been prevented from attending every stated meeting of Presbytery and Synod, but once by indisposition, and once from absence on a journey to Indiana and Illinois, in the fall of 1831. As a commissioner to the General Assembly I was a member of that body at Philadelphia in the years 1809, 1820, 1824, 1829; at Pittsburgh in 1835; at Philadelphia in 1837. In these Assemblies I never made a figure; was rather a silent member, unless attending to the special business on which I was particularly appointed."

At the disruption of the church in 1837–8 he adhered to the New-school General Assembly, and was a member of that body in 1850, 1852, and 1854, making ten Assemblies in which he sat as a commissioner. The last entry in his journal was made on January 31, 1855—"One circumstance more deserves special notice. I have been compelled to give up public duties, and all my pastoral relationship to the church. In connection with feeble strength, a nervous affection at the bottom of my stomach, after a short time speaking, prevents me from proceeding, weakening my articulation, and compelling me to cease altogether. Were it not for this, I could hold forth at least an hour, without much difficulty. But it is my Master's will that I should retire from the field and take my rest, after public service for more than half a century." His death occurred three years to a day after he penned these words. On Sabbath evening the 31st of January, 1858, he gently fell asleep in Jesus, in the eightieth year of his age.

"His manner of preaching," says Dr. Humphrey, "was plain and simple, without any attempt at fine style, or demonstration of the words of man's wisdom. His address was familiar, affectionate, and conversational. His style plain Saxon, highly scriptural and didactic. His voice was remarkably clear and melodious. His enunciation, though rapid, was distinct and impressive. In the prime of his life his discourses were usually from an hour to an hour and a half in length, but they were listened to with unabated, yea, increasing interest to the last. The first hour was taken up in expounding the text, and discussing the leading topic of the discourse; and when he had gotten the subject fully before the mind of his hearers, he would then enforce the whole by a most animated and moving exhortation. His manner was earnest and vehement, but never boisterous, and the effect upon his audience was overpowering. The house was usually filled to its utmost capacity. Under these most melting appeals the whole congregation were bowed upon their seats, and forcibly reminded one of a wheat-field after a storm had passed over it. There

18

would not be a dry eye in the whole house. Often times many could not refrain from weeping aloud, while others rejoiced before the Lord. Sometimes scores were convicted under one such discourse. He had at one time a continuous revival of seven years in one of his churches; nor were his labours confined to his own field, other churches enjoyed the fruits of his labours."

We have condensed this delightful autobiography from " Memoirs of the Rev. Thomas Cleland, D. D., compiled from his private papers, by Edward P. Humphrey and Thomas H. Cleland." His place in this Index is given to him on account of a letter published in the volume for 1834, on " Bodily Affections produced by Religious Excitement," in which he describes what he had himself felt and seen in 1801–3.

COBB, SANFORD H., was born in New York City in 1838; graduated from Yale College in 1858, and from Princeton Theological Seminary in 1862. In 1864 he became the pastor of the Reformed (Dutch) church in Schoharie, New York, where he is still labouring. In 1867 he contributed the article " Preaching to Sinners."

COLEMAN, LYMAN, was born in Middlefield, Massachusetts, where his father was a physician, on the 14th of June, 1796. He graduated at Yale College in 1817, and for three succeeding years was Principal of the Latin Grammar School at Hartford, Connecticut, and subsequently a Tutor at Yale for four years, where he studied theology. In 1828 he became pastor of the Congregational church in Belchertown, Massachusetts, and held the charge for seven years; afterwards principal of the Burr Seminary, Vermont, for five years; then Principal of the English Department of Phillips Academy for five years. The years 1842–3 he spent in Germany in study and in travel, and on his return was made Professor of German in the College of New Jersey, from which he received the degree of S. T. D. He continued here, and at Amherst, Massachusetts, and Philadelphia, the next fourteen years, in connection with different literary institutions. Dr. Coleman again visited Europe in 1856 and extended his travels to the Holy Land, the Desert, and Egypt, and since his return he has been Professor of Ancient Languages in Lafayette College, with his residence at Easton, Pennsylvania.

His principal published works are, 1. " The Antiquities of the Christian Church." 2. " The Apostolical and Primitive Church." 3. " An Historical Geography of the Bible."

4. "Ancient Christianity." 5. "Historical Text-book and Atlas of Biblical Geography."*

His contributions to this *Review* were in

1851. Antiquities of the Christian Church.

1866. The Samaritans, Ancient and Modern.

COLTON, ASA S., was born in Jefferson county, New York, in 1804; entered Hamilton College, New York, in 1824, and graduated in 1827. After teaching one year in Freehold, New Jersey, he commenced the study of theology in the Seminary at Princeton in the fall of 1828, and was licensed to preach by the Presbytery of Philadelphia in 1831. He was admitted to orders in the Protestant Episcopal Church in 1833, and served various parishes in Pennsylvania, Maryland, Delaware, and New Jersey, but much of his life has been devoted to the teaching of the higher mathematics, languages, metaphysics, and philosophy.

He is the author of "Successful Missions," a book for Sunday-schools; a pamphlet on "The Common Causes of Inefficieney in the Ministry;" a sermon on "The Decree of God concerning Murder," and some two thousand articles in magazines and newspapers under the signature of C. S. A. and A. S. C. He contributed to this *Review* in

1831. Ministerial Qualifications—Douglas on the Advancement of Society.

1832. German and French Philosophy.

1833. Progress of Ethical Philosophy.

1863. Mercer County Teachers' Institute.

1864. Thoughts of Marcus Aurelius Antoninus.

COLWELL, STEPHEN, was born in Charlestown, now Wellsburgh, Western Virginia, March 25, 1800; graduated at Jefferson College in 1818; was admitted to the Bar in his native State in 1820, and pursued his profession closely in a circuit embracing two counties in Virginia, two in Ohio, and two in Pennsylvania, for fifteen years; residing during that time seven years in Ohio, and lastly for eight years in the city of Pittsburgh. In 1836 he removed to Philadelphia, where he has remained since.

In Philadelphia he engaged in the manufacture of iron, and spent nearly all his leisure hours for thirty years in the study of Political Economy, and in studies connected with it, and in

* The materials for this notice are found in the genealogy of "The Coleman Family," and in "Biographical Sketches of the Members of the Class of 1817, Yale College."

process of that time collected the largest library perhaps in the country upon these topics.

The prosecution of these studies convinced him that egregions errors prevailed in the teachings on Political Economy, both in the books and in the lectures and literature of the subject. He denied that production, distribution, or consumption, or mere wealth, can be reduced to the form of science. The treatment of this subject, he shows must begin with MAN in social life, and must embrace man in all his social relations, such as his government, and the mutual duties of men to each other in a Christian country. In his Preliminary Essay to "List's Political Economy" he sets forth largely his objections to the leading works and doctrines of this so-called science.

Mr. Colwell has during the last twenty years written much on this subject, beginning with a pamphlet on the "Removal of Deposits of the United States from the Bank of the United States, by order of the President," in 1834. In 1851 he gave to the public "New Themes for the Protestant Clergy;" in 1852, "Politics for American Christians;" in 1854, "The Position of Christianity in the United States," and in the same year his great work on "The Ways and Means of Commercial Payment." Many of his publications were chiefly directed to passing events, and did good service in their day; the above will be permanently useful. He has lately made a gift of his library to the University of Pennsylvania, in view of a Chair of Social Science being created in that institution.

Mr. Colwell is an active member of the Presbyterian Church, and President of the Board of Trustees of the General Assembly. His contributions to this work were in

1841. The Poor of Britain—McCulloch's British Empire.
1842. The Smithsonian Bequest.
1843. Sweden.

COOKE, PARSONS, was born at Hadley, Massachusetts, on the 18th of February, 1800. He graduated at Williams College in 1822, and afterwards studied theology under the direction of the late Dr. Griffin, who was distinguished both as a preacher and an educator of preachers. His first pastorate was at Ware, where he was ordained on the 21st of June, 1826. The congregation over which he was placed was a new one, composed of very discordant materials, but he began his ministry with an unequivocal declaration of what he believed to be the gospel of Christ, and, with the blessing of God in the nine years of his ministry there, he moulded them into an harmonious and stable church. In April 1835 he resigned this charge and became pastor of a church at Portsmouth, New Hampshire, for a few months, and on the 4th of May, 1836, he was installed pastor of the First Congregational church in Lynn, Massachusetts, of which he continued to be the pastor till his death. "His society at Lynn, by building a church, had become embarrassed," says Dr. Nathaniel Adams, and to relieve them somewhat of the burden of his support, and help them through the crisis, he conceived the idea of establishing and editing a religious paper. The *Boston Recorder* then occupied the field, with an established reputation and a wide circulation, and he must have felt a consciousness of his power and the variety of his resources, to dare to hope for support from such an attempt. In 1839 he issued the first number of the *New England Puritan,* and its success fully justified his expectations. "His religious belief," says Dr. M. P. Braman, "as is well known, accorded substantially with that of the Puritan fathers of New England, for whom his reverence and attachment manifested themselves with a singular degree of prominence. The Puritan was to him the most honoured of all names, next to that of Christian. He could find no better title to bestow upon the weekly journal which he established, not long after his settlement in this place; and the propriety of which he intended to prove by the spirit and sentiments which should prevail in its columns. The class of men who bore this designation ranked in his esteem among the noblest order of confessors and sufferers, next to prophets and apostles and inspired teachers of Christianity. But his belief was not the offspring of tradition and reverence. He received their opinions upon no indiscriminating confidence in the excellence and loftiness of their character. He subjected their faith to the test of rigorous examination. He diligently sought the proofs by which it was sustained. It became almost as much his own as if he held them by the tenure of original discovery in the inspired records. It was the strong confidence which faithful research had given him in the grounds of his opinions, that contributed to the boldness with which he avowed them and stood forth in their defence. Some persons who entertain a similar belief with Dr. Cooke, but without the power of vindicating them from objections, proclaim them with a comparatively timid utterance. He girded on his armour and went forth into the arena with the confidence of a warrior who felt no distrust in his own skill, or the vigour of his arms; and who was certain that the weapons which he grasped were mighty through God to sustain him in the fiercest combat. He never withheld a doctrine because it was obnoxious to popular feeling. He did not disguise it to calm the fearful. He did not curtail it to satisfy the timid. He did not soften it to mitigate the scorn of the contemptuous. The natural sincerity of Dr. Cooke prompted him to a very explicit avowal of his sentiments. He was remarkably free from everything that looked like stratagem or artifice in effecting his purposes." His bodily frame was a representation of the spirit that reigned within. Large, massive, powerful in strength, suited to toilsome and ponderous employments. But during the latter years of his life he was a great sufferer, and exemplified in his own life the power of the doctrines he loved to teach. He saw not one stroke too much. When told that he would not probably survive a week, he exclaimed, "Bless the Lord!" "I hope I do not wish to die merely to get rid of pain!" "I am in a strait betwixt two, having a desire to depart and be with Christ, which is far better." "To die is gain." These were some of the thoughts that escaped from his lips shortly before he entered into his rest, on the 12th of February, 1864.

The degree of D. D. was conferred upon him by Lafayette College in 1848, and by Williams College in 1849. He was twice married. By his first wife he had no children; by his second, who was a daughter of Dr. Woodbridge, of Hadley, he had one son, to whom he gave the name of Parsons.

The *New England Puritan*, after a few years, was merged into the *Boston Recorder*, of which he continued to be one of the editors. He was also one of the founders of the *Boston Review;* but his most characteristic work is, "A Century of Puritanism and a Century of its Opposites, with Results contrasted to enforce Puritan Principles, and to trace what is peculiar to the People of Lynn to what is peculiar in its history," in one volume, 1855; which was followed by a second volume in confirmation of the first. He also wrote, "Modern Universalism Exposed;" "Hints to an Inquirer on the subject of Baptism;" "Recollections of Dr. Griffin;" besides a great many single sermons and pamphlets. To this *Review* he contributed two articles:

1843. Relation of the Gospel to Civil Law.

1844. Sacred Learning in the Primitive Church.

COPPINGER, WILLIAM, the Secretary of the American Colonization Society, revised and made additions to the article on African Colonization, in the volume for 1862. The name of the contributor is unknown.

COX, SAMUEL HANSON, was born at Leesville, New Jersey, on the 25th of August, 1793. His father was a member of the Society of Friends, but "was very different from the generality of Friends," and was often pained with "the looseness of principle which he observed among his people, and even their preachers, in regard to the truths of religion, the sanctity of the Scriptures, and the obligation of the Christian Sabbath." The early education of his mother was Presbyterian, and she coincided in sentiment with her husband. Young Samuel was encouraged by them to read the Scriptures, and finding how much the word of God varied from the teachings of those who professed to be guided by the inward light of the Spirit, he came to the conclusion that "Quakerism is not Christianity," and, after a severe mental struggle, yielded to his convictions of duty, and "on the 7th of March, 1813, professed his faith in Christ, and was baptized in the Second Presbyterian church, Newark, New Jersey." He was then twenty years of age, and had been studying law, but "shortly after this he came to the conclusion that God had called him to the work of the ministry, and he was licensed by the Presbytery of New York in the month of October 1816, to preach the gospel, and ordained to that office by the Presbytery of New Jersey, at Mendham, on July 1, 1817." He preached his first sermon in the Brick Church, New York, and in 1818 was enrolled among the honorary graduates of the College of New Jersey. In 1820 he became pastor of the Laight Street Presbyterian church in the city of New York—a charge which he held for thirteen years. In 1833 he visited Europe to recruit his health, and on the 10th of July, 1834, his house and church were ransacked by a mob on account of his having expressed his sympathy with the American Anti-Slavery Society. At this time he removed to Auburn, New York, and during the next two years was Professor of Sacred Rhetoric in the Seminary. In 1837 he accepted a call to the First Church, Brooklyn, New York, of which he continued to be pastor till 1854, when he was obliged by loss of voice to desist from public speaking. Since that time he has been President of the Ingham University for several years, and is now living in retirement in New York City.

Dr. Cox took a prominent part in the discussions that resulted in the division of the church in 1837–8, and many years after retained a virtuous indignation against "the abominable wickedness and fratricidal perjury of the exscinding acts of 1837 and 1838."* His talents and influence were exerted in favour of the New-school branch, and in 1846 he presided

* Interviews, p. 16, published in 1853.

as Moderator of its Assembly.   After the adjournment of the
Assembly, he made his second voyage to Europe as a delegate
to the Evangelical Alliance.

In 1823 the degree of D. D. was conferred upon him by
Williams College, and in a communication to the *New York
Observer* he ridiculed the honour, facetiously denominating its
symbols the "semi-lunar fardels." This epithet has obtained
a world-wide celebrity, but the Doctor, except by an occasional
horresco referens at the mention of the name, has borne the
honours thrust upon him meekly, and now in addition bears
the affix LL.D. which was given to him by Marietta College,
Ohio, in 1855, and by Columbia College, New York, in 1863.
He is the father of the Right Reverend Arthur Cleveland Coxe,
now Bishop of Western New York.   In 1833 he published
" Quakerism not Christianity; or Reasons for Renouncing the
Doctrine of Friends," in which we find the account of his early
life which we have transferred to our pages.   In 1842, "Theo-
pneuston; or Select Scriptures considered.   Adapted to be
useful to Bible-classes, Sabbath-school Teachers, and other
readers of the Word of God."   In 1853, " Interviews: Memorable and Useful; from Diary and Memory produced."   And
we learn that he is now engaged in writing a work to be
called, " Preferred Readings of Select Passages of the New
Testament, useful to Theologians, Preachers, and Pastors, as
well as to all intelligent Disciples who prefer to make no Mistake of the Passages, or of any other of the Sacred Text inspired of God for our instruction."

We cannot here enumerate the titles of the pamphlets and
sermons published by him.   He was one of the originators of
the *New York Observer*, and a valuable contributor.   In 1830,
his work entitled ." Regeneration, and the Manner of its Occurrence," was reviewed by Dr. Hodge in this work, to which
he wrote an article in reply, which was inserted in the October
number for 1831.

DAVIDSON, ROBERT, (son of Dr. Robert Davidson, pastor of the Presbyterian church in Carlisle, and President of
Dickinson College,) was born in Carlisle, Pennsylvania, Feb.
23, 1808.   He graduated in Dickinson College in 1828, and in
Princeton Theological Seminary in 1831.   In 1832 he took
charge of the McChord church in Lexington, Kentucky.   In
1840 he was made President of Transylvania University, and
the following year received the degree of Doctor of Divinity
from Centre College, Kentucky.   Resigning the Presidency in
1842, he was appointed by Governor Letcher, Superintendent
of Public Instruction for the State of Kentucky.   He was also

offered a chair in Centre College; and was subsequently elected to the Presidency of Ohio University. All these offers were declined from preference for the pastoral office.

Dr. Davidson's pastoral charges have been, the McChord or Second Presbyterian church in Lexington, Kentucky, 1832; the First Presbyterian church in New Brunswick, New Jersey, 1843; Spring-street church in New York, 1860; the First Presbyterian Church in Huntington, Long Island, 1864. In 1868, impaired health required a temporary intermission of the active duties of the ministry, since which time he has made his abode in Philadelphia.

He served as Permanent Clerk of the General Assembly from 1845 till 1850. For a score of years he has been a member of the Board of Foreign Missions; and since 1867, a Director of Princeton Theological Seminary. In 1864 he was appointed one of the Committee on the Hymnal. In 1869 he was one of the delegation to the General Assembly of the Free Church of Scotland, in the city of Edinburgh, when they were complimented with a Public Breakfast.

His published works are the following: "Excursion to the Mammoth Cave, with Historical Notes, 1838; "History of the Presbyterian Church in Kentucky," 1847; "Leaves from the Book of Nature, Interpreted by Grace," 1850; "Letters to a Recent Convert," 1853; "Elijah, a sacred Drama, and other poems," 1860; "The Relation of Baptized Children to the Church," 1866; "The Christ of God, or the Relation of Christ to Christianity," 1870.

Pamphlets—" The Bible, the Young Man's Guide;" "Reply to the (New-school) Manifesto;" "A Vindication of Colleges," (Inaugural); "The Study of History;" "A Plea for Presbyterianism;" "Presbyterianism, its place in History;" "History of the First Presbyterian Church, New Brunswick, New Jersey;" "The Evils of Disunion;" "A Nation's Discipline, or Trials not Judgments;" "On the Death of President Lincoln;" "History of the Presbyterian Church in Huntington, Long Island;" "Memoir of Governor Lewis Morris, of New Jersey;" "Piety not incompatible with the Military Life." To this list might be added Funeral Discourses, Sermons in the *National Preacher*, and numerous contributions to *McClintock's Cyclopædia* and divers periodicals; besides his share in the preparation of the Hymnal.

Dr. Davidson's articles in the *Princeton Review* are the following:

1849. Review of Dr. Stone's Life of Dr. Milnor.

19

1850. Review of Seymour's Mornings with the Jesuits—Review of Layard's Nineveh, and Hawks' Egypt.

1851. Review of Trench on Miracles.

1853. Review of Arthur's Successful Merchant, and Van Doren's Mercantile Morals.

DE BAUN, JOHN A., was born in Rockland county, New York, in March 1833. He graduated at Rutgers College in 1852, entered the Theological Seminary of the Reformed (Dutch) Church at New Brunswick, New Jersey, the same year, and was licensed in 1855. He immediately accepted a call to the Reformed Church of Oyster Bay, Long Island, and in 1858 he removed to Niskayuna, New York, and became the pastor of the united churches of Niskayuna and Lishas Kill. He has written frequently for different periodicals, chiefly on subjects connected with religion and theology, and furnished the article entitled, "A Plea and a Plan for Presbyterian Unity," in the volume for 1865.

DEMAREST, DAVID D., was born in Bergen county, New Jersey, in 1819; graduated from Rutgers College at New Brunswick in 1837; studied theology in the Seminary of the Reformed Dutch Church at New Brunswick, and was licensed to preach in 1840. After preaching about six months as assistant to the Rev. James Romeyn at Catskill, he was ordained and installed pastor of the Reformed (Dutch) Church of Flatbush, Ulster county, New York in 1841, which he resigned in 1843, and became the first pastor of the newly organized Second Reformed church of New Brunswick. In 1852 he removed to Hudson, New York, and took charge of the Reformed (Dutch) church there, and in 1862 he was elected Stated Clerk of the General Synod of the Reformed Church. In 1865 he was appointed Professor of Sacred Rhetoric and Pastoral Theology in the Theological Seminary of the Reformed Church located at New Brunswick. He received the honorary degree of D. D. from Princeton College in 1857, and has published a little volume with the title, "History and Characteristics of the Reformed Dutch Church." He contributed to this *Review* in

1856. Protestantism in Hungary.

DEWEY, CHESTER, was born in Sheffield, Massachusetts, on the 25th of October, 1784. After a youth spent in alternate labour on the farm and study in the common school, he fitted himself to enter the College at Williamstown in his eighteenth year, and graduated with honour in 1806. During his residence in the College he became the subject of those deep religious convictions by which he ever after ordered his life, and in 1807 he was licensed to preach by the Berkshire Congregational Association. After teaching and preaching a few months at Stockbridge and Tyringham, Massachusetts, he was appointed a Tutor in Williams College, and after two years service in that capacity was elected, at the age of twenty-six, Professor of Mathematics and Natural Philosophy. The sciences in those days were not marked out and their boundaries defined as now, and his department of instruction embraced the whole range of chemistry and the natural sciences. Here he entered upon his work with great zeal and enthusiasm, and began those collections of specimens for the illustration of botany, geology, mineralogy, and chemistry, which are now so large and valuable in that institution.

In 1827 he resigned the chair which he had occupied for seventeen years, and removed to Pittsfield, where he became Principal of a gymnasium for preparing young men for college and business pursuits, at the same time filling the chair of Chemistry in the Medical Colleges in Pittsfield and in Woodstock, Vermont. After nine years spent in this employment, he removed to Rochester, New York, and took charge of the Collegiate Institute in that city for fourteen years. In 1850, at the establishment of the University of Rochester, he was elected Professor of Chemistry and Natural History, and continued to discharge the duties of that chair for a little more than ten years, retiring from active duty at the ripe age of seventy-six. He was for forty years a constant contributor to *Silliman's Journal*, in which his researches on the *Carices*, or sedges, first appeared. He also wrote a "History of the Herbaceous Plants of Massachusetts," which was published by the State, and the article *Carices* in "Wood's Botany" was contributed by him. His last labour was the orderly arrangement of his large collection of sedges, which had been for many years accumulating on his hands, and copying out his meteorological journal. He died calmly of old age, on the 15th of December, 1867, in his eighty-third year. It is well said of him by Dr. M. B. Anderson, from whose "Sketch" this article is taken, " He appeared to study nature, not so much for the reputation which knowledge or discovery would secure to him, as from a tender affection for her various forms and aspects considered as exhibiting a grand connection of benevolent uses, means, and ends, revealing the goodness and wisdom of the Almighty." Up to the last years of his life he was constantly writing on scientific topics, and through his friend, Dr. J. H. McIlvaine, he contributed to the *Princeton Review* in 1863 and 1864, two articles, in which he combats and refutes the theories of Nott, Gliddon, Morton, and Agassiz, in regard to the unity of the human species.

1863. The True Place of Man in Zoölogy.
1864. Man's Place in Nature.

DICKINSON, RICHARD W., the eldest son of Charles Dickinson, late of New York, was born November 21, 1804; baptized by the Rev. Samuel Miller; brought up under the ministry of the Rev. Philip Milledoller, then pastor of Rutgers Street Presbyterian church, with which his mother was connected; placed at school under the care of the Rev. Platt Buffet, late of Stanwich, Connecticut; and on completing his preparatory studies, under John Walsh, of New York, entered the Freshman Class of Yale College in the 15th year of his age, and was graduated in the fall of 1823. But during that remarkable revival of religion (1820) in which Dr. Lyman Beecher and Rev. Mr. Nettleton assisted the pastors at New Haven, he, in company with many students, was arrested by God's grace; and at last, contrary to his predilections, deeply convinced that, instead of the law, to which he was looking forward, it was his duty to devote himself to the service of God in the gospel ministry. He entered the Theological Seminary at Princeton in December 1823; was licensed April 1827, by the Second Presbytery of New York, Dr. John M. Mason, Moderator at the time; and was ordained as an Evangelist in company with his fellow-student, Edward Kirk, in the Murray Street church, in the fall of 1827.

From this time he preached in different churches, received various invitations, and supplied in succession several pulpits. The Pearl Street church engaged his services during the absence of the Rev. Mr. Monteith, their excellent but infirm pastor; and after spending a winter at New London, Connecticut, in private study and occasional preaching, he supplied the pulpit of the First Presbyterian church of Philadelphia, of which the Rev. Dr. James Wilson was then the pastor. He was solicited to stand as a candidate for that pulpit after the decease of that eminent man; but a narrower and less arduous field seemed more advisable for one who had so recently left Princeton, and accordingly he accepted a unanimous call from the Presbyterian church at Lancaster, Pennsylvania, and was installed there, November 1829.

During his ministry in that church there was a revival of

great power, and the church greatly increased and prospered. Loss of voice ensued in consequence of over-exertions, and he was constrained to resign his charge in the fall of 1834. Having spent the following winter in Florida, and the next season, in travelling abroad, he resumed preaching on his return to New York, where he supplied the pulpit of the Reformed Dutch church, Market street, from December 1834 to September 1835, during the last year of the life of the lamented William McMurray, D. D.

In April 1836 he was called to succeed Dr. Woodbridge in the Bowery Presbyterian church—originally a colony from the Brick Church; and seventy-five families connected themselves with his congregation during the first six months of his ministry there. But utter failure of health again constrained him to resign.

Having thus secured to himself an indefinite period of retirement and quietude, he at last accepted an invitation to supply for a season the pulpit of the Laight Street Presbyterian church; and after having received a call to the Presbyterian church at Carlisle, Pennsylvania; a call from the church at Westport, Connecticut; to the Professorship of Ecclesiastical History and Sacred Rhetoric in the Theological Seminary, Bangor, Maine; the nomination to the chair of Mental and Moral Philosophy in the New York University, and an invitation to allow his name to be used for the Chaplaincy of West Point, he accepted a *second* unanimous call from the Canal Street Presbyterian church, New York, and was there installed October 22, 1839.

The following year the New York University conferred on him the degree of D. D. But his health again proved inadequate to the constant pressure of pastoral duty, and at the time of his resigning the charge of the Canal Street church, in the winter of 1845, there was little if any probability of his ever preaching stately again. In 1858 he was elected by the General Assembly Professor of Sacred Rhetoric and Ecclesiastical History in the Western Theological Seminary, Allegheny, Pennsylvania; but for various prudential reasons, deeming it not advisable to enter on an untried field, he remained in New York, until in November 1859, having been appointed by the Second Presbytery of New York to declare the pulpit of the Mount Washington Valley church *vacant*, he received a unanimous call to the pastorate of that church, his present charge. But during the period of his being *without charge*, his health having gradually improved, he occupied himself in supplying different pulpits, in accommodating pastors when sick or absent, but chiefly in writing for the press.

Among his works we may enumerate, "Religion Teaching by Example; or Scenes from Sacred History," 1848; "Introduction to the Life and Times of John Howard," 1849; "Responses from the Sacred Oracles, or the Past in the Present," 1850; "A Sketch of the late Walter Lowrie, Missionary to China," in Sprague's Annals, 1852; "The Resurrection of Christ, Historically and Logically Viewed," 1854. This however is but a very insufficient view of his literary labours. Even the titles of his articles in *The Presbyterian, Presbyterian Standard, The Literary and Theological Review*, edited by Dr. Leonard Woods, *The Theological and Literary Journal*, edited by David N. Lord, and other periodicals, would occupy too much space to find a place here. To the *Princeton Review* he contributed one article,

1854. The Bible not of Man.

DILLINGHAM, WILLIAM H., was born in Lee, Massachusetts, on the 3d of August, 1791. He received the rudiments of his education at Lenox Academy, in the neighbourhood of Lee, and at the age of fifteen entered the Sophomore Class in Williams College. In 1808 he came to Philadelphia, and studied law in the office of Charles Chauncey, who has left behind him the reputation of being not only a great lawyer but an honest man. After practising six years in Philadelphia, Mr. Dillingham removed to West Chester, the seat of justice of a neighbouring county, much resorted to in summer for its rural beauty, but known to many as the residence of Dr. Darlington, who never heard of its local attractions. Here he married, and entered heartily into all the schemes proposed for the public benefit, liberally supported all its institutions, religious, educational and scientific; and in 1837 was sent by his fellow-citizens to represent them in the Legislature.

In 1841 he returned to Philadelphia and was soon actively employed both as a legal counsellor, and in the management of its public institutions. His association with Dr. Darlington in West Chester had fostered a natural love for scientific pursuits, and in 1843 he was elected a member of the American Philosophical Society, of which he continued an interested associate till his death, which took place on the 11th of December, 1854. In that year he contributed to this *Review* a memoir of Peter Collinson, the correspondent of Bartram, who encouraged him in his labours, and made his discoveries known in Europe.

DOD, ALBERT BALDWIN, the son of Daniel and Nancy (Squier) Dod, was born in Mendham, New Jersey, March 24, 1805. His father was distinguished for mathematical taste and acquirements, and was by profession an engine builder. He was moreover a sort of universal genius—was a profound and accurate theologian, wrote poetry, and could scarcely turn his hand to anything in which he was not quickly at home. He resided at Elizabethtown, New Jersey, from 1812 to 1821, when he removed to the city of New York. On the 9th of May, 1823, he was killed by the explosion of the boiler on board the steamboat Patent, the machinery of which he had been employed to repair, and which, at the time of the explosion, was making an experimental trip on the East River.

The grandfather of Albert B. Dod, who originally resided in Virginia, but afterwards removed to New Jersey, was a man of highly endowed and cultivated mind, and educated his numerous family himself, without ever sending them to school. Thaddeus Dod, his grandfather's brother, was a graduate of the College of New Jersey in 1773, and was for many years an able minister of the gospel, and an efficient friend of education, in Western Pennsylvania. In 1810 or 1811, Daniel Dod was invited to accept the Professorship of Mathematics in Rutgers College, but declined it. Charles Dod, the brother of Albert, was Professor of Mathematics and Modern Languages in Jefferson College from 1837 to 1839, when he resigned the place to become a pastor. The family, for several generations, have been remarkable both for mathematical taste and talent.

Albert was the second son of his parents, and was one of eight children—five sons and three daughters. Of the sons, three became ministers, the others inherited or imbibed their father's taste for mechanics, and all keep up the reputation of the family for mathematics. Albert was like his father, not only in his mathematical taste, but in the versatility of his genius, and his quickness in mastering a difficult subject, amounting almost to intuition. From the time he knew how to read, he evinced a great fondness for books; and his brothers would often tell him that he ought to have been a girl, as he cared for nothing but to stay in the house and read. He was very affectionate in his spirit, and gentle in his manners, and always the favourite of the younger children. When his parents removed to Elizabethtown, he was seven years old; and from that time was kept constantly at school. He was fitted for College at a classical school in the town, taught by a Mr. Smith. When he was fourteen, his teacher told his parents that it was useless for him to attend *his* school any longer, as he was in advance of his schoolfellows, and was prepared to enter the Sophomore class at Princeton. His parents, thinking that he was too young to commence a collegiate course, concluded to send him to Dr. Armstrong, who had resigned his pastoral charge, and was then teaching a classical school in the neighbouring town of Bloomfield. He remained there, however, but one term, and spent the winter of that year at home—reading, and teaching the younger children of the family.

In the spring of 1821, being then fifteen years of age, he entered the Sophomore class in Princeton College, half advanced. He became hopefully pious the first year he was in College, and joined the church in Princeton. He graduated in the autumn of 1822, being seventeen and a half years old.

The Hon. Samuel L. Southard and Mr. Dod's father had, from early life, been intimate friends. Mr. Southard, who was then Secretary of the Navy, attended the Commencement exercises the year that Albert graduated, and immediately wrote to his father, congratulating him that he had a son of so much promise, and offering to advance him in the navy, if he would consent to enter it. But the son had already chosen the ministry as his profession, and he wished to be engaged in teaching until he should be of suitable age to enter the Theological Seminary. When this was communicated to Mr. Southard, he immediately wrote back that application had just been made to him for a teacher, by a gentleman of his acquaintance near Fredericksburg, Virginia, and recommended that the son of his friend should accept the place. He did so, and went the same fall in which he was graduated, and remained there, in circumstances very agreeable to him, between three and four years.

On his return from Virginia, he remained at home a few months, and in the autumn of 1826 became a member of the Theological Seminary at Princeton. The next year he accepted a Tutorship in Princeton College, still continuing his theological studies, as he had opportunity. He was licensed to preach, in the spring of 1828, by the Presbytery of New York, but retained his office as Tutor till 1829. In 1830 he was appointed to the Mathematical Professorship in the College—a place that was eminently congenial with his tastes and habits. This appointment he accepted, and discharged the duties of the office with signal ability and fidelity. Here he continued till his death, which took place, November 20, 1845. He died of pleurisy, after an illness of a week, having, during the whole time, maintained the utmost serenity of spirit.

Professor Dod was invited to take charge of several different congregations, but uniformly declined, from a conviction that his usefulness could not be promoted by leaving the College. He, however, preached a great deal; and his labours were frequently put in requisition to supply destitute pulpits in both New York and Philadelphia. He published nothing except his articles in the *Biblical Repertory*. The article on Transcendentalism was printed in a separate pamphlet, and attracted great attention.

He was married, in April 1830, to Caroline S., daughter of the late Hon. Samuel Bayard, of Princeton. They had nine children, seven of whom survived him.

The degree of Doctor of Divinity was conferred upon him by the University of North Carolina in 1844, and by the University of New York in 1845.*

"He was rather above the ordinary standard in height," says Dr. Hodge, "somewhat inclined to stoop; rather square-shouldered; but active and graceful in his movements and carriage. His head was unusually large; his forehead broad, but not high; his eyebrows massive and projecting; his eyes hazel, brilliant, and deep seated; his countenance intellectual and pleasing. His disposition was very cheerful and amiable, which rendered him, with his extraordinary conversational powers, peculiarly agreeable as a companion. His reputation as a talker threatened, at one time, to eclipse his fame in higher departments. But this was only the sparkling of a really deep and rapidly moving stream.

"He had a taste for literature and the fine arts, and considerable fertility of imagination, and was, I think, disposed to estimate these gifts at a higher value than his more solid mental qualities. To me it always appeared that his understanding, his power of clear and quick discernment, of analysis and lucid statement, and of logical deduction, was the leading power of his mind, to which his reputation and usefulness were mainly due.

"It was this that gave him his success and power as a teacher. There was nothing that he could not make plain. Provided his pupils had the requisite preliminary knowledge, he rendered the most abstruse departments of Mathematics so clear that his students became enthusiastic in their admiration of himself, and in their love for the science. It was his delight to unfold the *rationale* of all the processes of his department, and to elevate his pupils to the study of the philoso-

---

* This account of his life was prepared for Dr. Sprague's *Annals*, by a member of the family, and is here used with permission.

20

phy of every subject which he taught. He was, therefore, most successful with the more intelligent class of students; with the dull, as he had no fellow-feeling, he was prone to have too little patience. This mastery of his subject, and this superiority of his intellect, made him exceedingly popular as an instructor. When, on one occasion, he attended the annual examination of the Cadets at West Point, as a visitor, he evinced so clearly these powers of mind, that the Cadets and Professors united in an application to the Government for his appointment as Chaplain and Professor of Moral Philosophy. This incident shows how striking was the exhibition of talent, which any suitable occasion was certain to call forth.

"To this clearness and discrimination of mind is also to be referred his fondness for metaphysics, and his skill in the discussion of subjects connected with that department. Those of his writings which excited general attention, are on topics of this character. Reference may be made to the able articles in the *Princeton Review*, proceeding from his pen, in illustration and confirmation of his peculiar talents for philosophical discussion. His mind was always on the alert, and teeming with thoughts and suggestions. It was a common thing for him, when he entered my study, to say—'I was thinking, as I came along, of such or such a question,'—announcing some problem in mental or moral science. Indeed I do not know that I ever was acquainted with a man, who so constantly suggested important topics of conversation, or kept the minds of his friends more on the stretch. His consciousness of power in debate, no doubt, contributed to the formation of this habit; for the pleasure of discussion was in his case so great, that he would often start paradoxical opinions either for the sake of surprising his hearers, or exercising his skill in defending them. The talent to which I have referred was conspicuously displayed in all public assemblies. Had his life been spared, I doubt not he would soon have established for himself the reputation of one of the ablest debaters in our church.

" His best and most effective sermons are distinguished by the same character of mind. He undervalued, at least at one part of his life, emotional preaching. He did not seem to estimate aright how great and how permanent a good was effected by any preacher who calls into lively exercise the devotional feelings of his audience. Professor Dod aimed rather to lodge in the understanding some fundamental principle of truth or duty, which should become part of the governing convictions of the mind. He was accustomed to say that if he could make his hearers see that they are responsible for their faith, or that expediency is not the rule of right, or that things unseen are more real and powerful than the things that are seen, or some such general truth, he would do them far greater service than by any excitement of their feelings. His sermons were generally constructed on that principle; and many of them are of permanent value. His voice was melodious, and his delivery free and untrammelled by his notes, which were generally written out in full. Though his preaching, in the later years of his life, was generally addressed more to the understanding than to the affections, yet he had great emotional power, and could, when roused himself, control in an uncommon degree the feelings of his audience.

"Professor Dod has now been dead more than nine years. I have not yet ceased to mourn for his departure as a personal loss. I regarded him as one of the most gifted men of our church. His having chosen an academical instead of a pastoral career kept him in a measure aloof from our ecclesiastical courts, and turned his attention to science rather than to theology. But I have a strong conviction that he had in him rich stores of undeveloped resources, which, had it pleased God to prolong his life, would have rendered him one of the most eminent and useful ministers of our church."

His contributions to this *Review* were in

1835. Pinney's Sermons—Pinney's Lectures.

1837. Beecher's Views in Theology.

1838. Missionary Enterprise in the South Sea Islands—Phrenology.

1839. Transcendentalism, (the part of the article reviewing Cousin.)

1841. Analytical Geometry.

1842. Capital Punishment.

1844. Oxford Architecture—The Elder Question.

1845. Vestiges of Creation.

DOD, WILLIAM ARMSTRONG, is a younger brother of the late Prof. Albert B. Dod, a sketch of whose life and labours is given above. For an account of the family from which the brothers sprung, the reader is referred to the preceding article. Mr. Dod was graduated at the College of New Jersey in the fall of the year 1838. In 1840 he was appointed a Tutor in the College and discharged the duties of that position one year. He then entered the Theological Seminary, and after a three years course was licensed to preach in 1845. His first pastorate was at Port Richmond, Philadelphia: from thence he removed to Princeton, where he was pastor of the Second Pres-terian church, and in 1855 was appointed Lecturer on Architecture in the College of New Jersey. After a pastorate of several years he left the Presbyterian denomination and united with the Protestant Episcopal Church, and became rector of the Episcopal church at Princeton, till his health became impaired, when he retired to private life, and still resides at Princeton, New Jersey. In 1859 he received the degree of Doctor of Divinity from Columbia College, New York.

His contributions to the *Princeton Review* were in

1855. Church Architecture.

1856. Ruskin's Lectures on Architecture and Painting.

DUFFIELD, JOHN THOMAS, was born at McConnellsburg, Pennsylvania, on the 19th of February, 1823; was graduated at the College of New Jersey in 1841; entered the Seminary at Princeton in 1844; was elected Tutor in Greek in 1845; and Adjunct Professor of Mathematics in 1847. He was licensed by the Presbytery of New Brunswick in 1848; and in connection with duties in College was stated supply of the Second Presbyterian church for two years, commencing with October 1849, and was ordained to the ministry in 1850. In 1854 he was elected Professor of Mathematics, and in 1862 Professor of Mechanics and Mathematics, which is the title of the Chair he now fills.

While in charge of the Second Church he published a volume of sermons entitled "The Princeton Pulpit," and in 1866, a "Discourse on the Second Advent," with Notes and an Appendix. He received the degree of D. D. from the University of Indiana in 1862. The only article he furnished for this *Review* was in

1867. The Philosophy of Mathematics.

DUNN, ROBINSON POTTER.—There are some Christian lives unbroken by great events, and, happily, unvaried by marked defects, which, like a shining river, flow on from the outset to the close, affluent in gifts and graces—a noiseless benediction to the church and the world. Such emphatically was the course of the Rev. Robinson Potter Dunn. The son of an eminent physician of Newport, Rhode Island, he was born on the 31st of May, 1825; made spiritually alive in Christ Jesus in November 1838; admitted to the Congregational church of his native town, December 26, 1842; entered Brown University, September 1839; was ordained and installed as pastor of the Presbyterian church at Camden, New Jersey, November 1, 1848; accepted the chair of Rhetoric and English Literature at Brown University in the spring of 1851; and closed his brief and honoured career August 19, 1867, whilst on a visit to his parents at Newport.

The prominent events of Professor Dunn's domestic life were his early marriage, in 1848, to Maria, daughter of the late John Stillé of Philadelphia; her death, with that of her infant child, the following year; and his second union in January 1855, with his surviving wife, Mary Stiles, daughter of the Hon. A. D. Foster, of Worcester, Massachusetts.

These bare statistics constitute, in one sense, the history of a life. But what hand shall fill up the outlines with its true tracery of delicate beauty, and within the compass of a few sentences breathe into this frame-work of mere facts the mental, moral, and spiritual excellence which vitalized Professor Dunn's character, rendering it complete in Christ!

In the admirable memorial prepared by Dr. Caldwell, a few who knew him best—his pastor, teachers, co-labourers, and friends—have painted an exquisite portrait of him, evidently as truthful as it is beautiful. There we find him the cherished child of the household, endeared all the more to those around him by the sufferings incident to an extremely delicate mental and physical organization, which was the discipline alike of his youth and his riper years. But the mild lustre of his moral qualities shone with increased strength and purity under such influences. Docile, gentle, cheerful, intelligent, and singularly conscientious, it is not surprising that he was found from first to last, a perpetual joy to his parents. His mother's prayers and instructions received their crowning blessing in his devoted self-consecration to God at the age of thirteen; and thenceforward his path was as that of the just, which "shineth more and more unto the perfect day." In the simplicity of faith and love he received the gospel, and so walked in it ever upward and onward until he passed out of sight to be for ever with the Lord.

In the University, although the youngest member of his class, and in delicate health, he at once took the lead, and retained it until the last, graduating with the highest honours. The fact is significant in this connection, that he was the object of pride and pleasure to his classmates as well as his teachers, disarming all jealous competition by his genial kindness and frank, manly bearing.

His brief but happy pastorate at Camden furnished just evidence of his varied capacities for usefulness in the church of Christ, and of that magnetic power of affection which drew all hearts to him in love and admiration.

But, perhaps, all his original and acquired powers, his varied gifts and attainments, his profound researches, his graces of thought, style, speech, and manner, his deep, earnest, all-pervading piety, his ever-wakeful longing to be up and doing in his Master's service, found their most appropriate and ample field in the professorship at Brown University, which he held during the last sixteen years of his life.

The tokens of his superabounding acceptability and success in this vocation are so multiplied in the little volume before us, that they cannot be embodied at all in this brief notice, though they must elicit a tribute of gratitude to God that his grace and glory are made manifest from time to time in converting "earthen vessels" into "living temples of the Holy Ghost."

Such was Professor Dunn, and as such we may not consider the summons premature, though it was sudden, which through a brief illness, during a visit to his parents, called him to his heavenly home.

He contributed to the *Princeton Review* in

1858. English Hymnology.
1865. Eugenie and Maurice de Guérin.

ECKARD, JAMES READ, was born in Philadelphia, November 22, 1805. His father, J. Frederic Eckard, of the island of St. Thomas, was Danish Consul for the Middle States. His mother, Susan Read, was the daughter of Colonel James Read of Philadelphia, who took an active part in the Revolutionary war, both in the field, and as the Paymaster and a Commissioner of the Navy, and Secretary of the Marine Agency. Her uncle, George Read, was a signer of the Declaration of Independence.

Mr. Eckard was educated in Philadelphia, graduating from the University of Pennsylvania in 1823. He studied law with John M. Read, afterwards a Judge of the Supreme Court of the State. In December 1826 he began to practice law, and continued until the spring of 1830, when he commenced the study of theology, having made a profession of religion in September 1829, in the First Presbyterian church of Philadelphia. During this part of his life he was for several years active as a member of the Board of Directors of the Public Schools of Philadelphia, and also as a Director of the Society for Promoting Public Schools in Pennsylvania. He went to the Seminary at Princeton in 1831. Having offered himself as a missionary to the American Board, at their instance he left the Seminary in 1833, to sail to the island of Ceylon. In October 1833 he had been licensed by the Third Presbytery of Philadelphia. In

May 1833 he married Margaret E. Bayard of Savannah, Georgia, and was ordained in June by the Third Presbytery, in the church on Washington Square in Philadelphia. With his wife he sailed for Colombo in Ceylon in October 1833. On reaching Ceylon he was connected with the Mission Seminary at Batticotta. Early in 1835 Messrs. Todd and Hoisington were selected by the Ceylon mission to establish a new mission at Madura. Mr. Hoisington was unable to go, and exchanged positions with Mr. Eckard. The health of Mrs. Eckard was soon broken by the intense heat at Madura, and in 1836 they returned to Ceylon. At the close of 1843 they returned to New York by the way of England, touching at South Africa and St. Helena. This return was absolutely necessary to save the life of Mrs. Eckard. Mr. Eckard afterwards resided in Savannah as Principal of the Chatham Academy. He laboured at the same time for the religious instruction of the slaves, for which great facilities were afforded by their masters. This double work was too much for his health, and at the close of 1846 he returned to Philadelphia. Early in 1848 he under-took to re-establish the closed-up church on New York Avenue in Washington City. In July 1858 he received the degree of D. D. from Lafayette College, Pennsylvania, and, in October, was elected Professor of Rhetoric (afterwards changed to His-tory and Rhetoric) in that College. Before this, both he and the church had changed their connection to the (Old-school) Presbytery of Baltimore. He advised his people to unite with the F Street church, then under the pastoral care of the Rev. Dr. P. D. Gurley. They did so, after a brief attempt to con-tinue as a separate organization under the Rev. Dr. Hamner. The large and flourishing church now on New York Avenue is the result of this union.

Whilst connected with the College, Mr. Eckard began in 1860 to preach to a church newly organized at Asbury, New Jersey. In November 1867 he retired from this work, the church being then sufficiently strong to support a resident pastor.

When in Ceylon he published in the Tamil language an Essay on Faith and Justification. Also in English, a work called the "Hindoo Traveller," designed for natives educated to read English. It narrates the imagined journey of a young Hindoo through India, with extracts from, and refutations of, some of the Hindoo classical and sacred works which treat of the scenes described. On his return from India he published a small volume containing a narrative of some of the missionary operations there. He contributed to the *Princeton Review* an article on the "Logical Relations of Religion and Science," published October 1860.

EDWARDS, TRYON, son of Jonathan W. Edwards, an eminent lawyer of Connecticut, grandson of the younger, and great-grandson of the elder President Edwards, was born August 7, 1809, at Hartford in the State of Connecticut, where the family, from the early settlement of the colony, have been prominent and influential both in church and state. He was graduated at Yale College in 1828: and after studying law in New York, and theology at the Princeton Seminary, was settled as pastor of the First Presbyterian church in Rochester, New York, in 1834. In 1845 he accepted a call to the Second Congregational church in New London, Connecticut; and in 1867 to the First Presbyterian church in Hagerstown, Maryland, where he now resides. In 1832, while still in the Theological Seminary, a prize tract on "The advantages of Sabbath-schools" appeared from his pen, which was extensively published both in this country and abroad. And from that time he has contributed constantly, and in various forms, to the religious and literary press. Among his publications are, " An Appeal for the Sabbath," 1834; "The Doctrine of a Particular Providence," 1836; "On the Canon of the Old Testament," 1838; (these two in the *Christian Spectator*); "The Child's Commandment and Promise," (American Sunday-school Union), 1839; "Christianity a Philosophy of Principles," an Address at Williams College, in 1841; a Memoir of the Younger President Edwards, with his complete works, 1842; "Self-cultivation," 1843; and a Memoir of the Rev. Dr. Joseph Bellamy, with his complete works, 1850. Some of the published sermons and discourses of Dr. Edwards are, " The Worth of the Soul," 1836; "Reasons for Thankfulness," an important and valuable discourse on the early history of Rochester, New York, its churches, &c., 1836; " Monitions of the Judgment," 1838; "The Sinner's Character, Course, and End," 1838; "God's Voice to the Nation," and " National Sins," both occasioned by the death of President Harrison, 1841; "The Believer's Dying Message," 1842; "The Richest Treasure," (a discourse to one of the earliest bands of California emigrants), 1849; and "The Speed of Life impressing Probation," 1856. In addition to the works of the younger President Edwards and of Dr. Bellamy, Dr. Edwards has edited a volume entitled, " Charity and its Fruits," from the MSS. of the elder President Edwards, 1851; and has prepared and edited several collections designed especially for domestic culture, as " Poetry for Children and Youth,' 1851'; " Jewels for the Household," 1852; " The World's Laconics,' 1852; and the "Wonders of the World, 1855." Several of these works have passed through numerous editions, and have been republished in England. Dr. Edwards has also written several of the tracts or works issued by the American Tract Society: "The Advantages of Sabbath-schools," 1833; "The Time not Come," 1837; "I must Pray in Secret," 1840; "The Fatal Mistake, or the Midnight Shipwreck," 1850; "The Power of the Bible," 1856; "Take Care," (a prize tract for soldiers), 1861; and "The Good Fight," (also to soldiers), 1862. He has been a frequent contributor to the *Christian Spectator, New Englander, Biblical Repository*, and other periodicals of note, both literary and religious; and was, for many years, editor of the *Family Christian Almanac*, which, as published by the American Tract Society, had an immense circulation. In 1848 he received the honorary degree of D. D. from Wabash College. While a student at the Theological Seminary he contributed to this *Review* the article on "Hasty Admissions to the Church."

ELY, ELIAS P., a native of Connecticut, who graduated at the Theological Seminary of Princeton in 1832, wrote the article "On Independence of Thought," in the July No. for 1833. We have not been able to ascertain anything of his subsequent history.

ENGLES, WILLIAM MORRISON, was born in the city of Philadelphia, on the 12th of October, 1797. Of pious ancestry of English and Scottish descent, he inherited a vigorous physical frame, with corresponding moral elements of strength and solidity. His father was Captain Silas Engles, of the Revolutionary army, a citizen of high character in his day for intelligence and integrity. His mother was Anna Patterson, a lady of a family, both then and since, distinguished for intellectual gifts and attainments. He was the youngest of their children, and was baptized in the Scots Presbyterian church, which they attended, then under the ministry of the Rev. Dr. Annin.

His education, which was begun in the best schools of that period, was pursued in the University of Pennsylvania, in which his uncle, Dr. Robert Patterson, was at that time a distinguished Professor. At the Commencement, January 10, 1815, he stood among the first of his class, with the honour of the "Ethical Oration."

After his graduation, he studied theology for three years with the late Dr. Samuel B. Wylie, of the Reformed Presbyterian Church, and on the 21st of October, 1818, he ·was

21

licensed as a preacher of the gospel by the Presbytery of Philadelphia.

His first work in the ministry was a missionary tour, upon which he was sent by the Presbytery, in the Valley of Wyoming, where his preaching, which was then without notes, and had the freshness and zeal of a young evangelist, attracted great attention. He loved to look back to this period in after years, and often spoke of his adventures on horseback in that beautiful region, and of the families in which he was made welcome, forming friendships which continued through life. His earnestness and spirituality, combined with lively and agreeable manners, made many salutary and lasting impressions; and the experience which he gained was, no doubt, a valuable training for his subsequent work.

On his return to Philadelphia, he was soon called to a pastoral charge. A colony of English Independents, then worshipping in a building in Ranstead Court, familiarly called the "Tabernacle," having been led by various events to connect themselves with the Presbytery, were organized as the Seventh Presbyterian church, and Mr. Engles was called by them to be their first pastor. He was ordained and installed July 6, 1820, and continued in office until September 4, 1834, when a disease of the throat, which threatened to disable him from public speaking, led to his resignation.

The ministry of Mr. Engles was faithful and attractive. Although he did not visit his people as often as some pastors, yet his care for their spiritual good was shown in the appointment of special meetings for religious inquiry, as well as by fidelity in his round of duties. In the pulpit his manner was deliberate and quiet—didactic rather than hortatory; and his matter, which was always strictly evangelical, had more of the practical than the doctrinal element. Some of his sermons, after the lapse of many years, are still remembered as having made a deep and lasting impression; and among the converts due to his ministry, were two of the most distinguished jurists of the State. But whatever success of this kind he might have been capable of attaining, it would seem that the pulpit was not to be the sphere of his greatest usefulness.

The Presbyterian, from the editorship of which Dr. James W. Alexander was then about to retire, was placed under his direction, and from that time until the day of his death, a period of thirty-three years, he was the chief editor. Of his connection with that paper, his successor, Dr. Grier, lately said, "The history of *The Presbyterian* is the history of the

greater part of Dr. Engles's life. He found it weak, restricted
in its circulation, with an uncertain future, and surrounded by
rivals and opponents. He has left it securely established, with
a large and increasing list of subscribers, and with a character
for which it is very largely indebted to his hand."

In May 1838, four years after entering upon this editorship,
he was appointed editor of the Presbyterian Board of Publication, a post which he held from the time of its establishment
until the year 1863, during a period of twenty-five years.
After his withdrawal, and on the decease of the Rev. Dr. Phillips, he was elected President of the Board, in testimony of
his valued services, and was in that position at the time of his
death. The degree of Doctor of Divinity was conferred upon
him by Pennsylvania College about the time he was appointed
editor to the Presbyterian Board of Publication.

He was chosen Moderator of the General Assembly in the
year 1840, and at the close of its sessions appointed Stated
Clerk, a place which he filled during six years.

Those unacquainted with the state of Dr. Engles's health frequently wondered that one seemingly so robust should keep
himself aloof from ministerial duty. But those acquainted with
him knew that he suffered from heart disease, which manifested itself in giddiness and fainting, and that over-excitement
was liable to cause death at any moment. Frequent attacks
of this mysterious ailment warned him and his friends of his
danger. Often he would awake at night as in the very struggle of death. In the winter of 1866 an illness of another kind
brought him to the brink of the grave. But he had apparently
so rallied his strength that fears were beginning to be allayed,
when a fresh seizure, attended with congestion of the lungs,
made it plain to his physicians and to himself that the end was
near. He resigned himself prayerfully to what he felt to be
inevitable; submitted, though without hope, to the remedies
which were used; endured with patience the laboured breathing and suffocation, which taxed so painfully his still vigorous
frame; and at length, in one of the paroxysms of the disease,
ceased to live—expiring so suddenly, it was hard to believe
that his spirit was gone. He died on Wednesday night, November 27, 1867, after an illness of six days, in the seventy-
first year of his age.

On reviewing the life thus briefly sketched, we must look at
the eventful character of the period in which it was passed.
It was a period fraught with great movements. During the
last fifty years, the political map of the world had undergone

surprising changes in both hemispheres, affecting the interests of nations and races; human society passed through a new and marvellous phase of civilization in the arts and sciences, and Christianity had been diffused over the earth, even in heathen lands, as with the glory of the latter days. Dr. Engles was in a position such as few men have enjoyed to discern the signs of the times, and review events as they passed before him, not only in the world at large, but especially in his own church, which he was called habitually to survey. He became familiar with every event or question of general interest throughout its borders; he beheld several generations of pastors pass through its pulpits, and he lived to see its organization strengthen and extend itself, until its churches, missions, schools, and presses were scattered through the whole land and over the globe. And in all these scenes the part which he himself bore was by no means inactive or uninfluential. There may have been, and doubtless were, some more conspicuous figures before the church; and yet no one can even glance through its public records without seeing, that to erase that name and all that it represented, would be most seriously to mutilate its history.

As *Editor of the Presbyterian*, he made that journal what it soon became, the accepted organ of the Old-school. From the outset it became, in his hands, a trumpet of no uncertain sound. He rallied to its support the best writers in all parts of the church, acquired general confidence in it for its unswerving orthodoxy and evangelical sentiments, and imparted to it a tone of Christian dignity and respect toward surrounding denominations. His own contributions to its columns, as collected and preserved, fill several large albums; and the influence which he has quietly put forth from its editorial chair is beyond any power to estimate. During a whole generation he became a spectator and chronicler of public events, moulding and reflecting the mind of the church upon all current questions, not only in regard to its own doctrine and policy, but also in the related departments of morals, politics, philosophy, science, and literature. For thirty years he stood as in a watch-tower and bulwark of Zion, sounding the alarm and rallying to her defence, against all infidelity without and all heresy within her walls. He was every week a preacher at our firesides, and a herald of good tidings to our hearts.

In the other literary station which he filled, as *Editor of the Board of Publication*, his services were not less marked and valuable. That institution, indeed, might almost be said to have been the child of his brain. If the idea of it did not

actually originate with him, he was at least one of its active
founders, a leading member of its original Executive Committee, and during its history a ruling spirit in its counsels. Its
publications, for twenty-five years, bore the impress of his
mind and taste. Besides his editorial revision of the numerous
standard works which were issued, his own contributions to its
literature, in the form of abridgments, compilations, original
treatises, and tracts, reached a circulation amounting to thousands, and, in some instances, hundreds of thousands of copies,
and the mere testimonies to their value would themselves fill
volumes. Multitudes, indeed, owing to the wide circulation
which they obtained through the agencies of the Board, have
received good from him without knowing their benefactor;*
pastors who have his "Records of the Presbyterian Church"
on their shelves; sessions who have been instructed by his
tract on the "Duties and Qualifications of Ruling Elders;"
church members who have been stimulated by his "Hints to
Congregations;" Sabbath-schools in which his "Bible Dictionary" and children's books have been used; invalids and aged
people who have been comforted by his "Sick-Room Devotions;" retired Christian homes in which his "Book of Poetry"
and "Fountain of Wisdom" have blended entertainment with
instruction; while beyond the sphere of the church, in the army
and navy, his "Soldier's Pocket Book" and "Sailor's Companion" have cheered thousands of the sick, the wounded, and
the dying. The very titles of these works, and others, such as
"The World and its Influences," "Prevailing Errors," "Evenings' Entertainment," indicate the varied practical tendencies
of his writings, and the incalculable good which must have ensued upon their wide diffusion. As Editor of the Board of
Publication, for many years his labours were greatly lightened
by his brother, Mr. Joseph P. Engles, who was at the same
time Publishing Agent. Mr. Engles was an accomplished classical scholar, and unwearied in his endeavours to have everything accurate that passed under his eye, and to his care the
works going through the press were entirely committed. The
brothers met almost daily to consult upon their labours, and
after discussing the business matters, they seemed always to
have some pleasant anecdote or witty pun prepared for each
other, and often separated with a peal of laughter.

As a presbyter, too, he still served the church in its deliberative assemblies, and on all occasions requiring the applica-

* Until the issue of a late Catalogue of the Board, his own publications contained no hint of their authorship.

tion of its rules and principles in practice.   He was often consulted in regard to new and difficult questions of order or
policy.   His experience, good judgment, fairness, and equable
temper, made him, now and then, an accepted umpire between
conflicting parties in sessions or congregations; and in boards
and public bodies, when contending interests seemed incapable of adjustment, and both the wisdom and patience of the
disputants were exhausted, his more calm, sensible view, would
come in at the last moment, as a kind of reserve corps, to decide the doubtful battle.

As to the public character or reputation which he acquired
in these different positions, it was, as might be expected, in
keeping with the services he had rendered.   His theology
could hardly help being of a polemical cast.   He came upon
the stage in times when doctrine was valued as the only source
of duty, and sound words were more prized than decorous
forms; when opposite views and parties were forming upon
what were thought to be vital questions; and it was made an
ecclesiastical virtue to "contend earnestly for the faith once
delivered to the saints."   And his own opinions were so clear
and settled in his mind, so much to him the very word and
truth of God, that he could, as he did, throw his whole heart,
with all his powers, into their defence.

His love of harmony and desire for union among Christian
brethren were not less ardent than his zeal for truth.   As
much as was possible, he lived peaceably with all men; and
when controversy came, as it must come, sometimes with
friends no less than foes, he knew how to treat honourable opponents with due respect and fairness, and he claimed for himself the same meed of just consideration at their hands.

As a writer, his style reflected mainly the solid qualities of
his mind, and was dressed in that grave and stately diction
befitting the themes upon which he wrote.   His editorial articles, which could easily be recognized, were correct, lucid, and
judicious, at times relieved by some sportive sally or sedate
fancy, but always strictly spiritual in their tone.   And his
permanent works, if they cannot be cited as specimens of mere
fine writing, according to the reigning taste, have at least the
sober graces of a former and perhaps more earnest age, and
will long remain to do their silent work of usefulness, with no
line which any friend would now wish to blot.

On passing from the public to the more private aspects of
his character, we are at once struck with apparent contrasts.
There was a certain reserve, which to some was the most obvi-

ous trait, while by others it was not even perceived or felt, but which can only be justly rated in connection with its accompanying qualities. It is certain that if any thought him consciously cold or distant, they wronged one of the kindest hearts that ever beat. But while some who knew him only by reputation can scarcely be said to have known him at all, owing to this repellant, not repulsive, quality, others who knew him personally may have found it difficult even to recognize his public character, owing to a supposed inconsistency between it and certain of his private traits, with which they were more familiar.

The opponents of Calvinism have sometimes depicted its grave features as drawn into an habitual frown upon all that is bright and fair in the scene of life, and unable, with any native graciousness, ever to relax into a genial smile of human kindliness. But if there was ground for such a view in the founder of the system, or has been ground for it in any of his followers, too many other examples have shown it to be but a caricature; and among them none more strikingly than the one before us. This champion of orthodoxy, whom the stranger expected to find bristling with controversy, proved on acquaintance to be one of the mildest and gentlest of men. This leader of the straitest sect, without any peril or sacrifice of his principles, made Roman Catholics, Quakers, and Unitarians his warm, admiring friends. This believer in total depravity entered with the keenest zest into whatsoever things are lovely and of good report. A lover of books, he was also a true lover of men. A student of the Bible, he was not less a student of nature. While he enjoyed the doctrines and services of a supernatural religion, he still delighted with a calm pleasure in all objects of natural science and art; in birds, and shells, and ferns, of which he made rare collections; in exquisite specimens of taste and skill; in coins, and relics, new inventions, and things quaint and curious. His study, which was flanked with the heavy tomes of his grand old creed, contained upon its table the new poem or the freshly plucked flower; and the grave student himself could in a moment lapse into a playmate of little children, who flew to his arms with instinctive love. Young people did not simply venerate him at a distance, but perplexed their elders by a certain romantic freedom with which they gave him their confidence. Indeed, so much of this kind of youthfulness of feeling did he retain, with so little of the prejudice or infirmity of advancing years, that none who knew him can ever think of him as old.

He might often be seen, as many of us remember him,

passing out of the city on one of his solitary rambles to the banks of the Schuylkill, every nook of which he knew well; pausing here and there to talk with workmen about their craft, or to notice some simple thing in nature which others would have passed unheeded—a squirrel in the path, or bird upon the branch; and at length returning home again, as from the last walk that was taken, with a fragment of moss or an autumn leaf, and forgetting all fatigue in rapt admiration of its delicate tracery.

When good men die, we sometimes please ourselves by finding fit presages of their death in little incidents which would otherwise have been forgotten. It may not, therefore, seem trivial, in this instance, to mention coincidences which are certainly noticeable enough to appear providential. His last remark, on leaving the place of his life-long labours, was a pleasantry in allusion to the time, soon coming, when others would be speaking of him as he had just been speaking of some gone before him. His last editorial message to his readers, pondered by them after the hand that wrote it was cold in death, was that "Walk towards Zion," which now looks so much like a dying confession of faith. And his last private reading, left marked in his book of daily devotions, happened to be for that date upon the motto, " O grave, where is thy victory?"

But to understand fully that victory, as he was about to experience it, we must recall all that death meant to him, and in what spirit he encountered it. He met it as no unknown terror, but as the dread messenger, for whose coming, through many years, he had been daily waiting. The very beating of his heart had made it familiar to his thoughts. It was the shadow in which he walked on the bright earth by day, and the spectre which woke him, as with a mortal throb, at night. If ever any man habitually looked death in the face, it was he. And when therefore he came to that last conflict, the moral victory, which through Divine grace was to be achieved, was something more than the courage with which brave men are said to die in battle, amid the wild excitement of the moment; something more even than the rapture with which martyrs have clasped death as the angel of glory; it was the calm ascendency of reason and faith over sense, and doubt, and fear; it was the triumph of grace over nature, effected without noise or display, in lowliness and secrecy, alone with God.

All night long, in the pauses of that intense suffering, were heard broken prayers and whispered texts, and self-applied solaces, until at length, as if the moment had been reached when the sting of the monster was plucked away, and the spear shivered, came that utterance of an assured hope and faith, no more of this world, telling that the victory was won: "Dear Saviour, take me to thyself, and give me a crown of glory."

This sketch of his life we have adapted from the eloquent Discourse upon his Life and Services delivered by the Rev. Charles W. Shields, D. D. After twenty years of intimacy with Dr. Engles, we can only add our testimony to the justness of the portrait, and as far as we were able, have used the language of the discourse. Dr. Engles's only article in this periodical was contributed in

1833. On Dangerous Innovations.

EWING, FRANCIS ARMSTRONG, was named in memory of his maternal grandfather, the Rev. James Francis Armstrong, of Trenton, New Jersey, who was Moderator of the General Assembly of 1804, and died in 1816, having ministered to the Trenton church thirty years. His other grandfather was James Ewing, who held several public offices under Congress and the New Jersey Legislature, and was a ruling elder in Trenton at the time of his death in 1823. His son, and Dr. Ewing's father, was Charles Ewing, Chief Justice of the Supreme Court of New Jersey, who died in 1832.

Dr. F. A. Ewing was born in Trenton, September 1, 1806; graduated at Princeton College in 1824, and as Doctor of Medicine in the University of Pennsylvania in 1828. In 1840 he was ordained to the ruling eldership in Trenton, and was a devoted member of the Session until his death, which took place December 10, 1857. He made his first profession of faith during the ministry of Dr. James W. Alexander, who has written of him that "though a professional man by title, he was in fact and of choice much more a man of letters, and a recluse student of science. In the classical languages, in French, in the natural sciences, and in all that concerns elegant literature and the fine arts, he was singularly full and accurate. In matters of taste he was cultivated, correct, and almost fastidious. Music was his delight, and he was equally versed in the science and the art."* It may be added, that he was a well-read theologian, and one of the strictest adherents to the constitution of his church in doctrine, worship, and polity. In Dr. Alexander's "Letters" it is stated (1856), that Dr. Ewing projected the preparation of a vocabulary of the

* Dr. Hall's History of Trenton Church, p. 415.

22

English Bible, giving the variations that have taken place in the language since the translation was made. He did not live to execute this design, and the only publication that bears his name as author, is a volume of 400 pages, published by the American Sunday-school Union in 1835, entitled, "Bible Natural History; or a Description of the Animals, Plants, and Minerals mentioned in the Sacred Scriptures, with copious references and explanation of texts." For such a work, his knowledge, exactness, and taste, gave Dr. Ewing peculiar qualifications; and Dr. J. W. Alexander, reviewing it in the *Repertory* of October 1835, says, "We regard it for our own reference as being at once lexicon and concordance, and for these ends scarcely inferior to the best books on the subject, such as the *Biblische Naturgeschichte* of Rosenmueller. It is no small acquisition to a Bible-reader to have in a portable volume the quintescence of all that has been written on this topic."

The subject of Church Music, on which Dr. Ewing contributed an article to this *Review*, was one of his favourite branches of study and practice; for he not only delighted in the service of praise, but was always ready to give his assistance in conducting it with his voice, or in sustaining it by his delicate use of the organ. His defence of the use of instruments in our worship, as made in his article, rests mainly on the assumption that whilst the human voice produces the most perfect effects, the organ may be properly employed as subordinate and auxiliary, and may well be dispensed with when a congregation has been trained to a proper execution of the songs of praise. Since the date of that paper (1843), the controversy about instruments has almost yielded to the progress of custom in our churches, but when it was published, Dr. Ewing's sentiments, though so qualified by conditions, were guarded by an editorial note, to the effect that the *Repertory* must not be supposed to be committed by this part of the opinions of the contributor.

1843. Church Music.

FIELD, RICHARD STOCKTON, was born at Whitehill, in the county of Burlington, New Jersey, on the 31st of December, 1803. His father died in 1810, and the family removed to Princeton, where he was educated. He graduated at Princeton College in 1821. After reading law with his uncle, Richard Stockton, he was admitted to the bar in 1825. He at once removed to Salem, New Jersey, where he continued to pursue his profession until 1832, when he returned to Princeton, where he has since resided. For several years he represented the county of Middlesex in the Legislature of New Jersey. In 1838 he was appointed Attorney-General of the State, and filled that office until 1841, when he resigned. In 1844 he was a member of the Convention which framed the present Constitution of New Jersey. In 1855, when the State Normal School was organized, he was chosen President of the Board of Trustees of that institution, and has held the position ever since. Every annual report made to the Legislature, by the Board of Trustees, has been written by him. He has given much of his time and attention to popular education. For some years he was a professor in the law department of Princeton College, and delivered a course of lectures on Constitutional Law. In 1859 the degree LL.D. was conferred upon him by Princeton College. In 1862 he was appointed a Senator in Congress, to fill the vacancy created by the death of John R. Thomson, and resigned his seat in that body, in January 1863, for the purpose of accepting the appointment of United States District Judge, tendered to him by President Lincoln. This office he still holds. In 1869 he was chosen President of the New Jersey Historical Society, of which he was one of the founders.

In 1849 he published "The Provincial Courts of New Jersey, with Sketches of the Bench and Bar," being the third volume of the collections of the New Jersey Historical Society. A number of addresses delivered by him upon various occasions have also been published; among which are, "Address before the surviving members of the Constitutional Convention of the State of New Jersey;" "The Constitution not a compact between Sovereign States," delivered at Princeton, on the 4th of July, 1861. "Address on the Life and Character of Hon. Joseph C. Hornblower," Chief Justice of the Supreme Court of New Jersey; "Address on the Life and Character of Abraham Lincoln," delivered before the Legislature of New Jersey; "Address on the Life and Character of James Parker, late President of the New Jersey Historical Society."

Judge Field filled the several important positions which he was called to occupy, greatly to his own honour and to the good of society. New Jersey is probably more indebted to him for the success of its normal and common schools, than to any other man now living.

He contributed in 1852 an article to this Review, on "The New Jersey Historical Society."

FISK, EZRA, was born in Shelburne, Massachusetts, on the 10th of January, 1785. In 1801 he became the subject of an interesting work of grace, and attributed his conversion to some words spoken to him by Dr. Alexander, who was then making his first tour in the New England States. After a preparatory course of study under the direction of Dr. Packard, the pastor of the church of his native place, he entered Williams College, and was graduated in 1809; having been during his college course one of the little company of pious young men who met frequently for prayer in reference to missionary work, among whom were Mills and Richards. After graduating he studied theology under the direction of Dr. Packard, and was licensed to preach by the Franklin Association, on the 19th of April, 1810. After preaching some months as a licentiate he was ordained as an evangelist, and proceeded to Georgia, where he laboured for two years in districts comparatively destitute of the preaching of the gospel. In the autumn of 1812 he removed to Philadelphia, where he acted for some months as a city missionary. In August 1813 he became the pastor of the Presbyterian Church in Goshen, New York, where he laboured faithfully about twenty years.

In 1832 Dr. Fisk was compelled to intermit the greater part of his ministerial duties, on account of an affection of the lungs, and for relief he passed the winter of that year in the milder climate of Georgia. In his absence he received the appointment of Corresponding Secretary of the Board of Domestic Missions, but from a conviction that to fulfil its duties properly, it would require more labour than he was able to endure, he declined the appointment. In May 1833, he was elected to the Professorship of Ecclesiastical History and Church Government in the Western Theological Seminary, and after visiting the institution he accepted the chair, and obtained a release from his pastoral charge. Having taken leave of his people, and preached a Farewell Sermon to the Presbytery, he set out for his new field of labour. On the 2d of November he reached Philadelphia, and on the next day preached a sermon, which proved to be his last, in the lecture-room of the Second Presbyterian Church. Immediately after preaching he became sick at the stomach, and on the day following had a high fever, accompanied with excruciating pain in the head, accompanied with other unfavourable symptoms, and after an alternation of hopes and fears, he departed this life on December 5, 1833, in the forty-ninth year of his age; and his remains was removed, by request of his former charge, and deposited amid the ashes of his beloved people at Goshen.

In 1825 the degree of Doctor of Divinity was conferred upon him by Hamilton College; and in 1830 he presided as Moderator of the General Assembly. His published works consist of an Oration delivered at Williams College in 1825; a Lecture on the Inability of Sinners ; the Farewell Sermon on leaving Goshen, and a series of articles on Mental Science in the *Christian Advocate,* and the following articles written for this work :

1830. Character of the Present Age.
1831. What Constitutes a Call to the Gospel Ministry.
1832. Character of the Present Age.

FORSYTH, JOHN, was born at Newburgh, New York, and was fitted for college at the Academy of his native city. He was graduated at Rutgers College, but completed his literary and theological course at the University of Edinburgh. In 1835 he was ordained pastor of the Second Associate Reformed Church of Philadelphia (now the Second U. P. Church, in Race Street). In 1837 he was called to be pastor of Union Church, Newburgh, and at the same time he was elected Associate Professor of Biblical Literature in the Theological Seminary of the Associate Reformed Church in that city. In 1847 he was elected Professor of Latin in the College of New Jersey, and discharged the duties of that office until 1853, when he was recalled to Newburgh by the Associate Reformed Synod of New York, having been again elected to the Professorship of Biblical Literature and Church History in the Theological Seminary. In 1844 he received the honorary degree of Doctor of Divinity from Rutgers College, and in 1864 he was appointed Lecturer on History in the College of New Jersey. Though his connection with the Seminary ceased in consequence of the union which formed the United Presbyterian Church, he has continued to reside in his native city.

He has furnished to the Review the following articles :

1843. Alison's History of Europe.
1845. The Fall of the Jesuits.
1846. Whewell's Elements of Morality—The Evangelical Alliance.
1849. The Apostolic Constitutions—Ignatius and his Times.
1850. Macaulay's History of England—The Life of Calvin.
1851. Œcolampadius—The Slavonic Nations—The Vaudois Church.
1852. Five years in an English University.
1853. Merle d'Aubigné's Reformation in England.
1857. Annals of the American Pulpit.

1861. Annals of the American Methodist Pulpit.
1862. Memoirs of Philip De Mornay.
1863. The Fathers of Ross-shire.
1865. Arabia—Unitarian Annals.
1866. The Great Schools of England.

GASTON, WILLIAM, was born at Newbern, North Carolina, on September 19, 1778. He was of Huguenot descent by his father, but brought up by his mother, who was a Roman Catholic. In 1794 he entered the Junior Class of the College of New Jersey, and graduated in 1796 with the highest honours of his class. He then studied law in his native town, and was admitted to practice at the bar in 1798. In the summer of 1800 he was elected to the Senate of North Carolina, where he soon became conspicuous for his talents and usefulness. From 1813 to 1817 he represented his State in Congress, and signalized himself by his opposition to the war loan of 1815; and by a speech in reply to one of his colleagues who had made a motion to expunge "the previous question" from the Rules of the House. This speech, delivered in 1815, is reprinted in the volume for 1835, on account of its "interest and importance to all who are concerned in ecclesiastical proceedings." In 1834 he was made a judge of the Supreme Court of North Carolina, and though at that time the Constitution of that State required its judges to qualify themselves for office by taking an oath to preserve the Protestant religion, yet such was the confidence in his rectitude that little opposition was made to his taking his seat on the bench and dispensing with that formality.

1835. The Previous Question.

GOSMAN, ABRAHAM, was born at Danby, Tompkins County, New York, on the 25th of July, 1819. He did not begin his classical studies till the fall of 1839, and was graduated at Williams College in 1843. The next year he entered Princeton Seminary, and went through the prescribed three years course, remaining another year upon a fellowship, after completing the regular course. In the session of 1850–51 he assisted Dr. J. Addison Alexander in the Hebrew department, and in May 1851, he was ordained to the ministry, and installed pastor of the church at Lawrenceville, New Jersey, his present charge. The degree of D. D. was conferred upon him in 1862 by the College of New Jersey.

Dr. Gosman was chosen to complete "The History of the Israelitish Nation," from Samuel to the Babylonish Captivity, left incomplete by Dr. Archibald Alexander. He has also been engaged in translating and editing a portion of Lange's Commentary on Genesis and Deuteronomy. He is the author of the following articles:

1850. Neuman's Hebrew Commonwealth.
1854. Pearson on Infidelity.

GRAHAM, SAMUEL LYLE, was born at Liberty, Virginia, on the 9th of February, 1794. His father was a younger brother of the Rev. William Graham, the preceptor of Dr. Alexander; and his mother belonged to the Lyle family, which has also furnished some distinguished ministers to the church. When a boy he attended the common school; and in the vacations worked upon the farm, for his father was a farmer. When he was about fourteen years of age his father concluded to give him a liberal education, and the Rev. James Mitchell having opened a private school in the neighbourhood, he was sent to it, and initiated into the mysteries of the Latin grammar. After about a year's attendance there, he was transferred to the New London Academy, where he studied two years longer; and in May 1812 he entered Washington College, at Lexington. Here he was led to close in with the gracious promises of mercy in the gospel, and made a public profession of religion, uniting with the church in Lexington. In April 1814 he was graduated with the highest honours of his class, and after leaving college he acted as tutor six months in the family of Judge Nash of Hillsboro, North Carolina. In 1815 he entered the Seminary at Princeton, and was licensed to preach the gospel by the Presbytery of New Brunswick, on the 29th of April, 1818.

After his licensure he acted for some months as a missionary in Indiana, but finding that his health would not endure the climate, and that the field of labour was less promising than he expected, he returned to Virginia, and engaged in missionary labour in Greenbriar and Monroe counties. In 1821 he removed into North Carolina, where he was ordained by the Presbytery of Orange, and took charge of the Oxford and Grassy Creek churches. This arrangement continued till 1828, when he resigned the charge at Oxford, and assumed the pastoral care of the Nutbush church in conjunction with Grassy Creek. Over these churches he was installed on the 3d of November, 1822. In 1830 and 1831 these churches were visited by gracious revivals, and he was accustomed ever afterwards to look back to this period as the most successful and delightful of his life.

In 1832 he was elected to the chair of Ecclesiastical History in the Union Theological Seminary, Virginia, but he did not accept the appointment. In 1833 he was honoured with the degree of D. D. by Union College, Schenectady, New York. In 1838 he was again elected to the professorship in the Union Theological Seminary, and the two Synods being entirely harmonious in the choice, he regarded it as a call of Providence, and removed to Prince Edward in the autumn and entered upon his duties. After filling the professorship ten years, he became painfully affected by the small number of students in the Seminary, and became anxious to resign, that some more popular instructor should be put in his place. With this feeling pressing upon his mind, he resigned in the spring of 1851, intending to devote the remainder of his life to pastoral duty. It was not, however, the will of God that this resolution should be carried into effect. On the 29th of October, 1851, he departed this life, in the fifty-eighth year of his age.

Dr. Benjamin H. Rice, who was then the pastor of the College Church of Prince Edwards, coming into his room a short time before his death, said to him, " Dr. Alexander has got home before you!" alluding to his death, the news of which had just reached him. Immediately the dying man raised himself in bed, and in a tone triumphant even in its feebleness, cried out, " Oh, is it possible—is it so—I had almost shouted Glory. Heaven has seldom received from earth such an inhabitant!" After this he lived but a few hours. The opinion formed of Dr. Graham by his brethren in Virginia may be estimated from the position in which they placed him. Though not an eminently brilliant man, he was a faithful, laborious, and able minister of the gospel, respected and loved by all who knew him. " He was always," says Dr. Sprague, " a great favourite of Dr. Alexander ; and that of itself is no mean praise."

His contributions to the Review were,

1845. Review of Bishop Ives's Sermons.

1847. Review of Carson on Baptism—On the Reading of History.

GREEN, ASHBEL, was born at Hanover, New Jersey, on the 6th of July, 1762. His father, the Rev. Jacob Green, was a native of Massachusetts, a graduate of Cambridge College, and pastor of the Hanover Church for forty-five years. Thorough instruction in the Bible and Shorter Catechism was among the blessings inherited by him from godly parents. He received the elements of his education in a school kept by his father, but was not expected to receive a collegiate education. His early fondness for books, however, was soon noticed by both father and mother, and he was encouraged to prosecute his studies as far as their circumstances would admit.

At the age of sixteen he was the teacher of a classical school; but dismissed his school to rally with others around the standard of his country. After teaching school for parts of three years he entered the Junior Class of Princeton College. He united with the church while a student at college, having, as he hoped, experienced a saving knowledge of Christ just before going to Princeton. It is a remarkable fact, showing also his own decision in coming out on the Lord's side, that for a time he was the only pious student in the institution. He was the first scholar in his class, and was graduated in 1783 with the honours of the valedictory oration. The oration was delivered in the presence of General Washington and of Congress; and the orator gained great credit by adroitly addressing General Washington, and congratulating him on his success in conducting the war to a close. While at college he was instrumental in reviving the College literary societies, the *Whig* being the one to which he himself belonged. He says in his Autobiography, "I used to think and say that I derived as much benefit from the exercises of the Whig Society as from the instructions of my teachers." P. 141. Immediately after graduation he was appointed tutor in the College; and as Dr. Witherspoon was on a mission to Britain to secure benefactions, the whole instruction of the College devolved upon Dr. Smith and himself. After two years he was appointed Professor of Mathematics and Natural Philosophy, which office he held about the same length of time. Whilst connected with the College, he resolved to devote his life to preaching the gospel of Jesus Christ. His theological studies were directed by Dr. Witherspoon, whose friendship and confidence he possessed in a high degree. He says, "to Dr. Witherspoon, more than to any other human being, I am indebted for whatever of influence or success has attended me in life." His first public service was in the church at Princeton in 1785. He next preached twice in Philadelphia; and the Second Presbyterian Church forthwith sent him a call as colleague to the Rev. Dr. Sproat, then nearly seventy years of age. Before moving permanently to Philadelphia, he supplied for a time the church at Lawrenceville, New Jersey. The Independent Congregation in Charleston, South Carolina, also wished him to become their

23

pastor, but he declined. He was called to Philadelphia in
1786, and would have refused to accept the call but for the
earnest and decided advice of Dr. Witherspoon. His ordination occurred in May 1787; and he entered upon a ministry
destined to be highly successful and of long continuance.

His reputation as a preacher has come down to the present
generation in honourable and undisputed tradition. When he
first commenced his ministry, Dr. Miller, who was a young
man in Philadelphia, and an attendant on his church, bears
the following testimony: "He was eminently popular. No
minister in the city approached him in this respect. Crowds
flocked to hear him, more than the place of worship could
contain. His evening services especially were attended by all
denominations, and that not once or a few times only, but
from one year's end to another, and for a course of years with
unabating interest. And truly his discourses were so rich in
weighty thought, so beautiful in their language, and so
powerful in delivery, that they were well adapted to attract
and gratify all hearers of intelligence and pious taste."

In 1789 the First Presbyterian Church in New York
desired to obtain his services as colleague with Dr. Rodgers.
Dr. Green says, "I immediately wrote in answer that no
consideration could take me from the people whom I served,
and that any attempt to do it would most certainly prove
abortive. *Ministerial coquetry I have always abhorred.*"

In 1792 the title of D. D. was added to the name of Ashbel
Green in the Minutes of the General Assembly. This title
was conferred upon him by the University of Pennsylvania,
probably at the preceding commencement, when he was only
twenty-nine years old. The degree of LL.D. was conferred
upon him in 1812 by the University of North Carolina.

During his ministry here very many were added to the
church. At one communion season about fifty were received.
In short, there can be no doubt that the basis of all Dr.
Green's usefulness in the church was his commanding
character as a minister of the gospel. His public services in
the Presbyterian church while pastor in Philadelphia, will
show his influence, wisdom, perseverance, and energy. The
subject of forming a "General Assembly" was engaging the
attention of the church at the period of Dr. Green's settlement in Philadelphia. The Synod of 1787, after considering
the draft of a constitution for the church, issued a pamphlet
forming the basis for the deliberations of the Synod of 1788,
at which meeting the Constitution was ratified and adopted.
In these deliberations Dr. Green took part, and he was one of

a committee of three, appointed to superintend the printing of the Constitution, &c. Two years after, at the age of twenty-eight, he was elected a delegate to the Second General Assembly in 1790, and introduced the motion for a correspondence with the Congregational churches. He says, "As I had been informed that good had resulted from a Convention of Presbyterian and Congregational ministers before our Revolutionary war, I made a motion that the intercourse between us and the New England churches should, with their approbation, be renewed. I am responsible, therefore, for the correspondence between them and us, which has subsisted to the present time."

In 1792, Dr. Green was elected, "without his knowledge or even suspicion," chaplain of Congress, and was re-elected by every successive Congress till the removal of the seat of Government to Washington in 1800; so that he continued chaplain, in connection with Bishop White, for eight years. This office brought him in contact with all the great men of the day, and gave him an influence in general society. In 1798, the Assembly adopted certain regulations guarding against the introduction of foreign ministers, which proved unpalatable to the Presbytery of New York, and a request was made the next year for a reconsideration. Drs. Rodgers and McWhorter powerfully advocated the reconsideration, but Dr. Green encountered these veterans in debate on the floor of the Assembly, and by his eloquence and arguments won the day. In 1802, the College building at Princeton having been burned down, Dr. Green was appointed to write an address to the public, which was widely circulated, and he also used his personal influence in obtaining a considerable amount of money in Philadelphia. No man probably did as much towards restoring the College edifice. In 1802, the Assembly resolved to prosecute the work of missions more systematically, and appointed a Standing Committee on Missions. Of this committee Dr. Green was chairman, and he served for ten years, until called to Princeton College in 1812. The work of managing this great department fell in a great measure upon Dr. Green. The responsibilities and labours demanded by this office were discharged with that wisdom, perseverance, and energy which entered so largely into the composition of his character, and which so eminently qualified him in after-life to assist in reorganizing the missionary operations of the church upon their present basis. In 1803, the trustees of Princeton College unanimously elected him Professor of Theology in that institution; but he declined the appointment, notwithstanding the importunate solicitations of Drs. Rodgers, McWhorter, Tennent, and others. In 1804, the Assembly recommended the publication of a monthly Magazine, the prospectus for which was written by Dr. Green. It was called *The Assembly's Magazine*, and at the beginning of the third volume he became the exclusive editor. In 1805, Dr. Green transmitted to the Assembly a paper on the education of candidates for the ministry, which originated the system of measures finally resulting in the organization of the Board of Education. At a later period, he says in his autobiography— " In concert with the professors in the Seminary and College, we formed an Education Society; not only for pious youth, but for those not pious, if moral and talented." This subject was always very near his heart. In 1805, Dr. Green, after persevering and assiduous labours, was permitted to see the completion of the new Presbyterian church in the Northern Liberties. He preached the opening sermon; and by his zeal in the whole enterprise approved himself a staunch friend of church extension. In 1810, he commenced the course of Catechetical Lectures to the young, which have won for him so deserved praise. About the same time, the Philadelphia Bible Society was formed, and Dr. Green wrote the address, which was the *first public movement* for the Bible cause in the United States.

His agency in establishing the Theological Seminary at Princeton was among the most prominent acts of his life. He was chairman of the committee which drafted a plan for the constitution of the Seminary. He was appointed the first President of the Board of Directors, an office he held until his death. He laid the corner-stone of the building, was the agent in disbursing its funds, and from time to time collected money for the institution. On one occasion he collected in Philadelphia $4400. His forethought procured an additional quantity of land for the institution, presenting as a donation of his own, two acres which cost him $400. The sum of his own private benefactions was not short of $2000. He was instrumental in obtaining its act of incorporation in 1823, and was one of its trustees until his death. He was in fact, more than any other man, the father of the Seminary. After he reached the age of four-score years, on a calm review of life, he recorded the following expressive declaration :—" I consider the agency I have had in providing ministers of the gospel for the church, and in securing the means for their adequate instruction and for an attention to their personal piety, as *the most important service* I have ever rendered to the church of Christ."

In the midst of a useful ministry and eminent public services, Dr. Green was chosen President of Princeton College in 1812. His administration was marked by at least three characteristics: 1st. The increased prominence given to *religious instruction.* Dr. Green was the first President who caused the Bible to be introduced as a regular collegiate study. He also established a weekly meeting of the students for prayer and exhortation. In 1815, a remarkable revival of religion visited the institution, in which about fifty young men were brought by the grace of God to acknowledge Christ as their only hope. Dr. Green says: "Besides the general revival, there were at different periods under my President-ship, but chiefly under the last two or three years of it, a number of conversions of those who were without religion when they entered college." 2d. Dr. Green's administration was also distinguished by the *thoroughness of his discipline.* 3d. The college course of studies was also improved. The two upper classes had not, since the revolutionary war, been in the habit of attending to the Greek and Latin Classics. He resolved without delay to "return to the primitive usage," and contributed much to supply the preëxisting deficiencies. The remark of Dr. Miller is certainly correct: "The incum-beney of Dr. Green as head of the College of New Jersey, will will ever be considered by all competent judges as forming a memorable and highly important era in the history of that seat of learning."

In 1822, Dr. Green resigned the Presidency of the College, and removed to Philadelphia. At the urgent solicitation of his brethren, he became the editor of the *Christian Advo-cate,* a monthly periodical which had been started two years before under the name of the *Presbyterian Magazine.* This work was continued through twelve volumes, in which the editor displayed the fertility of his active, well-disciplined mind, the extent of his learning, the acuteness of his critical powers, his devotion to the interests of the kingdom of Christ, and his special attachment to the Presbyterian church. The best history of the Presbyterian church during those twelve years is to be found in the pages of the *Christian Ad-vocate.* Although Dr. Green was three-score years of age when he commenced editing the *Advocate,* he attended to other duties of a public nature. He commenced writing out in full his "Lectures on the Shorter Catechism,"* which are a

---

* Reviewed by Dr. Alexander, in vol. for 1830, p. 297.

monument of his talents and his theology. He frequently preached for his brethren, and assisted in administering the communion. ·He says: "I preached as often as I was able, and on an average once a week for many years." One of the interesting incidents in the life of this venerable theologian, was his supplying the pulpit of the African Presbyterian church for the space of two years and a half. Dr. Green also lectured for two winters to the Sabbath-school teachers on the portion of Scripture on which they were to hear their pupils on the next Sabbath after the lecture. He also visited, conversed and prayed with many persons in sickness and distress. A weekly prayer-meeting of his ministerial brethren was kept up for twenty years in his study. And during his residence in Philadelphia, he attended the meetings and took an active part in the deliberations of the various public bodies of which he was a member, especially the Boards of Missions and of Education.

Dr. Green's services in the judicatories of our church, after his coming to Philadelphia, formed an important part of his useful career. In 1824, he was elected Moderator of the General Assembly. He was prominent in council and action in reorganizing the Board of Education, in organizing the Board· of Foreign Missions, and in prosecuting the measures which resulted in the division of the church in 1837–8. Altogether he was a member of the General Assembly twenty-nine times.

The last regular sermon preached by this venerable man, was in the African church at Princeton, on July 16th, 1843, in the eighty-second year of his age. One of the greatest theologians of the times, he becomingly ended his ministry by preaching the gospel "to the poor."

In 1846, overcome by the infirmities of age, he was conducted into the General Assembly which had so often been the theatre of his earnest zeal for truth and for its universal diffusion. As he entered, the Assembly and audience spontaneously arose to do him honour; and Dr. Hodge, the Moderator, addressing him appropriate words of Christian salutation, he responded with patriarchal gravity and took a seat assigned to him. After listening to the proceedings for about half an hour, he retired in the presence of the rising and deeply affected audience, who felt that they would never see him more in the flesh. On the 19th of May, 1848, this venerable servant of Christ departed this life in the 86th year of his age. Death found him in the act of prayer with hands raised upward to the God of his salvation.

In the following year there was published "The Life of Ashbel Green, V. D. M., begun to be written by himself in his eighty-second year, and continued till his eighty-fourth; prepared for the press, at the Author's request, by Joseph H. Jones, pastor of the Sixth Presbyterian church, Philadelphia." It is an interesting work, and was reviewed by Dr. James W. Alexander in the October number for 1849. His place in this Index is given on account of two addresses which he made to the students of the Theological Seminary at Princeton in

1831. Address to the Students of the Theological Seminary at Princeton, May 16, 1831.

1835. Address delivered to the Theological Students of the Princeton Seminary, at the close of the semi-annual Examination, May 1835.

GREEN, HENRY WOODHULL, was born on the 20th of Sept., 1804, at Maidenhead (now Lawrence), in the county of Hunterdon (now Mercer), N. J. His father Caleb Smith Green, a highly respectable and intelligent farmer, and for many years an elder of the Presbyterian church in Lawrenceville, was a grandson of the Rev. Caleb Smith of Newark Hills and his wife Martha Dickinson, a daughter of the Rev. Jonathan Dickinson. He continued at school in his native village until he was fourteen years of age, receiving his early classical education at the academy of the Rev. Isaac V. Brown, now under the charge of Rev. Mr. Hammill. Here he prepared for college under the special instruction of Mr. John Maclean, since president of the College of New Jersey. In the fall of 1818, he entered the Junior Class at Princeton, where he graduated with honour at the early age of sixteen. In December 1821, he commenced the study of the law in the office of Mr. Charles Ewing, with whom he continued to read until Mr. Ewing was appointed Chief Justice, with the exception of seven months spent at the Law School in Litchfield, Connecticut, under the instruction of Judge Gould. He then entered the office of Mr. Garret D. Wall, and finished his legal studies with him in November 1825. He was thereupon licensed as an Attorney-at-law, and continued to practice in Trenton for twenty-one years. In 1832 he was appointed Recorder of the City of Trenton; he held and exercised the judicial functions of this office for five years. In 1838 he was appointed by the Legislature reporter of the decisions of the Court of Chancery of the State; he was reappointed in 1840 and held the office until the expiration of his term. In 1842 he was elected a member of the House of Assembly of New Jersey as a representative from Mercer county. In 1844 he was elected a member of the Convention to revise the Constitution of the State, and participated in its deliberations and debates. In 1845 he was appointed a commissioner with Hon. Peter D. Vroom, Hon. William L. Dayton and Hon. Stacy G. Potts, to collate and revise the statute laws of the state. The work was executed and published in 1847. In 1846 he was appointed Chief Justice of the Supreme Court of the state, and at the expiration of his term of office, in 1853, was reappointed. On the 14th of March 1860 he was appointed Chancellor; whereupon he resigned his office of Chief Justice and entered immediately on the new duties thus imposed upon him. In the spring of 1866 he resigned his office on account of his health, which had become enfeebled by his intense and unremitting labours, and imperatively demanded repose. A voyage to Europe, from which he returned after five months absence, proved of essential benefit. In 1867 he was appointed by the Legislature a member of a commission to revise the laws of the state relative to taxation; this work was executed and the commission reported the following year. Chancellor Green is universally esteemed one of the most accomplished jurists, and one of the ablest and most upright judges which the state has produced.

He has always been a devoted friend of the institutions at Princeton, and a warm supporter of the Presbyterian Church, of which he has been an elder for several years, and in whose judicatories he is always an influential member. When the Mason Library was in controversy between the Presbyterian and Associate Reformed Churches, he was charged with the management of the case on behalf of the former. The investigations which he made at that time in denominational history, left a profound impression upon his mind of the unhappy dissensions in the Presbyterian family, and made it one of the most ardent desires of his life that they might be amicably and harmoniously terminated, if this could be done without compromise of principle or any sacrifice of truth and duty. He has been a Trustee of Princeton Theological Seminary since 1833, and the President of the Board since 1860. At the opening of the Princeton law-school in 1847, he was invited to deliver the introductory address. In 1850 he received the degree of LL.D. from the College at Princeton, and at the same time was elected a member of its Board of Trustees. He is a brother of Mr. John C. Green of New York City, one of the most liberal benefactors of both the College and the Seminary.

In 1868 he contributed to this *Review* the article on the Trial of the Rev. William Tennent.

GREEN, WILLIAM HENRY, a nephew of the foregoing, was born at Groveville near Bordentown, in the state of New Jersey, on the 27th day of January, 1825. He graduated at Lafayette College in Easton, Pennsylvania, in 1840, where he remained for a short time as Tutor. He pursued his theological studies in Princeton, and upon the completion of his course in 1846 was made assistant teacher of Hebrew. After remaining three years in this capacity, during a portion of which he supplied successively the pulpits of the First and Second churches in Princeton, he became the pastor of the Central Church in Philadelphia. In 1851 he was elected Professor of Oriental and Biblical Literature in the Theological Seminary at Princeton, as successor to Dr. J. Addison Alexander, who was transferred to the chair of Ecclesiastical History. In 1859 the title of his Professorship was changed to that of Oriental and Old Testament Literature. In 1861 he published a Grammar of the Hebrew Language; in 1863, a Hebrew Chrestomathy; in 1866, an Elementary Hebrew Grammar; in 1863, "The Pentateuch Vindicated from the aspersions of Bishop Colenso;" and in 1870 he translated Zöckler's Commentary on the Song of Solomon for the American edition of Lange's Commentary.

The following articles were written by him:

1850. Keil on Joshua.

1851. Delitzsch on Habakkuk—Kurtz on the Old Covenant.

1852. The Prophet Obadiah expounded—The Jews at K'aefung-foo.

1853. Theology of the Old Testament—The Religious Significance of Numbers.

1854. Recent Commentaries on the Song of Solomon—Ebrard on the Apocalypse—Origin of Writing.

1855. Nahum's Prophecy concerning Nineveh—Jewish Exposition of Malachi—Monuments of the Umbrian Language—Demotic Grammar—Lepsius and Brugsch's Travels in Egypt—Comparative Accentual System of Sanscrit and Greek.

1856. Kurtz's History of the Old Testament—The Money of the Bible—The Sacred writings of the Parsis.

1857. Tischendorf's Travels in the East—Spiegel's Pehlevi Grammar—The Book of Job—New Edition of Horne's Introduction to the Scriptures—The Scope and Plan of the Book of Ecclesiastes—Albania and its People.

1858. Hoffman's Prophecy and Fulfilment.

1859. The Book of Hosea—Christology—The Old Testament Idea of a Prophet.

1860. The Text of Jeremiah.

1861. The Fulfilment of Prophecy—The Alexandrine and Sinaitic Manuscripts.

1862. The Matter of Prophecy.

1863. Date of the Book of Chronicles.

1864. Davidson's Introduction to the Old Testament—Modern Philology.

1865. The Structure of the Old Testament.

1866. Relations of India with Greece and Rome—Dr. Williams's New Translation of the Hebrew Prophets.

1867. The Position of the Book of Psalms in the Plan of the Old Testament—The Hebrew word Yashath.

GREGORY, DANIEL SEELY, is a native of the town of Carmel, Putnam county, New York, and was born on the 21st of August, 1832. The name of his great-grandfather Elnathan Gregory, 1757, stands first of that name as a graduate of the College of New Jersey, and Daniel Seely, 1857, is at present the last. After graduation, and while a student at the Seminary, he acted as Tutor in Rhetoric in the Session 1859–60, when he completed his course at the Seminary. After licensure he settled as pastor at Galena, Illinois, but was driven eastward by an attack of ague in 1863. He then accepted the charge of the Second Church of Troy, New York, where his labours were very greatly blessed, and several hundred added to the membership of the church. In 1867 he was induced to accept a call to the Third Congregational Church of New Haven, Connecticut, but the climate brought upon him a recurrence of the disease which had lodged in his system, and in 1869 he removed to South Salem, New York, his present field of labour. The articles he wrote for the *Repertory* excited more than ordinary interest at the time of publication. They were,

1866. The Preaching for the Times.

1868. The Pastorate for the Times—Studies in the Gospels—Matthew the Gospel for the Jew.

HAGEMAN, JOHN FRELINGHUYSEN, Counsellor-at-law, was born in the village of Harlingen, in Somerset county, a few miles north of Princeton, New Jersey, where his father, Dr. Abraham P. Hageman, a practising physician, lived and died. He was graduated at Rutgers College in 1836, and read law with Judge Field and Governor Vroom until he was admitted to the bar in 1839. He opened a law office in Princeton, where he has resided and pursued his profession until the present time. In 1850 he was a member of the Legislature of the state, having been elected from the county of Mercer, on general ticket, to the House of Assembly. Since 1851 he has been a Ruling Elder in the First Presbyterian church of Princeton, and a Trustee of the Theological Seminary of the same place.   He has been accustomed to write for the secular papers, and for eight years from 1859, especially during the war, he, with other gentlemen, contributed to the editorial department of the *Princeton Standard*.

In 1862 he was nominated by Governor Olden to the Senate, for Prosecutor of the Pleas for the county of Mercer.   The disquieted state of the country at that time gave increased importance to this office, especially at the capital of the state, and he accepted the appointment, and held the office for the term of five years, when he declined a re-nomination tendered by Governor Ward.   The celebrated trial of Charles Lewis in 1863, who was convicted and executed for the murder of James Rowand of Princeton—a remarkable case of circumstantial evidence, which was published in pamphlet; and the several bribery indictments against members of the Legislature, and of its lobby in 1866, were among the most important and exciting criminal cases which occurred during his term.   While holding this official relation to the state, he and all the other Prosecutors in the state were interrogated by the Corresponding Secretary of the New York Prison Reform Association, on the subject of the Administration of Criminal Law.   He and Courtlandt Parker, Prosecutor of Essex county, were the only ones who responded, and their responses were published in the Special Report of that Association in 1867.   It was in reference to that Report that he contributed, by request, an article for this *Review:*

1868. Prisons and Reformatories.

HALL, BAYNARD RUSH, was the son of Dr. John Hall, an eminent surgeon in Philadelphia.   He was a wealthy man, and died when his son was four years old, and only a small portion of· the property left him by his father ever came into his possession.   He was born in Philadelphia in 1798, and commenced his collegiate course in the College of New Jersey, but completed the course at Union College, from which he graduated with distinguished honour in 1820.   His relatives wished him to study law, but his own inclination was for the ministry, and he entered the Seminary at Princeton in the fall of the same year.   He had at the age of twenty-two married a Miss Young of Danville, Kentucky, and as soon as he left the Seminary he set out for the West, and obtained a Professorship in the University of Indiana, at Bloomington.   He seems to have left the West in 1831, and till 1838 was stated supply of the church at Bedford, Pennsylvania, and also taught an academy there. He then became successively the Principal of Academies at Bordentown and Trenton, New Jersey, and at Poughkeepsie and Newburgh, New York, and in 1852 removed to Brooklyn and became Principal of the Park Institute. The last few years of his life he spent in preaching the gospel to the poor, and he died on the 23d of January, 1863, leaving a widow and two children in destitute circumstances.

In 1842 the degree of A. M. was conferred upon him by the College of New Jersey; and in 1848, the degree of D. D. by Rutgers College. His first publication was a "New and Compendions Latin Grammar," and in 1843 he published "The New Purchase, or Life in the Far West," and "Something for Everybody," and in 1847, "Teaching a Science; the Teacher an Artist,"* and "Frank Freeman's Barber's Shop." As a writer he is acknowledged to display great versatility of talent and genius, and his works are pervaded by a religious spirit, and have a place in all our libraries of popular literature. For this periodical he wrote an article in

1842. On Theories of Education.

HALL, EDWIN, is a son of Ira Hall, M. D., and was born in Granville, Washington county, New York, on January 11, 1802. He graduated at Middlebury College in 1826, and acted as Tutor there in 1827–8. After preaching some time to the churches at Glen's Falls and Sandy Hill, New York, he became pastor of the First Congregational church in Norwalk, Connecticut, and continued in the charge twenty-three years, from 1832 to 1855, when he accepted the chair of Professor of Theology in Auburn Theological Seminary, which he continues to fill at the present time.

His published works are an "Ordination Sermon," 1833; "Law of Baptism," 1840; "Refutation of Sundry Baptist Errors," 1841; "The Puritans and their Principles," 1846; "Remonstrance and Complaint of Fairfield West Association," in the Bushnell Case, 1850; the part on the Atonement in the "Appeal of Fairfield West," and "Speech on the Bushnell Case before the General Association of Connecticut, at Danbury," in 1852; and "Examination of the Latest Defences of Dr. Hickok's Rational Psychology," in the *American Presbyterian and Theological Review*, in 1863. He is also the author of various Temperance Sermons and Addresses; and the "Review of Dr. Hickok's Rational Psychology," in the volume for 1861 is written by him.

* This work was reviewed by Dr. James W. Alexander in the volume for 1848.

HALL, JOHN, was born in Philadelphia on the 11th of August, 1806, graduated at the University of Pennsylvania in 1823; and in December 1827 was admitted to practise at the Philadelphia bar. In 1829 he made his first attempt at authorship in a translation, with notes, of Milton's Latin Letters, which was published by Littell. In 1832 he relinquished the practice of law, with a view to devote his life to the ministry; and being elected a manager, and afterwards Secretary of the Mission Work of the American Sunday-school Union, his training for the ministry was chiefly in the course of active work in this service. He was Editor of the "Sunday-school Journal," and the "Youth's Friend;" revised the first five volumes of the "Union Questions on the Bible," and prepared the seven subsequent volumes of the series; he produced nine original works and compiled six others, which have now a place upon the Catalogue of the Union. In 1839 he was licensed to preach by the Presbytery of Philadelphia, and in May 1841, he received a call to the First Church in Trenton, New Jersey, which he accepted, and entered upon his duties on the Sabbath immediately following that on which the pulpit was vacated by the late Dr. J. W. Yeomans, who preceded him. Mr. Hall was ordained and installed by the Presbytery of New Brunswick on the 11th of August, 1841, and no inducement has been able to make him engage in labour in another field. When he entered upon his pastorate in Trenton, the First had been the only Presbyterian church for more than a century. Out of it have now been formed three other large congregations in the city, and a small one in the neighbourhood, besides a mission chapel.

In 1850 the degree of D. D. was conferred upon him by the College of New Jersey. In 1852–3 he delivered a course of lectures in the Princeton Theological Seminary, filling a temporary vacancy in the chair of Pastoral Theology; and in 1853 the General Assembly elected him Professor of Pastoral Theology and Sacred Rhetoric in the Western Theological Seminary at Allegheny City, but he did not accept the appointment.

In addition to the works he prepared for the American Sunday-school Union, nine volumes appear on the Catalogue of the Presbyterian Board of Publication, viz: "The Chief End of Man," "The Only Rule," "Minor Characters of the Bible," "The Virgin Mary," "The Sower and the Seed," "Forgive us our Debts," "Sabbath-school Theology," and the "Life of Mrs. Sherwood." Besides these he is the author of a "History of the Presbyterian Church in Trenton," Sermon on the Death of

Mrs. Armstrong, and the brothers James W. and J. Addison
Alexander; Sermon before the Young Men's Association of
New York; Oration before the Society of Cincinnati of New
Jersey; several discourses in *National Preacher* and other
periodicals; papers in *American Quarterly Review, North
American Review*, and various religious and literary journals,
besides contributions to newspapers—a habit dating back in
boyhood.   But the most extraordinary of his works is the publication of the series of "Familiar Letters," which passed between himself and Dr. James W. Alexander, during a period
of forty years, beginning when they were boys, and only ending
with the life of Dr. Alexander.   Such an uninterrupted friendship is rare, and a correspondence preserved through so many
years is probably unique.   It is a delightful and instructive
volume for a leisure hour.   His articles published in the
Princeton Review are:
    1830. Memoir of Oberlin, (last two paragraphs by J. W. A.)
    1831. Arabs of the Desert.
    1832. Duty of the Church in relation to Sunday-schools.
    1834. Religious Obligations of Parents.
    1836. Life of Harlan Page.
    1840. Education in Europe.
    1842. Primitive Christian Worship, (last paragraph by J.
W. A.)
    1843. The Familiar Study of the Bible—The President's
Message.
    1844. Mental Cultivation.
    1845. Henderson on the Vaudois.
    1848. Life of Elizabeth Fry—The Sandwich Islands.
    1854. Present State of Oxford University.
    1856. The Bible, the Missal, and the Breviary.
    1858. Life of Cardinal Mezzofanti.
    1864. Life of Governor Winthrop.

    HAMILTON, WILLIAM, was born at Garvagh, in the
county of Londonderry, Ireland, on the 18th of February, 1807.
His studies were pursued chiefly in the schools and collegiate
classes of the Royal Belfast Academical Institution.   After
completing his theological studies, he opened a private school
in Belfast, from which he was removed to the Institution, on
the resignation of the celebrated Dr. Henry Montgomery, as
Head Master of the English Department.   In 1844 Mr.
Hamilton resigned this important and lucrative situation, and
came out to Canada as a missionary of the Free Church of
Scotland.   In 1847 he removed to the United States, and was

for some time Professor of the Latin Language and Literature in Hanover College, Indiana, from which, we believe, he received the honorary degree of D. D. Subsequently Dr. Hamilton entered the Reformed Dutch Church, and was sometime pastor of the New Prospect Church, Ulster county, New York. Latterly he has resided in Canada, and is now living there without pastoral charge. His only contribution to the *Princeton Review* is an article in the July No. of 1868, on "Ireland—the Church and the Land," in which the recent measures of Church and Land Reform were anticipated and foreshadowed.

HAND, AARON H., was the son of an elder in the Third Presbyterian church of Albany, New York, and was born in that city on the 3d of December, 1811. He graduated at Williams College in 1831, and received his theological education at the Princeton Seminary. The first seven years of his ministry were spent in Georgia and Florida; he was then three years at Berwick, Pennsylvania; and for the last seventeen years has been pastor of the church at Greenwich, New Jersey. He received the degree of D. D. from Lafayette College in 1858, and contributed to this journal in

1867. The Rejection of Christ by the Jewish Rulers and People.

HARRISON, GESSNER, was born in Harrisonburg, Rockingham county, Virginia, on the 16th of June, 1807. He was the son of Dr. Peochy G. Harrison of that county, quite a distinguished physician. At the age of eight years he was sent to the best school the town afforded, and there commenced the study of the Latin language. At the age of eighteen he entered the University of Virginia, then just opened, in the year 1825. Here, by assiduous attention to his studies and the proper use of no ordinary powers of mind, he acquired a fund of information hardly to be expected from his previous preparation. Though intending to follow the profession of medicine, he paid great attention to both Greek and Latin, with such success as to win for him the admiration of his Professor Mr. George Long, now of the University of London, England. Mr. Long resigned the Professorship of Latin and Greek in 1828, and the subject of our sketch was chosen to succeed him, he being then only twenty-one years of age. At the age of twenty-six he became a member of the Methodist Church, and was characterized by habits of piety throughout his whole life. He continued to perform the duties of both professor of Latin and Greek until 1856, at which time the school of Ancient Languages was divided—he remaining professor of Latin. He resigned this professorship in 1859, and established an academy, which he conducted successfully until the time of his death, which took place on the 7th of April, 1862, having then almost reached his fifty-fifth year. His principal works were "An Exposition of some of the Laws of the Latin Language," and "Greek Prepositions and Cases of Nouns." Both these works have been very highly complimented by English, German, and American scholars. His work on the Laws of the Latin Language was reviewed by the late Isidor Lœwenthal in the July number for 1852, and elicited a reply from Dr. Harrison in the number for October.

1852. Laws of Latin Grammar.

.

HART, LL.D., JOHN·SEELY, was born in Old Stockbridge, Berkshire county, Massachusetts, on the 28th of January, 1810; but when he was only two years old, his father, with some other families, removed into Pennsylvania, and settled in Providence township, on the Lackawanna, which was then a wilderness. Here he continued till 1823, when his father acquired a mill-privilege at Laurel Run, then about two miles above Wilkesbarre in the valley of Wyoming. When a boy he was very sickly, and adjudged unfit for any employment requiring physical strength; so arrangements were made to get him educated for a teacher, and in his fifteenth year he entered the Wilkesbarre Academy. By diligent use of the opportunities afforded him here, in three years he was well-fitted for college, and had acquired robust health. In the fall of 1827 he entered the Sophomore Class of the College of New Jersey, and graduated in 1830, with the first honours of his class. After graduation he taught one year in the Academy at Natchez, Mississippi, and in the fall of 1831 entered the Theological Seminary at Princeton. During the last two years of his attendance at the Seminary, he acted as Tutor in the College, and in 1834 he was appointed adjunct Professor of Ancient Languages. Mr. Hart was licensed to preach the gospel by the Presbytery of New Brunswick in 1835; but in the following year he was induced to become proprietor of Edgehill School, and regarding it as a permanent field of usefulness, requested the Presbytery to take back his license, which was formally cancelled.

Mr. Hart continued in the management of the Edgehill School five years; and in September 1842 he was elected Principal of the High-School of Philadelphia. While in connection with the school, in 1848, the degree of LL.D. was conferred upon him by the University of Miami. In this institution he continued until 1859, when he became editor of the periodicals of the American Sunday-school Union, in connection with which he commenced the publication of the *Sunday-school Times*, of which he is still senior editor. For the last eight years he has been Principal of the New Jersey State Normal School, at Trenton, N. J., at which place he resides.

Dr. Hart has been busy with his pen. Besides his Annual Reports of the Philadelphia High School and of the New Jersey Normal School, amounting to many large volumes, and his continual contributions to the periodical press, he has published the following works: 1. The Golden Censer; Thoughts on the Lord's Prayer. 2. Thoughts on Sabbath-Schools. 3. Removing Mountains; or, Life Lessons from the Gospels. 4. Counsels for the School-Room. 5. In the School-Room; Chapters in the Philosophy of Education. 6. Prayers for the School-Room. 7. Mistakes of Educated Men. 8. Spencer and the Faery Queen. 9. Female Prose Writers of America. 10. Class-Book of Prose. 11. Class-Book of Poetry. 12. English Grammar. 13. English Grammar, (Part I. Introductory). 14. Constitution of the United States, (An Exposition for Schools). 15. Mythology for Schools. 16. Composition and Rhetoric. He is the author of the articles subjoined.

1835. Jenkyn on the Atonement.
1836. The English Bible.*
1838. Tyndal's New Testament.
1865. The Revised Webster.
1866. Common Schools—Normal Schools.
1868. The English Language.

HASTINGS, THOMAS, Mus. Doc., was the son of Dr. Seth Hastings, and was born in Washington, Connecticut, on the 15th of October, 1784, but removed to Oneida county, New York, in 1796. In 1822 he published at Albany his "Dissertation on Musical Taste," and in 1824, he became editor of the *Western Recorder*, which was published at Utica, New York. While in this position he contributed two articles to the *Princeton Review*, on "Church Music." In 1832 he removed to New York City, where he still resides; and during his residence there he has by lecturing, teaching, and writing, done much to elevate the taste in Church Music.

* This article is erroneously attributed to Dr. Joseph Addison Alexander on page 90.

25

His principal publications are, "History of Forty Choirs," "Mother's Hymn Book," "Devotional Hymns and Poems," "Musica Sacra," "Spiritual Songs," "Selah," "Hastings's Collection," "Manhattan Collection," "Sacred Lyre;" and in connection with the late William B. Bradbury, the "Psalmodist," "Choralist," "Mendelssohn," and the "Psalmister." He has also edited various musical works for religious societies and for church organizations.

1829. Church Music.
1830. Church Music.

HELM, JAMES I., was born in East Tennessee on the 25th of April, 1811. He is a graduate of Greeneville College, Tennessee, and studied theology in the Princeton Seminary three years, completing his course in 1834. He was pastor of the Presbyterian church at Salem, New Jersey, twelve years, after which he devoted some years to teaching, and was twice elected President of Washington College, Tennessee. In 1859 he left the Presbyterian Church and joined the Protestant Episcopal Church, and since then has been minister of the parish of Sing Sing, New York. He contributed to this *Review* in 1843, an article on the Westminster Assembly of Divines.

HENRY, JOSEPH. He is of Scotch Presbyterian descent; his grand-parents on both sides landed in New York the day before the battle of Bunker's Hill. His maternal grandfather, Hugh Alexander, was a man of remarkable ingenuity, and settled in Delaware county, N. Y., where he erected a mill and prepared all the apparatus, even the grinding-stones, with his own hands. During the progress of the war, however, he was driven from his mill by the Indians, and became an artificer in the continental army, and afterwards a manufacturer of salt at the springs of Salina. His paternal grandfather, Wm. Henry, or Hendrie, as the name was spelled in Scotland, settled on a farm in Albany county. He was a man of reading, especially in the line of Presbyterian theology and Scotch history. He lived to the age of upwards of ninety, and was wont to give in his late days an account of the appearance of Charles Stuart as he entered Glasgow in 1745.

The subject of this sketch was born in Albany, but having lost his father at an early age, he was adopted by an uncle, and sent, at the age of seven years, to live with his grandmother and to attend school at Galway, in Saratoga county. Here he remained until the age of fourteen, the latter part of the time being spent in a store, attending school in the afternoon. He showed no aptitude for learning, or for excelling in the ordinary sports of boyhood. This, however, was mainly due to his having accidentally and secretly obtained access to the village library, where he became so fascinated with works of fiction, perhaps on account of the stolen access to them, that he spent most of the time in reading, which was devoted by other boys to active sports. He became the story-teller to his comrades, and on one occasion, while on a visit to his mother in Albany, was taken to the theatre by a relative, and on his return amused his young companions by reproducing with them the two plays which had formed the evening entertainment.

On his return to Albany, after the death of his uncle, he was apprenticed to his cousin to learn the trade of a jeweler, but after he had been two years in this occupation, and before he had acquired sufficient skill to support himself by the art, his relative gave up the business and he was set loose from regular employment, and gave himself up, almost entirely, to light reading and the amusement of the theatre. In this course he was suddenly arrested by opening a book which had been left upon the table by one of the boarders at his mother's house. A single page of this produced a remarkable change in his life. It gave a new direction to his thoughts, and called forth mental characteristics, of which he had previously supposed himself entirely deficient. He resolved at once to devote his life to the acquisition of knowledge, and immediately commenced to take evening lessons from two of the professors in the Albany Academy. He also became a pupil of the celebrated Hamilton, who visited this country for the purpose of introducing the method recommended by Locke for teaching languages, endeavouring, in the meantime, to support himself by such chance employment as he could obtain. In this, however, he was not successful, and he abandoned this course for that of a teacher of a country district school. After spending seven months in this occupation he entered as a regular pupil of the Academy, where he remained until his means were exhausted and then returned to school teaching, and at the expiration of his second term again renewed his connection with the Academy. After continuing his studies here for some time he was, through the recommendation of Dr. T. Romeyn Beck, Principal of the Academy, appointed private tutor to the family of Gen. Stephen Van Rensselaer, the Patroon of Rensselaerwyck. His duties in this position occupied him only about three hours in the day, and the remainder of his time was spent as an assistant to Dr. Beck in his chemical investigations, and in the study of anatomy and physiology under Drs. Tully and Marsh, with a view to graduating in medicine. His course of life, however, was suddenly changed by an offer, through the influence of Judge Conkling, with whom he had become a favourite, of an appointment on the survey of a route for a state road from the Hudson river to Lake Erie, through the southern tier of counties. His labours in this work were exceedingly arduous and responsible. They extended far into the winter, and the operations were carried on in some instances, amid deep snows in primeval forests.

Having finished the survey with the approbation of the commissioners, on his return to Albany he was offered the position of engineer on a canal in Ohio, and of director of a mine in Mexico, but the professorship of mathematics in the Academy having fallen vacant, he was elected to fill the chair; having, however, become enamoured with the profession of an engineer, he very reluctantly accepted the position in accordance with the wishes of his friend, Dr. Beck. The duties of the office, however, did not commence for five or six months, and this time he devoted to the exploration of the geology of New York with Prof. Eaton of the Rensselaer School. He entered upon his duties in the Academy in Sept. 1826, and after devoting some time to the studies of mathematics and other subjects pertaining to his professorship, he commenced a series of original investigations on electricity and magnetism, the first regular series on Natural Philosophy which had been prosecuted in this country since the days of Franklin. These researches made him favourably known, not only in this country but also in Europe, and led to his call, in 1832, through the nomination of Dr. Maclean, to the chair of Natural Philosophy in the College of New Jersey at Princeton.

In the first year of his course in this college, during the absence of the professor of chemistry, Dr. Torrey, in Europe, he gave lectures in Natural Philosophy, Chemistry, Mineralogy, Geology, Astronomy, and Architecture. In the chemical course he was assisted by Dr. George Maclean. In teaching these multifarious branches, he was unable during the first year at Princeton to continue his investigations, but after that time he commenced anew where he had left off at Albany, and prosecuted his original researches until he was called to his present position in Washington. In 1835 he was elected Professor of Natural Philosophy in the University of Virginia. The offer was a tempting one, since the emoluments connected with the professorship in the Virginia University were greater than perhaps in any other in the country, while the salary at Princeton was small, and scarcely sufficient to support his family, and to meet other demands upon him. He was, however, reluctant to leave the place where he had experienced so much affectionate kindness and encouraging appreciation. It may be mentioned perhaps as an interesting fact, that the Hon. Samuel M. Southard, at one time Secretary of the Navy, and one of the trustees of the college, to whom he had presented the case, said, in reply, "if you live to the ordinary age of men, you will see a rupture between the North and South, and in that case your position in Virginia may not be agreeable." Though this remark was prophetic, it produced but little effect on the Professor, and the matter was compromised on other grounds. He was allowed by the trustees of the college a full salary, a new house, and a years' absence in Europe, nine months of which he spent principally in London, Paris, and Edinburgh. His previous researches had given him a favourable introduction to the savants of these cities, and he returned to prosecute his investigations with enlarged views and more efficient apparatus, procured during his tour in Europe.

In 1846 he was requested by some of the members of the Board of Regents of the Smithsonian Institution, then just about to be organized, to give his views as to the best method of realizing the intentions of its founder. In compliance with this request he gave an exposition of the will, and of the method by which it might most efficiently be realized. On account of this exposition, and his scientific reputation, he was called to the office of Secretary or Director of the establishment. Unfortunately, Congress had attempted to organize the Institution without a due appreciation of the terms of the will. This gave rise to difficulties and expenditures on local objects, particularly to the commencement of a very expensive building, which have much retarded the full realization of what might have been produced by the plan originally proposed by Prof. Henry. He has, however, by constant perseverance in one line of policy, brought the Institution into a condition of financial prosperity and wide reputation. Indeed it is scarcely too much to say that no institution of a scientific character, established by the benevolence of an individual, has done more to render the name of its founder generally and favourably known throughout the civilized world.

At the time of the organization of the Light House Board of the United States, Prof. Henry was appointed by President Filmore one of its members, and still continues as such in the capacity of Chairman of the Committee on Experiments. During the war he was appointed one of a Commission, together with Prof. Bache and Admiral Davis, to examine and report upon various inventions and propositions, intended to facilitate the operations against the enemy, and to improve the art of navigation. On the death of Prof. Bache, he was elected President of the National Academy of Sciences, established by an act of Congress in 1863, to advance science and to report upon such questions of a scientific character as might be connected with the operations of the Government. He is a member of various societies in this country and abroad, and has several times received the degree of LL.D., the last time from Cambridge, Mass.

Professor Henry was married in May 1830, to Miss Alexanander, of Schenectady, the sister of Professor Alexander, of Princeton, and from the ardent devotion of his wife, and the fraternal sympathy of her brother in his pursuits, he has received assistance and support beyond that which usually falls to the lot of men. The most peaceful, and to himself the most profitable, part of his life, was that spent in Princeton, for which place, and the College connected with it, he retains the warmest attachment. He left Princeton with the intention of returning to his professorship as soon as he should be able to organize the Smithsonian Institution, but in this he was disappointed,—he could not leave without losing all the fruits of his labours.

The following is a brief enumeration of his scientific investigations and discoveries.

1. A sketch of the topography of the State of New York, embodying the results of the survey before mentioned.

2. In connection with Dr. Beck and the Hon. Simeon De Witt, the organization of the meteorological system of the State of New York.

3. The development, for the first time, of magnetic power, sufficient to sustain tons in weight, in soft iron, by a comparatively feeble galvanic current.

4. The first application of electro-magnetism as a power, to produce continued motion in a machine.

5. An exposition of the method by which electro-magnetism might be employed in transmitting power to a distance, and the demonstration of the practicability of an electro-magnetic telegraph, which without these discoveries was impossible.

6. The discovery of the induction of an electrical current in a long wire upon itself, or the means of increasing the intensity of a current by the use of a spiral conductor.

7. The method of inducing a current of quantity from one of intensity, and *vice versa*.

8. The discovery of currents of induction of different orders, and of the neutralization of the induction by the interposition of plates of metal.

9. The discovery that the discharge of a Leyden jar consists of a series of oscillations backwards and forwards until equilibrium is restored.

10. The induction of a current of electricity from lightning at a great distance, and proof that the discharge from á thunder cloud also consists of a series of oscillations.

11. The oscillating condition of a lightning rod while transmitting a discharge of electricity from the clouds causing it, though in perfect connection with the earth, to emit sparks of sufficient intensity to ignite combustible substances.

12. Investigations on molecular attraction, as exhibited in liquids, and in yielding and rigid solids, and an exposition of the theory of soap bubbles. [These originated from his being called upon to investigate the causes of the bursting of the great gun on the U. S. steamer Princeton.]

13. Original experiments on, and exposition of the principles of acoustics as applied to churches and other public buildings.

14. Experiments on various instruments to be used as fog signals.

15˙ A series of experiments on various illuminating materials for lighthouse use, and the introduction of lard oil for lighting the coasts of the United States. This and the preceding in his office of chairman of the Committee on Experiments of the Light House Board.

16. Experiments on heat, in which the radiation from clouds and animals in distant fields was indicated by the thermo-electrical apparatus applied to a reflecting telescope.

17. Observations on the comparative temperature of the sun-spots, and also of different portions of the sun's disk. In these experiments he was assisted by Professor Alexander.

18. Proof that the radiant heat from a feebly luminous flame is also feeble, and that the increase of radiant light by the introduction of a solid substance into the flame of the compound blowpipe, is accompanied with an equivalent radiation of heat, and also that the increase of light and radiant heat in a flame of hydrogen by the introduction of a solid substance, is attended with a diminution in the heating power of the flame itself.

19. The reflection of heat from concave mirrors of ice, and its application to the source of the heat derived from the moon.

20. Observations, in connection with Prof. Alexander, on the

red flames on the border of the sun, as observed in the annular eclipse of 1838.

21. Experiments on the phosphorogenic ray of the sun, from which it is shown that this emanation is polarizable and refrangible, according to the same laws which govern light.

22. On the penetration of the more fusible metals into those less readily melted, while in a solid state.

Besides these experimental additions to physical science, Professor Henry is the author of twenty-two reports giving an exposition of the annual operations of the Smithsonian Institution. He has also published a series of essays on meteorology in the Patent Office Reports, which, besides an exposition of established principles, contain many new suggestions, and among others, the origin of the development of electricity, as exhibited in the thunderstorm; and an essay on the principal source of the power which does the work of developing the plant in the bud, and the animal in the egg.

He has also published a theory of elementary education, in his address as President of the American Association for the Advancement of Education, the principle of which is, that in instruction the order of nature should be followed, that we should begin with the concrete and end with the abstract, the one gradually shading into the other; also the importance of early impressions, and the tendency in old age to relapse into the vices of early youth. Youth is the father of old age rather than of manhood.

He was successful as a teacher, and never failed to impart to his students a portion of his own enthusiasm. His object was not merely to impart a knowledge of facts, but mainly to give clear expositions of principles—to teach the use of generalizations—the method of arriving at laws by the process of induction, and the inference from these of facts by logical deduction.

His papers in the *Princeton Review* are,

1841. The British Scientific Association.

1845. The Coast Survey—Observations on Colour Blindness.

HODGE, CHARLES, the originator, editor, and leading contributor of this *Review*, was born in 1797, in Philadelphia, where his grandfather, a merchant of Scotch-Irish descent, had settled in 1730. His father was Dr. Hugh Hodge, a physician of great promise and large practice, who died at the early age of forty-three, leaving a widow and two sons. To the influence of this mother, a lady of rare excellence and endowments, both the distinguished brothers are greatly indebted for the mental and moral culture, to which they owe, under God, much of their fame and usefulness.

The subject of this notice passed his early life in his native city. At twelve years of age he commenced his classical studies at the academy in Somerville, N. J., and afterwards pursued them at a school in Princeton. He entered the Sophomore Class of Nassau Hall in 1812, the year when Dr. Ashbel Green became President, and immediately took a high standing, and on graduating delivered the valedictory oration. During a memorable revival in the College in 1815, he, with many others, (among them the present Bishops McIlvaine and Johns, of the Episcopal Dioceses of Ohio and Virginia) made a profession of religion. The next year, the three friends, Hodge, McIlvaine, and Johns, entered the Princeton Theological Seminary; and the affectionate intimacy, then begun and confirmed, has continued to the present day.

It was probably owing to Dr. Alexander's advice and influence that Dr. Hodge turned his attention to that form of his professional life, in which he has been so distinguished. That revered friend, "who early discerned his talents, and seems to have ever regarded him more as a beloved son than even as a cherished pupil,"* induced him, not long after he left the Seminary as a student, to accept the appointment, in it, of assistant teacher of the Original Languages; and in 1822 the General Assembly elected him Professor of Oriental and Biblical Literature. Soon after his election, by the advice of the Professors and Directors of the Seminary, he went abroad for the advantages of European universities, and spent parts of three years in Paris, Halle, and Berlin, resuming his duties in Princeton in 1828. After filling that chair for more than twenty years, he was transferred to the Professorship of Exegetical and Didactic Theology; Dr. Alexander, on account of his age and impaired health, desiring relief. And on the death of Dr. Alexander, in 1852, Polemic Theology was added.

The first number of the *Biblical Repertory* was issued by him in 1825. At the outset it was restricted to selections from foreign works in the department of Biblical Literature. But on his return from abroad it was deemed expedient to enlarge its scope, and *Princeton Review* was added to its title. The "association of gentlemen," who then consented to assume with him its responsibilities before the public, formed a truly brilliant and effective corps. Their varied talents, learning and temperaments, the peculiarities of each admirably supplementing and harmonizing with those of the others, at once

* Life of Dr. Archibald Alexander, page 381.

26

gave the *Review* a prominent position among the leading quarterlies of the age. Little did they realize what an influence in moulding and sustaining the opinions of numbers in and out of the church was then set in motion. While it was published as the work of an association, the editor not only had the chief care, but also contributed the largest number of articles, on the greatest variety of subjects, besides preparing the best portion of the "Notices," which to many so greatly enhanced the value and interest of each number. His associates unquestionably gave to it a very important part of its reputation and success. The value of the contributions by the Drs. Alexander, Dr. Miller, Professor Dodd, and others, cannot be overestimated. But circumstances devolved upon him the chief labour, and made him the principal exponent of its plans and aims. So they felt, and such has been the general sentiment. It was not only projected by him, but also styled "Mr. Hodge's work." Dr. Addison Alexander once said playfully to a friend, who was urging him to write upon a particular theme, "Dr. Hodge, you know, frames our constitution, and then we enact the laws; you must get him to open on that subject." And the editor himself said, in 1865, that "he had carried it as ball and chain for forty years, with scarcely any other compensation than the high privilege of making it an organ for upholding sound Presbyterianism and the honour of our common Redeemer."*

These forty years comprised a period of as great agitation and anxiety as any other of equal extent in the history of American Presbyterianism. "New Divinity" and "New Measures" were beginning to assume a positive and polemical attitude. Voluntary societies, seeking to embrace the various Presbyterian as well as Congregational bodies, were supposed to be spreading these "novelties" throughout our church, and to this state of things the *Review* was principally directed. Its most prominent feature, that which has elicited the most general interest, has been its discussion of questions connected with these subjects; the burden of which has fallen chiefly upon Dr. Hodge, as will appear, by a glance at the list of his articles,

---

* "In the year 1825 a quarterly publication was issued at Princeton, under the title of the *Biblical Repertory*. It was projected and undertaken by Professor Hodge, under whose auspices it has continued to flourish till this day. * * * Through good and evil report, it has pursued its way, and has contributed more than any other agency to make known those opinions which belong to what some have chosen to call the Princeton school. * * * Its pages contain ample discussions of all matters relating to the defence of Calvinism and Presbytery, the policy of the Church, the charities of the age, new divinity, new philosophy, and new measures." *Dr. Alexander's Life*, pp. 393-394. See also p. 67 of this *Index*—and vol. xxxvii., p. 657 of the *Review*.

in the sequel of this notice. These discussions, covering so much of the field of theology and ecclesiology, attracted as much attention, and exerted as wide an influence as almost any of the kind in the last half century.* They aimed to propagate no new system of doctrine, but simply to vindicate that contained in our standards; and this they did with great force and clearness. We have no "Apologies" that could take their place. They have served as much as any with which we are acquainted to correct erroneous views of the Calvinistic system, and to preserve doctrinal integrity in the church. Professor Shedd but expressed a general opinion, when he declared, in the Assembly of '68, "Dr. Hodge has done more for Calvinism than any other man in this country.† To engage in such a vindication, was a task by no means to be coveted, even when the principles involved were supposed to lie at the foundation, and to be essential to the power of religion. But such defences have often, under God, resulted in a more definite understanding and wider reception of the truth. And for this, Divine providence seems to have especially qualified him. His natural temperament, his early training, and the years he devoted to the critical study and teaching of God's word,‡ laid a broad foundation for the service. And the church in the future, we doubt not, will look back gratefully to this "life work," as Dr. Shedd styled it, of him who originated, and in so great part sustained this *Review.*

His articles were not confined to theological discussions. During the earlier years of the *Repertory*, Dr. Miller, who then filled the chair of Church Government in the Seminary, contributed the leading papers in defence of Presbyterian church polity. Subsequently Dr. J. Addison Alexander pre-

---

* We need here but refer to the articles on "The Knowledge of God;" "The Ground of Faith in the Scriptures;" "What is Christianity;" "Inspiration;" "Original Sin;" "Imputation;" "Free Agency;" "Human Ability;" "The Atonement;" "Regeneration;" "Sacraments;" "Finney's Theology;" "New Divinity Tried;" "Park's Theology of the Intellect and Feelings;" "Stuart" and "Barnes on Romans;" "Beman on the Atonement;" "Beecher's Great Conflict;" "Bushnell's God in Christ;" "Vicarious Sacrifice;" "Baird's First and Second Adam," and various others.

† "Debates," p. 95.

‡ "He is the greatest and best theologian who has most accurately apprehended the meaning of Scripture, and by comparing and combining its statements, has most fully and correctly brought out the whole mind of God, on all the topics on which the Scriptures give us information, as is best fitted to commend them to the apprehension and acceptance of men, and most skilfully and effectively defended them against the assaults of adversaries. In this work there is abundant scope for the exercise of the highest powers and the application of the most varied and extensive acquirements." "Theology of the Reformers," Essay vi. John Calvin, by Principal Cunningham, p. 296.

pared those brilliant, learned, and effective essays and reviews on this subject, which attracted so general attention and interest. Dr. Hodge was at first indisposed to take any part in the Prelatic controversy, because, as he once intimated, "the scriptures are so clear on it, while the testimony of the fathers is so ambiguous." When, however, Dr. Miller's health declined, Dr. Hodge was called to lecture for a time on Ecclesiology, that department being intimately related to his own. In 1845 more than usual attention was called to some aspects of the subject, by discussions in the church on Romish baptism. The action then taken by the General Assembly being so different from what many had regarded as the doctrine of the Presbyterian and other Protestant churches, an earnest but temperate paper by him appeared in the July number of that year's *Repertory*, which was replied to in the *Presbyterian*, and in the *Watchman of the South*. This seems to have induced that series of able articles on "Theories of the Church," "Idea of the Church," and kindred themes, some of which were reprinted in Edinburgh, with notes by Dr. Hanna and an introduction by Principal Cunningham. During the same period he wrote the reviews on the "Oxford Tracts," "Mr. Goode's Vindication of the doctrine of the Church of England on the validity of Presbyterian Ordination," and "Bishop McIlvaine's Sermons" in which he vindicated the true idea of the church, and exposed the ritualistic theory, which makes the church and the ministry the channels of grace, and strikes at the roots of the most vital doctrines of religion. In 1855, the *Church Review* in a criticism upon his "Address before the Presbyterian Historical Society," called the author's attention to what was represented to be an unanswerable argument, by his old friend Bishop McIlvaine, in favour of the "Permanency of the Apostolic office." Dr. Hodge at once replied in one of his most effective articles, with great courtesy to his friend, but utterly demolishing the argument. These and a number of hardly less useful discussions on "Presbyterian Liturgies," the "Rights of Ruling Elders," and kindred topics, comprise one of the most valuable portions of this department of the *Review*.

Another class of his contributions related to the prerogatives and duties of the church in developing its life, preserving its purity, and exerting its influence. The rise and spread of doctrinal novelties had early drawn attention to the agencies by which the ministry was to be trained and sent forth. According to the theory of the church prevalent in New England, these were entirely outside of ecclesiastical organizations.

The Presbyterian Church had its Boards, but the advocates of voluntary societies called in question the right or competency of church courts to exercise such supervision and control; and they used every means not only to prevent the formation of a new Board of Foreign Missions, but also to do away with existing ones. As the decision of this might soon determine the doctrinal character of the church, it gave rise to a very serious and wide-spread controversy. The discussion in favour of Ecclesiastical Boards, in opposition to Voluntary Societies, in the *Repertory*, commenced in the first volume of the "new series." The replies to Professor Stuart of Andover did not indeed go into the real question, but they prepared the way for that full consideration of the subject that soon became necessary; when it underwent so thorough an examination, and the policy of ecclesiastical control received so complete a vindication, that it seems to have become finally settled. To this result the articles of Dr. Hodge largely contributed. Subsequently the right of church courts to entrust this work to Boards, even of their own appointment, was controverted by some of the friends of ecclesiastical control, and Dr. Hodge vindicated it with great force. In this connection may also be noticed his papers on the extent of the control to be exercised over Missions and Mission Churches, and the superintendence of Foreign Missions, which discuss principles of great interest and importance with reference to the work of the church.

Others of his contributions on the policy of the church related to measures for its reform. In the controversy, which resulted in the division of 1838, the Princeton Association, although in doctrinal sympathy with their Old-school brethren, was charged with an unfaithful liberality. Dr. Hodge as the chief exponent of this "moderate party," and the author of the articles on the "Act and Testimony," "Mr. Barnes' trial," "The exscinding of the three Synods," &c., received a full share of the censure of both extremes. The same may be said of his part in the re-union movement. We need not revert to these controversies at this time. It may be noticed, however, in passing, that although regarded as so "moderate" and "time serving" in 1837–8, he is considered in 1867–9 an ultraist for adhering to the same principles; the church not being disposed at this time to go even so far as the "moderates" then went. The tone of these discussions was very fraternal and conciliatory, as no little regret was felt in differing from brethren with whom there had been for the most part so cordial a sympathy.

The remaining point under this general head had reference to the relations and duties of the church in respect to the country.   As early as 1855, some of our Southern friends who had taken extreme ground on the policy of Boards, raised a further question as to the prerogatives of the church respecting matters that had secular relations and bearing.   Dr. Hodge, in the *Review*, earnestly opposed the extreme action carried by a small majority at Indianapolis.   A harmonious understanding, however, seemed to have been reached, after the warm though courteous debate at Rochester in 1860. But when the church in 1861 apparently leaned over to the opposite extreme, he still adhered to the principles of the Rochester action.   No articles from his pen have attracted more general attention, or called forth more praise and censure, than those on the state of the country and affiliated subjects. During the excitement of the times, the radical friends of the North and the ultra friends of the South, criticised him with unmeasured severity; but the church and the country appears to be gradually returning to his moderate position.   He has fully explained his views, and defended his course on these questions, in the article on "The Princeton Review and the State of the Country."

From these topics we pass to mention briefly a different, but valuable class of Dr. Hodge's papers, on such questions as "Sunday Mails," "Slavery," "Abolitionism," "Conscience and the Constitution," "Temperance," "New Translation of the American Bible Society," "Christian Economics," "Diversity of Species," and many others, which may be seen in the appended list.   Although directed to temporary aspects of these subjects, the discussion is treated on such broad, comprehensive principles, and in so able a manner, that they greatly enhance the permanent value of the *Review*.

Before concluding this notice we must call attention to a series of articles of special importance, although they cover some of the ground already gone over.   In 1835 he commenced giving an annual review of the proceedings of the General Assembly of our Church.   From the excitement of the public mind at the time, they soon began to be looked for with as much interest as any of his more elaborate articles; so much so that one of his associates said, "there is no inducement to prepare a good article for the July number, because every one turns at once to that on the General Assembly, which absorbs all the interest."   They not only contained a clear and condensed account of the state of the church, the origin, modifications and operations of its various Boards, agencies and seminaries; its legislative enactments, judicial decisions, and general recommendations; but also a summary of all the discussions of the most important controversies in the church, such as its division and re-union, the elder and quorum questions, demission of the ministerial office, examination of ministers, Romish baptism, marriage question, appeals and complaints, declaration and testimony, state of the country, which were warmly contested in their day, and still having practical interest. Altogether they present a full view of the proceedings of the church during a most important period. They give a concise but clear representation of the opposite views advocated in these various questions, with impartial criticisms upon them. Dr. Hodge's extensive knowledge of the general history of church doctrine, polity and policy, as well as his sound judgment, candour and moderation, peculiarly qualified him for this work. Here may be found some of his ablest and most valuable suggestions on important questions connected with the prerogatives and practical working of the church. The advocates of opposite extremes in exciting times, may not agree with some of his arguments and conclusions, yet even when we differ from him in opinion, his calmness and impartiality in presenting both sides, glossing over nothing, exaggerating nothing, and his dignified fraternal courtesy, make them historically very valuable. For often what is objected to, during the excitement of debate, will afterwards be highly appreciated by those who have not mingled in the conflict. A better service for the information of the coming generation of ministers could hardly be rendered, than that of collecting and republishing this series of articles on the General Assembly.

This notice has been prepared under some embarrassment. The time has not come for a full expression of opinion and feeling respecting the life and character of its subject. Yet the publisher and public would feel it to be a strange omission in this "Index to the authors of the *Review*," not to make some mention of its originator and efficient editor, whose contributions comprise more than one-fifth of its pages, and have commanded the greatest attention, exerted the widest influence, and rendered the most important service. The prevalent impressions of his intellect and erudition, the soundness and penetration of his judgment, his candour and conscientiousness, have been formed as much perhaps from this *Review*, as from any other source. Most of its readers would say, "*Si quæris monumentum, circumspice.*" To regard him, however, only as he has here made himself known and felt, he might be presumed to have been distinguished chiefly as an able and accomplished theologian, remarkable for his skill in didactic and polemic discussions. But this is a very subordinate aspect of his true character and real power. Since 1835 Dr. Hodge has been eminent in various departments of authorship. His "Constitutional History of the Presbyterian Church in the United States," which aims to exhibit its true character in regard to the principles on which it was founded, both as to doctrine and order, was a work, in the estimation of many, much to be desired. In yielding to the request of some of our most judicious clergymen and laymen that he would prepare it, he rendered a most valuable service to the church, as well as added to his own reputation. He also published, at the solicitation of the American Sunday-School Union, "The Way of Life," in which he has given a clear, simple, and very able exhibition of the evidences and teachings of the Scriptures as the word of God. This work contains one of the most satisfactory doctrinal and practical expositions of the gospel plan of salvation in our language; and has rendered valuable service to inquirers after the way of life, having gone through many editions in this country and Great Britain. The works, however, which first gave him general reputation as an author, were his expositions of the books of the New Testament. In 1835 he published his Commentary on the Epistle to the Romans, which, from the state of the church, and the character of the work, combining, as it did, rare exegetical tact, with fine analytical power, interpreting the principles and reasonings, as well as the words and phrases of the sacred writers, attracted unusual attention, not only in this country but also abroad. Subsequently he was induced to unite with Dr. J. A. Alexander in preparing a series of notes on all the books of the New Testament; he agreeing to write those on the doctrinal and epistolary parts, and Dr. Alexander those on the historical and prophetical books. Dr. Hodge had completed his part on First and Second Corinthians and Ephesians, when Dr. Alexander's unexpected decease put an end to the undertaking. As exegetical, doctrinal, and practical expositions, they have been held in the highest estimation by general and professional students of the sacred Scriptures.

But during these labours through the press, his real life-work and power have been in far higher and better relations and efforts. Dr. Hodge has been for full half a century employed in training successive generations of young men for the sacred ministry—devoting his time and energies, with ever accumulating experience and resource, to the most difficult and responsible office in which a Christian minister can be engaged. He has become the Theological Professor, by pre-eminence, of our Church; known in this and other lands as the erudite and devout guide and counsellor of our rising ministry. No other man has held such a place and influence in these relations. Those only whose privilege it has been to listen to his instructions and counsels, to be led by him in the devotions of the class-room and the oratory, to hear him in the Sunday conference, to feel the power of his gentle and generous sympathy in perplexity and sorrow, can know comparatively anything of the best elements of his character. But such, if no others, will be able, as they look back over the critical and interesting history of the last forty years of our church, to form some adequate estimate of the value of having one, so qualified and trained, providentially placed in the position, which he has held as the founder and editor of this *Review*.

The following is the list contributed by him to this series:

1829. Introductory Lecture—Public Education—Reply to Dr. Moses Stuart's Examination of the Review of the American Education Society.

1830. Reply to Dr. Moses Stuart's Postscript to his Letter to the Editors of the *Biblical Repertory*—Regeneration and the Manner of its Occurrence—Review of an Article in *The Christian Spectator* on Imputation.

1831. Sunday Mails—Sprague's Lectures to Young People—Doctrine of Imputation—Remarks on Dr. Cox's Communication.

1832. Hengstenberg on Daniel—The New Divinity Tried.

1833. Suggestions to Theological Students—Stuart on the Romans.

1834. Lachmann's New Testament—The Act and Testimony.

1835. The Act and Testimony—Barnes on the Epistle to the Romans—The General Assembly—Narrative of Reed and Matheson.

1836. Rückert's Commentary on Romans—Slavery—The General Assembly.

1837. Voluntary Societies and Ecclesiastical Organizations—Bloomfield's Greek Testament—General Assembly.

1838. Oxford Tracts—State of the Church—The General Assembly—West India Emancipation.

1839. Clapp's Defence of the Doctrines of the New England Churches—General Assembly—Dr. Dana's Letters—Testimonies on the Doctrine of Imputation.

1840. Latest Forms of Infidelity—Presbyterianism in Virginia—Dr. Hill's American Presbyterianism—New Jersey

27

College and President Davies—The General Assembly—Discourse on Religion by Mr. Coit.

1841.—Bishop Doane and the Oxford Tracts (with J. A. A.)

1842. The Theological Opinions of President Davies—Milman's History of Christianity—The General Assembly—Rule of Faith.

1843. Rights of Ruling Elders—The General Assembly.

1844. General Assembly of the Church of Scotland (with J. A. A.)—Claims of the Free Church of Scotland—The General Assembly—Abolitionism.

1845. Beman on the Atonement—Thornwell on the Apocrypha—Schaff's Protestantism—The General Assembly.

1846. Theories of the Church—Is the Church of Rome a part of the Visible Church?—General Assembly—Neill's Lectures on Biblical History—Religious State of Germany—The late Dr. John Breckinridge—Life and Writings of Dr. Richards.

1847. Pinney's Lectures on Theology—Support of the Clergy—General Assembly (with Dr. Hope)—Bushnell on Christian Nurture.

1848. Doctrine of the Reformed Church—General Assembly—Dr. Spring on the Power of the Pulpit (with J. A. A.)

1849. American Board, Special Report of the Prudential Committee—Bushnell's Discourses—The General Assembly—Emancipation.

1850. Memoir of Walter M. Lowrie—The General Assembly—Prof. Park's Sermon.

1851. Civil Government—Remarks on the *Princeton Review*—The General Assembly—Prof. Park and the *Princeton Review*.

1852. The General Assembly.

1853. Idea of the Church—The General Assembly—Visibility of the Church.

1854. Beecher's Great Conflict—Dr. Schaff's Apostolic Church—The Church of England and Presbyterian Orders—The Education Question—The General Assembly.

1855. Memoir of Dr. Archibald Alexander—Bishop McIlvaine on the Church—Presbyterian Liturgies—The General Assembly.

1856. The *Church Review* on the Permanency of the Apostolic Office—The *Princeton Review* and Cousin's Philosophy—The General Assembly of 1856—The Church, its Perpetuity.

1857. Free Agency—The General Assembly—The American Bible Society and its New Standard—Inspiration.

1858. The Church—Membership of Infants—The General Assembly—Adoption of the Confession of Faith—The Revised Book of Discipline.

1859. The Unity of Mankind—Demission of the Ministry—The General Assembly—Sunday Laws.

1860. What is Christianity?—The First and Second Adam—The General Assembly—Presbyterianism.

1861. The State of the Country—The Church and the Country—The General Assembly.

1862. Are there too many Ministers?—England and America—Diversity of Species in the Human Race—The General Assembly.

1863. The War—The General Assembly—Relation of the Church and the State.

1864. Can God be known?—The General Assembly.

1865. Nature of Man—Principles of Church Union, and the Re-union of Old and New School Presbyterians—President Lincoln—The General Assembly—The *Princeton Review* and the State of the Country and the Church.

1866. Sustentation Fund—Bushnell on Vicarious Sacrifice—The General Assembly.

1867. The General Assembly.

1868. Presbyterian Re-union—The Protest and Answer.

HODGE, ARCHIBALD ALEXANDER, the eldest son of Dr. Charles Hodge, was born at Princeton, N. J. in July 1823; graduated at the College of New Jersey in 1843; and after acting one year as Tutor, he entered the Princeton Theological Seminary. On leaving the Seminary he was ordained as a missionary, sailed for India in August 1847, and was stationed at Allahabad two years, but owing to the ill-health of his wife he returned in May 1850, and in 1851 accepted the charge of the church of Lower West Nottingham, Maryland; and in the fall of 1855 resigned this charge for that of Fredericksburg, Va. While here he composed his "Outlines of Theology," which were published in 1860; but upon the breaking out of the war in 1861, he removed to the north, and became the pastor of the church at Wilkesbarre, Pa. In May 1862 he was elected by the General Assembly to the Chair of Didactic, Historical, and Polemic Theology in the Western Theological Seminary, and he removed to Allegheny City in the fall. In 1867 he published his work on "The Atonement," and in 1869 his "Commentary on the Confession of Faith." In 1862 the College of New Jersey conferred upon him the degree of D. D. He contributed in

1851. The Vedantists of Young Bengal.

HOOKER, EDWARD WILLIAM, was born at Goshen, Connecticut, on the 24th of November, 1794. He was the son of Asahel ·Hooker, a descendant in the eighth generation of Thomas Hooker of Hartford, one of the Puritan Fathers. His mother was Phœbe [Edwards] Hooker, a granddaughter of President Jonathan Edwards, of the College of New Jersey. Mr. Hooker was graduated at Middlebury College, Vermont, in 1814, and completed his course in theology at Andover Theological Seminary in 1817, and was licensed to preach the gospel by the Presbytery of Londonderry. On August 15, 1821, he was ordained and installed pastor of the Green's Farm church, Fairfield, Connecticut, and continued in this charge till January 27, 1829, when he entered the service of the American Temperance Society, becoming, with Dr. Nathaniel Hewit, Associate General Agent, and editor of a weekly paper published by that society. At the close of the year he again resumed ministerial labour, preaching on temporary engagements with several churches, till the 22d of February, 1832, when he was installed pastor of the church in Bennington, Vermont. In this charge he continued twelve years, when he accepted the Chair of Sacred Rhetoric in the Theological Institute of Connecticut, into which he was inducted on the 25th of August, 1844. After some years he again resumed ministerial work, and became pastor of the church in South (formerly East) Windsor; a church of which his great-great-grandfather, the Rev. Timothy Edwards, had been the first pastor. This charge he resigned for one at Fairhaven, Vermont into which he was installed August 20, 1856, and concluded his labours as pastor in November 1862, but continuing to preach as opportunity offers till the present time, 1870, residing at Newburyport, Massachusetts. In 1840, the degree of D. D. was conferred upon him by Williams College, Massachusetts.

His labours as a preacher were small in comparison with what he accomplished as an author, but to enumerate even the titles of his works would take more space than we can here devote to them. The American Tract Society, the Massachusetts Sunday-school Society, the Presbyterian Board of Publication, the Congregational Board of Publication, publish volumes or tracts written by him. There are few quarterlies or monthlies of much repute, that were published during his long and active life, that did not receive some contributions from his pen. He was often called to preach upon particular occasions, and his sermons and addresses, if collected, would make several volumes; among them are six addresses on Music, which embody the history of sacred and secular music in this country, one of which was delivered before the American Musical Convention in New York in 1845. In the *Temperance Annual*, published in New York in 1849, there is a Sketch of the Life and Services of Nathaniel Hewit by him. His only contribution to this periodical was made in

1854. Review of the Life and Labours of St. Augustine.

HOPE, MATTHEW BOYD, was born in Mifflin county, Pennsylvania, on the 31st of July, 1812. He entered Jefferson College in the year 1825, and graduated in 1830, when he was only seventeen years of age. He then studied theology at the Seminary at Princeton till 1832, and having concluded to go out as a missionary to India, studied medicine at the University of Pennsylvania in the two following years, and was licensed and ordained as a missionary by the Presbytery of Huntingdon in 1835. He received an appointment from the American Board of Commissioners for Foreign Missions, and laboured two years at Singapore, an island off the northern extremity of the Malay peninsula, where he was sun-stroke, and on partial recovery was recommended by his physicians to return to his native land. The homeward voyage was beneficial to him, and he was able in a short time to act as agent for the Colonization Society, and in 1839 he was appointed Financial Secretary to the Presbyterian Board of Education, and in 1842 Corresponding Secretary. In this office he continued till 1846, but in 1845 was elected to the professorship of Belles Lettres and Political Economy in the College of New Jersey, a relation which he held till his death. From the time of his return from India he was perpetually suffering from neuralgia, a violent pain passing from one member of the body to another, till finally it reached his heart; and after half an hour of suffering, on the morning of the 17th of December, 1859, its pulsation ceased, before his physician could reach him. His funeral sermon was preached by President Maclean; and shortly after, a Memorial Discourse, by Dr. Atwater, which was published in the *Nassau Literary Magazine*. During his funeral all the places of business in Princeton were closed, as a mark of respect.

Dr. Hope was a man of great simplicity of manner, direct yet full of genial kindness, and which in him was not manner alone, but the native offspring of an earnest life—a life too full of solemn purpose, and too deeply impressed with a conviction of its own brevity to spend a moment upon the art of appearances. A broken constitution hindered him from executing much which otherwise he would have done, but notwithstanding such a serious obstacle, the amount of work which he went through would have been felt to be laborious by a healthy man. It was often subject of wonder to his friends, how with his continual ailments he succeeded in thinking with so much power and effect. Often in the midst of preaching or lecturing he would be seen to press his hand to his forehead and pause, while the fixedness of his features evinced the struggle with pain. A few seconds, and that expression would melt away, and the current of his argument return to its channel. For many years his life was the contest of a strong and enterprising intellect to effect its purposes through, and often in spite of, a frail and hopelessly shattered body.

In addition to the toils of an exciting department, Dr. Hope frequently preached in the adjoining cities, as well as in his place in chapel, and spent much time and exhausting labour for the financial interests of the College. Several of his later years were concerned with carrying out that endowment scheme, whereby a large number of scholarships were founded for the aid of indigent students. And while the enlargement of the plan of instruction in Princeton was largely due to Dr. Maclean, it was Dr. Hope who initiated those efforts for securing the means of carrying it out, which have since his death exceeded even the bounds of his expectation.

But the chief element of his character, and the one which can never be separated from recollections of him, was his deep and active piety. Of this none who ever came in contact with him could fail to be aware. At the daily college prayer-meetings he was always in his place, unless detained by some unavoidable cause. And although for the last year of his life disabled from preaching, he never ceased to take his turn in conducting and addressing that meeting. The fervor of those addresses will not be forgotten by any who ever listened to them. The very pain with which they were frequently delivered went to enhance their earnestness and solemnity.

Although not a brilliant man, nor of extraordinary scholarship, yet as a faithful and effective worker, and a benign Christian power, Princeton has never enjoyed the labours of a superior to Dr. Hope.

His name appears upon the title-page as publisher of this *Review* from 1840 to 1848, and he continued to take charge of its financial matters for Dr. Hodge till his visit to Europe in 1856. The following articles were written by him.

1833. Foreign Missions.
1834. Mr. Irving and the Modern Prophetic School.
1839. Malcolm's Travels in South-Eastern Asia.
1840. Historical Composition.

1841. Relation between the Scriptures and Geology—General Assembly of 1841.

1843. Education in Bengal.

1844. Religious Melancholy.

1849. Robert Burns, as a Poet and as a Man—Prison Discipline.

1850. Prof. Bachman on the Unity of the Human Race—Harrison on the English Language—Prof. Agazziz's New Hypothesis.

1852. Apologetics.

HOPKINS, ERASTUS, was born at Hadley, Massachusetts, in 1810; received his classical education at Dartmouth College; studied theology at Andover and Princeton Seminaries; became pastor of the Beech Island church, near Charleston, S. C., three years; removed to Troy, N. Y., where he was pastor of the Second Church from 1838 to 1842; was for seven years President of the Connecticut River Railroad Company, and has represented the town of Northampton in the Massachusetts Legislature several years. In 1840, while in Troy, he published "The Family a Religious Institution," and is the author of a great number of pamphlets and periodical articles. In 1833 he contributed to this *Review* the article on African Colonization.

HUBBARD, AUSTIN O., was born in Sunderland, Massachusetts, August 9, 1800. In 1804 his parents removed to Stanstead, Canada East, where, at the age of seven years, he was the subject of a remarkable interposition of Divine providence. The settlement was then new, and covered with dense forests, his father was engaged in building, and on one occasion sent him with his hired man to the mill for lumber. On their return he rode on the cart, with a load of some two tons weight. In going down a steep hill he was shaken off, and one of the wheels passed directly over his body. He was badly hurt, but recovered in a few days. He was, however, ever after subject to occasional derangement of the bowels, and after his decease in 1858, a post mortem examination showed a displacement of the colon, which must have been the result of the accident.

His early opportunities of education were limited to the common schools of the new settlement. He was prepared for college at Amherst Academy, Massachusetts; graduated at Yale in 1824; studied theology under the direction of the Baltimore Presbytery in Maryland, and was licensed by them in 1826. After preaching some time, he was ordained as a missionary to labour in Frederick county, Maryland, where he preached two or three years. From 1833 to 1834 he was engaged as a student and an assistant teacher in Princeton Seminary. In 1833 he married Mary A. Graydon, daughter of William Graydon, Esq., of Harrisburgh, Pennsylvania, who died in 1834. After her death he came to Stanstead, and remained there with his brother until 1835, supplying the Congregational church during the time. He afterwards laboured three years as a missionary in Melbourne, C. E., during which time he married his second wife, Julia A. Hayes, daughter of the Rev. Joel Hayes, of South Hadley, Massachusetts. ¡In 1841 he was installed as pastor of the church in Hardwick, Vermont, where he remained as pastor about three years, and resided there about two years afterwards; in 1845 he took charge of a church in Barnet, Vermont, where he remained as a preacher until 1851. He continued to supply neighbouring churches for some two or three years, and removed to Craftsbury, Vermont, in 1854, and supplied the church in that place until the death of his wife in 1857, when from this afflictive bereavement and his constitutional infirmities he became hopelessly insane, and was taken to the Asylum in Brattleboro', Vermont, where he died in August 1858. His insanity took the form of despondency. He dwelt much upon his unfaithfulness; feared that he had not been sufficiently earnest in the cause of his Divine Master, but all who knew him felt assured that all was well with him. His remains were brought to Stanstead and interred in the family burying-ground.

The late Mr. Nevins, of Baltimore, preached his ordination sermon at Taneytown, Maryland, and the Rev. President Wheeler, of Burlington College, preached his installation sermon at Hardwick, Vermont. He was the author of a small English Grammar and five discourses on the Sabbath. He reviewed in

1834. Perkins on Ability.

INGLIS, DAVID, is the son of the late Rev. David Inglis, of Greenlaw, Berwickshire, Scotland. He is a graduate of the University of Edinburgh, where he also received his theological education. He was licensed to preach in 1845, and immediately afterwards came to this country. After itinerating some time in Michigan and Illinois, he returned to New York and supplied the Mount Washington church about six months, then settled as pastor of the church at Bedford, Westchester county, N. Y. Here he continued till 1852, when he visited some of his relatives in Canada, and was induced to accept the pastorate of the St. Gabriel street church in Montreal; and in 1855 resigned that charge for the McNab street Presbyterian church in Hamilton, where he has remained till the present time.

While in the United States he was a diligent contributor to its periodical literature, and wrote a series of biographical and historical sketches of the Scottish Church for the *New York Observer.* He is the author of "Crown Jewels," published by the Nelsons of Edinburgh, and in 1864 he received a prize from the American Tract Society for the tract entitled "The Soldier's Best Friend." He contributed to this *Review* in

1852. The Early History of Christianity in the British Isles.

JACOBUS, MELANCTHON WILLIAMS, was born September 19, 1816, at Newark, N. J. He entered Princeton College (Sophomore Class) in his 15th year, and was graduated in his 18th year with the first honours of the College. After an interval of a year at home, he entered the Theological Seminary at Princeton in 1835, and having completed his course, he was invited to remain as an assistant to Prof. J. Addison Alexander, in the Hebrew department. He acted in this capacity during an academic year. When the year was drawing to a close, he received a unanimous and urgent call from the First Presbyterian Church of Brooklyn to become its pastor. The church was involved in the struggle which ensued upon the rupture in 1838 in the General Assembly, and it fell to his charge to build it up amidst very peculiar difficulties. He was installed pastor in the fall of 1839. In January 1840 he was married to the eldest daughter of Samuel Hayes, M. D., of Newark, N. J. He laboured successfully in Brooklyn during eleven years, in which time the church was well established as one of the most flourishing churches of the Presbytery. A beautiful and expensive edifice was erected on Fulton street, which was afterwards vacated for a more quiet and central part of the city; and a superior sanctuary of stone was built on the corner of Clinton and Remsen streets, which is still occupied by the congregation of that church.

In the fall of 1850, the health of the pastor broke down under the severe duties of the charge; and the church made liberal provision for releasing him, and supplying his pulpit, for a year's absence in foreign travel. He went with his wife through Europe, into Egypt and Palestine and Syria to Damascus, returning by Constantinople and Greece, and arrived at home in September 1851, after a year's journeying among classic and Bible lands, to the great advantage of his health. During his absence, the General Assembly of the Presbyterian Church, at their session in May 1851, elected him as "Professor of Oriental and Biblical Literature" in the Theological Seminary at Allegheny, Pa. He was now thirty-six years of age. Finding his health inadequate for the pulpit and pastoral work, and feeling himself called of God to enter upon the new field, in an interior climate, with furniture such as he was known to possess for the professorship, he entered upon his duties in Allegheny in the opening of the year 1852. The Presbytery of New York, when called upon to dissolve the pastoral relation, made most complimentary notice of his laborious and successful work in Brooklyn, and few will forget the touching speech of the venerable Dr. Spring in making the motion.

Already in Brooklyn in 1848, during the toil of his pastorate, he had prepared and published his first volume of "Notes on the New Testament," entitled "Matthew, with the Harmony." This volume was received with so much public favour, and with the Catechetical Question Book accompanying, supplied so important a need, that, in the Professor's chair, with larger and richer materials from Bible lands, where he had made personal observation with advantage, he issued a second volume, "Mark and Luke," in May 1853.

In 1856 he published a very valuable Commentary on John; and this was followed in 1859 with a still more elaborate Commentary on the Acts of the Apostles. In 1862 the Notes on the Gospels were republished in Edinburgh, Scotland, by Messrs. Oliphant & Son. Their very extensive circulation in this country, and the great favour with which they were received in the churches, warranted the British publishers in this undertaking.

In 1864-5, the two volumes on Genesis were issued from the press of the American publishers, the Messrs. Carter of New York. They evince great labour and research, and in a brief space furnish a mass of material. And his special fitness for this latest work, where so many great questions were to be grappled, at the threshold of Divine Revelation, was already indicated by his review of "Bush on Genesis" in the *Princeton Review*, in 1839.

In 1852 the degree of D. D. was conferred upon him by Jefferson College, and he was honoured with the degree of LL.D. by the College of New Jersey in 1867. He was Moderator of the General Assembly in 1869.

He is the author of " Letters to Governor Bigler (of Pennsylvania) on the Common School System" in controversy with
Bishop O'Connor of the Roman Catholic Diocese of Pittsburgh ;
also of a tract on "Universal Salvation," published by the
Presbyterian Board of Publication in Philadelphia.

In February 1858, Dr. Jacobus was called to the pastorate
of the Central Presbyterian church of Pittsburgh, (formerly
the Fifth Presbyterian church, which had been dissolved,) and,
beginning with a membership of nineteen persons, he has
gathered around him, during ten years, a flourishing and well-
established church, which he still continues to serve, in addition to the duties of his Professorship.

The following articles are from his pen :

1839. Bush on Genesis.

1845. Concordances.

JONES, JOEL, was of Puritan ancestry, being a lineal
descendant of Col. John Jones, one of the judges who signed
the death-warrant of Charles I., and who married one of the
sisters of Oliver Cromwell. He was born at Coventry, Connecticut, on the 26th of October, 1795. His father, Amasa
Jones, was largely engaged in mercantile business and in farming, and intended his son to follow the same pursuits, but he
early manifested a great love of learning, and with the advice
of his mother, who was a daughter of the Rev. Dr. Joseph
Huntington, it was concluded to give him a collegiate education. In the year 1813 he was admitted to the Freshman
Class in Yale College, and graduated in 1817, receiving the
second honours of the class and the Berkleian prize. He then
pursued the study of the law, first with Judge Bristol of New
Haven, and subsequently at Litchfield, where Judges Reeves
and Gould were Professors. He was admitted to practice in
Luzerne county, Pennsylvania, and settled at Easton. He
rapidly became known as a very learned man in his profession, and when, in 1830, a Commission was appointed to revise
the Civil Code of the State of Pennsylvania, he was designated
one of the Commissioners, in conjunction with the late Thomas
I. Wharton and the elder Rawle. In 1835, he accepted a
nomination from Governor Wolf to an Associate Judgeship on
the Bench of the District Court for the City and County of
Philadelphia. On the removal of Judge Pettit to another position, Judge Jones became the President Judge of the Court,
and continued to be so until the year 1848, when he was
elected to the Presidency of Girard College. He occupied the
latter post nearly two years, and shortly after vacating it, was

elected to the Mayoralty of the City of Philadelphia. Upon the expiration of his term of office, he returned to the practice of the law; in which he continued to the time of his death, which occurred on the 3d of February, 1860, in the full assurance of a glorious immortality.

His professional acquirements were of a diversified and extensive range, including not only the English Common Law, but the Civil Law of Rome and the modern European systems. The compilations of Justinian were no less familiar to him as subjects of study, than the Commentaries of Coke. Indeed, from his taste for antiquities and for comparative jurisprudence, he was not only peculiarly qualified, but intellectually inclined to explore the doctrines of the law to their historical sources, and gather around them, in tracing their development, all the accessories which history and learning could supply. This was to him a loving labour, for he regarded the law as a lofty science, and its practice as the application of ethical principles by a trained logic. No client could ever leave his office, and no colleague part from a consultation with him, without having his idea of a true lawyer elevated and expanded.

His reports as a Commissioner to revise the Civil Code of the State, exhibit his accurate habits of thought and expression; his "Manual of Pennsylvania Land Law" is a model of a condensed and perspicuous law-book. But the acquirements of Judge Jones extended beyond even the widest range of professional attainment. He was, from his youth upward, a scholar and a thinker, and there was scarcely a department of severe knowledge which he had not penetrated. His acquisitions as a linguist have been seldom equalled; with him, the study of a language was only subordinate to the conquest of its literature. It was not the language, but its contents, that he sought. As a classical scholar he was full and accurate. Latin had for him long ceased to be a dead language, and his thrice bound Greek Testament, with its well-worn leaves and copious pencilling on the margin, was his constant companion, even in the briefest intervals of professional business. As an accomplished Hebraist his reputation has extended abroad. He had pushed his studies with success into the Oriental tongues, and spoke fluently most of the modern languages of Europe. These studies were the discipline and appliances by which he qualified himself to grapple with difficult and lofty themes. Theology he esteemed as the sum of all science; biblical studies were the delight and solace of his life; his knowledge of biblical criticism, antiquities, and interpretation, was profound.. His library contained an unusually rich collection of the writings of the Christian Fathers, and with these, as with all the other books in his valuable collection, he had familiarized himself. '

As a Judge, his recorded opinions attest his judicial ability, and the uniform courtesy of his judicial demeanor will live among the traditions of the bar.

In the various ecclesiastical Boards, of which he was an active and punctual member, his literary and legal opinions, always freely bestowed, were invaluable. In the church, of which for several years he was a ruling elder, his characteristics were fidelity, humility, conscientiousness, an edifying fervor and unction, and a blameless and holy life. The prayer-circle found him always at his post; and while leading its devotions, with his rich scriptural phraseology, drawn from a heart imbued with the mind of the Spirit, and alike removed from the language of literature or conversation, the scholar and the lawyer for the time so wholly disappeared in the humble Christian, that the lowliest worshipper found himself in sympathy.

Judge Jones was a member of the Historical Society of Pennsylvania, and of the American Philosophical Society. In the year 1848 the degree of LL.D. was conferred upon him by the College of New Jersey. He was the author of a Treatise on the Land Titles of Pennsylvania. Besides a number of public-spirited articles in the daily press which were never attributed to him, Judge Jones contributed largely to the *Theological and Literary Journal*, to the Baltimore *Literary and Religious Magazine*, and the *Spirit of the Nineteenth Century*; also to *The Jewish Chronicle*.

.The "Story of Joseph; or, Patriarchal Age," with copious and valuable notes, he published for the orphans of Girard College. He translated from the French, "Outlines of a History of the Court of Rome and of the Temporal Power of the Popes, with original Notes." He also originated a work, to which he gave the title of "*Literalist*," now in five octavo volumes, which is a republication of works on prophecy, written in England, which he imported, and with some revision caused to be published in Philadelphia. The essays in the end of the fifth volume, signed "Philo Basilicus," were the production of his pen; also some of the notes on Sirr's "First Resurrection." .This work he had the satisfaction of knowing was the means of awakening the minds of Christians to what he considered sound views of prophecy.

A little treatise on "The knowledge of one another in the

future State," was also given to the press; but the best labours
of his life he considered as contained in his "Notes on Scripture," which in his last illness he directed to be published, and
which was edited by his widow, and published by Alfred Martien of Philadelphia, in 1860. A few years afterwards, by
request, the addition of "Jesus and the Coming Glory" was
made to the title. It was his purpose to take up one or more
of the Epistles of Paul, and from them develope his view of the
person of our glorious Lord, considered in the threefold character of the Son of God, or Second Person of the Trinity, the
Son of Man, his Adamic character, and as the Christ or Head
of the redeemed Church, or that glorious kingdom of kings and
priests which our Lord will associate with himself in the government of the Universe; but the answer to his oft-repeated
prayer, "Show me thy glory," arrested his pen. His contributions to the *Princeton Review* were

1836. On the Perpetuity of the Church.
1837. On Protestantism—Civil and Religious Liberty.

JONES, JOSEPH HUNTINGTON, brother of the preceding, was born in Coventry, Connecticut, August 24, 1797.
His great thirst for knowledge and aspirations for some pursuit
more intellectual than that of a farmer or a merchant early
determined him to begin a course of liberal study. He graduated at Harvard University in 1817, with George Bancroft,
Caleb Cushing, Asa Cummings, Stephen H. Tyng, Alva Woods,
and other men of mark.

While at the University he was at one time in imminent
danger of being led astray by the erroneous teachings of the
Unitarian leaders of that day. But he had a praying mother
—a woman of great force of character, who wielded a vigorous
pen, and whose thorough acquaintance with the doctrines of
the Bible qualified her to warn and instruct, and to save her
son from the snare. To that godly mother were the members
of this family chiefly indebted for the honour and usefulness
which they attained. One, who knew them well, wrote: "It
was especially upon the minds and hearts of her children that
she left the deepest impression of her character. They re-
sembled her physically. Her ways of thinking, her very tones
of voice they caught. Her prudent caution, her natural reserve, her adherence to principles were theirs. And every
one of them was brought into the church, and the youngest
since her happy death; and most of them are filling and
adorning positions of distinguished usefulness. One is an
eminent jurist, worthy of the place once occupied by a Mar-

shall. One is a clergyman known in all the church for his abilities and amiable virtues. One was the lovely wife of a minister whose sun went down before it reached its noontide. One died in hope, the wife of an army-surgeon, and was buried by the waves of the Mississippi. And two others, in the spheres in which they move, are serving their generation according to the will of God. That mother is gone; but her influence lives in her children, and will be transmitted to her children's children to the remotest times. Such a life as she led is immortal."

After taking his first degree Mr. Jones was for a time employed as Tutor in Bowdoin College, Maine. Having been brought by divine grace to a saving knowledge of Christ, he turned his thoughts to the sacred ministry; and after much prayer, not without many doubts and perplexities, he was forced to the conclusion that "necessity was laid upon him" to preach the gospel. He completed his course of study in divinity at the Princeton Theological Seminary, where he spent one year, 1823–4. He was licensed as a probationer, September 19, 1822, at Braintrim, Bradford co., Pa., by the Presbytery of Susquehanna; and was, by the same Presbytery, ordained as an Evangelist, April 29, 1824, at Wilkesbarre, Luzerne co., Pa. On the 1st of June, 1824, he began his labours in the Presbyterian church at Woodbury, New Jersey, and was shortly installed as pastor, having been received into the Presbytery of Philadelphia, June 8, 1824, by certificate from the Presbytery of Susquehanna. That church was, at this time, almost extinct, and steps were about to be taken to dissolve it. Mr. Jones entered on his duties with great zeal and activity, and "threw his whole soul into the work of the Lord." By the raciness and fervour of his preaching, his constant attention to pastoral visiting, and his personal efforts for the salvation of sinners, new life was infused into the church, the moral aspect of the town was changed, and during the short year of his ministrations, which was in every good sense a year of revival, thirty-three were added to the roll of communicants—thirty-one on confession, of whom eleven were baptized. Within the same period fourteen infants were baptized. At the same time he supplied the feeble church of Blackwoodtown, which shared the blessing enjoyed by that of Woodbury. Thus he was the instrument of saving one church, and probably two churches, from extinction.

Before the expiration of a year he was called to the pastorate of the Presbyterian church at New Brunswick, New Jersey, of which he announced his acceptance, April 21, 1825.

Having been received from the Presbytery of Philadelphia by the Presbytery of New Brunswick, April 26, 1825, he was duly installed pastor on the second Wednesday of July following. Here he remained thirteen years, preaching " in season, out of season," and " from house to house," proving himself to be " a workman that needed not to be ashamed." His ministry was honoured of God by at least three seasons of religious awakening, namely, in 1832, 1833, and 1837, the last of the three being one of the most remarkable revivals known in this country during the present century. Of the fruits of that work of grace about one hundred and fifty persons were enrolled as communicants. The results of his labours are thus briefly but significantly summed up.

Three hundred and thirty-eight received on confession, of whom one hundred and seven were baptized;—on certificate, one hundred and sixty-five were received, and three hundred and thirteen infants were baptized. In February 1837, this congregation entered their new and beautiful house of worship just in time to accommodate the great increase of hearers, and the large accession to the number of communicants.

Having received an urgent invitation from the Sixth Presbyterian church in Philadelphia, his pastoral relation with the church at New Brunswick was dissolved, April 24, 1838, and upon his reception by the Presbytery of Philadelphia he was shortly after installed pastor of the Sixth Church. In this field of labour he continued twenty-three years. Beginning with a church reduced so low that a resuscitation was deemed well nigh impossible, and struggling with difficulties that would have discouraged ordinary men, a manifest blessing crowned his efforts. He gathered in three hundred and seventy-seven on confession, of whom seventy-nine were baptized, and two hundred and seventy-two by certificate, and by baptism brought into the visible fold three hundred and sixty-four infants. Wherever he went, the infants were baptized, the lambs of the flock were cared for in the family and in the Sabbath-school, the sick and bereaved were visited and comforted, the poor found in him a helper, the inquiring a safe guide, and those who were sunk in deep waters the needed sympathy and aid. Having had a deep experience in the varied trials of the Christian life, and in conflicts with the powers of darkness, in addition to a familiar practical acquaintance with the word of God, he was well fitted to be a Christian teacher. Always in delicate health, and often the subject of painful religious depression, produced by physical causes, he was never idle, but toiled on through darkness and light, a faithful steward in his Lord's service. He was a model-pastor.

On the 28th of May, 1861, that he might be able to give his whole time to the Secretaryship of the Committee on the Fund for Disabled Ministers, &c., his pastoral relation to the Sixth Presbyterian Church of Philadelphia was dissolved. For seven years he had already served the church in this cause without compensation; and now for five years more the Fund was to be saved from charge by the private bounty of several who were anxious to see this work advanced. In the Report for 1867, Dr. Jones writes: "The cause having been sustained for fifteen years from its inception, with little expense to the church, it was obviously proper that, like other institutions, this, when able, should support itself. During the past year, therefore, the sum which has been contributed annually by a few friends to sustain the Secretary has been drawn from the treasury. And although every article of subsistence has become doubly expensive since this agency began, yet the stipend, which was inadequate at first, has not been increased. In the meanwhile, all the labour of visiting the churches, or making collections, diffusing information, and of managing this whole concern, has been performed in the least expensive manner, without any charge for office-rent or for assistance rendered by others. Letters in answer to many inquiries of interested persons, official communications with Presbyteries, appeals to neglectful churches, solicitations of donations and bequests, words of sympathy in cases of special affliction, and expressions of thanks for marked favours done to the cause, have called for no little exercise of the mind and of the pen. Few have an adequate conception of the amount of effort demanded in meeting the claims of such an agency on the Secretary."

This last work of Dr. Jones' life may be regarded as in some respects his noblest and best. For what he achieved in this cause, he deserves the lasting gratitude of the church, and in the eternal world many "will rise up and call him blessed." He died suddenly, as it were with the harness on, December 22, 1868.

He was married in 1825 to Miss Anna Maria Howell. In 1843 he received the honorary degree of Doctor in Divinity from Lafayette College.

Of his principal work, "The effects of Physical Causes on Christian Experience," Dr. J. W. Alexander wrote: It is "a valuable and entertaining book."* Dr. Jones also published a

---

* It was reviewed by Dr. W. J. R. Taylor in the volume for 1860.

Memoir of the Rev. Ashbel Green, D. D., a History of the Revival at New Brunswick in 1837, and several Sermons. His only article to the *Repertory* was in
1839. The Present Distress.

JUNKIN, GEORGE, was born in a stone farm-house which is still standing near to the present town of Kingston, in Cumberland county, Pa., on the 1st of November, 1790. His father, Joseph Junkin, was born near the same place in 1750, and his mother, Eleanor Cochran, was a native of Franklin county. Both branches of Dr. Junkin's ancestry were attached to the covenanting section of the Scottish Church; and Dr. Junkin's great-grandparents were of those who took refuge in Ireland from the persecution of the Stuarts.

The youth of Dr. Junkin was passed upon his native farm in Cumberland county, but in 1806, the family removed to Mercer county, which was then sparsely settled, and contained the lingering remnants of the Leni Lenappe Indians. In 1809 he entered Jefferson College, Pa., and graduated in 1813. During his college course he attended chiefly upon the ministry of Dr. John McMillan, the apostle of Western Pennsylvania, and sometimes upon that of Dr. Ramsay, of the Associate Church. In an autobiography, begun but not completed, he dates his first religious convictions, and also, he thinks, the renewal of his heart, as early as 1799, in his tenth year. Thenceforward he maintained regular habits of secret devotion. Under Dr. McMillan's preaching his religious impressions were often quickened, but he mentions the ministrations of his pastor at Mercer, the Rev. James Galloway, (subsequently his brother-in-law) as the instrumentality employed by the Spirit of God in giving him such clear and satisfactory views of the plan of salvation, and of his personal acceptance in Christ, as led to a public profession of religion during his college course in 1811. In 1813 he entered upon the study of theology with Dr. Mason, in New York, and was licensed to preach the gospel by the Associate Reformed Presbytery of Monongahela, on the 16th of September, 1816, and preached his first sermon in the court-house at Butler, Pa.

After licensure he spent a few months in missionary labour in the states of New York, Pennsylvania, and Maryland, and was ordained at Gettysburg on the 29th of June, 1818. In the early part of the next year he accepted a call to the united congregations of Milton and Pennel, (McEwenville, Pa.) a charge which he held for eleven years—marked by abundant labours, the influence of which is felt to this day. Here he edited *The Religious Farmer*, an agricultural and religious bi-monthly in 1828-9; and in 1830 he accepted the position of Principal of the Pennsylvania Manual Labour Academy at Germantown, where he toiled assiduously two years; but a charter having been granted to Lafayette College in 1832, he accepted the Presidency, and with the greater part of the scholars removed to Easton, where it was located. During his presidency the college acquired reputation and strength. In 1841 he accepted the Presidency of Miami University, and removed to Oxford, Ohio, but on Dr. Yeoman's resigning the Presidency of Lafayette College in 1844, he was recalled, and resumed the position of President till 1848, when he became President of Washington College, Virginia. Here he remained till 1861, when, on the students raising the rebel flag upon the college, he declared, "I will never hear a recitation, or deliver a lecture under a rebel flag," and left for ever the state of Virginia. He then made his residence in Philadelphia, preaching frequently in churches of all denominations, and reducing to writing the results of studies which he had not leisure to write out in his more active life. In the last seven years of his life his labours were very abundant in the cause of temperance, in opposition to Sabbath desecration, and even in mollifying the public indignation against the rebels who had driven him from their soil. He acted as chaplain to the Widows' Home, and his last sermon was preached in the Magdalen Asylum, about a week before his death. His last illness was short. On Monday morning he became seriously ill, and died on Wednesday, the 20th of May, 1868. The General Assembly was then in session at Albany, and when the news of his death reached them on the 27th, Dr. E. P. Humphrey offered the following resolution, which was adopted unanimously by a rising vote:

"This General Assembly having heard, since our sessions began, that the Rev. Dr. George Junkin has departed from life, record with sadness our sense of loss in his death, and our memory of the long and signal service he has rendered the Church, as a teacher, an author, a defender of the faith, and an exemplary patriot, in times of trial and perplexity, when the foundations of order in the State and in the Church were overturned.

"The Stated Clerk is hereby directed to communicate this minute to the family of the deceased."

Though Dr. Junkin was by birth attached to "the straitest sect of our religion," yet at an early period he evinced great catholicity of sentiment, and through life he never allowed his

denominational preferences to keep him from labouring with
other Christian sects in any good work.   When he applied for
license from the Associate Reformed Presbytery of Monongahela, he avowed his belief in the unrestricted communion of
God's people, and at first they refused to license him, but upon
his asking to be dismissed to another presbytery they rescinded
their refusal.   He was, however, no latitudinarian in opinion,
and professed no tolerance for those in the church who pro-
mulgated opinions and advocated practices not in accordance
with its standards.   He was an active promoter of the measures that led to the disruption of the church in 1838; and the
wisdom of that course now appears evident, for that harmony
of opinion which enables the church again to unite has been
greatly promoted by the observation of thirty years of separate
action by the divided body.   Dr. Junkin for many years maintained a great influence in the church courts, sustained by his
thorough knowledge of every subject on which he attempted
to speak, and the keen logic with which he exposed the fallacies in the arguments of his opponents.   In 1844 he was Moderator of the General Assembly.   In 1833 he received the
degree of D. D. from Jefferson College, and in 1856 that of
LL.D. from Rutgers College, he having that year, by request,
delivered the annual address before the literary societies of
that college.   In 1866 he was appointed Emeritus Professor of
Political Philosophy in Lafayette College, an institution to
whose success he had devoted the best days of his life.

He was very happy in his domestic relations.   In early life
(June 1819) he married Miss Julia Rush Miller, of Philadelphia, with whom he enjoyed thirty-five years of uninterrupted
domestic happiness, and by her had eight children, all of whom
were a comfort to their parents.   His daughter Eleanor became the wife of Prof. Thomas J. Jackson, who afterwards signalized himself as the rebel General "Stonewall" Jackson.
Margaret has acquired an honourable place among American
Female Poets.   Of his sons, John M. is a practising physician
in Easton; Joseph died in his twenty-sixth year; George is a
lawyer in Philadelphia, an elder in the church, and one of the
Trustees of the General Assembly; Ebenezer D. is pastor of
a large congregation in Virginia, and William F. is pastor
of a church in Danville, Kentucky.

Dr. Junkin performed an amazing amount of work in his lifetime.   His preaching record shows that he preached a larger
number of sermons than most pastors do; whilst his toils in
building up and reviving colleges, in laborious agencies, in
ecclesiastical labours in the church-courts, in the professor's

chair, at the editor's desk, and through the press, in his numercus books, sermons, and essays, make us wonder how he could find the time and endure the labour of doing so much.

He published *The Educator*, a periodical, in 1838; "The Vindication, containing a history of the Trial of the Rev. Albert Barnes, by the Second Presbytery and by the Synod of Philadelphia," in 1836; "A Treatise on Justification," in 1839. "The Little Stone and the Great Image; or Lectures on the Prophecies," in 1844; "The Great Apostasy; a Sermon on Romanism," in 1853; "Political Fallacies," 1862; "A Treatise on Sanctification," 1864; "The Tabernacle, or the Gospel according to Moses," 1865. In 1854 he contributed to this journal a review of Dr. Cannon's Pastoral Theology.

KOLLOCK, SHEPARD KOSCIUSKO, was born at Elizabeth, New Jersey, on the 25th of June, 1795. His ancestors were Huguenots, who were driven into Germany, and from thence emigrated to America, and settled in the State of Delaware. In many respects this family were remarkable. The father lived till he was· eighty-eight years of age, and the mother till she was ninety, and they had nine children, to all of whom the kindness of Providence was abundantly manifested. The eldest son was Dr. Henry Kollook, one of the most distinguished preachers of his day ; the youngest, Dr. S. K. Kollook, the subject of this sketch; while five of his daughters were married to men whose names are familiar to most of us, namely, Chief Justice Frederick Nash, of North Carolina, Dr. William A. McDowell, Dr. John McDowell, Dr. Joseph Holdich, and Dr. John Witherspoon.

· His father was an officer in the Revolutionary army, and greatly admiring the personal and military character of the Polish leader Kosciusko, gave his name, together with his own, to his youngest son. In childhood, Shepard was carefully instructed in the truths of Christianity, at home, and prepared for college by Dr. Henry Mills, afterwards a professor in Auburn Seminary, New York. He entered the College of New Jersey in September 1809, and graduated in 1812, with high honours. Up to this time he had lived without Christ, but in 1813 it pleased God to grant a remarkable revival to the church in Elizabethtown, and Mr. Kollock, after two months deep anxiety, found peace in believing. Under the new feelings thus produced he was led to give himself to God in the ministry of the gospel, and commenced the study of divinity under the direction of his brother-in-law, the Rev. John McDowell; and after some further instruction under his brother, Dr. Henry Kollook, he was licensed to preach the gospel by the Presbytery of South Carolina, in June 1814, when he was hardly nineteen years of age.

After preaching three years in South Carolina and Georgia he received a call to the church in Oxford, North Carolina, and was ordained by the Presbytery of Orange on the 2d of May, 1818; but he soon after accepted the appointment of Professor of Rhetoric and Logic in the University of North Carolina, and resigned the charge. In 1825 he became pastor of the church in Norfolk, Virginia, and continued in it about ten years; he then returned to New Jersey, and for three years acted as agent for the Board of Domestic Missions. He then became pastor of the church in Burlington till 1848, when he took charge of the church in Greenwich, till worn out with age and infirmity he resigned and took up his abode in Philadelphia in 1860. As a means of support he was placed by the trustees of the General Assembly upon a foundation created by the late Elias Boudinot for the support of a preacher to the benevolent institutions of the city.

He was a successful minister of the gospel in all his charges; and the writings that he has left behind him display culture of no common order. In justification of this assertion we refer to his " Hints on Preaching without Reading;" to his " Pastoral Reminiscences," which have been translated into French and published in Paris; and to the following articles which he contributed to this journal.

1852. The Bards of the Bible—Eloquence of the French Pulpit.

1853. Character and Writings of Fenelon.

1854. Character and Writings of Pascal—St. Ignatius and the Jesuits.

1856. Character and Writings of Nicole—Sidney Smith as a Minister of Religion.

LEUSDEN, JOHN, was professor of Hebrew in the University of Utrecht from 1649 to 1699. He was one of the best Oriental scholars of his age; and as allusions are frequently made in theological works to the Chaldee Paraphrase and Jewish Targums, a translation was made from his works, to give information in regard to them, for the use of those who have no need to consult the more elaborate works on the subject.

1834. Chaldee Targums.

LEWIS, TAYLER, was born at Northumberland, Saratoga county, New York, in 1802, and graduated at Union College,. Schenectady, in 1820. He studied law in Albany, and practised law in Washington county, New York, though devoting most of those years to classical and biblical study. He was made Professor of the Greek Language and Literature in the University of New York in 1838; and called to the same professorship in Union College in 1849. He received the degree of LL.D. from Union College in 1844.

He has written and published the following books: 1. Nature and Ground of Punishment; 2. Plato contra Atheos, or the Platonic Theology; 3. The Six Days of Creation; 4. The World Problem; 5. The Divine Human in the Scriptures; and edited the books of Genesis and Ecclesiastes for the American edition of Lange's Commentary. Besides these, he is the author of a large number of published discourses, and numerous articles in the *Biblical Repository, Bibliotheca Sacra, Methodist Quarterly, Presbyterian and Theological, Mercersburg, North American*, and other reviews. He contributed to this periodical in

1851. Absurdities of Modern Education.

LOEWENTHAL, ISIDOR, was born of Jewish parents in the city of Posen, in Prussian Poland, in 1826. He was the oldest of a family of eight children. His father, like many other of the same people, was indifferent to matters of religion, but observed, from custom only, the ceremonies and rites of his ancestral faith. His mother was a strict adherent to the traditions of the Rabbis, and at the same time instructed her children carefully in the principles of morality. His parents bestowed upon him an education more liberal than their circumstances and the number of their children might seem to warrant. He was first placed at a Jewish school where he learned the first principles of science, and to repeat prayers which he did not understand. After a few years he left this school, and then attended the *soi-disant* Christian schools and gymnasia of his native city. In these religion was taught like other branches of science, as a thing of which it was necessary for a man to know something in order to get along in the world. The manner in which religion was taught in the gymnasium may be known from the following extract from one of his letters: "We had two recitations (in religion) weekly, which I was not obliged to attend. We studied Greek, but were never told that the Gospels and Epistles of the New Testament were written in that language. We studied Hebrew—read Isaiah—were taught to admire his style, which accord-

ing to our professor's opinion was almost equal to that of
Homer.   I was early enough taught to look upon the greatness of the Jews—Philo, Spinosa, and Mendelssohn; and the
Christians, Voltaire, Rousseau, Hume, and Bolingbroke.   I
was told of the fanatics Milton and Locke, and of the discoveries of Newton, a genius who, notwithstanding his greatness,
could not rid himself from the common superstitions of the
greater part of mankind.   I was taught to give as much credit to the Bible as to the work of some ancient Greek who
wrote on National History."   Such was the character of the
training Mr. Loewenthal received in the professedly Christian
schools and gymnasia of his native city.

After completing the course of study of the gymnasium—
which is about equal to that of our college—he entered a mercantile house in Posen as clerk.   But merchandizing had no
attractions for him—his tastes led him in a different direction.
In the midst of books he was happy, and no where else.   He
had a strong desire to enter one of the German universities,
but what interfered is not known.   While acting as a clerk he
formed associations with educated young men of his own age,
who had imbibed liberal political sentiments.   This was in
1844. and 1845, when there was great political agitation
throughout continental Europe, and which culminated in the
upheaval of 1848.   These young men were in the habit of
meeting secretly for the discussion of political questions, reading
essays, and rehearsing poetry of their own composition, usually
political in its character.   Mr. Loewenthal was so bold as to
publish a piece of poetry in one of the public journals, which
brought him under the displeasure of the authorities.   Learning that he was in danger of arrest, and knowing the fate that
awaited him in such an event, he hastily fled from his native
city, and after many difficulties and narrow escapes reached
Hamburgh, whence after much trouble he succeeded in getting
a passport, and sailed for New York, where he landed in the
latter part of the summer of 1846.   Here he was a stranger,
not possessed of much means, and ignorant of the language of
the people, except what little he had learned on board the
English vessel in which he had crossed the Atlantic.   He endeavoured first to find employment in New York and failed;
then he visited Philadelphia with the same want of success.
He then went into the country and sought employment from
the farmers, but was again disappointed, although he offered
his services to several for whatever they chose to give him.
His funds were now almost exhausted, and he became despondent.   At last he invested the small amount of funds that re-

mained to him in a few notions, and started out as a pedler. His stock was small—as a small basket was by no means filled by it. In this capacity, in November 1846, he came to the house of the late Rev. S. M. Gayley, near Wilmington, Delaware, drenched with rain, and suffering with cold. Mr. Gayley kindly asked him in to warm himself, and gave him his dinner. After disposing of some of his wares to Mrs. Gayley he was about to depart, when Mr. Gayley seeing that he was thinly clad for the season, and the day was cold, asked him to tarry for the night, which invitation he gladly accepted. Upon inquiring as to his home, occupation, &c., Mr. Gayley discovered that he was well acquainted with the ancient classics— also Hebrew—several modern languages, also that he had studied some philosophy and mathematics. His sympathies were drawn to the young stranger, and he persuaded him to remain at his house until he would make an effort to obtain employment for him more congenial to his tastes and wishes than his present one. Mr. Gayley, among others, wrote to George Junkin, D.D., then President of Lafayette College, Easton, Pa., also to his own nephew, the Rev. S. A. Gayley, now of West Nottingham, Maryland, who was then in the Junior class of the same institution; the result of which was the formation of a class in modern languages in the college, and the employment of Mr. Loewenthal as the teacher. His fees were sixty dollars for the session. To save him expense, Mr. S. A. Gayley agreed to take him into his room, share with him his bed, and generally aid him in any way he was able. The Faculty directed him to have his board in the College refectory. The offer thus tendered him he gladly accepted. About the 1st of January, 1847, he started for Easton, where he immediately entered upon the discharge of his new duties. During the six or seven weeks that Mr. Loewenthal resided in Mr. Gayley's family, the latter was totally ignorant of the race and lineage, also of the religious views and feelings of the former. During their conversations, this subject was never touched. It was not until he received a long letter from Mr. Loewenthal in the following July, that he became aware that he was a descendant of Abraham, also that during his residence at his house, "the veil was taken away" from his mind—that he had become convinced of the truth of Christianity, and after much mental conflict and deep sorrow for sin, had found peace in believing on Jesus. In the letter above referred to, he gives the agencies employed by the Holy Spirit to bring about this change. After stating the influences by which he was surrounded in his early life, which we have already given, the condition of the Jewish

30

mind on the subject of religion, and the character of the Christianity with which he had been surrounded—Popery with image worship, and a nominal Protestantism without life, having no power over the heart and conscience, ministered to by a card-playing, ball, and theatre-visiting clergy, he described the darkness of his own mind, when God in his kind providence brought him to Mr. Gayley's house. He says: "It was at your house, by your earnest prayers (at family worship,)— to which I first went, half from curiosity—half from politeness —by your humble supplications, that I was awakened to apprehend my danger, to consider that I had an immortal soul. I began to open the Bible. I was astonished. I waited with eagerness, morning and evening, for the summons to family worship, to hear you pray; I was more and more convinced that I was on the wrong path." During the time he was at Easton, Mr. Gayley corresponded regularly with him, and frequently in his letters gave him religious advice, although ignorant at the time of the peculiar state of Mr. Loewenthal's mind. These kind words happened to be exceedingly appropriate to him, as the letter above referred to shows. In the following fall he made a public profession of his faith, was baptized by his father in the gospel, and received into the membership of the Rockland Presbyterian church, to which Mr. Gayley was then statedly ministering.

Mr. Loewenthal entered the Senior class of Lafayette College the following year, and graduated with his class. After gradnation he acted as Tutor in the college for a short time. In the fall of 1848 he accepted an offer from Dr. Samuel Miller, to take the position of teacher of languages in the collegiate school at Mount Holly, N. J., which he accepted. Here he remained until the fall of 1851, when he entered the Princeton Theological Seminary. Here he took the full course, graduated with honour, and was licensed by the Presbytery of New Brunswick. After completing his theological studies he offered himself to the Board of Foreign Missions of the Presbyterian Church to go to India—to Affghanistan—as a missionary, and was accepted, and sailed for his field of labour about the 1st of August, 1855.

His eminent linguistic acquirements had become known among the colleges of this country prior to his sailing for India; and several of them endeavoured to secure his services —all of which he declined. As a linguist he had few if any equals in this country. In mathematics and philosophy he was equally proficient. But all his talents were unreservedly given to God. The Society of Inquiry of the Seminary selected him as their essayist at the commencement at which his class graduated. His subject was "India as a missionary field," and was afterwards published in the *Princeton Review.*

He reached Peshawur in 1855, and immediately addressed himself to the acquisition of that difficult language, the Pushtoo, which he soon mastered. He had completed a translation of the New Testament into it, and was about commencing that of the Old Testament, for which labour his thorough knowledge of the Hebrew and the oriental languages so admirably fitted him, when he met his death by violence, on the 27th of April, 1864, in the thirty-eighth year of his age. It appears that Mr. Loewenthal suffered much from headache, and was in the habit of going out very early to get the air. On the morning he was shot, he had got up about three o'clock, and went to walk in the verandah, when the watchman, taking him for a thief, as he alleges, discharged his carbine, killing him instantly. He could preach with ease in Pushtoo, Persian, Cashmere, Hindustanee, Arabic, and in fact in all the languages and dialects of the country which he had selected as his field of labour. Perhaps no man in India had so great a knowledge of Asiatic literature, and few were so completely master of the manners and customs of the natives and oriental politics. His intellect was of the highest order, and his method of studying all subjects was exhaustive. His library, the collection of years, was one of the richest in manuscripts and rare books in India. It was astonishing the amount of intellectual labour he accomplished. Three or four hours rest was all that he allowed himself. In addition to his linguistic labours, he contributed many valuable papers to English and American quarterlies, also instructive letters to the missionary periodicals of the church, full of valuable information. He also carried on an extensive correspondence and regular preaching in the Bazaar. In controversy with Mohammedans in these exercises he was a master. The only rest he sought was in passing from one of these labours to another. It was astonishing how his fragile physical organism could stand such unremitting intellectual labour, but although in stature diminutive, almost a dwarf, he had the strength of will and power of endurance of a giant.

In the social circle he was a charming companion. With a perfect command of our language he combined a mind thoroughly cultivated and richly stored with knowledge, fine powers of illustration, a genial humour, and great conversational powers.

We have sketched nothing here but his outer history from the time of his making a public profession of his faith in Christ to the time of his death. But there is another history, the history of his religious experience, that our space forbids us to touch upon. This is more fully given in his correspondence with the late Rev. S. M. Gayley, his father in the gospel, than can be found anywhere else. He unbosomed himself more fully and freely to him on these subjects than to any other human being. He always spent his vacations at Mr. Gayley's house. Their correspondence was frequent and voluminous. The materials found in these letters should not be permitted to lie in oblivion. Some person competent to the task should prepare his life and give it to the church in a permanent form. It would form a volume intensely interesting, suggestive, and instructive.

They both now rest from their labours, and are again united in that presence where there "is fulness of joy," where no longer "through a glass darkly, but face to face they can see their Saviour as he is," and can contemplate without a cloud the glories of his person and the greatness of his work, topics which so often formed the subject of their correspondence and conversation while here upon earth.

The following articles were written by him:

1852. Harrison on the Latin Grammar—The Origin of Language—The Gymnasium in Prussia.

1853. Life and Studies of C. G. Zumpt—Education in the High Schools of Germany.

1854. India: its Past and Future.

1855. Exegesis Heb. vi. 4–8—Christianity in India.

1858. The Present State of India.

LORD, JOHN CHASE, was born at Washington, New Hampshire, on the 9th of August, 1805. His father, the Rev. John Lord, A. M., was the pastor of the Congregational church there, and he received the name of Chase from the family of his mother. He graduated at Hamilton College, New York, in 1825, and immediately after came to Buffalo, where he studied law, and practised successfully about two years. In 1831 he commenced the study of theology at Auburn Seminary, and after completing his course, was about two years settled in Genesee, Livingston county, when, in 1835, he was called to the Central Presbyterian Church, Buffalo, New York, of which he is still the pastor. The edifice in which he now preaches is the second built for him during his ministry, and is said to be the largest audience room of any Protestant church in the United States. About a thousand members have been received into the church during his pastorate.

In 1852 he was Moderator of the General Assembly, when it met at Charleston, South Carolina.

He is the author of "The Popular Objections of Infidelity, stated and answered, in a series of Lectures addressed to the Young Men of Buffalo," 1838; a volume of Lectures delivered before various associations at different times, published in 1851; and a volume of occasional poems, published in 1868; besides a great number of sermons, essays, and contributions to periodicals, he wrote for this *Review*, in 1841, an article on Sanctification and Christian Perfection.

LORD, WILLIAM W., a younger brother of Dr. John C. Lord, was born in western New York about 1818, studied one year in the Theological Seminary at Auburn, 1842–3, and one year in the Seminary at Princeton, 1843–4, and is now Rector of a Protestant Episcopal church at Vicksburg, Mississippi. He is the author of two volumes of poetry, the last of which is an epic poem, entitled, "Christ in Hades," published in 1851. He is the author of the following articles:

1845. The Reign of the Saints.
1846. The Law of Human Progress.

LORD, D. D., WILLIAM HAYES, son of Rev. Nathan and Mrs. Elizabeth King (Leland) Lord, was born at Amherst, New Hampshire, in 1824. In 1828 his father, who had for twelve years been the beloved and admired pastor of the Congregational church at Amherst, entered upon the Presidency of Dartmouth College, which he so worthily held for thirty-five years. William, the fifth son, was graduated at Dartmouth in 1843, completed his theological course at Andover in 1846, and September 20, 1847, was ordained and installed over the Congregational church at Montpelier, Vermont. In this ministry he has continued until the present time, (May 1870,) although often solicited to take charge of important city churches in the Middle and Western States. From an early period in his ministry, he has been recognized as one of the ablest and most influential clergymen of his state, and his position at the Capitol has made his influence widely felt in matters of public policy as well as in the cause of religion. His published sermons and addresses are quite numerous. In 1869 he contributed to this *Review* the article entitled "Romanism at Rome," and in the time included in this Index,

1868. Liberal Christianity.

LOWRIE, JOHN C., is the eldest son of the late Hon. Walter Lowrie, the first Corresponding Secretary to the Board of Foreign Missions. At an early age he entered into political life, and after serving the State of Pennsylvania seven years in its Senate, and six years as its representative in the Senate of the United States, and acting as Secretary to the Senate twelve years, in 1836 he renounced all aspirations for political power, honour, or emolument, and accepted the office of Corresponding Secretary to the Western Foreign Missionary Society, which was then struggling into existence, and gave three of his sons to the service of the foreign field. John C. Lowrie, the eldest, was graduated at Jefferson College in 1829; took the usual three years course at the Western Theological Seminary, and was licensed to preach by the Presbytery of Ohio, in the First Church of Pittsburgh, on the 21st of June, 1832. He afterwards studied one term at the Princeton Seminary, and was ordained as a missionary by the Presbytery of Newcastle, in the First Church of Philadelphia, on the 23d of May, 1833, and was sent out by the Western Foreign Missionary Society to Northern India, but his health failing, he returned to America in 1836, and in 1838 was made Assistant Secretary to the Board of Foreign Missions, the Western Foreign Missionary Society having in 1837 been merged in this Board. From 1845 he was also minister of the Forty-second street Presbyterian church in New York city, till 1850, when he was elected one of the Corresponding Secretaries of the Board of Foreign Missions, which office he fills at the present time. He was Moderator of the General Assembly in 1865.

He is the author of "Two Years in Upper India," and a "History of the Foreign Missions of the Presbyterian Church," besides a great many reports and sermons. To this journal he contributed in

1838. India.
1840. Buxton on the Slave Trade.
1850. Return of Missionaries.
1858. Revolt of the Sepoys.
1864. The Superintendence of Foreign Missions.
1867. The Training and Distribution of Missionaries.

LOWRIE, WALTER H., son of Matthew B. and Sarah Lowrie, nephew and namesake of the Hon. Walter Lowrie, late Secretary of the Board of Foreign Missions of the Presbyterian Church, was born in Armstrong county, Pennsylvania, March 31, 1807, during the removal of his father's family from Butler county to Pittsburgh, Pa. He received his education in the Western University of Pennsylvania, at Pittsburgh, under the Rev. Drs. Bruce, Black, E. P. Swift, and John H. Hopkins, afterwards Protestant Episcopal Bishop of Vermont, graduating in June 1826. He began the study of law immediately afterwards; part of the time with Hon. Charles Shaler, and part of the time with the Hon. Walter Forward, and was admitted to the Bar in Pittsburgh, Pa., August 4, 1829. On August 20, 1846, he was appointed by Gov. Francis R. Shunk to the Judgeship of the District Court of Allegheny county, Pa., made vacant by the elevation of Judge Grier to the Supreme Court of the United States, and occupied this position until elected to the Supreme Court of Pennsylvania, in October 1851. This being the first election of Judges in the Commonwealth, (previously they were appointed by the Governor,) the five then newly elected to the Supreme Court resorted to the lot to fix the term of office for each. By this, Judge Lowrie was allotted a twelve-year term. The last six years of this period he filled the office of Chief Justice. The term expired in December 1863. For a few years after, he resumed the practice of law in Pittsburgh. In the winter of 1868–69 he removed to Philadelphia and still resides there.

Judge Lowrie served some years, beginning with 1836, as ruling elder in the Second Presbyterian Church of Pittsburgh,. (where his father had been ruling elder before him.) He was a delegate to the General Assembly in 1838, the year of the disruption of the church, and remained with the Old-school branch. The degree of LL.D. was conferred upon him by Washington College, Pa. in 1856.

He has been a contributor to several other journals, monthly and quarterly, besides the *Repertory*. Several communications to the American Philosophical Society, on the "Origin of the Tides" and on "Cosmical Motion," have been published in pamphlet form.

He is best known by his judicial opinions, amounting to many hundreds, most of which are reported in Harris', Casey's and Wright's Reports, in Grant's Cases, and in the Philadelphia Reports. Many of them contain very thorough historical and philosophical discussions of complicated judicial questions, pervaded by a pure and decided tone of individual and social morality and order. Not a few of these are of general interest, and those who give attention to social philosophy, even though not "learned in the law," would find in them much useful matter. The following cases are cited as good, though perhaps not the best examples.

In the case of *Miller* vs. *Fichthorn*, 7 Casey's Rep. 252, we

have a discussion of the admissibility of oral, in aid, or in con-
tradiction of the written evidence of the matter in dispute:
and a philosophical vindication of the usage and right of the
people to clothe their transactions in a garb of their own
making, though unknown to the law, and of the duty of the
courts to interpret them, however uncouthly dressed, so as to
reach their real meaning and enforce the same, if not contrary
to law.

The most difficult questions in the law of habeas corpus are
carefully treated in many opinions. Two interesting cases are:
Williamson vs. *Lewis*, 3 Wright's Rep. 9; and *Commonwealth*
vs. *Wright*, 3 Grant's Cases, 437. The opinion in the first of
these cases is a thorough historical investigation of the nature
of the writ; showing that its sole purpose is to discharge a
person from any custody not judicial, where there is no legal
cause of detention; or to put him under judicial custody or
under bail if there is such cause, so that his case may be tried
in due course of law, and he not restrained of his liberty by any
power which has no authority to try him. That it can never
be used where one is confined under judicial sentence or judgment; and that it institutes no conflict between one judge or
court and another. In the second case, it is shown that this
remedy as a State writ applies when a person is restrained of
his liberty even by a federal officer not officially authorized,
and that such has always been understood to be the law. That
it is the State habeas corpus laws that are guarantied to the
people by the declaration of the federal Constitution, that this
writ shall not be suspended except in case of rebellion or
invasion.

In the opinion in the case of *Keenan* vs. *Commonwealth*, 8
Wright's Rep. 55, the definition of murder in the first degree
is cleared of some confusion, and the plea of intoxication as
excuse or palliation of crime is discussed.

Nesbit vs. *Commonwealth*, 10 Casey's Rep. 398, is the case
of a servant driving his employer's carriage to church on the
Lord's-day, and decided to be no breach of the law. The
opinion shows that the civil institutions of the country must
protect its religious institutions, and the morality and civilization which grow out of them. That our laws do not go beyond
that. They enforce no duty *as religion,* but only as part of
the customs and morality of the people. This subject is illustrated in other cases, as *Murray* vs. *Commonwealth*, 12 Harris' Rep. 270; *Scully* vs. *Commonwealth*, 11 Casey's Rep. 511,
and especially, *Mohney* vs. *Cook*, 2 Casey, 342.

The three following cases all relate to dissensions and divisions in churches. *McGinness* vs. *Watson*, 5 Wright's Rep. 9, is the secession of a majority of a congregation (Seceders) because unwilling to follow its Synod into the union that constituted the United Presbyterian Church. *Suter* vs. *The Reformed Church*, 6 id. 503, and *Winebrenner* vs. *Colder*, 7 id. 204, are instances of the secession of majorities of congregations from the associate bodies of churches to which they belonged for the sake of popular preachers who were not of the association. One rule is applied to all these cases. Dissensions in churches are to be tried according to their own law as it existed before the dissension began. In the case of independent churches by their own peculiar laws; and in the case of associate churches by this and their associate law together. These laws are to be learned from the history, the customs, and the written institutions of the body. Recognizing that every such body has an inherent right of legislation within its sphere, and may exercise it for the purpose of maintaining and enlarging its influence and increasing its membership, it is shown that all its members and even majorities of congregations who secede on account of such acts, done in an orderly way, cease to be members of the association or of any of its congregations, and abandon all their rights therein.

The importance of these cases will be felt by every one who engages in the study of such questions, which are often very difficult of solution.

The following articles were contributed by him :

1860. Inductive and Deductive Politics—The Dissolution of Empires.

1861. The Natural Grounds of Civil Authority.

1864. Buckle's History of Civilization—Man's Mental Instincts.

1868. Social Liberty.

MACDONALD, JAMES M., is a native of the state of Maine; received his preparatory education from John Adams, LL.D., at Andover, Mass., and entered the Freshman Class at Bowdoin in 1828. At the close of the Sophomore year he removed to Union College, from which he graduated at the age of twenty in 1832. He was licensed to preach the gospel on the 6th of August, 1834, and ordained pastor of the Congregational Church, Berlin, Ct., on April 1, 1835. In 1837 he accepted the charge of the Second Congregational Church, New London, Ct., and was installed on the 13th of December. He continued here till May 5, 1841, when he was installed pastor of the Presbyterian church at Jamaica, Long Island, by the

31

Presbytery of New York.   During his pastorate here he declined several calls to other churches, but was induced to accept the charge of the Fifteenth Street church in New York City in 1850, and was installed on the 16th of April.   In the spring of 1850 he received a call to the First Church in Princeton, N. J., which he declined, but on its being renewed in September he accepted the call and was installed into the charge on the 1st of November.   In this charge he has continned till the present time.

His life has been eminently a literary one.   His first publication was a Sermon occasioned by the duel between Cilley and Graves, in 1838.   This was succeeded by a small volume entitled, "Credulity, as Illustrated by Impostures in Science," &c. in 1843.   In 1846 he published a "Key to the Book of Revelation," which reached a second edition in 1848.   In 1855 the first edition of "My Father's House" was published, and it has now reached the fifth edition in this country, and been re-published in London and Glasgow.   In 1856 he published "The Book of Ecclesiastes Explained," and during this long period of authorship he has been a constant contributor to periodicals, and has published a great variety of sermons and funeral discourses, among which we may mention his "Two Centuries in the History of the Presbyterian church of Jamaica, Long Island, and the article in the *Bibliotheca Sacra*, "Irony in History; or, Was Gibbon an Infidel?"   His articles in this *Review* are,

1855. Faber on the Locality of Heaven—Dr. I. S. Spencer's Sketches and Sermons.

1858. Historical Value of the Pentateuch.

1863. Faith, a Source of Knowledge.

1865. Census of 1860.

McGILL, ALEXANDER TAGGART, was born at Canonsburgh, Pennsylvania, on the 24th of February, 1807.   He was graduated at Jefferson College in 1826; and remained at the same institution two years longer, teaching the Latin language.   He then removed to Milledgeville, Georgia, and became Principal of the Baldwin Academy, for one year, as he pursued the study of law.   In 1830, he was admitted to the Bar of Georgia, and immediately afterwards received several important appointments from the government of that state.   In 1831 he relinquished these for the ministry of the gospel.   Returning to Pennsylvania, he entered the Theological Seminary of the Associate, now United Presbyterian Church, the oldest institution of the kind in this country, then located at Canons-burgh, now at Xenia, Ohio.

In 1835 he was ordained to the ministry at Carlisle, Penn-sylvania, and installed pastor of three churches in one charge, extending over three adjoining counties.   In 1838, immedi-ately after the separation of Old-school and New-school in the General Assembly he transferred his connection to the former, and became pastor of the Second Presbyterian church of Car-lisle, Pa.   In 1842 he was elected by the General Assembly Professor of Ecclesiastical History and Church Government in the Western Theological Seminary at Allegheny, Pa.   Beside the duties of this chair, he taught Hebrew, and most of the branches in Biblical Literature, five years, from 1847 to 1851; part of the same time acting as pastor of the Second Presbyte-rian church, Pittsburgh.   Persevering in the service of that Seminary, through its darkest days of poverty and depression, he declined the chair of Theology offered him in the Seminary at New Albany, and another chair in the new Seminary at Cincinnati, with Drs. Rice, Hoge, and others; also, the Presi-deney of four different Colleges, and calls to many important churches, east and west.

At length, his failing health induced him to accept a posi-tion, which had been twice offered him, in the Theological Seminary at Columbia, South Carolina; and in 1852–3 he entered on his duties there.   But finding that the climate would be too debilitating, he consented to a re-election by the General Assembly of 1853 to his old chair at Allegheny.   In 1854 he accepted the nomination of the Board of Directors of the Theological Seminary at Princeton to the chair of Ecclesiastical, Homiletic, and Pastoral Theology, as it is now entitled, and was transferred accordingly by a vote of the Gen-eral Assembly.   At the urgent desire of Dr. J. Addison Alex-ander in 1859, Church History was added to his chair, and became the title of it in 1860, but in 1861 he returned to the chair he had originally accepted at Princeton.

He was Moderator of the General Assembly in 1848; Per-manent Clerk, from 1850 to 1862; and has been Stated Clerk, from 1862 to the present time.   He was a member of the Committee on Revision of the Book of Discipline, along with Drs. Thornwell, Breckinridge, Hodge, and others, appointed in 1857; and has been Chairman of a new Committee for this object since 1866.   He received the title of D. D. in 1842 from Marshall College, Pa., and that of LL.D. in 1868, from the College of New Jersey.   Many of his Sermons and Addresses have been published from time to time, and various pamphlets.

His lectures in a controversy with Bishop O'Connor, Roman Catholic, at Pittsburgh, in 1853, were widely published in the newspapers and magazines of that time. Contributions have been made by his pen on a great variety of subjects in the papers of the Church, mostly without his name; but he has avoided regular authorship.

As yet none of his Lectures have been published. In 1853 he completed the article entitled "Sketches of Western Pennsylvania," which had been begun by Dr. Carnahan, and in

1865. Mason and Dixon's Line.

McILVAINE, JOSHUA HALL, was born in 1815 at Lewes, Delaware; graduated at the College of New Jersey in 1836; entered Princeton Seminary in the same year, and remained there till 1840. In 1844 he organized the Westminster church of Utica, N. Y., and was its pastor about five years. His next charge was the First Church of Rochester, of which he was pastor twelve years. In 1859 he was invited to deliver the Oration before the two literary societies of the College of New Jersey, and chose for his subject, "A Nation's Right to Worship God," and in 1860 he was elected to the chair of Belles Lettres in that institution. This position he held until 1870, but during his professorship he was constantly engaged in preaching on the Sabbath in the neighbouring cities; and he is now pastor of the High Street Presbyterian church, Newark, N. J.

He is a Fellow of the American Oriental Society, and in 1858 delivered a course of Lectures on Comparative Philology, the Sanskrit Languages, and the Arrowhead Inscriptions, before the Smithsonian Institution; and in 1870 he gave a course of Lectures on Social Science in the University of Pennsylvania. He is the author of "Elocution: the Sources and Elements of its Power," and contributed the following articles:

1859. A Nation's Right to Worship God.
1861. Covenant Education—American Nationality.
1862. The Church and the Poor.
1867. Malthusianism.

McKINNEY, DAVID, was born in Mifflin county, Pennsylvania, October 22, 1795; graduated at Jefferson College in 1821; studied theology at the Seminary in Princeton; was licensed by the Presbytery of Philadelphia in April 1824, and ordained and installed in Erie, Pa., in May 1825.

In 1835 Mr. McKinney took charge of the congregations of Sinking Creek and Spring, in the Presbytery of Huntingdon;

and in 1841 he was transferred to the church in Hollidays-
burg, in the same Presbytery.   In 1852 he resigned his pastoral charge and removed to Philadelphia, where he established
the *Presbyterian Banner.*   In 1855 he removed the *Banner*
to Pittsburgh, having purchased the *Presbyterian Advocate*
and added its subscription list to that of the *Banner.*   In 1864,
having parted with the *Banner,* Dr. McKinney established the
Family Treasure, a monthly journal, which he conducted for
three years.   Parting with this journal, he accepted the position of Librarian and Treasurer for the Board of Colportage of
the Synods of Pittsburgh and Allegheny.   In the service of
this Board he still continues.   He was also a joint proprietor
and editor of the *North-western Presbyterian,* published at
Chicago for some years.   The degree of D. D. was conferred
upon him by his *alma mater.*

. In 1850 he contributed to this *Review* the article on a Cheap
Presbyterian Newspaper.

MACLEAN, JOHN, eldest son of Dr. John Maclean, the
first Professor of Chemistry in the College of New Jersey, and
of his wife, Phœbe Bainbridge, was born in Princeton, N. J.,
March 3, 1800; entered the College at Princeton in the spring
of 1813, and was admitted to the first degree in the Arts in
the autumn of 1816.   In the autumn of 1818 he was appointed
a Tutor in the College, and he was at this time a student in
the Theological Seminary of Princeton.   In 1822 was made
Teacher of Mathematics and Natural Philosophy, and in 1823
was chosen Professor of Mathematics.   In 1829 he was transferred to the chair of Ancient Languages, and at the same time
was chosen Vice-President of the College.   In December 1853
he was chosen President of the College, and entered upon the
duties of his office on the 28th of June, 1854.   In December
1857 he tendered to the Board of Trustees his resignation, to
take effect at the ensuing Commencement in June; at which
time he gave up his connection with the College, after a service, in various offices, of fifty years.

He was several times a member of the General Assembly of
the Presbyterian Church.   When the division took place in
1838, he was a member of the Assembly, and wrote the letters
to the Foreign Churches.   He was also a member of the
Assemblies of 1843 and 1844, and he wrote the answers to the
protests against the decisions of these Assemblies, respecting
the Elder or Quorum question, and also respecting the right of
ruling elders to impose hands in the ordination of ministers.
On three other occasions he was a commissioner to the Assem-

bly, and took an active part in the proceedings. In 1837 he wrote a review of the proceedings of the Assembly for that year, in which review he defended the action of the Assembly; but he was careful not to use any expressions which could be regarded as impeaching the veracity or the motives of those from whom he differed in opinion; and no exception was ever taken to the spirit or to the language of the Review, in any mention made of it by those of the opposite side. It was first published in *The Presbyterian,* and afterwards in a pamphlet form. In 1844 he published in *The Presbyterian* ten letters on the Quorum or Elder Question, which were collected and printed in a pamphlet, together with three letters on the "Imposition of Hands." In 1829 he published a Lecture on a Common School System for New Jersey. In 1831 he published in the *New York Observer* a revision of Prof. Stuart's Prize Essay on Temperance, which led to an animated discussion; and subsequently he published several other articles on the same subject in that and in other papers. In 1853 he published two letters on "The True Relations of the Church and State to Schools and Colleges." In 1854 he published the address delivered by him when he was inaugurated as President of the College. Five or six sermons delivered by him in the College Chapel have also been published; and occasionally articles from his pen, on different topics, have been given in the public papers.

His contributions to the *Repertory and Princeton Review,* in addition to some short notices of books, were an article on "Common Schools," and a review of "Bacchus" and "Anti-Bacchus," two works on Temperance, which were written and originally published in England.

1833. Common Schools.
1841. Bacchus and Anti-Bacchus.

MARCH, FRANCIS ANDREW, eldest child of Andrew and Nancy Parker March, was born in Millbury, Mass., October 25, 1825, and studied in the public schools of Worcester, Mass. Hon. Alfred D. Foster, one of the Examiners of these schools, sent him to Amherst College, (1841), and in 1845 he graduated with the highest honours. He then taught two years in Leicester Academy, Mass., and two years as Tutor in Amherst College. He prosecuted the study of law in the office of Butler, Barney & Butler, New York City; was there admitted to the bar in October 1850, and began practice with Gordon L. Ford, Esq. In December 1851 he was attacked with bleeding at the lungs and sent South to die; spent the winter in Cuba, then went to Florida; taught three years (1852–1855) in Fredericksburg, Virginia; went to Easton, Pennsylvania, as Tutor in Lafayette College in 1855; was appointed Adjunct Professor of English Literature in 1856, and Professor of the English Language and Comparative Philology in 1858. This professorship he still holds. It is claimed as the first in this country in which extended and systematic study of the English Language in the English Classics, in the light of modern Philology, was co-ordinated with that of Greek and Latin. He was honoured with the degree of LL.D by the College of New Jersey in 1870.

He published a "Method of Philological Study of the English Language," 1865; "A Parser and Analyzer for beginners, with diagrams and suggestive pictures," 1869; "A Comparative Grammar of the Anglo-Saxon Language; in which its forms are illustrated by those of the Sanskrit, Greek, Latin, Gothic, Old Saxon, Old Friesic, Old Norse, and Old High German," Sampson Low & Co., London, 1870; "An Anglo-Saxon Reader, with philological notes, vocabulary and a brief Grammar," Harper & Brothers, New York, 1870. He has also contributed a great number of philological articles to the leading Reviews in America and to the *Jahrbuch für Rom. und Englische Literatur*, Berlin, 1859, 1860, 1861.

Professor March has heard the college classes in Constitutional Law and in Mental Philosophy. His earliest publication was in connection with these branches: "The relation of the Study of Jurisprudence to the origin and progress of the Baconian Philosophy," *New Englander*, October 1848. He published and advocated a plan of pacification for the country, in the *New York Times* and *The World*, 1860–1861. He has contributed to the *Princeton Review* two articles on Sir William Hamilton, which were thought to contain the first elaborate exposition of the difficulties in applying Hamilton's views to the facts of Perception. They attracted appreciative attention and notice from M. Cousin, Dr. Hickok, Dr. H. B. Smith, and other masters. The last paragraph in the July number is from the Editor of the *Repertory*.

1860. Sir William Hamilton's Theory of Perception—Sir William Hamilton's Philosophy of the Conditioned.

MARTIN, W. A. P., was born in 1827 in the state of Indiana; graduated at the State University in 1846; studied theology under Drs. Mathews and Wood at New Albany; sailed for China in 1849, and laboured as a missionary at Ningpo ten years. He assisted as Interpreter in the negotiation of the

American Treaty in 1858, and in 1859 accompanied the American Minister to Peking. After a short visit to the United States he returned to Peking and founded the Presbyterian Mission in that city in 1863. During this period he was engaged also in translating and preparing works on International Law and Natural Philosophy for the use of the Chinese government, and assisted in translating the Scriptures into the Court dialect of the Chinese language. In 1867 he was appointed to the professorship of International Law and Political Economy in the University newly established by the emperor, and his present residence is Peking, China. In 1870 the degree of LL.D. was conferred upon him by the University of New York. In 1862, when on a visit to the United States, he contributed the article on the Ethical Philosophy of the Chinese.

MATTHEWS, JAMES, was born in county Down, Ireland, on the 19th of May, 1820, and emigrated to this country in 1831. In 1836 he united with the Third Presbyterian church in Pittsburgh, and graduated at Jefferson College in 1843; and after studying theology at New Hagerstown, O., was licensed to preach by the Presbytery of Pittsburgh in 1846. For a few months he preached at Laurel and Savage, Maryland, and in the spring of 1847 removed to Kentucky and took charge of the churches of Carlisle, Millersburg, and Old Concord, over which he was ordained by the Presbytery of Ebenezer. In 1854 he was elected Professor of Languages in Centre College, Danville, and continued in the professorship till 1867, when he resigned, and became Principal of the Presbyterial Academy at Logansport, Indiana, which, together with the pastorate of the Second Presbyterian church, is his present charge.

The life of Dr. Matthews has not been one destitute of stirring incident. About twenty years ago he signalized himself in an oral controversy with Elder Benjamin Franklin of Cincinnati, on "Predestination and the Foreknowledge of God," which was afterwards published in a volume of 450 pages. And during the late war he acted four years as chaplain to the 19th Regiment of Kentucky Volunteers. He was a member of the General Assembly of 1853 and of 1867, in which he delivered a speech upon the "Constitutional Powers of the General Assembly," which was afterwards published, and has been highly commended. He received the degree of D. D. from Centre College in 1867, and while in the service, in 1863, wrote the article upon Religious Instruction in the Army.

MATTHEWS, JOHN, was born in Guilford county, North·
Carolina, on the 19th of January, 1772. His father, who in
early life had emigrated from Ireland, was a farmer in moderate circumstances, and from conscientious motives never held
slaves. There was little opportunity to give his son a good
education, and when a boy he was sent to learn the trade of a
wheelwright, and afterwards worked at the business of a house-
carpenter and cabinet-maker, but even then he evinced an
insatiable thirst for knowledge, and all the leisure he could
spare from his employment was devoted to reading. About the
age of twenty be commenced a course of regular study in the
school of the Rev. Dr. David Caldwell, the pastor of the church
with which he was connected, and part of the time he lived in
Dr. Caldwell's family, paying his board by exercising his me-
chanical skill in making various articles for his teacher, among
which was a carriage, a pulpit for the church, and a planet-
arium, which is said to be still preserved as a relic in the
family.

In March 1801, in his thirtieth year, he was licensed to
preach the gospel by the Presbytery of Orange, and next winter he crossed the desert country to Natchez, Miss., and acted
as a missionary there. · In April 1803 he returned to North
Carolina, and shortly after received a call to the churches of
Nutbush and Grassy Creek, which he accepted, and continued
here till 1806, when he removed to Martinsburg, Virginia, and
after little more than a year he resigned this for the charge at
Shepherdstown, Va. Here he continued till 1836, preaching
as stated supply of this church, and that of Charlestown, and
frequently also at Harper's Ferry. He then gave up his
charge at Charlestown and took Martinsburg in its place,
dividing his time between Martinsburg and Charlestown till
he removed to Indiana. At this period he was very popular
as a preacher, and in 1823 the trustees of Washington College,
Pa. conferred upon him the degree of D. D.

Influenced by his reputation as an eloquent preacher, when
the Theological Seminary was established at Hanover, Indiana,
he was invited to become Professor of Theology, and in opposition to the wishes of many of his friends he accepted the
appointment. Like Dr. Alexander, he had not enjoyed the
advantages of a collegiate education. He was " uncommonly
familiar with the classics,"* but his knowledge had been
acquired by hard study, unassisted and alone. "It seemed to
me," says another who knew him well, " that there was not a

---

* Dr. James Wood.

32

verse in the Bible that he had not investigated, so as to form a matured opinion in regard to it."* He was therefore well prepared for the work he had undertaken; and with a vigorous mind sharpened by its conflicts with difficulties, he threw his whole soul into the work, and at the close of his seventeen years of trial and labour, the verdict of his brethren, and we have no doubt of his Lord, was, " Well done."

Dr. Matthews was tall and spare rather than fleshy. He was an example of temperance in eating and drinking. In his manner he was grave and dignified, but not morose and assuming. He had a happy talent in administering reproof. While at Hanover he was passing by one of the college students who was cutting wood; the student, not knowing he was near, and being vexed about something, uttered a profane oath. Dr. Matthews approached him, and said very kindly, "That is good exercise you are taking this cold morning." He then asked him if his axe was dull; and taking hold as if to examine it, he commenced chopping the stick of wood, to the great amusement of the young man, till he had cut it through, then turning to the student he said, " See there now I have cut that stick without fretting or swearing, and why could not you do the same ?" The young man apologized for his profaneness, saying, " I did not know that you were near, sir." " Yes, but God is always near, and hears every word you say—you ought to remember that," was the answer.

Dr. Matthews laboured without intermission almost to the close of his life. He had been urged to submit to a surgical operation for an internal malady, and finally consented to it, but the operation proved fatal at the very moment of its being performed. He died at New Albany on the 19th of May, 1848, in the seventy-seventh year of his age.

Dr. Matthews was twice married, and left a family of nine children, six of whom were graduates of colleges, and three of them ministers of the gospel. His most important publications are his "Letters on the Divine Purpose," and " The Influence of the Bible." In 1844 he contributed to this *Review* the article on " Ecclesiastical Polity."

MILLER, SAMUEL, was a son of the Rev. John Miller, a native of Boston, Massachusetts, who, after being licensed to preach the gospel, visited Delaware and Maryland, and having accepted a call from the churches of Dover and Duck Creek Cross-Roads, (now Smyrna, Delaware,) passed over forty years

* Dr. James M. Brown.

in the same charge. He had nine children; and Samuel, who was the eighth, was born on the 30th of October, 1769. He was not sent to any school or public seminary, but was educated by his father under the parental roof, till he was eighteen years of age, when he entered the Senior Class of the University of Pennsylvania, on the 21st of July, 1788, and graduated at the close of the session in the following year with the first honours of the class. The next two years were devoted to theological study under the direction of his father, and on the 19th of April, 1791, he was taken on trials by the Presbytery of Lewes, and licensed on the 13th of October, 1791. His father had died in July of that year, and on the first two Sabbaths after his licensure he was appointed to supply the churches made vacant by his death, but as soon as he was free from presbyterial appointments, he hastened to Carlisle and put himself under the care of the Rev. Charles Nisbet, D. D., then President of Dickinson College, for further theological instruction.

Mr. Miller remained in Carlisle till the beginning of May 1792, when he accepted an invitation to preach in a vacant church on Long Island. In passing through New York, to fulfil this appointment, he called on Dr. Rodgers, an old friend of his father, who had formerly been settled at St. George's, Delaware, and was prevailed upon to tarry two weeks, and preached repeatedly in the city, and after returning to Delaware supplied the pulpit of the Dover and Duck Creek church till the beginning of June. In April the Presbytery met at Laurel, when a call was put into his hands from the Dover and Duck Creek church, but he had received an invitation to preach again in the New York church, and without accepting the call, he proceeded again to that city in the month of June, and preached there every Sabbath for a month with great acceptance. Being desirous to visit the Eastern States, from which his family had come to Delaware, he now set out on a leisurely tour through them, and did not return to New York till the end of September.

The second visit to New York resulted in a call to the church in that city, and after receiving his dismission from the Presbytery of Lewes, he returned to make his permanent abode there, in January 1793. The First church in New York had then two buildings, one in Wall street, and the second the Brick Church, in which the pastors, Drs. Rodgers and McKnight, preached alternately, but had only one board of trustees and one bench of elders. Dr. McKnight's health being somewhat impaired, a third pastor, Mr. Miller, was called to the collegiate charge, in order that three services might be kept up each Sabbath in the two churches. The usual routine of public service seems to have required at first, and for several years, only one sermon each Sabbath, but that sermon twice delivered. "From the commencement of his ministry," says Dr. Sprague, "Mr. Miller enjoyed a reputation in some respects peculiar to himself. Besides having the advantage of a remarkably fine person, and most bland and attractive manners, he had, from the beginning, an uncommonly polished style, and there was an air of literary refinement pervading all his performances, that excited general admiration, and wellnigh put criticism at defiance. He was scarcely settled before his services began to be put in requisition on public occasions; and several of those early occasional discourses were published, and still remain as a monument of his taste, talents, and piety."

Among these is his first published sermon, which was preached before the Tammany Society of New York, on the 4th of July, 1793, and published at their request. In it he says that "It is a truth denied by few, at the present day, that political and domestic slavery are inconsistent with justice, and that these must necessarily wage eternal war. . . . The American patriot must heave an involuntary sigh at the recollection that, even in these happy and singularly favoured republics, this offspring of infernal malice, and parent of human debasement, is yet suffered to reside." The same sentiments were expressed in equally strong language in the fifth of his published discourses, an oration delivered April 12, 1797, before the Society for Promoting the Manumission of Slaves, and Protecting such of them as have been or may be liberated. He entered heartily into all the popular movements of his day, to such a degree as to cause regret in after life; and among the resolutions he made when he came to Princeton was, "On coming to Princeton in 1813, I resolved to begin a new course in regard to politics. I resolved to do or say as little as could be deemed consistent with the character of a good citizen—to attend no political meetings—to write no political paragraphs —to avoid talking on the subject much either in public or private—to do little more than to go quietly and silently to the polls, deposit my vote and withdraw; and in the pulpit never to allow myself, either in prayer or preaching, to utter a syllable from which it might be conjectured on which side of the party politics of the day I stood."

On his first settling in New York, Mr. Miller simply took boarding, but in 1796 he prevailed upon his brother, Dr. Edward, to give up his practice in Dover, Delaware, and come to New York, where the two brothers kept house together. This arrangement continued till October 1801, when Mr. Miller was married to Miss Sarah Sargent of Philadelphia, who from this time took charge of all his household matters. In 1809 the collegiate relation in the First Church was broken up, and in the division of labour that ensued Mr. Miller became the pastor of the Wall street church. During the first nine years of his pastorate he published eight discourses, but in January 1804 he published a work of a more ambitious character, which had cost him much labour, and made him generally known both in America and Europe. This was "A Brief Retrospect of the Eighteenth Century," in two octavo volumes, in which he gave a review of the progress that had been made in science, politics, history, art, philosophy, and religion, in every part of the globe. This drew to him the attention of scholars throughout the world, and brought upon him a great foreign correspondence; and in testimony of its approbation, the University of Pennsylvania, from which he graduated, conferred upon him the degree of D. D. It was not usual that any one so young should bear this title, and he was by some styled "the boy doctor."

During his residence in New York several attempts were made to draw him from the pastoral office, by the offer of the Presidency of a College, particularly by the University of North Carolina, and Hamilton College, N. Y., but he resisted all their offers. He had however, in conjunction with Dr. Ashbel Green, been greatly instrumental in founding the Princeton Theological Seminary, and in 1813, when the General Assembly elected him to the second professorship in that institution, he did not feel at liberty to reject the appointment. On the 29th of September, 1813, he was inaugurated into the chair of Ecclesiastical History and Church Government, and returned to New York for his family; but here he was seized with a violent inflammatory fever, which degenerated to typhus, and he did not again reach Princeton till the third of December.

In regard to how he taught and how he lived after he came to Princeton, we have the privilege of presenting to our readers the reminiscences of a student who once sat at his feet, and who was afterwards associated with him in that triad of instructors which made the Seminary at Princeton illustrious.

"Dr. Miller came to Princeton in 1813 and retained his connection with the Theological Seminary in that place until his death in 1850. No one not intimately acquainted with him during this important period of his life can duly appreciate his character. None knew him so well as his students and colleagues. By strangers he was often misunderstood. He had always the demeanor and carriage of a polished gentleman. But there was also the appearance of precision and formality about him, which made the impression on casual acquaintance that he was deficient in emotion, cheerfulness, and vivacity. This, however, was a great mistake. He was always cheerful, and the life of every social reunion. The professors of the College and Seminary were accustomed to meet once a fortnight for social intercourse and the discussion of matters of interest at the moment. These meetings were often rather dull and prosy, until Dr. Miller made his appearance. As soon as he entered every one would brighten up, and conversation was sure to become animated and instructive. It is a common impression that Dr. Miller was destitute of humour. But this too is a mistake. He had a fund of anecdotes which he was accustomed to tell with great effect. On every Friday evening the professors and students were accustomed to meet for the discussion of some topic previously assigned. On these occasions Dr. Miller would convulse the audience by some appropriate anecdote. This neither of his colleagues ever did or could do, but they enjoyed the benefit and the pleasure. The writer is almost ashamed to say how often in Princeton, even yet, some pithy sentence or witty saying is introduced by the words, 'as Dr. Miller used to say.' But even this trait of his character sheds a pleasing lustre on his memory.

" Dr. Miller as a professor was diligent, faithful, and instructive; and to an extraordinary degree kind and forbearing. Our class, one of the earliest, tried his patience a good deal. We were not bad, but boyish. One particularly, afterwards one of the most distinguished and useful ministers of our church, the late Dr. William Nevins of Baltimore, was so full of fun and wit, that he kept us in a constant titter. The good Doctor wore out his lead-pencil in thumping the desk to make us behave, but was never irritated. He made allowance for us as boys, knowing that we loved and reverenced him. There was one unfortunately constituted member of the Seminary, whom the Doctor had found it necessary privately to admonish, and who was often positively disrespectful. Dr. Miller never resented, and did not even seem to notice it. To the credit of the students it should be stated that this is the only case of intentional disrespect of a student to a professor, of which the writer, during the fifty years of his connection with the Seminary, has any recollection.

"Dr. Miller's self-control was exhibited on all occasions. At the ministers' meetings above referred to, it could not fail that at times the discussions should be animated, and decided diversity of opinion be elicited. It so happened that one evening Dr. Miller took one side, and all the other gentlemen, to the number of six or eight, the opposite. The Doctor had, therefore, for some two hours to sustain the contest against arguments and queries directed against him from all sides. He never for a moment lost his self-command or evinced the slightest irritation. When the discussion was over and the Doctor had left the room, Dr. James W. Alexander gave expression to the feeling of all present, by exclaiming, ' How beautifully Dr. Miller behaved this evening!'

"The deep reverence and affection entertained for Dr. Miller arose from a conviction of his thorough goodness. There are different kinds of good men. Some are good in one aspect and not in another. The Germans say a man is a Strass-engel and Haus-teufel, an angel in society and the opposite at home. But apart from such extremes, there are often great inconsistencies in really good men. Some are good ministers, but not good fathers or neighbours. Some are good God-ward, but not so good man-ward. Some have good feelings, but are not governed by principles; while others have good principles and very unlovely dispositions. Dr. Miller was thoroughly good; good in every aspect, because he was good in principle. It was this that made him generous, faithful, kind, and devoted to his duties. In him as in other men, as his friends at times observed, the first impulse was wrong. Most men would yield to that impulse and afterwards repent. With Dr. Miller it was immediately suppressed, and the right thing almost uniformly said or done. The fact that for over thirty years he was intimately associated with colleagues to whom he never said an unkind word or exhibited an unkind feeling, is proof enough of his habitual self-control. He bore with the infirmities of other men without calling on them to bear with his. It is not said that he was perfect, but we record the facts of our own experience. It is a melancholy satisfaction to lay even this late and withered garland upon his tomb.

"Dr. Miller's association with Dr. Alexander, a man so differently constituted, served to bring out in the clearest light the peculiar excellencies of his character. Dr. Alexander had extraordinary emotional power—the power of expressing and exciting feeling. This is a gift which perhaps more than any other gives its possessor ascendancy, especially in the sphere of religion, over those who come under his personal influence.

Dr. Miller cheerfully, uniformly, and sincerely recognized this and all other endowments of his venerated colleague. Indeed he was disposed if not to exaggerate the gifts of Dr. Alexander, at least unduly to depreciate his own. In the summer of 1819 Dr. Alexander delivered to the then senior class a lecture which so impressed his pupils, that Dr. William Nevins said to his classmates that it was a shame they should enjoy such instructions and do nothing to secure the same advantage for others. He, therefore, proposed that we should endeavour to found a scholarship, to be called 'The Scholarship of the Class of 1819.' To this the class assented, and a committee was appointed to inform the professors of our purpose. When the committee waited on Dr. Miller, Dr. Nevins with his characteristic naive frankness told him the whole story, and dwelt on the enthusiasm cherished by the students for Dr. Alexander. Dr. Miller, having heard him through, expressed his pleasure in view of what the class had done, and then lifted his hand and said, 'My young friend, I solemnly believe that Dr. Alexander is the greatest man who walks the earth.' When we left the Doctor's study, Nevins said to his associates in the committee, 'Well, if Dr. Alexander be the greatest, Dr. Miller is surely the holiest man who walks the earth.' We were boys then; but this incident serves to show how Dr. Miller was regarded by his pupils.

"There is one other incident which is perhaps almost too sacred to make public. Yet as it is eminently characteristic, and casts, as it seems to the writer, a halo round the dying bed of a distinguished servant of God, we may be pardoned for referring to it. The last interview we had with Dr. Miller was a short time before his death. He was very weak, but was sitting in his study in a large chair, propped up with pillows. He referred in his usual tone of self-depreciation to his life as a professor in the Seminary, and said of Dr. Alexander, that his memory would be a means of grace to the Seminary as long as the institution existed, and then added these words, 'As for me, I have nothing to do but to wrap my rags about me, and slink into the grave.' Holy man! In him doubtless was verified the words of the Lord, 'He that humbleth himself shall be exalted.'"

On the 7th of January, 1850, Dr. Samuel Miller died, in peace with God and man, surrounded by a family by whom he was loved and venerated, and watched over by her who had been the faithful partner of his life. "Of all the deaths I ever knew," wrote Dr. J. W. Alexander to his friend Dr. Hall, " this is the most surrounded by all the things one could desire." His sufferings were not severe; and no cloud intervened to hide the glories which the eye of faith had during his long life set before him. We cannot however here enter into particulars. Those who desire to know more of him and his times, can be amply gratified in an admirable "Life," in two volumes, prepared by one of his sons. In the *Annals* of Dr. Sprague, who was an intimate friend, there are also many loving memorials. . To these works we must refer for a list of his writings, but there are a few volumes on which his reputation will chiefly depend, and which ought to have a place in every good library, which we will enumerate.

1. A Brief Retrospect of the Eighteenth Century, 2 vols., 1803. 2. Letters on the Constitution and Order of the Christian Ministry, 2 vols., 1807, 1809. 3. Letters on Unitarianism, 1821. 4. Letters on Clerical Manners and Habits, 1827. 5. An Essay on the Warrant, Nature, and Duties of the Office of the Ruling Elder in the Presbyterian Church, 1831, 1843. 6. Infant Baptism scriptural and reasonable, 1834. 7. Presbyterianism the truly Primitive and Apostolical Constitution of the Church of Christ, 1835. 8. The Primitive and Apostolic Order of the Church of Christ vindicated, 1840. 9. Letters from a Father to his Sons in College, 1843. 10. Thoughts on Public Prayer, 1849.

His papers in this periodical are,

1830. Review of Cooke on the Invalidity of Presbyterian Ordination—Remarks on certain Extremes in pursuing the Temperance Cause—Use of Liturgies.

1831. The Temperance Society—Works of John Howe—The People's Right defended.

1832. Memoir of Rev. J. S. Christmas.

1833. Brittan on Episcopacy.

1834. Remarks on the Epistles of Ignatius.

1835. The Present State and Prospects of the Presbyterian Church*—New Ecclesiastical Law—Episcopacy tested by Scripture—Annual of the Board of Education.

1836. Christian Union—Title of the Sabbath—Toleration—Mitchell's Church Member—Thoughts on Evangelizing the World.

1837. Decline of Religion.

1838. Attention to Children—Henry's Christian Antiquities (with J. A. A.)

1839. Bible-Class Manual—Dr. Griffin's Sermons—The Intermediate State.

1842. Stone's Life of Red Jacket.

* See Note, p. 66.

33

MILLER, JOHN, son of Dr. Samuel Miller, was born at Princeton in 1819; graduated at the College of New Jersey in 1836; entered the Theological Seminary at Princeton in 1838; and was licensed to preach by the Presbytery of New Brunswick in 1842. In 1843 he was ordained pastor of the church at Frederick City, Md., which he resigned in 1848, and spent the next year in travel in Europe. On his return he received a call to the Eleventh or Vine street church in Philadelphia, and during his pastorate his people built the West Arch street church, into which they entered in 1854. In 1855 he removed to Virginia, and is now pastor of the Washington street church, Petersburgh, Virginia. In 1846 he published a 12mo volume on "The Design of the Church, as an Index to her real Nature and the true Law of her Communion;" and reviewed in this periodical in
1845. Palmer on the Church.

MILLER, SAMUEL, Junior, son of Dr. Samuel Miller above, was born at Princeton, N. J. in 1816, and graduated at the College of New Jersey in 1833. After a short tour in Europe to restore his health, he acted as Tutor in the College eighteen months; studied law, and was admitted to practice at the Philadelphia bar in 1838. While at the bar he published the "Presbyterian Church Case" in 1839, and the d'Hauteville Case in 1840. Giving up the practice of law he entered the Seminary at Princeton in 1842, and was licensed to preach in 1844. In 1845 he was ordained as an Evangelist and became stated supply of the churches of Mount Holly and Columbus, to which was added Tuckerton and Bass River in 1857. He was also Principal of the West Jersey Collegiate School from 1846 to 1857. In 1850 he was installed pastor of the Mount Holly church, and these other charges were gradually reliuquished to other pastors, and he now devotes his time to Mount Holly alone. He received the degree of D. D. from his *alma mater* in 1864; and in 1869 he published the Life of . his father in two volumes 12mo. He wrote for this periodical in the volume for
1840. The Presbyterian Church Case.

MOFFAT, JAMES CLEMENT, is a native of the south of Scotland, and came to this country in 1833, with the intention of following his profession as a printer; but soon after landing he was introduced to Professor Maclean of Princeton, and learning from him that he was qualified to enter the Junior Class in the College of New Jersey, his love of learning

prompted him to embrace the opportunity of receiving a collegiate education. He entered the Junior Class in 1833 and
was graduated in 1835, and an offer being then made to him to
engage as a private tutor to two boys about to study at Yale
College, he accepted the proposal, and had the privilege of
attending the course of lectures in that institution. His pupils
distinguished themselves there by their abilities, and one of
them is now ranked among the most eminent Greek scholars in
Europe, where he has long resided.

At the end of about two years Mr. Moffat returned to
Princeton as Greek Tutor, in which capacity he continued till
September 1839, when he accepted the appointment to the Professorship of Greek and Latin in Lafayette College, then under
the presidency of Dr. Junkin. In the spring of 1841 he removed with Dr. Junkin to Miami University, Ohio, where he
had been called to the department of Latin, and subsequently
Modern History was added to his work. In the spring of
1851 he was licensed to preach the gospel; and in the summer
of next year he taught Greek and Hebrew in a theological
school which had a short existence in Cincinnati.

Having been elected to the Professorship of Latin and History at Princeton, he returned to that place in the spring of
1853. Upon the resignation of Dr. Carnahan and the election
of Dr. Maclean to the presidency, several changes were made
in the faculty, and Dr. Moffat was transferred to the Chair of
Greek, which he held for a period of seven years, retaining
still the lectureship of History, until a professor was appointed
to that department. In 1861 Dr. Moffat was elected by the
General Assembly to the Chair of Church History in the Theological Seminary at Princeton, his present appointment. He
is the author of an " Introduction to the Study of Æsthetics"
and a "Life of Dr. Chalmers," and has now in the press a
" Comparative View of Religions." He lately became editor
of the *Princetonian*, a weekly newspaper published at Princeton, N. J.

His contributions to this *Review* are:

1839. Cory's Ancient Fragments.

1856. Macaulay's History of England—Egyptology.

1857. Grote's History of Greece—The Aim of History—
The Historical Epoch of Abraham—Popular Education.

1858. St. Hilaire on the Reformation in Spain—Harrison
on the Greek Prepositions.

1859. Political Education.

1861. Antiquity of the Book of Genesis—Rawlinson's Hero-
dotus—Motley's Dutch Republic.

1862. Christian Enterprise.
1863. University Education.
1864. Latin Christianity.
1865. Early History of Heathenism.
1867. The Oriental Churches—The British Churches under Cromwell.
1868. Lord's Old Roman World.

MOMBERT, J. ISIDOR, is a native of Germany, of Hebrew lineage, educated in England, from whence he emigrated to Canada, and came into Pennsylvania in 1857. Our knowledge of him begins with a translation of "Tholuck on the Psalms," which he adapted to the English version with the approbation of Dr. Tholuck, and which was published by Martien in 1858. In 1859 he was made rector of St. James Protestant Episcopal church at Lancaster, Pa., and continued in the charge till 1869, when he returned to Germany, and is now rector of St. John's American Episcopal church, Dresden, with his residence at Villa Emma, Strehlin, in the suburbs. He received the degree of D. D. from the University of Pennsylvania. Dr. Mombert is the editor and translator of the volume of Lange's Commentary containing the catholic epistles of James, Peter, and Jude; and he contributed to this periodical the following articles:

1865. Are James the son of Alpheus and James the brother of the Lord identical?—An Account of Extreme Unction—The First Miracle of Christ.
1866. The Raising of Lazarus.

MONOD, ADOLPHE FREDERIC THEODORE, was a son of the Rev. John Monod, a native of Geneva, who was many years pastor of the Reformed church in Paris, and dignified as a chevalier of the Legion of Honour, and President of the Consistory. He had seven sons and three daughters. Three of his sons became eminent ministers of the gospel, and the four who devoted themselves to secular pursuits were distinguished for ability and integrity in their own spheres. Adolphe was born at Copenhagen on the 21st of January, 1802; received his education at the National Academy of Geneva; and in 1826 and 1827 became pastor of a French Protestant congregation in Naples, and chaplain to the Prussian ambassador. From 1827 to 1831 he was pastor to the National Protestant church in Lyons. When here, he was personally brought to know that the form of godliness was different from its spirit and reality; and in the church of which he was pastor, he insisted that a distinction should be observed there between the openly profane and those who made a credible profession of religion, and debarred the scandalous from the communion. For this he was deposed by the Consistory, of which he was president, and from 1831 to 1836 he continued in Lyons, but as pastor of an independent church. In 1836 he accepted the appointment of Professor of Sacred Eloquence in the Seminary at Montauban, and continued in this position till 1848, when he accepted a call to the National Protestant church in Paris, as assistant to his brother Frederic, and when his brother withdrew from the National establishment in 1849, he continued to be sole pastor, and in defence of his course published the pamphlet, *Pourquoi je demure dans l'Eglise établie.* He died on the 6th of April, 1856, aged fifty-four. During the last two years of his life he was a great sufferer.

The work by which he is best known is his *Lucille, ou la Lecture de la Bible,* which has been translated into many languages. His Sermons are published in four volumes, two of which were published in his lifetime. They abound in eloquence. Of one of them, " Compassions de Dieu pour les Chrétiens inconvertis," Michelet said, " Ceux qui l'ont entendu en tremblent encore." While at Montauban he wrote a Preface to Dr. Hodge's Commentary on the Romans, which had been translated into French by his brother, Dr. Horace Monod. During the last fifteen years of his life he was the French correspondent of *The Presbyterian.* In 1841 the degree of D. D. was conferred upon him by Jefferson College, and in 1842 by the College of New Jersey. He has been called the Bossuet of the Protestant pulpit, and was the most eloquent preacher in France in his day. His labours also were very abundant, and never confined to his own pulpit, but while at Lyons and Montauban he did a great work of evangelization in the surrounding country. A translation of one of his Introductory Lectures is given in the April No. for 1843.

MOORE, THOMAS V., was born in Newville, Pa., on the 1st of February, 1818. He commenced his collegiate course at South Hanover College, Indiana, and graduated at Dickinson College, Pa. in 1838. After spending a year as an agent of the Pennsylvania Colonization Society, he entered the Princeton Seminary, and completed his theological course in 1842, when he accepted a call to the church in Carlisle. In 1845 he removed to Greencastle, and in 1847 he accepted the charge of the church in Richmond, Virginia, in which he continued till 1868, when he became pastor of the church in Nashville, Tennessee, his present charge.

His principal works are a "Commentary on the Prophets of the Restoration," New York, 1856; "The Last Days of Jesus," about 1858; "God's University: or, the Family a School, a Government, and a Church, a Prize Essay for the Philadelphia Society for Juvenile Delinquency;" "The Culdee Church," and "The Corporate Life of the Church;" besides two lectures in the "Book of Evidences," delivered before the University of Virginia, and various articles in the *Methodist Quarterly*, North and South. His contributions to this *Review* are,

1844. The Missionary bearing of Calvinism.
1848. Howison's History of Virginia.

MOTT, GEORGE SCUDDER, is a native of New York City, and born on the 25th November, 1829. His parents were members of the Rutger Street church, and he united with that church in his fourteenth year, at which time Dr. Krebs was the pastor. He pursued his classical studies at the University of New York, graduating in 1850; after which he entered the Theological Seminary at Princeton, and was licensed as a preacher by the First Presbytery of New York, April 1853. In October of the same year he was ordained pastor of the Second Presbyterian church in Rahway, New Jersey, and continued in the charge five years. He then accepted a call to the church in Newton, where he continued nine years, and in 1869 removed to Flemington, N. J., his present charge.

He is the author of several books and tracts published by the American Sunday-school Union, among which is the book called "The Perfect Law," now translated into Spanish and Portuguese, and the tract "Holding on to Christ," which has had a very large circulation. The Board of Publication publishes a work of his on "The Prodigal Son," and several tracts. To this *Review* he contributed in

1863. Paul's Thorn in the Flesh.

MUIR, WILLIAM KENNEDY. This devoted young minister was a native of Scotland, took a high position in the University of Edinburgh, where he graduated with honour, and afterwards in the New College at Edinburgh, where he pursued his theological course. Here his thorough devotion to study affected his health, and seeking to renew it by change and rest from laborious study, he went to Egypt, where he associated himself with the missionaries of the United Presbyterian Church from the United States, and for a period of nearly two years devoted himself thoroughly to the work of acquainting himself with the condition, and especially the spiritual needs of that people, and to endeavours, as far as in his power, to do them good.

All this was to him a work of love. His habits of close observation and patient research enabled him to lay up a valuable store of knowledge—rich instalments of which were furnished in a series of articles for the *Repertory*, under the title of "Christian Work in Egypt."

Recovering his health, he desired to devote himself wholly to the work of the ministry, and for this purpose returned to Scotland in 1868, where he was licensed to preach the gospel, and ere long accepted with all the ardour of his nature, chastened and sanctified by Christian principle, a proposition of the Colonial Committee of the Free Church to enter upon labours in Australia. Just before sailing for Scotland he entered into the marriage relation with a Miss Rufka Gregory, a Syrian young lady, who had been raised and trained in the family of the late excellent missionary of the American Board in Syria, the Rev. Mr. Whiting. With this young lady, and with strong hopes of usefulness, he set forth immediately after the marriage in Scotland for his new field, and on their arrival in Australia, March 1, 1869, he was immediately settled in a newly formed and most promising congregation at Easternwich. But how mysterious the ways of Providence! On the very first Sabbath after his ordination, when he preached with great unction and power, he shortly after ruptured a blood vessel, never occupied his pulpit again, and in a short time sunk to a most lamented grave.

He was a ripe scholar of the Hebrew tongue, and of very general research and attainments. His crowning excellence, especially toward the close of his life, was his ardent piety, and his consecration of all to the service of Christ.

1868. Christian Work in Egypt.

NEANDER, JOHANN AUGUST WILHELM, was born at Gottingen, of Jewish parents, on the 15th of January, 1789. While receiving his education in the gymnasium at Hamburg he was converted to the Christian faith, and assumed the name of Neander, (the Greek for *new man*) at his baptism. He prosecuted his studies in theology successively at Halle, Gottingen, Hamburg, and Heidelberg, where in 1812 he was made Professor Extraordinary of Theology, but in the same year he was called to a similar office at Berlin. His life was devoted chiefly to researches into the history of the church.   In 1832–3 he issued his "History of the Apostolic Church," in two volumes.   From 1825 to 1845 his "Universal History of the Christian Religion and Church," in five volumes.   In 1835 he issued a "Life of Jesus in its Historical relations," in refutation of the work bearing a similar title by Strauss.   A chapter of his great work was translated and published in the volume for 1832, on the Rites and Worship of the Early Christian Church.

NORDHEIMER, ISAAC, was a native of Bavaria, and of Hebrew extraction.   He obtained the degree of Doctor of Philosophy from the University of Munich.   In 1836 he was made Professor of Arabic, Syriac, and other Oriental languages, in the University of the City of New York, and at the time of his death, November 3, 1842, he was also Teacher of Hebrew and German in the Union Theological Seminary.   He is the author of a History of Florence, and of a Hebrew Grammar and Chrestomathy, which at once achieved for him a high reputation for oriental scholarship.   He also began the preparation of a Hebrew and Chaldee Concordance to the Old Testament, but died before it was completed.   He wrote the article on Fürst's Hebrew Concordance in the volume for 1839.

OWEN, JOSEPH, was born in Bedford township, West Chester county, New York, on the 14th of June, 1814.   His parents attended the ministry of the Rev. Jacob Green, who manifested a great interest in him when a boy. He graduated at the College of New Jersey in 1835, was Tutor in the College in 1836, and after taking the three years course at the Princeton Theological Seminary, he was ordained as a missionary and sailed to India in 1840.   He remained there without visiting his native country till 1869, but he is now in Scotland revigorating his system by its cool breezes, and is expected in the United States in the fall of 1870.

His labours in India have been mainly at Allahabad station, and much of his time has been devoted to translating the Scriptures and preparing a Commentary on the Old Testament in Urdu.   During the Sepoy mutiny a great portion of what he had prepared on the Psalms was destroyed, and had to be recomposed; but we learn that before he left India his Commentary on Isaiah had been issued.   In addition to preaching and superintending the press he has acted as Secretary to the North India Bible Society and the Tract Society.   He contributed, while in the Seminary at Princeton, in 1839, the article on China.

PACKARD, FREDERICK ADOLPHUS, oldest son of Asa and Nancy (Quincy) Packard, was born at Marlborough, Massachusetts, September 25th, 1794. He traced his ancestry, through both parents, up to respectable settlers who came from England during the early emigrations to the Puritan colonies, and in both lines the families had always borne the character of sober, educated, God-fearing citizens. His own father was for many years the minister of Marlborough, and afterwards of Lancaster in the same state, where he ended his life, honoured and respected for shrewd mother-wit and strength of character.

Mr. Packard had his early education at a school in Wiscasset, Maine, was graduated at Harvard College in 1814, and soon afterwards went to Northampton and began the study of law in the office of Ashmun and Strong. Here he found a delightful society open to him, and entered heartily into the intellectual and social life of what was then perhaps the leading town of western Massachusetts. Admitted to the bar, he settled himself in 1819 for the practice of his profession in Springfield. Here he remained for nearly ten years, securing a very promising position as a lawyer, and editing during most of the time the *Hampden Journal.* In 1822 he married Elizabeth Dwight, second daughter of John and Sarah (Dwight) Hooker, thus connecting his own with two others of the old and honoured families of New England.

During this time he also interested himself actively and earnestly in Sunday-schools, superintending one in Springfield, establishing a county Sunday-school society, holding meetings and raising money to promote its work, and keeping up frequent communication with the American Sunday-school Union, then just established in Philadelphia. This led to his visiting Philadelphia in 1828 to attend a meeting of the friends of that society, when he made the personal acquaintance of some of its managers. He was soon after invited to come into the service of the Society as Recording Secretary and Editor of Publications. This invitation he accepted, and removed to his new home in 1829, where he resided the rest of his life. He was then thirty-five years old. He had in Springfield an assured income, the most encouraging prospects of success and eminence at the bar of his native state, and a happy home among his wife's early friends. The duties of his new position were untried, the position itself a new one, to which he must give its form; the salary was limited, and the social advantages few; he had no relatives or early friends in the city. Yet he believed that he was called of God to a place of usefulness, and it

34

became a clear duty to go.   He went, and from that time he never looked back or regretted the choice he had made.   He entered heartily into his work, and devoted his life to the cause of the education of children and the elevation of the poorer and criminal classes.

The principal duty of his new position was the editing of all the publications of the Society.   Every book which the Society issued from 1829 to 1867 (and we think no single exception need be made) passed under his eye, and was by him prepared for and carried through the press.   The number of these books is over two thousand, and of them some fifty were not only edited but written by him.   Besides this he edited the periodicals of the Society, the *Sunday-school Journal*, afterwards the *Sunday-school World*, and the *Youth's Friend*, afterwards the *Youth's Penny Gazette*, and still later the *Child's World;* writing constantly in them himself and selecting material from a wide range of reading.   He also prepared for twenty-five years the Annual Report of the Society, and attended regularly the meetings of the Board of Managers and Committee of Publication, of both of which he was secretary.   These were his formal duties, but in addition to these, how much influence he exerted in shaping the course of the Society and building up its extensive business by his judgment, energy, and high principle, how much in forming the standard of service within it by his steady example of industry and devotion, no one can estimate.   He was strongly and intelligently attached to the fundamental idea of the Society, that of denominational union for objects common to all evangelical Christians, and successfully defended it in a controversy with the late Bishop Potter of Pennsylvania.   He believed with his whole heart in Sunday-school education, within the sphere for which it was originally undertaken, and for the work which in large towns and in unformed communities it can best perform.   Throughout his life he was always ready to take part in it himself, by teaching, by lecturing to teachers, or in any way which he thought would do good.

Nor was his activity confined to this one department of Christian labour.   He interested himself early in the general secular education of the young, and studied carefully the working of our common school system.   One of his latest publications was an examination of the actual condition of the system in four states of the Union, designed to call attention to the wide difference between the theory and the practice, and to stimulate thoughtful people to earnest effort after greater efficiency and thoroughness.   He was for several years a Director of the Girard College for Orphans, and was twice strongly urged to become its president.   The condition of the neglected and criminal classes also enlisted his benevolence in efforts to secure for them the wisest treatment of kindness and severity in due proportion.   For many years a Manager of the House of Refuge, he was deeply interested in its welfare, and often conducted the Sunday services there as well as at Girard College.   He was also for twenty-one years the editor of the *Journal of Prison Discipline*, and has left in it a monument of his zeal and wisdom in dealing with that difficult subject.   The Pennsylvania system, as it is called, of separate confinement, he heartily approved and advocated in the Journal.

The labours thus imperfectly sketched filled a busy life of thirty-eight years in Philadelphia.   It is impossible to estimate how much was added to them by his extensive correspondence with friends in this country and in England.   His letters were rapidly written, but singularly rich in thought—full of discussions of public matters and elevated subjects, full also, those written to personal friends, of the best feelings of a noble heart. He contributed also abundantly to daily papers and to magazines, chiefly to the *Princeton Review*, and when the Union League of Philadelphia was established, being presented with membership by a friend, he wrote a number of plain political tracts which it published.   Such an amount of work he accomplished only by constant and intense application.   He was in his office every day of his life, except when occasionally absent from home, and during three short periods of sickness, for as much as seven hours, often for eight—generally the only person in the building on public holidays.   In the summer he always carried his work with him and kept up constant communication with the office.   Of course, he acquired great facility in performing his special duties, but he always kept himself beforehand, so far as possible, with his work.

In 1840 he was sent by the Society to England, to establish closer communication with the London Sunday-school Union, and obtain some aid from it for the work then entered upon in the Mississippi valley.   His mission was successful in its main object, and secured for him the life-long friendship of a number of excellent people who sympathized with him in his Christian labours.   Among these was the family of Samuel Bagster, Esq. and W. H. Watson, Esq., one of the secretaries of the London Society.

Mr. Packard had a strong frame and an excellent constitution.   The great simplicity and regularity of his habits secured him a remarkable degree of health.   Every day, in all weathers and wherever he was, he took a walk of an hour and a half or two hours, simply for exercise. His rapid gait, with head slightly bent and eyes generally fixed on the ground, together perhaps with his never wearing an overcoat in the coldest weather, made him often an object of curious inquiry to those who did not know him. Among his friends he was well known as remarkable for activity and vigor. To the last year of his life he kept the ruddy complexion and the soft brown hair, turned gray only underneath at the side of the forehead, of his youth. During the thirty-eight years which he spent in Philadelphia he was confined to the house only three times, once by a sprained ankle, and twice from operations on his diseased lip, before his last sickness.

To this activity of body was joined a similar youthfulness and healthiness of disposition. He seemed never to lose his sympathy with young people, and always enjoyed their enjoyment. Full of humour, he entered keenly into all pure and good-tempered fun, and enjoyed a good joke upon himself as well as any he made upon others. He loved children and they loved him. His own remember him in their early days as a most delightful playmate, never losing his authority, but never keeping them at a distance, and, as they grew older, he was still their most trusted, respected, and *enjoyable* friend, ready with sympathy and help in their trials, delighted with their successes, always wise and kind in counsel, reproof, or encouragement.

Perhaps the most striking characteristic of his mind was its activity in practical matters. He never devoted himself to abstract or scientific study, and seemed to have no taste for it. Some of his friends regretted, and he at times, later in life, seemed almost to regret, that he had not given himself to some pursuit which would have trained his mind more severely, and enabled him to contribute something substantial to the sum of human knowledge. But that was only in a pause of his work, in the conversation of a quiet hour. He would go back from it to his daily pursuits and throw himself into them with all the zeal and energy of his nature, untroubled by such doubts or regrets. And no one can think that his life was thrown away. The need of just such work as he did was overwhelming, and, however he might have been fitted for some other, perhaps higher, function, there can be no doubt of his fitness for this. His mind was intensely active—to that the variety of subjects which he investigated, the number and fruitfulness of his suggestions and contrivances in carrying on his editorial duties, the power of his intellectual influence over so many and

such different minds, abundantly testify.   It was also well-
balanced and sound in its judgments, capable of originality and
appreciating it in others, but not led away by novelty, far more
conservative indeed than radical.   His whole inclination was to
the practical rather than to the theoretical.   Seeing the want,
more than twenty years ago, of a dictionary of the Bible for
Sunday-school teachers and scholars, he set to work, though
not trained in such studies, and not thoroughly master of the
original sources, and with great labour prepared one himself,
one which was very widely circulated and exceedingly useful.
So in other things; it was always the practical result that engaged his attention.   However good the theory of our common
school system was, however praised by foreigners and boasted
of by Americans, it did not satisfy him unless it actually
accomplished results proportioned to the labour and expense.
It was much the same in his judgment of character.   To him a
man was worth what he could do by his virtue and intelligence, and he paid little heed to family or station or wealth
compared with that.   This caused some to think him hyper-
critical and some illiberal, but he judged himself by as severe
a standard.   With all this practicalness, he was keenly alive
to beauty and to all pure pleasures.   An article of his in the
Princeton Review for October 1863, on " The Beautiful Things
of Earth," was a revelation to many who knew its authorship
of a hitherto unexpected side in his character.   Even those
who knew him best were surprised to find that he had noticed
so closely and felt so vividly the common pleasures that are
offered to us so freely in our daily life.

It is not well to attempt any analysis of his religious character, which was to him a sacred matter between himself and
God, but a few words should be said about his church connec-
tions and his religious life as it bore upon others.   It was
while he was living in Springfield that he became a Christian,
and he joined the First (Trinitarian) Congregational church of
that place.   When, soon after he came to Philadelphia, a church
of that order was formed there, the Clinton street church, he
transferred his membership to it by letter of dismission, but on
its dissolution, he sent back his letter and remained a member
of the Springfield church during the rest of his life.   For many
years he attended worship in a Presbyterian church, first in
that on Clinton street, while Dr. Joel Parker was settled there,
then in Calvary church on Locust street, after he had moved
into its neighbourhood.   But for the last few years of his life
he attended services regularly at St. Mark's (Episcopal)
church, being attracted thither first by the preaching of Dr. E.

A. Washburne, which he greatly enjoyed. He found that no objection would be made to his regularly communing there without being confirmed, and he soon came to feel himself quite at home and happy in the new relation. It should be added, that, probably by a not unnatural effect of increasing age on a conservative disposition, he felt more confidence in the steady government and uniform ritual of the Episcopal order than in the comparative freedom and variableness of Congregationalism. This certainly shows, as many other things did, his liberality towards all forms of evangelical Christianity, and with few persons did he more enjoy religious intercourse than with a cousin, of most beautiful Christian character, who died in the Unitarian faith a few months after him. It seems but the simple truth to say, that an earnest zeal to to serve and glorify Christ, his Lord, was the mainspring of his active life from the time of his decision to come to Philadelphia. Naturally of a quick temper and positive mind, he became humble and self-distrustful, yet was always on the watch for opportunities to do good, fearless in what he thought to be his duty, and resolute in his struggle against sin and immorality. His strength of will was sanctified in the service of Christ and became a holy energy in the work of righteousness. Early in life he was involved in a bitter quarrel, which turned partly on a question of veracity, between him and another, and broke off all intercourse between them. A few years before his death he wrote to that man, requesting a reconciliation, as they were both drawing near the sunset of life, and was delighted to receive an answer in the same spirit of charity. In his family and in his business, in ordinary intercourse and in times of excitement, he seemed to all who knew him a true Christian gentleman.

Mr. Packard continued actively at work, going to his office daily, until June 22d, 1867. The cancerous growth upon his lower lip had been increasing for more than a year, unchecked by a severe operation upon it in the previous summer, and steadily undermining his strength. That afternoon he felt too weak to go back to his office as usual, and from that day he never left the house until his death. He had been prepared for such an event, and for months had left his business every day in such a state that he need not, if he felt unable, return. He was confined to his room at once, and, the light darkened, his face bandaged and daily dressed, unable to take food except through a glass tube, unable to read or to bear reading or lengthened conversation, he lingered for five months. During this time he was obliged to take morphine in large quantities, and, in addition to his weakness and physical pain, was tormented by sleepless nights and the wretched visions of a brain affected by the opiate. It was a terrible trial to his faith and patience, and his sensitive nature felt it most keenly, but the grace of God never shone more brightly than in that darkened chamber of suffering. All who were about him there, even those who had repulsive duties to perform, felt the attractive power of his Christian character. The poor body might become feeble and even poisonous, but the soul beamed from within it like "a star confined into a tomb." He prayed earnestly but submissively for release, and at length it came. The disease reached in its progress the muscles by which he swallowed and he could take no more food. Still, a mere skeleton as he was, he lingered two whole days without a drop of nourishment. At last, on the morning of November 11th, 1867, the long agony was over, and he "fell asleep in Jesus."

The list of his public works is as follows:—"The Daily Public School in the United States," J. B. Lippincott & Co., 1865; "Life of Robert Owen," Ashmead & Evans, 1866.

The following were published by the American Sunday-school Union:

Annual Reports, 1829–1839, 1841–1855; Catharine Gray, Affectionate Daughter-in-law, 1833; Hadassah the Jewish Orphan, 1834; Murdered Mother, Refuge, Infidel Class, 1835; Anchor, Life of Peter, Susan Ellmaker, 1836; Union Spelling-book, 1838; Life of Mary A. Hooker, 1840; Two Ways and Two Ends, Home of the Gileadite, 1841; Kinsale Family, Teacher's Harvest, 1842; Great Aim of Sunday-school Teacher, 1843; Life of Solomon, Proverbs of Solomon, 1845; Consecutive Union Question books on the Gospels, 1846–8; Six Days' Wonder, 1847; Light and Dark Path, 1848; Light and Love for Nursery Group, 1851; Sunday-school Phenomena, 1852; Union Primer, 1853; Union Bible Dictionary, 2d ed. 1855; Boy's Picture Gallery, 1856; Teacher Taught, 2d ed., Teacher Teaching, The Rock, 1861; Penny Question-book, 1862; and some eighteen others without dates affixed.

His contributions to the *Princeton Review* were as follows:

1841. Religious Instruction in Common Schools.
1842. Irish School System.
1843. English School Systems.
1850. Religion and Insanity.
1851. Public Libraries.
1857. Public Lectures.
1863. The Beautiful Things of Earth.
1865. Horace Mann.

PATTERSON, ROBERT, was born near Letterkenny, Ireland, on the 20th of January, 1820. He had received the rudiments of a good education and adopted the mercantile life; and in 1847 he emigrated to the United States and opened a store in Philadelphia. Here he was received into the communion of the First Reformed Presbyterian church, then under the joint pastoral care of the late Dr. Samuel B. Wylie and his son, and became a teacher in the Sabbath-school, which was under the superintendence of Mr. George H. Stuart. Mr. Stuart soon perceived that he had more than common abilities as a teacher, and with the coöperation of the pastors encouraged him to prepare himself for the ministry, and in 1849 he entered the Seminary of the Reformed Presbyterian Church. In May 1851 he was licensed to preach the gospel by the Reformed Presbytery of Philadelphia, and on the 17th of June he was ordained and sent on a missionary tour through the churches to enlist them in a plan of Systematic Benevolence for the support of Home and Foreign Missions. In 1854 he acted as one of the secretaries in the great Missionary Convention held in New York, on the occasion of the visit of Dr. Duff, and accompanied him on his tour through the United States. On June 27 of that year he was installed pastor of the First Reformed Presbyterian church in Cincinnati; and in October 1857 he exchanged this for the First Reformed Presbyterian church in Chicago. During the war he often visited the field as one of the Army Committee of the Young Men's Christian Association of Chicago, and Mr. Stuart being fully convinced of the energy with which he could carry out anything he undertook, frequently engaged him in making tours through the country to raise supplies, and one especially with the Rev. George J. Mingins to the Pacific Coast in 1864, which was very successful. .

Dr. Patterson was not slow to perceive the power that the press exerts upon the people of this country, and has employed it extensively and perseveringly in the service of the gospel. He has published over four hundred tracts, sermons, essays, and letters, and been a regular contributor to the pages of the *Banner of the Covenant*, *The Evangelical Repository*, *The Preacher*, *The Western Presbyterian*, *The Presbyter*, and *The Family Treasure*. His discussions are all in a popular style, and some of them have attained a wide circulation. Of "The Fables of Infidelity," a volume in which Atheism, Pantheism, and Ritualism are discussed, thirteen thousand copies have been sold. Over four hundred thousand copies of his Sabbath letters and sermons have been printed in German and English;

while his Christian Commission articles have been used to a great extent. He has now published a work entitled "Scientific Suggestions," being a criticism of those alleged facts in Mathematics, Astronomy, Geology, Chemistry, Physiology, Phrenology, Physical Geography, Ethnology, &c., which are said to be in conflict with the teachings of the Bible, a chapter of which was published in advance as an article in this *Review*.

In prosecuting the work of the Christian Commission he became convinced that the restricted communion and liturgy of the Reformed Presbyterian Church was unwarranted and unedifying, and got a dismission from the Reformed Presbytery of Chicago on the 15th of January, 1867, and is now pastor of the Jefferson Park church, Chicago, in connection with the Presbyterian Church of the United States.

1868. Antiquity of Man.

PLUMER, WILLIAM SWAN, was born at Darlington, Pennsylvania, in 1802; graduated at Washington College, Va. in 1825, and in the same year entered Princeton Theological Seminary. He was ordained pastor of the Presbyterian church at Danville, Va. in 1827, and subsequently had charge of the churches at Warrenton, N. C., Briery, Petersburg, and Richmond, Va., and the Franklin street church in Baltimore, Md. In 1854 he was elected by the General Assembly to the Chair of Didactic and Pastoral Theology in the Western Theological Seminary, which he held till 1862, for some years in conjunction with the pastorate of the Central church in Allegheny City; but a popular opposition to him, on account of his want of sympathy with the government in the suppression of the rebellion, compelled him then to resign, and during the next three years he made his residence chiefly in Philadelphia and Pottsville, Pa., supplying vacant churches, and superintending the printing of five or six volumes of his works, enumerated below. In 1866 he was elected Professor of Theology in the Theological Seminary at Columbia, S. C., his present appointment.

He was Moderator of the General Assembly in 1838, and received in the same year the honorary degree of D. D. from Washington College, Va. and the College of New Jersey; and that of LL.D. in 1857, from the University of Mississippi.

In 1837 he established the religious newspaper called *The Watchman of the South*, and conducted it eight years; and he is the author of the following works on practical and doctrinal religious subjects. 1. Substance of an Argument against the Indiscriminate Incorporation of Churches and Religious Socie-

35

ties, 1 vol. 8vo. 2. The Bible True and Infidelity Wicked, 18mo. 3. Plain Thoughts for Children, 18mo. 4. Short Sermons to Little Children, 18mo. 5. Thoughts Worth Remembering, 8vo. 6. The Saint and the Sinner, 18mo. 7. The Grace of Christ, 12mo. 8. Rome against the Bible and the Bible against Rome, 18mo. 9. Christ our Theme and Glory: Inaugural Address, 8vo. 10. The Church and her Enemies. 11. The Law of God as contained in the Ten Commandments, Explained and Enforced, 12mo. 12. Vital Godliness, 12mo. 13. Jehovah-Jireh: a Treatise on Providence, 12mo. 14. Studies in the Book of Psalms: being a Critical and Expository Commentary, with Doctrinal and Practical Remarks on the entire Psalter, royal 8vo. 15. The Rock of our Salvation, 12mo. 16. Words of Truth and Love, 18mo. 17. Sermons and Select Remains of Rev. William Nevins, D.D., 12mo. 18. An Abridgment of Stevenson on the Offices of Christ, 16mo. Besides these, and several pamphlets, he has contributed largely to the periodical literature of the country, among which contributions we acknowledge the following:

1834. Revivals of Religion.

1848. Religious Instruction of Slaves—Swedenborgianism—Duelling.

1849. The Inquisition.

1850. Algernon Sidney.

1851. Life of Socrates.

1854. Is the Church of Rome idolatrous?

1864. The late Rev. James Hoge, D. D.

POND, ENOCH, was born in Wrentham, Massachusetts, on the 29th of July, 1791; was graduated at Brown University in 1813; ordained pastor of the church at Ward (now Auburn,) Mass. in 1815, and continued in the charge about thirteen years. During this time the church was favoured with two remarkable revivals of religion, in which about one hundred and sixty persons were added to the church, and from being weak and inefficient it became one of the most flourishing churches in Worcester county.

In June 1828 Dr. Pond relinquished his charge at Ward and removed to Cambridgeport, in order to assume the editorship of the *Spirit of the Pilgrims*, which had just been established. He edited the first five volumes of this work, and wrote two-thirds of the articles published in them.

In June 1832 he accepted a call to become Professor of Theology in the Seminary at Bangor, Maine, and filled this professorship twenty-three years, at the same time teaching Ecclesiastical History. In 1855 he resigned the Chair of Theology, and was transferred to that of History, which he has retained till the present time.

Dr. Pond has been a diligent writer. We give the abridged titles of twenty-four volumes which have emanated from his pen. 1. Monthly Concert Lectures. 2. The World's Salvation. 3. Memoir of President Davies. 4. Memoir of Susan Anthony. 5. Memoir of Count Zinzendorf. 6. Memoir of John Wickliffe. 7. Morning of the Reformation. 8. No Fellowship with Romanism. 9. First Principles of the Oracles of God. 10. The Mather Family. 11. Pastoral Theology, (two editions.) 12. Pope and Pagan. 13. Review of Swedenborgianism, (two editions.) 14. Plato and his Works. 15. Manual of Congregationalism, (two editions.) 16. Review of Bushnell's God in Christ. 17. Life of Increase Mather, and Sir William Phipps. 18. Ancient Church. 19. Memoir of John Knox. 20. The Wreck and the Rescue. 21. The Church, (two editions.) 22. Memoir of Joseph Stone, Esq., of Ward. 23. Lectures on Christian Theology. 24. A Text-Book of Ecclesiastical History. Besides these, there are a few pamphlets which attracted considerable attention when published: "A Reply to Judson on Baptism," which passed through three editions; "Apology for Religious Conferences," with a Rejoinder in Reply to Dr. Bancroft of Worcester; "Letters to Rev. Samuel Nott;" "Review of Unitarian Tracts;" "Exhibition of Unitarianism," and about twenty sermons, of which some were published in *The National Preacher.*

There were very few magazines or religious newspapers published in this country to which Dr. Pond has not contributed; he is also the editor of several works, and a great number of Tracts published by the different publication and tract societies were written by him. He is the author of the following articles:

1862. Augustine.

1864. The Works of Plato—The Russian Church.

1866. The Missionary Enterprise and its bearing on the Cause of Science and Learning.

1868. Spectral Appearances, their Causes and Laws.

PROUDFIT, JOHN WILLIAMS, was the son of the Rev. Alexander M. Proudfit, D. D., who was pastor of the Associate Reformed Presbyterian church at Salem, New York, from 1795 to 1835. He was born in the village of Salem on the 22d of September, 1803; was educated at Union College, Schenectady, N. Y., and entered the Seminary at Princeton, New Jersey, in 1823, being then in the twenty-first year of his age.

"He was then," says Dr. Dickinson,* who was a member of
the same class, ."tall, imposing in person, with an expansive
brow, and dark deep-set eyes. On conversing with him it was
easy to perceive that he had not neglected the advantages
which Union College, under the auspices of the late President
Nott, afforded; still less the home influences amid which his
boyhood was trained. There was a thoughtful seriousness in
his mien, a conscientious studiousness, a prayerful sense of his
dependence on God, which indicated a maturity of preparation,
both mental and spiritual, for the theological course on which
he had then entered. So far as our recollection serves us,
there were few, if any, of our class at Princeton Seminary more
respected, or of whose probable future a more favourable estimate was made. Nor were we disappointed. Having acquired
fixed habits of study, he ultimately became familiar with the
Greek and Latin fathers of the church, as well as with the
best classical authors, and his mind stored with the treasures,
it might be said, of ancient and modern learning; while his
fondness for the languages was so decided that he always preferred the original Scriptures to the English version for daily
use—so that when it became incumbent on him to instruct in
the Greek language, it was his aim to perfect his pupils in the
Greek Testament—those, in particular, who might have been
looking forward to the pulpit. Having been very diligent and
circumspect during his own college days, he was hardly less
strict with his students; and if he might have made too little
allowance for youthful indiscretions, it was because he was no
less solicitous for their future standing in society than their
present scholarship. It was his practical judgment that education should never be divorced from religion—the mental
powers cultivated to the neglect of the moral. Whatever studies were to be pursued, exercise secured, company or travel
enjoyed, it should alike be in subordination to the moral law of
man's being; and either, without the daily recognition of our
dependence and accountability, is virtual atheism. Aware,
too, of the great advantage of social intercourse with men of
letters to the practical development of educated mind, he was
wont to avail himself of his opportunities for the interchange
of thought on important points of inquiry, and seldom returned
from a visit or a journey without having added something to
his mental stores, to be used as occasion might serve, either
for the illustration and defence of a truth, or to advance some
useful cause; and thus his frequent correspondence, for which
he had acquired more than ordinary facility, was marked alike

* In *The Presbyterian* of April 16, 1870.

by the extent of his observations and the justness of his reflections.

"Early taught by parental precept and example the necessity of prayer to both advancement in the Divine life and effective preparation for usefulness, he referred every matter to
God, cultivated a devout frame of mind, attained to rare
excellence in prayer—adoration, thanksgiving, confession, sup-
plication. In this relation there is a diversity of gifts, and
though all may be alike reverent and devout, alike weighed
down by a sense of their own or the needs of others, yet all
comparatively have not the same freedom and fulness, much
less the same aptitude and scriptural richness in prayer.

"He had, moreover, experienced the power of *the truth* in
his own soul, and hence looked on the rescue of the soul—its
discipline for usefulness in this life, and preparation for the
life to come, as the great end of the preached word. In accordance with this view his sermons were written, or trains of
thought for the pulpit arranged; and if he lacked the qualities of voice so essential to popular attraction, he was always
wrapped in his subject, and at times impressive; while his
sermons, written with due study and prayer, afforded ample
material for reflection, and led in not a few instances to blessed
results. We might refer to some that we heard—such as that
on the text, 'Occupy till I come,' and another on the text, 'I
beheld Satan fall as lightning from heaven;' but we are not
aware of his having published more than three; one entitled
'The Sanctuary Consulted in the Present Crisis,' the other,
'The Two Lives,' on the occasion of the installation of his
nephew, the Rev. William Irving, at Rondout, and the last at
the funeral of Dr. Strong, formerly Professor of Mathematics
in Rutgers College. It has sometimes occurred to us that he
effected as much by opportune conversation with individuals
as by his occasional discourses. In this respect he was unusually gifted, and time and again cheered by hearing of some
good done.

"At Newburyport, Mass., the place of his early settlement,
October 4, 1827, as pastor of the Federal Street Presbyterian
church, he was most assiduous in his preparation for the pulpit; his Sabbath services, and weekly meetings, and pastoral
visits, were warmly appreciated; about three hundred and
forty were added to the church; and the tie between his people and himself grew stronger until, in 1833, the state of his
health rendered it advisable to resign his charge.

"Before this, and during his connection with the church to
which we have referred, he went abroad; and while recruiting

his exhausted strength by foreign travel, aided in furthering the incipient Evangelical movement in Switzerland and France, about the year 1831. This, in connection with subsequent labours in this country, after his return, was spoken of by competent judges, both at home and abroad, as contributing in no small measure to the formation of what is now known as '.The American and Foreign Christian Union.'

"In 1834 he was elected to the Professorship of Latin and Latin Literature in the University of New York, of which the late Dr. James Matthews was then Chancellor. This he retained until 1841, when, in consequence of the troubles in which the University became involved, he, with several other of the Professors, resigned.

"About this time, the College at which he was graduated, and where his qualification for teaching was early appreciated by his appointment to a Tutorship, (which he held for a year or two after leaving the Seminary at Princeton,) conferred on him the degree of Doctor of Divinity.

"In 1841, Dr. Proudfit accepted the Professorship of Greek and Greek Literature,in Rutgers College at New Brunswick, N. J.; and it was while retaining this office through nearly twenty years that he spent the most useful portion of his life. During this period he contributed articles to the *Bibliotheca Sacra* and to the *Princeton Review;* also to the *Independent*, New York *Evening Post*, and the *Ledger;* and became the editor of the *New Brunswick Review*, which, though able contributors had been secured, encountered local prejudice from its incipiency, and even under more favourable auspices could hardly have been sustained, when several, if not all of our prominent periodicals laboured under pecuniary embarrassment.

"Aside from the leisure he was able to secure for writing on different important subjects, he had frequent opportunities for preaching, which he was forward to embrace, whether to officiate in the College chapel, to supply a vacant church, to assist a brother, or to go to some out-of-the-way and unoccupied field of Christian labour. Well do we recollect his solicitude for the highest interests of the members of his class. Scholars they should be—excelling in every branch embraced in the curriculum of the College; but not to the neglect of the highest of all sciences—that of the mind and will of God. In this respect he was not unlike the late President Frelinghuysen, with whom he often walked for exercise in the intimacy of Christian fellowship, and cordially united in sustaining meetings for prayer—faithful to the moral and religious interests of the students. His influence, too, so far as it extended, was that of the scholarly mind in union with the courtesy and kindness of the Christian parent, manifest in the training of many a youth for usefulness in his day, aside from those members of his own household, who, in remembrance of his teachings, his prayers, his example at the time of their own consecration to God's service, and of the influence they are now exerting in their respective fields of ministerial duty, will bear witness that personal friendship has not-warped our judgment.

"But not long after Dr. Proudfit's retiracy from his professorship, a post of duty awaited him which could never have entered into the programme of his life's work. An imperative call for armed men resounded through the land! In this momentous crisis, among the Northern clergy, perhaps, no one was more decided and fearless in the expression of his scriptural views in relation to the nature of the contest in which the nation was plunged than Dr. Proudfit; and from that crisis there was no hesitancy in his course—no abatement in his zeal. His two sons voluntarily offered their services, and became chaplains—one as chaplain in the Second New Jersey volunteers—the other in the United States hospital at Portsmouth Grove, Rhode Island—while their father promptly began his labours—and at his own expense—among the soldiers assembling in the camps. Afterwards, as chaplain, he conducted daily religious service at Fort Wood—labouring also in hospitals, and in various ways for the spiritual, mental, and physical good of the army. At last, at the instance of General Brown, he assumed the chaplaincy at Bedloe's Island, New York harbour, where, during his term of service, no less than about fifteen thousand wounded soldiers (and among them no small proportion of rebel prisoners) were confined; and where he remained till the overthrow of the rebellion—making no discrimination between the loyal and disloyal—supplying them alike with suitable reading—conversing with each in turn, so far as practicable—holding religious meetings; and then again, smoothing the pillow, moistening the lips, and whispering words of peace to the dying soldier; thus proving that Dr. Proudfit was governed by principle, not passion; by Christian sympathies, not partisan aims; and thus furnishing a signal example of voluntary humility and self-denial.

Feeling now the necessity of bodily relief, and deferring to the judgment of his physician, he again went abroad, and this time proceeded directly to the south of Europe; and though he recruited but slowly, it appears from the testimony of his son, who accompanied him, that by his observations and interviews with prominent Christian men in different places, he aimed to acquaint himself with the varying phases of error and superstition, to ascertain the condition of foreign churches and the spiritual needs of the people, in order that he might devise ways and means for the diffusion of Christian knowledge, and thus subserve the cause of Christ abroad as well as at home. Speaking French with facility, he preached in several foreign chapels, and to the galley-slaves in Toulon. He was absent about two years, from 1865 to 1867; and on his return, communicated the results of his observations and doings to the First Presbytery of New York, with which he was connected.

Perfectly familiar with the word of God, and ever on the alert to preach Christ, he was the first to conduct stated religious service in the Lunatic Asylum on Blackwell's Island, New York; in the county jail at New Brunswick; among canal boatmen of the Delaware and Raritan Canal, detained by closing of the lock at New Brunswick on the Sabbath; and often preferred preaching where the means of grace were not known. And with what quiet diligence he kept on the even tenor of his way in doing good as opportunity served—by preaching, by prayer, by a letter of counsel or of condolence—by a word in season, or by an act of kindness; with what meekness he submitted to misrepresentation, or bore calumny; with what resignation he aimed to glorify God in suffering his holy will; with what serene confidence he referred his future to Him who seeth the end from the beginning; and how habitually he communed with God, and walked humbly with God, is best known on earth only by those who were most intimate with him in the relations of private life.

"The second day after his confinement to bed by a cold which ultimated in pneumonia, one of his nephews referred to 2 Corinthians v. 9—'Wherefore we labour, that whether present or absent, we may be accepted of him'—quietly said, 'That has been our *ambition*, (used in the sense of the original,) uncle.' 'Yes,' he replied, 'and *shall be for ever!*' He died at New York City on the 9th of March, 1870.

"When Dr. Proudfit's death was so unexpectedly announced, we felt as if we had been deprived of a privilege—that of listcuing to his dying utterances—for he had loved to converse on the great things pertaining to God and the soul—a man of deep spiritual experience and heavenward aspirations; but the nature of his disease obstructed his voice. As in the case of Whitfield, whose bones still rest beneath the pulpit of the church which witnessed our departed brother's youthful labours for Christ, he too had borne his willing and untiring testimony to the gospel of the grace of God—had worked while 'it is called day,' and when the night came, he had nothing to do but calmly fall asleep in Jesus."

The three following articles are from his pen:

1851. Inspiration and Catholicism.

1852. The Heidelberg Catechism and Dr. Nevin—The Apostles' Creed.

RANKIN, JOHN C., was born May 18, 1816, near Greensboro', North Carolina. His early preparatory studies were directed by an older brother, the Rev. Jesse Rankin, then of Salisbury, now of Lenoir, N. C.; but most of his progress at this stage was made while teaching school, on which he entered at the age of seventeen. He had the benefit of a partial course in the University of North Carolina, at Chapel Hill, but was not graduated. Leaving there in 1836 he entered the Theological Seminary of Princeton, New Jersey, in September of the same year, where the usual three years course of study was pursued. Before closing his connection with the Seminary he was accepted as a missionary of the Presbyterian Board of Foreign Missions, but prior to embarking, spent nearly one year in visiting the churches of the West as an agent. In June 1840 he was married to Sarah T., daughter of the Rev. David Comfort, of Kingston, N. J., and in August of the same year sailed for India. After reaching his destination he soon acquired such a knowledge of the native language as to speak and write it with fluency. Besides some minor contributions to the native press, he wrote and published in the Urdú language in 1845 an extended reply to a learned and formidable Mohammedan book against Christianity; in the mean time teaching and preaching among the heathen with much earnestness and efficiency. In the midst of these labours, after spending five years on the plains of India, his health failed, and he was compelled to resort to the Himmaleh Mountains in the hope of restoration, and finding but little benefit from a residence there of eighteen months, he returned to this country in 1848. In the autumn of 1851 his health was sufficiently restored to justify him in taking a pastoral charge, and in September he was installed by the Presbytery of Elizabethtown over the church in Baskingridge, N. J., of which he is still the pastor. In 1867 he received the honorary title of D. D. from the Trustees of the College of New Jersey. His contributions to this *Review* have been,

1851. Foreign Missions and Millenarianism.

1854. Thoughts for the Ministry.

36

1856. Armenianism and Grace.

1861. The Mode of Baptism—The Subjects of Baptism—A Practical View of Infant Baptism.

RICE, JOHN HOLT, was born near New London, Virginia, on the 28th of November, 1777. When only four years old he had read a considerable part of the Bible, and in his eighth year he began to learn Latin in a school which had been opened by his uncle, the Rev. John Holt, in Bottetourt county. On account of the failure of his uncle's health, the school was only continued about a year, after which he was sent to several schools, till about the age of fifteen he entered Liberty Hall Academy, of which the Rev. William Graham, who has already been noticed as the teacher of · Dr. Alexander, was the Principal. When Mr. Archibald Alexander assumed the Presidency of Hampden Sidney College, he engaged Mr. Rice, who was now in his nineteenth year, as a Tutor, and he immediately entered upon his duties. Mr. Alexander was unable till the close of May 1797 to enter upon his, but he then brought with him another Tutor, Conrad Speece, and the intimacy now formed among these remarkable men only closed with their lives. Mr. Rice continued in the situation till the spring of 1799, when he spent some six months in the family of the father of Dr. Benjamin M. Smith, in the study of medicine, but in the autumn of 1800, being again solicited by Dr. Alexander to resume his Tutorship, he returned to the College, commenced the study of theology under his direction, and was licensed to preach the gospel by the Presbytery of Hanover on the 12th of September, 1803.

On the 5th of April, 1803, he received a call to the church of Cub Creek, and was ordained on the 29th of September following, but still continued his connection with the College. In 1804 he resigned the Tutorship, having removed his family to a small farm which his father-in-law had enabled him to purchase. His labours here were very arduous, as the people composing his congregation were scattered over the whole of Charlotte county and had three distinct places of worship, but he continued with them till April 1812, when he removed to Richmond, Virginia, and began the First Church there. In 1819 he was honoured with the degree of D. D. by the College of New Jersey, and in 1823 he was elected its President, but in the same year he was unanimously appointed Professor in the Union Theological Seminary, which he accepted, and resigned his charge at Richmond. His duties here were of the most onerous character. "The number of students increased from seven to upwards of fifty. He had but one assistant in instruction. He taught Theology, Church History and Government, and for a part of the time, the Interpretation of the New Testament Scriptures. The vacations of six weeks each, besides the whole of one and parts of other sessions, were occupied in travelling to solicit funds. During the sessions he supplied the vacant pulpit of the church in the vicinity at least half the time, and on the alternate Sabbaths was usually engaged in preaching at some of the churches in the surrounding country. Thus he had little time for his family or his company. Having entered the new Seminary building in November 1825, while yet not entirely finished, and while the premises were but partially reclaimed from the forest, he combined utility with exercise for recreation, in most vigorous labour, digging up stumps and removing dirt accumulated by the excavations for the buildings. He set the example for his own precepts, and pleasantly urged on the students the benefit of varying their labours on Greek and Hebrew roots, by labours on those of the oak and the hickory. He generally wrought in this way for half an hour or an hour before breakfast, and would often come into the house with his forehead and cheeks and clothes bathed in perspiration. His meals were his only seasons of relaxation. His plain but hospitable house was ever open to strangers; and his extensive acquaintance and increasing reputation brought visitors to him from all parts of the country."* Thus he continued till 1830, when on a tour in the North to collect money for the Seminary, he contracted a severe cold from which he never recovered, though he conducted the studies of the students through the following session. As the season advanced his bodily and mental distress increased, but on the 3d of September, 1831, while his friends were surrounding his bed, waiting his departure, he experienced a singular relief. Turning suddenly to Mrs. Rice he threw his arms around her neck, and looking in her face with a clear bright eye, he exclaimed, "Mercy is triumphant!" and passed into the joy of his Lord.

Mr. Rice was tall and well-proportioned. He used but little gesture. Sometimes his hand would remain in his coat bosom through nearly the whole of his discourse. But often, as he waxed warm in speaking, his whole chest would seem to partake of his emotion. His voice was another mode of expressing his emotions, and the deep tones of solemn earnestness, indicative of pent up feeling, would awaken in his hearers emo-

* Dr. Benjamin M. Smith, in Sprague's *Annals.*

tions far more correspondent than could be enkindled by any amount of gesticulation. His preaching was commonly extemporary, but sometimes he had notes covering about a foolscap page. He had no time to write sermons, though his pen was never idle. His literaray abilities were first manifested in the *Virginia Religious Magazine*, and in 1815, he issued the *Christian Monitor*, the first publication of the kind that had appeared in Richmond, Va. In 1818 this gave place to *The Virginia Evangelical and Literary Magazine*, which was chiefly sustained by his abilities till 1829. In 1830 he addressed a series of Letters to Ex-President Madison, showing that it is the duty of the government to favour religion, on account of the beneficial influence it exerts upon the prosperity of the country. Besides these he published various sermons and discourses, and contributed to the *Princeton Review* the following articles:

1829. Correspondence of the General Assembly with Foreign Churches.

1831. Review of Professor Stuart's Letter to William E. Channing, D. D.

RIGGS, ELIAS, was the son of the Rev. Elias Riggs, who had been for many years pastor of the church at New Providence, New Jersey. Here his son was born on the 19th of November, 1810. At an early period he manifested very studious habits, and at eleven years of age he commenced the study of the Hebrew language. In 1825 he entered Amherst College, and graduated with honour in 1829. While at College, in addition to the prescribed studies, he prosecuted the study of Hebrew, with the cognate dialects of Chaldee and Syriac, and commenced the study of modern Greek, French, and Spanish. After graduation he entered the Andover Theological Seminary, and was licensed to preach the gospel in 1832. In this year he published a Manual of the Chaldee language, and his early inclination for the study of these languages was undoubtedly a providential preparation for the work of Bible translation to which much of his life has been devoted. He was ordained at Elizabeth, N. J., on the 20th of September, married in the same month, and embarked at Boston as a missionary to Greece, on the 30th of October, 1832. He reached Athens on the 23d of January, 1833, and remained with the late Dr. King over a year, to perfect himself in modern Greek, and established a missionary station at Argos in May 1834. He remained here till a law was enacted that pictures of the Virgin Mary and of the Saints should be hung up in the school-rooms and the children taught to worship them. This broke up all the Protestant schools, and in November 1838 he removed to Smyrna, still continuing to labour among the Greek population. In 1843 he transferred his labours to the Armenians, and commenced the translation of the Scriptures into their language. This he completed; and with the aid of Dr. Long on the New Testament and of native scholars on the whole Bible, made the only complete version that exists in the Bulgarian language. In 1847 he published a Grammar of the Modern Armenian Language, and a Vocabulary of the Words used in Modern Armenian not found in the Ancient Armenian Lexicon; and Notes on the Grammar of the Bulgarian Language. In 1856, Outlines of a Grammar of the Turkish Language, as written in the Armenian character.

He removed to Constantinople in 1853, and has continued to reside there, with the exception of two years, 1856 to 1858, when he visited the United States. In the *Eclectic Magazine of Foreign Literature*, for May 1862, there is a beautiful group of the Bible translators, Drs. Goodell, Schauffler, and Riggs, with a sketch, to which we have been somewhat indebted for this article. His only paper in this periodical was transmitted through his friend, the late Dr. Magie:

1852. Did Solomon write the Book of Ecclesiastes?

SCHAFF, PHILIP, was born at Coire, Switzerland, on the 1st of January, 1819. He was educated at the college of his native city, and prosecuted his studies at the gymnasium at Stuttgart, and the Universities of Tübingen, Halle, and Berlin, and in 1842 he was Lecturer on Theology in the University of Berlin. The German Reformed Synod in the United States, in October 1843, having thought it desirable to have a suitable representative of German theology in this country, applied to their German brethren for one, and at the recommendation of Drs. Neander, Hengstenberg, Tholuck, Müller, Krummacher, and others, he was invited to the United States. During the first twenty years he made his residence at Mercersburg, Pa., acting as Professor of Church History and Exegesis in the Seminary, and in 1863 he removed to New York, to edit Lange's Commentary and to superintend the printing of the last two volumes of his Church History. Since his residence in New York he has delivered a course of Lectures on Ecclesiastical History in the Theological Seminary at Andover; and in 1868 he was elected Professor of Church History in the Hartford Theological Seminary, and in May 1870, Professor of Theological Encyclopedia and Symbolism in the Union Theological Seminary. In 1863 he revisited Europe, and in 1869 he was sent by the Evangelical Alliance of America to extend an invitation to the leading divines in Europe to attend a general Conference to be held in New York in September 1870, in which he met with great success, as may be seen from the publishêd report.

. Before coming to this country he had acquired a good reputation in Germany by his treatise on "The Sin against the Holy Ghost," published at Halle in 1841, and his "Historical Essay on James the Brother of the Lord," published at Berlin in 1842.   His first published work in this country was an address on the "Principle of Protestantism as related to Romanism and the Present State of the Church," which was translated from the German by Dr. Nevin, and was the beginning of the controversy in regard to what is called "Mercersburg Theology," which has been frequently adverted to in this *Review*.   His great works however are his "History of the Apostolic Church, with a general Introduction to the Study of Church History," first published in German at Mercersburg in 1851, and republished with additions and improvements at Leipsig in 1854, translations of which have been made into Dutch and English.   This was followed by his "History of the Christian Church," the two first volumes of which were written by him in German, and translated from the manuscript by the late Dr. E. D. Yeomans; and the third of which was published in 1867.   In 1864 he began the translating and editing of Lange's Exegetical, Doctrinal, and Homiletical Commentary on the Scriptures, of which nine volumes have now been published.

During the preparation of these great works he has always been engaged in preaching the gospel, in writing books for Sabbath-schools, and in labouring to convince the people, both from the pulpit and by the press, of the duty and benefits flowing from the observance of the Sabbath as a day dedicated to the service of God.   Several volumes of this class have been published by him.   We may enumerate his "German Hymn-book," consisting of Selections of Hymns from all ages of the Christian Church, accompanied by remarks on the Authors and History of the Hymns, Philadelphia, 1859.   "Essay on the Moral Character of Christ," or the Perfection of Christ's Humanity a Proof of his Divinity, Chambersburg, 1861. Essays on Slavery and the Bible, 1861.   Katechismus, with Scripture Parallels and Hints to Teachers, Chambersburg, 1861.   A Catechism for Sunday-schools and Families, Philadelphia, 1862.   Christlicher Katechismus, Philadelphia, 1863. The Anglo-American Sabbath, New York, 1864. The Christ of the Gospels and the Romance of M. Renan, London, 1864. The Person of Christ the Miracle of History, Boston, 1865; this has been translated into French, Dutch, and German. Christ in Song; a Collection of Hymns of Immanuel, selected from all Ages, New York, 1869, and republished in London.

He has also endeavoured to make the German and English populations better acquainted with each other's thoughts and feelings, by such works as "America; a Sketch of the Political, Social, and Religious Character of the United States of America," two Lectures delivered at Berlin in 1854, and translated into English and published in New York in 1855. " Germany : its Universities, Theology, and Religion," Edinburgh, 1850, Philadelphia, 1857. "The Civil War, and the Christian Life in America," Berlin, 1865, which has been translated into English and Dutch.

Dr. Schaff was editor of *Der Deusche Kirchen Freund* from 1848 to 1859, and has contributed largely to periodical literature, both in German and English. The following articles were written by him:

1863. The Anglo-American Sabbath.

1864. The Union of Church and State—St. Jerome—The Donatist Controversy—Lange's Theological and Homiletical Commentary.

1865. The Hagiology and Hagiolatry of Romanism.

1866. The Patristic Doctrine of the Eucharist—The Monophysite Churches of the East.

1867. Gregory the Theologian.

SCHANCK, JOHN STILLWELL, spent his childhood and youth on a farm in Monmouth county, N. J. A strong desire for knowledge induced him at the age of seventeen to seek and obtain the opportunity to attend, for a few months, the lectures of Prof. Henry and Dr. Torrey on Natural Philosophy and Chemistry at Princeton. So far from satisfying him, this only stimulated him to seek further educational advantages, and he shortly after repaired to the then celebrated Academy at Lenox, Mass., to prepare for college. He entered the College of New Jersey at Princeton in the autumn of 1838, and was graduated in 1840. He immediately commenced the study of medicine, and received his medical diploma from the University of Pennsylvania in 1843. He settled in Princeton, and there pursued the practice of medicine with a fair measure of satisfaction to himself and many friends. Meanwhile the Trustees of the College, in 1847, invited him to deliver a few lectures to successive classes on Zoölogy, and in 1857 he was elected Professor of Chemistry, the successor of one of the eminent men whose humble assistant he had been twenty-three years before. He shortly after relinquished the practice of medicine, and now, 1870, is Professor of Chemistry and Natural History in the College of New Jersey. In 1866 the degree of LL.D. was conferred upon him by Lafayette College; and he is the author of the article in the volume for

1865. What is the Use of Breathing?

SCOTT, WILLIAM M., was born in Jefferson county, Ohio, in 1817; graduated at Jefferson College, Pa., and commenced the study of law in Kentucky. While preparing for the Bar he attended a series of religious meetings at the Franklin Springs church, near Frankfort, Ky., which resulted in his making a profession of faith in Christ, and joining the Pisgah church in West Lexington Presbytery. He soon after gave up the study of law and entered the Theological Seminary at Princeton, N. J. in 1843, and after a three years' course was licensed to preach the gospel by the West Lexington Presbytery. In 1847 he was elected Professor of Ancient Languages in Centre College, Danville, Ky., and having accepted a call to the First Presbyterian church in that place, he was ordained by the Presbytery of Transylvania in 1848. In January 1856 he accepted a call to the Seventh Presbyterian church in Cincinnati, Ohio, and held this relation till 1859, when the General Assembly elected him Professor of Biblical Literature and Exegesis in the Theological Seminary of the Northwest, at Chicago, Ill. His health had been gradually declining for some time, and in the autumn of 1861 he visited Princeton, N. J., in the hope probably of regaining his health, but it soon became evident that he was far gone in consumption, and on 22d of December, 1861, he died at the residence of his father-in-law, Dr. Charles Hodge, whose eldest daughter he had married, leaving three sons surviving.

A correspondent of *The Presbyterian Herald* wrote of him as follows: "Dr. Scott was a superb teacher, plain, accurate, and interesting. He made everything clear to the dullest brain; enthusiastic, earnest, and skilful in judicious praise, he excited the interest and study of the content intellect. Of commanding personal appearance, and sternly conscientious in the discharge of his duties, but full of interest in, and considerate friendship for, his students, he not only gained their respect but won their love. I confidently assert that no Professor was more respected or beloved by his students than William

M. Scott; and through his influence many young men now gratefully acknowledge that, under God, they were brought to a new and higher life.

"Professor Scott was above the average of preachers. Full of burning zeal for his Master's cause, and of consuming love for his fellow-men; gifted with a most striking and affecting voice, admirably used; learned not only in Biblical and Theological learning, but in all profane wisdom and science, and using his knowledge with rare skill; of dignified presence and earnest and impressive, though sometimes awkward manners; having reached through labour a cultivated and elegant style, he was a delightful and most instructive preacher. His earnest piety and great gift of prayer, added to his other qualities, made him peculiarly successful during periods of religious excitement. His personal temperament, his ready sympathy and overflowing kindness, his softness of voice and manner, rendered his pastoral visits to the sick-room most cheering, refreshing, and soothing, to both body and mind. His brave yet moderate, earnest yet charitable, advocacy of every good work made him extremely useful not only in the church but in the state. He was a useful citizen in the truest sense. He accomplished much, but he indicated greater deeds hereafter. God knows best when to remove to a better world; humanly speaking, he was taken in the beginning of true and real labour.

"A life spent in Christian service has fitly ended in a death of triumphant faith in Christ. No terrors were around his couch. The lengthening shadows of life's evening were but the forerunners of the ineffable glories of an eternal dawn. He who preached Christ to sinners has gone to receive his reward. May we, to whom he preached, meet him in that heaven, through the grace of the same Saviour."*

He furnished the following articles to this periodical:

1850. English Diction.

1857. The Argument from Prophecy for Christianity.

SCRIBNER, WILLIAM, brother of the well known publisher, Charles Scribner, was born in city of New York, January 20, 1820. He received his preliminary education in New York City, and at the Lawrenceville High School, N. J. Shortly before he left this school for college a deeply interesting though not extensive revival took place, and he and his brother, who

* For the materials for this biography we are indebted to *The Presbyterian Historical Almanac* for 1863, by Joseph M. Wilson.

37

was also a pupil of the institution, were among the first subjects of the work of grace. He first went to the University of
the City of New York, and afterwards to the College of New
Jersey, where he graduated in 1840. He then entered upon
his theological studies at Princeton Seminary, and was licensed
to preach the gospel by the Presbytery of New York, April 19,
1843. . Upon leaving the Seminary in 1843, and while still a
licentiate, he went to Columbia, Pa., and supplied the pulpit
of that church for several months in the absence of its pastor,
the Rev. Robert Dunlap. Having fulfilled this engagement, he
accepted a call to the church of Stroudsburg, Pa., and continned its pastor until April 1849. Hoping to recruit his
health, which his labours and a severe affliction had impaired,
he now spent some time in Europe, returning home in the
spring of 1850. He then laboured for a while as a stated supply, first for a church in the neighbourhood of New York City,
and afterwards for the church of South Salem, N. Y., after
which he accepted a call to the church of Bridesburg, Pa.,
over which he was installed by the Second Presbytery of Philadelphia. In connection with his pastoral labours in this
place, he devoted much time to the superintendence of a parochial school which he had established at the beginning of his
ministry among this people. Resigning his pastorate in December 1854, he consented, notwithstanding his enfeebled
health, to take charge of the church at Red Bank, N. J., where
his installation took place, February 1855. Here he was
mainly instrumental in the erection of a new church. His
connection with this church continued three years, when his
health proved altogether inadequate to the work he was undertaking, and he was compelled to resign. Since he gave up
his last charge he has resided at Plainfield, N. J., with the
exception of being absent at various times in the West, and
once in Europe, which he again visited with the hope of regaining health. During his first visit to the West he supplied
the First Presbyterian church of Des Moines, Iowa, for five
months.

He contributed to the *Princeton Review* in

1868. Progress of Doctrine in the New Testament.

SEELYE, JULIUS H., was born at Bethel, Connecticut, in
1825; graduated at Amherst College in 1849; studied theology at Auburn Seminary, N. Y. and at Halle, Germany,
and on his return became pastor of the Reformed Dutch
church, Schenectady, till 1859, since which he has been Professor of Mental and Moral Philosophy in Amherst College.

He is the translator of Schwegler's History of Philosophy in Epitome, and in 1862 he contributed to this *Review* an article in defence of Dr. Hickok's Rational Psychology from the strictures of Dr. Edwin Hall.

1862. Dr. Hickok's Philosophy.

SHARSWOOD, GEORGE, was born in Philadelphia in 1810; graduated at the University of Pennsylvania in 1828; and was admitted to the bar in 1831. He served three years in the Pennsylvania Legislature, and in 1845 was made a Judge of the District Court, and was President Judge from 1851 to 1867, when he was elected an Associate Judge of the Supreme Court of the State. The degree of LL.D. was conferred upon him by the University of the City of New York, and also by Columbia College.

From 1850 Judge Sharswood has been Professor of Law in the University of Pennsylvania, and he has contributed largely to the literature of the science by his works, as well as by his numerous decisions. In 1854 he published "Professional Ethics," a Compend of Lectures on the Aims and Duties of the Profession of the Law, which has now attained the third edition. In 1856 he published "Popular Lectures on Commercial Law." In 1870 also, "Lectures Introductory to the Study of the Law," and has edited a great many law works. His edition of Blackstone, which was published in 1859, is very highly commended. Judge Sharswood is an elder of the Presbyterian Church and one of the Trustees of the General Assembly, and in 1853 he wrote for this periodical an article on Religious Endowments.

SHEDD, WILLIAM GREENOUGH THAYER, was born at Acton, Massachusetts, in 1820; was graduated at the University of Vermont in 1839, and at Andover Seminary in 1843. From 1843 to 1845 he was pastor of the church at Brandon, Vermont, and from 1845 to 1852 Professor of English Literature in the University of Vermont; from 1852 to 1854 Professor of Sacred Rhetoric and Pastoral Theology in Auburn Seminary; and from 1854 to 1861 Professor of Ecclesiastical History and Pastoral Theology in Andover Seminary. In 1862–3 he was associate pastor of the Brick Church in New York, and from 1863 has been Professor of Biblical Literature in Union Theological Seminary, New York City.

He has published the following *original works:* "Philosophy of History," 1856; "Discourses and Essays," 1856, 2d ed. 1861; "History of Christian Doctrine," 2 vols. 1863, 3d ed. 1869, republished in Edinburgh, 1865; "Homiletics and Pastoral Theology," 1867, 4th ed. 1869, republished in Edinburgh, 1869. *Translations*—Theremin's Rhetoric, translated from the German, 1850, 2d ed. 1859; Guericke's Church History, translated from the German, 2 vols., 1857, 1870. *Edited works*—Coleridge's Complete Works, with Introductory Essay, 1853; Augustine's Confessions, revised, with Introductory Essay, 1860; McCosh's Intuitions of the Mind, with Introductory Note, 1866; Garbett's Dogmatic Faith, with Introductory Note, 1870, and the book of Mark in the American edition of Lange's Commentary. Dr. Shedd is the author of several articles in the *Bibliotheca Sacra* and *American Theological Review*, and the following Discourses by him have been published in pamphlet form : Intellectual Temperance, 1844; The True Method of Preaching, 1850; Ministerial Education, 1855; God's Knowledge of Man, 1862; The Guilt of the Pagan, 1863; The Union and the War, 1863; Commemorative Discourse upon Dr. Pease, 1864; The Bondage of Sin, 1865. He contributed in

1863. The True Tone in Preaching, and the True Temper in Hearing.

SHIELDS, CHARLES WOODRUFF, was born in New Albany, Indiana, in 1825; graduated at the College of New Jersey, in 1844; studied theology three years at the Princeton Seminary; became for a short time pastor of the church at Hempstead, L. I., from which he accepted a call in 1850 to the Second Church in Philadelphia, and continued in that charge till December 1865, when he was elected Professor of the Relations of Religion to Science in the College of New Jersey, and had Modern History added to his department in 1870. On the death of Dr. E. K. Kane, the Arctic Explorer, in 1857, he pronounced a funeral eulogy at the obsequies, which was so much admired that he has been often called into requisition to portray the departed, and his Memorial Discourses for Dr. Darragh, Hon. Joel Jones, and Dr. William M. Engles, have been published. His most characteristic work, however, is " Philosophia Ultima," published in 1861. In 1855 he published "The Book of Remembrance: a Pastor's Gift for the New Year." In 1862, "A Manual of Worship suitable to be used in Legislative and other Public Bodies, compiled from the Forms, and in accordance with the common usages of all Christian Denominations." In 1863, " The Directory for Public Worship and the Book of Common Prayer, considered with reference to the Question of a Presbyterian Liturgy." And in 1867, "The Book of Common Prayer and

Administration of the Sacraments and other Rites and Ceremonies of the Church, as amended by the Westminster Divines
in the Royal Commission of 1661, and in Agreement with the
Directory of Public Worship of the Presbyterian Church of the
United States;" and in the same volume, "Liturgia Expur-
gata; or, The Prayer Book Amended according to the Presbyterian Revision of 1661, and Historically and Critically revised." The degree of D. D. was conferred upon him by the
College of New Jersey in 1861. He has written the following
articles for this periodical:

  1858. Positive Philosophy of Auguste Comte.
  1862. The Philosophy of the Absolute.

SKINNER, THOMAS HARVEY, was born near Harvey's
Neck, in North Carolina, in·1791; graduated at the College of
New Jersey in 1809; was licensed to preach the gospel at
Morristown, N. J., December 16, 1812, and ordained and
installed pastor of the Second Presbyterian church in Philadelphia, as colleague to Dr. Janeway, on June 10, 1813. He was
pastor of the Fifth Presbyterian church, Philadelphia, from
1816 to 1832, when he became Professor of Sacred Rhetoric in
Andover Theological Seminary. From 1835 to 1848 he was
pastor of the Mercer street Presbyterian church in New York
City, and in 1848 he was appointed Professor of Sacred Rhetoric, Pastoral Theology and Church Government in the Union
Theological Seminary, his present position. He received the
degree of D. D. from Williams College in 1826, and LL.D.
from the College at Marietta, O. in 1855.

His published works are, 1. Religion of the Bible. 2. Aids
to Preaching and Hearing. 3. Religious Liberty. 4. Hints
to Christians. 5. Thoughts on Evangelizing the World.
6. Religious Life of Francis Markoe. 7. Vinet's Pastoral
Theology and Homiletics, which he translated and edited
with Notes. 8. Discussions in Theology, his latest work, and
occasional Sermons. He contributed in

  1830. The Means of Repentance.

SKINNER, THOMAS HARVEY, Junior, the son of
the above, was graduated at the University of New York in
1840; licensed to preach the gospel in 1843; and ordained
and installed pastor of the Second Presbyterian church, Paterson, N. J. In 1846 he accepted a call to the West Presbyterian church, New York City; and in 1856 was transferred to
the church at Honesdale, Pa. In 1859 he took charge of the
Reformed Dutch church in Stapleton, Long Island, in which he

continued till 1868, when he accepted the pastoral care of the First Presbyterian church, Fort Wayne, Indiana, his present charge. The degree of D. D. was conferred upon him by the College of New Jersey in 1867. He contributed the following articles:

1860. The Bible its own Witness and Interpreter.
1866. The Trinity in Redemption.
1867. Sanctification.

SMITH, EDWARD B., is a native of Virginia, born in 1833; graduated at the University of Virginia as Master of Arts in 1854; Assistant Instructor in Mathematics in the University, 1855–7; Principal of the Piedmont Academy until 1861; Lieutenant-Colonel of Ordnance in the Confederate service to 1865; Professor of Mathematics in Richmond College since 1867. He is the author of several religious and scientific papers in the Reviews. To this *Review* he contributed in 1868. Mathematics as an Exercise of the Mind.

SMYTH, THOMAS, was born in Belfast, Ireland, and educated at Queen's College, Belfast, and in London, and studied one session (1830–1) at the Theological Seminary at Princeton. On leaving the Seminary he preached some time at Pensacola, Florida, and in 1832 he received a call to the Second Church in Charleston, S. C., of which he has continued to be the pastor till the present time, (1870.) In 1843 the degree of D.D. was conferred upon him by the College of New Jersey, and during his long pastorate his literary labours have been very extensive. In Allibone's Dictionary of Authors there is a list of twenty works from his pen, and besides these he has written and published a great many sermons, pamphlets, and newspaper articles. 1. Lectures on the Prelatical Doctrine of the Apostolic Succession, 1841. 2. Ecclesiastical Catechism of the Presbyterian Church, 1841. 3. Presbytery and not Prelacy the Scriptural and Primitive Polity, 1843. 4. Claims of the Free Church of Scotland on American Christians, 1843. 5. Ecclesiastical Republicanism, 1843. 6. History of the Westminster Assembly, 1844. 7. Calvin and his Enemies, 1844. 8. Name, Nature, and Functions of Ruling Elder, 1845. 9. Prelatical Rite of Confirmation examined, 1845. 10. Union to Christ and his Church, 1846. 11. Solace for Bereaved Parents, 1848. 12. Unity of the Human Race Proved, 1850. 13. Young Men's Christian Associations, 1857. 14. Church Manual, 1857. 15. Well in the Valley, 1857. 16. Presbyterian Tracts, 1857.

17. Why do I live? 1857. 18. How is the World to be
Converted? 1857. 19. Faith the Principie ot Missions, 1857.
20. Obedience the Life of Missions, 1858.

Dr. Smyth has also collected in Europe and America a
very valuable library, which he has given to the Theological
Seminary at Columbia, S. C.

The articles furnished by him to this periodical are,
1839. Mammon and Anti-Mammon.
1849. The Principle of Secrecy.
1850. Secret Societies.
1860. Theories of the Eldership.

SPEER, WILLIAM, was brought up in Pittsburgh, Pa.,
having been born in the adjoining county, Westmoreland,
April 24, 1822.* After a short stay at Jefferson College, Pa.,
he went to Kenyon College, Ohio, where he enjoyed the tuition
and care of Bishop McIlvaine, Dr. William Sparrow, and others,
and graduated in 1840. He studied medicine till 1843, in
which year he was elected Resident Physician at Will's Hospital, Philadelphia. His health had, however, been broken
down by over-confinement and study, and in the latter part of
his medical course having been led to find the way of salvation through Christ, he concluded to study for the ministry of
the gospel, as the best and most direct way in which to serve
his Master. He studied theology at Allegheny Seminary, and
was licensed to preach in April 21, 1846. Though offered the
Presidency of Austin College, Texas, the. pastorate of the
Fourth Church of Louisville, Ky., and a chaplaincy for seamen
at New Orleans, he obeyed an urgent call from the Board of
Foreign Missions to go to Canton, China, and sailed for that
port July 20, 1846. After learning the language and performing much arduous labour, his wife and child became vic-
tims to the climate, and he himself was prostrated with chronic

* His grandfather, the Rev. William Speer, was the youngest son in a large
and influential family; the only daughter in which was Elizabeth, the mother
of James Buchanan. President of the United States. He was a minister remarkable in his day for deep and tender piety, refined taste, and thorough scholarship. "His method of treating his subjects," says Rev. Dr. David Elliott, "was
sometimes too profound and abstruse for those whose minds were not disciplined
to thought." His life as a pastor was chiefly spent at Chambersburg, Pa.,
Chillicothe, Ohio, (where he was the first chaplain of the Territorial legislature,) and at Greensburg, Pa., then the centre of a cultivated and superior population. Mr. Speer was the ardent friend of education; a trustee of Washington
College; probably the most active friend in the West of Princeton Theological
Seminary, for which, by appointment of the General Assembly, in the year 1810
and subsequently, he repeatedly collected aid; and was the first Vice-President
of the Board of Directors of the Western Theological Seminary at Allegheny.
His only son is Dr. James R. Speer, who has been for nearly half a century an
eminent physician and surgeon in Pittsburgh, Pa.

disorder of the liver and digestive organs, from which the physicians pronounced it impossible for him to be cured in that
tropical climate, he returned to the United States in 1850.
The Board of Education soon engaged his services in representing that cause in Western Pennsylvania and the neighbouring States; for the success of which he received most cordial acknowledgments from Dr. Van Rensselaer.   But the end
of the way in which God had led Mr. Speer was manifest when
in the years 1851-2 the Chinese from Canton province began
to pour into California by thousands, in search of its gold, and
the Board of Foreign Missions in the latter year again called
upon him to go to preach to them Christ, in their own language.   To the Presbyterian Church belongs the credit of the
first missionary efforts upon this continent for that race whose
millions are hereafter to be so vastly important to its agricul-
ture, its manufactures, its commerce, and the national and religious influence of our own country over Asia and other parts
of the world.   Mr. Speer promptly met this great emergency
by courses of lectures addressed to the American people, which
awakened universal interest on the Pacific Coast, and were
reported at length in the newspapers and distributed in this
and other countries.   He commenced preaching regularly in
Chinese, opened a night-school for the young men, gave occasional lectures to them on astronomy, &c.; opened a dispensary
for the sick, who were very numerous on account of the bad
food and treatment on shipboard, and engaged in the distribution of tracts and scriptures by a colporteur, and the publication of a newspaper, entitled *The Oriental,* printed in English
on one side and lithographed in Chinese on the other.   He was
often called also to be the counsellor and advocate of the Chinese in difficult matters.   When the classes and parties inimical to them succeeded in passing through the legislature in
1855 a law designed to drive them from the mines and ruin
them, they refused to employ the legal talent of the State, and
pressed the missionary into the work of securing its repeal.
By an organization of those friendly to them, and the energetic
use of proper means, this object was at the next session tri-
umphantly accomplished; and the Chinese were freed from the
greatest calamities, the question of the possibility of degrading
and enslaving them was settled, the establishment of a slave
State on the Pacific Coast was prevented, and the first settling
of a flood of evil arrested which might have affected the institutions of our Pacific States, the result of our late civil war,
and the character of our nation.   The importance of these
efforts was recognized at the time by some of our leading pub-

lic men; among others by the Hon. W. H. Seward, then in the
Senate of the United States, who wrote to Mr. Speer, saying,
"accept assurances of the sincere respect with which you have
inspired me by your resolute assertion of the principles of
human freedom and political justice, and be assured that I
shall not fail to coöperate with you whenever occasion shall
offer." Completely exhausted in health by these manifold
labours, occupying all the day and often much of the night,
Mr. Speer sought, rest by a visit to the Sandwich Islands,
where he spent some months, part of the time engaged in
labours for the benefit of the Chinese who are immigrating
thither, which, says the Rev. Dr. Damon, in a recent article in
The Friend, published at Honolulu, "awakened a deep and
abiding interest in behalf of the Chinese." He was however
compelled by the progress of disease in the lungs to abandon
the work. The next eight years were spent in efforts to recruit,
which it pleased God to bless, and also in active missionary
labour, partly in the Gulf States of the South, but chiefly in
Wisconsin and Minnesota.

After the death of Rev. Dr. Chester, in 1865, the Board of
Education, at its meeting in December, called Mr. Speer to
the position of Corresponding Secretary; and since the re-con-
stitution of the Board, by the union of it to the "Permanent
Committee on Education," which was the organ of the late
New-school branch of the church, whose seat was at New
York, he has been unanimously elected to the same office
under the re-united church. The degree of D. D. was conferred upon him by Centre College, Kentucky, in 1866.

Dr. Speer has written largely for the press. Articles from
his pen have appeared in many of the leading magazines and
newspapers, religious and secular, of the country, more especially in the *Missionary Chronicle*, *Home and Foreign Record*,
and other publications of the Boards of the Church. Some of
those in *The Oriental* exercised much influence in explaining
the necessities of the Chinese in this country, removing prejudices against them, and enlisting the sympathies and efforts of
Christians of every denomination, and thinking people, in their
behalf. Among his special productions are pamphlets entitled,
"Remarks of the Chinese Merchants of San Francisco upon
Gov. Bigler's Message," &c., 1855; "An Humble Plea, addressed to the Legislature of California, in behalf of the Merchants from the Empire of China to this State," 1856; "An
Answer to the Common Objection to Chinese Testimony, and
an Earnest Appeal to the Legislature of California for their
Protection by Law," 1857; "The Lessons of 1860, a Discourse

38

before the Young Men's Christian Association of St. Paul, Minn., at their Fourth Anniversary," St. Paul, 1861; and several recent tracts in furtherance of the objects of the Board of Education. The Annual Reports of the Board have been carefully prepared with the object of exhibiting its varied and beneficent influence; and a special and complete review of the history of the Board, entitled "A Practical Summary of the Principles and Work of the Board of Education of the Presbyterian Church from its Establishment in 1819 till the Present Time" (56 pp. 8vo.) was drawn up for its fiftieth anniversary, which was held at the General Assembly in New York in 1869. A work, entitled, "The Oldest and Newest Empire: China and the United States," has recently been published by Dr. Speer, which embodies much of the results of his experience in his missionary work among the Chinese in this country, and is designed to disseminate information useful to our people and to that race in connection with the immigration to this continent. His articles are,

1853. China and California.
1867. Western Presbyterianism.

SPRAGUE, WILLIAM BUEL, one of the most remarkable living authors, remarkable for the amount of his writing, the facility and felicity with which his work is done, and extensive influence for good, was born in Andover, Connecticut, October 16, 1796, where his relatives still reside. When a mere boy he was at the house of a distant relative, and she permitted him to take home some manuscript sermons of the former pastor of the church. That was the beginning of a passion for the collection of autographs, which has grown with his life until now his treasures exceed those of any individual or institution in this country, and probably there are few private collections in the world more extensive and valuable than his.

He was fitted for college partly at Colchester Academy, and partly under the Rev. Abiel Abbot, of Coventry, and entered Yale in 1811, graduating under President Dwight in 1815. Nearly a year was now spent by him as a private tutor in a branch of the Washington family in Virginia.

Three years, from 1816 to 1819, he was a student of theology in Princeton Seminary, and the library of that venerable institution has upon its shelves a thousand volumes, chiefly of pamphlets bound, which he has presented as a token of his filial gratitude. In 1819 he was settled at West Springfield, Mass. as a colleague of the venerable Dr. Josephp Lathrop, whose granddaughter became his wife. After ten years of distinguished usefulness in the ministry he was called to the Second Presbyterian church of Albany, N. Y. There he spent forty years of almost unexampled industry, fidelity, and success, performing an amount of pastoral labour, pulpit duty, and private study, that has scarcely a parallel in the annals of the Church.

Twice he has visited Europe, where his reputation as. a scholar and divine had preceded him, and being brought into easy contact with the wisest, best, and most cultivated people abroad, he formed a wide and delightful acquaintance, which has since been kept up by a correspondence that would fill volumes.

Called upon to grace the festivities of our colleges, to preach upon special public occasions, such as ordinations, dedications, and the funerals of distinguished persons, he has at the request of others given to the press about *one hundred and sixty* sermons and addresses, more probably than any other living divine. His published volumes are, 1. Letters on Practical Subjects to a Daughter, 1822, numerous editions in this country and in Great Britain, also published with the title "The Daughter's Own Book." 2. Letters from Europe, 1828. 3. Lectures to Young People, 1830.* 4. Lectures on Revivals, with an Introductory Essay by Dr. Leonard Woods, 1832.† 5. Hints designed to Regulate the Intercourse of Christians, 1834.‡ 6. Lectures illustrating the Contrast between True Christianity and various other Systems, 1837. 7. Life of Edward Dorr Griffin, 1838. 8. Letters to Young Men, founded on the Life of Joseph, 2d ed. 1845, 8th ed. 1854. 9. Aids to Early Religion, .1847. 10. Words to a Young Man's Conscience, 1848. 11. Visits to European Celebrities, 1855. 12. Annals of the American Pulpit; or Commemorative Notices of Distinguished American Clergymen of Various Denominations from the Early Settlement of the Country to the close of the year 1855, with Historical Introductions, 8vo., in nine volumes.§ He is also the author of twenty funeral sermons published in pamphlet form, and over a hundred discourses on various occasions, and prefaces, introductions, and memoirs for other works, sufficient to fill several volumes.

The *Magnum Opus* of his life, and with which his name will be associated in the history of the Church, is the "Annals of

---

* Reviewed by Dr. Hodge, 1831.   † Reviewed by Dr. John Breckinridge, 1832.
‡ Reviewed by Dr. J. W. Alexander, 1834.
§ The volumes of "Annals" were reviewed as they successively appeared, by Dr. Forsyth in 1857, 1861, and 1865, and by Dr. J. W. Alexander in 1858.

the American Pulpit," in ten volumes, 8vo., Carter & Brothers, New York. This work he began at the age of fifty-two, when most men begin to think of relief from literary labour. With industry appalling to weaker men, and perseverance that never fainted, he addressed himself to the task of rescuing from oblivion the personal history of every individual minister, of every Christian denomination, from the first settlement of this country, whose usefulness had made him distinguished in the church to which he belonged. The information to be wrought into history was mainly to be found by personal inquiry and correspondence. He wrote and received tens of thousands of letters; and all the letters he received are carefully preserved in volumes. Through seventeen years of steady toil he pursued this work, at the same time writing fresh sermons every week, fulfilling every pastoral duty, visiting his large congregation systematically and more frequently than is common, keeping open house with a hospitality that had no limit, and never denying himself to calls that became almost incessant upon a man so distinguished and so generous.

Admonished by the advance of years that he could not expect to have vigour for efficient pulpit service much longer, he decided to resign his pastoral charge. This he did toward the close of the year 1869, and he has now removed to Flushing, New York, near the city, where he is passing in dignified retirement the evening of his useful life.

As a preacher he is earnest, persuasive, affectionate, and instructive; as a writer, vigorous, fluent, and elegant; as a man, genial, gentle, accomplished, loving and beloved; shrinking from public service yet constantly called into it; timid as a child and resolute as a lion, he has the heart of a woman and the head of a man. His biography will form a fitting conclusion to his own Annals of American divines; for among them all there never lived a purer or better man than the subject of this sketch.

His contributions to this *Review* are,

1833. On the Deportment of Candidates for the Ministry—Cox on Quakerism.

1834. The Bible the Christian's Standard—Decorum Due to Public Worship—Reflections on the Life and Character of Balaam.

1863. Dr. Nicholas Murray.

SPRING, GARDINER, was the son of the Rev. Samuel Spring, D. D., and was born at Newburyport, Mass., on the 24th of February, 1785. In the year 1799 he entered Yale Col-

lege, and graduated in 1805.   His religious impressions in
early life had often been vivid, but though at this time he saw
many of his fellow-students pressing into the kingdom, he felt
that he had no part or lot in the matter.   He had made up
his mind to follow the legal profession, and immediately after
leaving college entered the law office of Judge Daggett of New
Haven.   He had no money, but procured a loan of two hundred and fifty dollars, got the place of precentor in the church
occupied by the Rev. Moses Stuart, and by this and the fees
from a singing-school, he calculated that he would be able to
keep himself from want.

During the autumn an offer was made to him to go out as a
classical and mathematical teacher to the island of Bermuda,
which he accepted, and remained on the island fifteen months,
at the same time pursuing his legal studies under the direction
of the late Chief Justice Esten.   After a few months stay on
the island he returned to Newburyport, and on the 25th of
May, 1806, got married to Miss Susan Barney, with whom he
immediately returned to the island, but fearing the breaking
out of war with Great Britain, in the fall of 1808 he returned
to the United States.

On the 15th of December of that year he was admitted to
practice at the bar, and opened an office in New Haven.   He
had no cause for discouragement, and his success was equal to
his expectation.   But from the second evening after his marriage he had maintained morning and evening worship in his
family, and the religious impressions of his youth had been
gradually returning.   On the 24th of April, 1809, he united
with the church under the pastoral care of the Rev. Moses
Stuart, and on the following commencement at Yale College,
when he took his degree of A. M., he chose for the theme of
his oration the " Christian Patriot," but as yet he contemplated
no change in his professional career.   On the morning after
the commencement he heard a sermon by the Rev. John Mason, D. D., from the text, "To the poor the gospel is preached,"
and when he left the church he could think of nothing but the
gospel, and resolved, if the providence of God should prepare
the way, to become a preacher.

Arrangements were soon made for his family and he set out
for Andover, and after eight months study he was licensed to
preach the gospel.   In May 1810 he passed through New York
with a view to visit the General Assembly which was then
holding its sessions in Philadelphia, and was asked to preach in
the Cedar Street church.   A number of persons from the Brick
church had been present, and on his return from Philadelphia

he received a unanimous call to become its pastor. This was accepted, and on the 8th of August, 1810, he was installed into the charge. Sixty years have transpired since then, and with him many changes have taken place, but few are of such a · nature as to interest the general reader. By his prudence, diligence, and piety, he has always drawn around him a wealthy, intelligent, and devoted people, who have laboured with him in the gospel. Three times he has visited Europe, where he was received with distinction. After fifty-four years of married life his beloved wife Susan died. She had born to him fifteen children, and it was then his conviction that he would never be able to love another, but in little more than a year after her death, on the 14th of August, 1861, he was married to Abbe Grosvenor Williams. In May 1861 he was a member of the General Assembly which met in Philadelphia, and there offered a resolution, commonly called the "Spring resolution," which has had some effect both upon the church and the country. Civil war between the North and South was then imminent, and a portion of the Assembly were anxious to preserve the integrity of the church, even though the Union should be rent in two, and were opposed to any resolution in which all who were willing to adopt her standards could not join. Dr. Spring offered a resolution which declared the obligation of the church "to promote and perpetuate, so far as in us lies, the integrity of the United States, and to strengthen, uphold, and encourage the Federal Government in the exercise of all its functions under our Constitution; and to this Constitution, in all its provisions, requirements, and principles, we profess our unabated loyalty." This resolution became the act of the Assembly.

During his long pastorate he has been continually using the press as an auxiliary to the preaching of the gospel. His first publication was a sermon on "Faith and Works," preached before the New York Widows' Society in 1811; this was followed by a New Year's sermon in 1815, entitled, "Something must be done," which reached a fourth edition. In the same year he published "Essays on the Distinguishing Traits of Christian Character," which has had a large circulation in English and been translated into French. Passing over some sermons and pamphlets, in 1820 he wrote the Life of Samuel J. Mills, which was reprinted in Scotland and at Andover. His tract on the "Sabbath a Blessing to Man" has been translated into Modern Greek and Italian. In 1826 he published "Internal Evidences of Inspiration," and in 1827, a "Dissertation on the Means of Regeneration," which was the occasion

of considerable controversy. A volume of miscellanies, entitled, "Fragments from the Study of a Pastor," was reviewed
in this work by Dr. James W. Alexander in 1839, and "The
Obligations of the World to the Bible," by some one unknown.
"The Attraction of the Cross" was noticed by Dr. James W.
Alexander in 1846; and the "Bible not of Man," by Dr. Dickinson in 1848; in the same year his work on "The Power of
the Pulpit" was reviewed by Dr. J. Addison Alexander and
Dr. Hodge, to which Dr. Spring replied in a pamphlet, "Strictures on the *Princeton Review*." To these may be added,
"The Mercy-Seat," which has been republished in Scotland;
"The Contrast," in 1855; "The Mission of Sorrow," 1862;
"Pulpit Ministrations," 1864. For further information on all
points we refer to "The Personal Reminiscences of the Life
and Times of Gardiner Spring," published in 1866. His only
contributions to this *Review* are an article entitled, "God himself the Ultimate End of all Things," and an address to the
Theological Students of Princeton Seminary, both in the volume for 1832.

STORRS, RICHARD SALTER, Junior, is the third in
succession who has borne this name, and been dignified with
the title of D. D. The grandson was born at Braintree, Massachusetts, on the 21st of August, 1821; graduated at Amherst
College in 1839; and after some time spent in reading law
devoted himself to the ministry, and completed his theological
course at Andover in 1845. In the same year he took charge
of the Harvard Congregational church at Brookline, Mass.,
but in November 1846 he accepted a call to the Church of
the Pilgrims in Brooklyn, New York, which has continued to
be his field of labour.

In 1856 he delivered the Graham Lectures: on the Wisdom,
Power, and Goodness of God, as manifested in the Constitution
of the Human Soul, at the Brooklyn Institute, which were
published in a 12mo. vol., 1857, and he has published a few
occasional discourses. He delivered a lecture before the students in the Seminary at Princeton, which was given for publication in the *Review:*
1867. The Aim of Christianity for those who accept it.

STUART, MOSES, was born at Wilton, Connecticut, on the
26th of March, 1780. His father was a farmer, and intended
his son to follow the same profession, but in his fifteenth year
he was sent to an academy at Norwalk, Conn., merely to perfect himself in the English branches, and the teacher was so

impressed with his remarkable powers of mind that he urged him to prepare for college. He immediately commenced the study of Latin, and in three days was able to take his place in a class that had been studying the grammar for months. In 1797 he entered the Sophomore Class of Yale College, and graduated in 1799 with the highest honours. The next three years were devoted to teaching school and reading law, and in 1802 he was admitted to the bar at Danbury, Conn. About the same time he was chosen Tutor in Yale College, a position more congenial with his disposition, and he accepted the appointment, and performed its duties till the autumn of 1804. " Wishing one day to procure some appropriate book for the Sabbath, he borrowed of President Dwight a volume of Macknight on the Epistles. Though at first he read it for mere literary gratification, yet, as he proceeded, he came to regard the truth in its high practical bearings, and finally, after a season of severe conflict, bowed both his intellect and his heart, as he believed, to the teachings of the Holy Spirit."* There can be little doubt that this work also led him into the class of investigations in which he afterwards distinguished himself.

Having now relinquished all desire to follow the law as a profession, he began the study of theology under Dr. Dwight, and after preaching about two years as a probationer, received a call to the church at New Haven, and was ordained on the 5th of March, 1806. He entered upon the duties of his pastorate with that energy which distinguished all his operations, and during its three years and ten months two hundred persone were admitted to the church, of whom only twenty-eight were received upon certificates from other churches.

An offer was made to him at this time of the Professorship of Sacred Literature at Andover, and though he felt himself unqualified for the place, having only begun the study of Hebrew, yet in reliance upon the blessing of God in connection with his own diligent efforts, he accepted the appointment, and was inaugurated professor on the 28th of February, 1810. Here began the great business of his life, and from this time until 1848, when he resigned the professorship, he produced those works which have had so important an influence upon the interpretation of the Sacred Scriptures over the whole world.

"His life had a somewhat abrupt termination. As he was taking his daily walk he fell in the street and fractured the bone of his wrist. The pain and confinement which this occasioned rendered him unable to withstand a severe cold which

* Sprague's Annals, vol. ii. p. 476.

subsequently came upon him, and passing into a typhoid fever
quickly put an end to his life. During his illness his mind
was part of the time clear and active, and his interest in matters of public concern seemed unabated. When his physician
expressed to him the hope that his sickness was not unto
death, he replied, 'Unto the glory of God—but unto death.'
He expressed no desire to live longer, except for the sake of
his family and the execution of a work which he had projected
in his favourite department of study. He died on the 4th of
January, 1852, in the seventy-second year of his age."*

When he entered upon his professorship he could have had
no presentiment of the work that was before him. He had to
prepare himself for the work, and provide the materials as he
was able to use them. Grammars, reading-books, and even
types and printers had to be prepared for the service. As he
advanced in knowledge himself these improved in character,
and not the least important service that he rendered to Biblical
criticism was the translation into English of the works of
the learned German scholars, Jahn, Ernesti, Winer,† Hug, and
Gesenius. "The department," says Professor Stowe, "was
nothing when he began, and before he closed his career it became the leading branch in all systems of theological culture,
and mainly by his example and efforts."

Dr. Wendell Holmes gives an outside view of him as "tall,
lean, with strong bold features, a keen, scholarly, accipitrine
nose, thin expressive lips, great solemnity and impressiveness
of voice and manner. He was my early model of a classic
orator. His air was Roman, his neck long and bare like
Cicero's, and his toga—that is, his broadcloth cloak—was carried on his arm whatever might have been the weather, with
such a statue-like grace that he might have been turned into
marble as he stood, and looked noble by the side of the antiques
of the Vatican." Professor Stowe thus describes his appearance in the lecture-room: "A countenance ever changing with
every change of inward emotion; his movements all abrupt,
elastic, and full of vigour, and never for a moment at rest; he
gave one the impression of an exuberance of life and spirit,
that could not possibly be concealed or restrained, but must
find vent in some way. There was an earnestness and hearti-
ness in his manner that was always childlike, and sometimes
almost boisterous; and his excess of vitality often flowed out
in the oddest kind of gestures, which, if not the most graceful,
never lacked expressiveness. Withal he was very much of a

* Sprague's Annals, vol. ii. p. 477.
† Reviewed by Dr. Joseph Addison Alexander in 1835.
39

gentleman, and never rude or coarse; and, when the occasion called for it, his deportment was of the most bland and polished type. Not a little of the interest of his lectures depended on his perfectly unique, and inimitable, and indescribable manner in the lecture-room. Who that has ever seen him lecturing can ever forget the picture? And who can ever reproduce it, so that others can see it at second-hand? He was as earnest to communicate as he was to acquire. The pleasure of attaining was no greater than the pleasure of imparting—nay, he found it more blessed to give than to receive. The lecture-room was his paradise, and the circle of admiring pupils his good angels. The delight was mutual. It was thus that he inspired the enthusiasm which he felt himself. It was wonderfully contagious."

The work that Professor Stuart performed was enormous. We will not attempt to give the titles of his compilations and translations, all of which were noticed when issued by the *Princeton Review*, but in 1832 he published his Commentary on the Epistle to the Hebrews; in 1833 his Commentary on Romans, which is reviewed by Dr. Hodge in the volume for that year; in 1844, his Commentary on the Apocalypse; and in 1850–2, his Commentaries on Daniel, Ecclesiastes, and Proverbs. "Of these," Professor Stowe says, "all his works were better fitted for the oral instructions of the lecture-room than for the printed page pondered in the closet. His readers can never feel the kindling enthusiasm that was never wanting among his hearers. His writings abound with knowledge; they are rich in information of the most varied kind, but the digressions, the repetitions, the egotisms, the general want of compactness, which give vivacity to a lecture, rather deaden the impression of a book. His books will always be valuable for the stores of learning they contain—they will be exhaustless magazines for the supply of other minds, but they can never be extensively popular. It is worthy of remark that his later writings—those which he elaborated after he had ceased to lecture—such as the Commentaries on Proverbs and Ecclesiastes, are much less liable to the above criticisms than the books which he composed in the acme of his strength and in the zenith of his power and activity as a lecturer."

For further information concerning his life and writings see Sprague's Annals and Allibone's Dictionary of Authors. He took exception to Dr. Carnahan's article on the American Education Society, and wrote an Examination of the Review in the October No. for 1829, to which he wrote a Postscript, which appeared in the January No. for 1830.

TAYLOR, WILLIAM J. R., was born in 1823; graduated at Rutger's College in 1841, and at the Theological Seminary at New Brunswick, N. J., in 1844. He then became successively pastor of the Reformed (Dutch) churches in New Durham, Jersey City, Schenectady, and Philadelphia; and in 1862, Corresponding Secretary of the American Bible Society. During the late war the chief care of Bible distribution in both armies was intrusted to him, and from the peace till 1869 the Bible work in the entire South. He is now pastor of the Clinton Avenue Reformed church, Newark, N. J. He is the author of "Louisa, a Pastor's Memorial," published by the American Sunday-school Union in 1862, and several occasional discourses, and has been a frequent contributor to periodical literature. He reviewed Dr. Joseph H. Jones's work, "Man, Moral and Physical," in the volume for 1860.

TODD, JOHN A., is a native of Somerville, N. J. His parents were members of the Reformed Dutch Church, and after receiving his preliminary education he was sent to Rutger's College, where he graduated in July 1845. He studied theology in the Seminary of the Reformed Dutch Church at New Brunswick, completing his course in July 1848. On September 26, 1848, he was ordained to the ministry and installed pastor of the Reformed Dutch church at Griggstown, N. J., which charge he held upwards of six years, when he accepted a call to the church at Tarrytown, N. Y., into which he was installed on May 1, 1855, where he has continued till the present time.

As a writer he is best known by his sermon on "The Character and Death of Washington Irving," whom he knew as a neighbour, and his "Memoir of the Rev. Peter Labagh, D. D. with Notices of the Reformed Protestant Dutch Church in North America,"* but he has been an active contributor to the periodical literature of the country. In 1868 he was honoured with the degree of D. D. by Rutgers College. For this work he wrote a review of "The Higher Christian Life," by the Rev. W. E. Boardman.

1860. The Law of Spiritual Growth.

TUCKER, MARK, son of David Tucker, and his wife, Eunice Tallman, was born in Whitestown, New York, on the 7th of June, 1795; entered Union College at Schenectady, N. Y., in 1808, where he received his first degree in

---

* Noticed in the volume for 1860, p. 571.

1811; studied divinity with Drs. Nott and Yates, and was ordained to the ministry, and settled as pastor over the Presbyterian church in Stillwater, N. Y., in 1814. After some years he removed to Northampton, Massachusetts, and took charge of the Congregational church (then undivided) in that venerable town; and afterwards laboured in the pastoral office in Troy, N. Y., Providence, R. I., and Wethersfield and Vernon, Conn. For the last few years he has been withdrawn from active labours, and is now living with his children in Wethersfield, Conn. He received the honorary degree of D. D. from Williams College in 1831.

Dr. Tucker has published a number of sermons, but his life has been devoted to the pastoral work, in which he has been a diligent and successful labourer. He is the author of the article in the volume for

1835. The Moral Influence of the Cross.

TYLER, SAMUEL, was born October 22, 1809, in Prince George's county, Maryland, on a tobacco plantation. He went to country schools until he was twelve years of age. He was then sent to the academy of the Rev. James McVean, at Georgetown, D. C. At this school he became, for one so young, a remarkable Latin and Greek scholar. In 1827 his father removed him to Middlebury College, Vermont. Becoming convinced that the collegiate course would only retard his progress in knowledge, he visited other New England colleges, and finding his opinion confirmed, he returned to Maryland, and began the study of law at Frederick City, under John Nelson, afterwards Attorney-General of the United States. He was admitted to the bar in 1832, and soon got into practice. Devoting most of his time to his profession, he nevertheless studied almost everything. Reid's "Inquiry" led him to study metaphysics.

In 1844 he published his "Discourse of the Baconian Philosophy," and in 1848 a second edition. In 1846 he wrote and published his "Burns as a Poet and as a Man." In 1858 he published his "Progress of Philosophy," and a second edition in 1868. For the first edition, South Carolina College, and also Columbia College, New York, made him LL.D.

Sir William Hamilton, having become familiar with his philosophical writings, sent him, in 1852, his *Discussions;* and the second edition he sent, in 1855, by a student from Edinburgh. Upon the death of Sir William Hamilton, Mr. Tyler, at the solicitation of the friends of Prof. Fraser, recommended him as his successor, and several other professors of philosophy in British universities asked and received from Mr. Tyler testimonials of their fitness before their elections.

In 1852 Mr. Tyler was chosen, with two other lawyers, by the Legislature of Maryland, to simplify the Pleading and Practice in all the courts of the State. The Preliminary Procedure and Pleading are his sole work. It is embodied in "Tyler's Pleading." It is the most successful of law reforms.

Mr. Tyler is now senior Professor in Columbia College Law School at Washington City, and engaged in active practice as a lawyer.

His papers in the *Princeton Review* are,

1836. Balfour's Inquiry.
1840. The Works of Lord Bacon.
1841. The Life of Lenhart the Mathematician.
1843. Psychology—Influence of the Baconian Philosophy.
1844. Agricultural Chemistry.
1846. Bush on the Soul.
1852. Cosmos by Humboldt.
1855. Sir William Hamilton and his Philosophy.
1858. De Tocquevillle and Lieber as Writers on Political Science.
1859. Sir William Hamilton.
1860. The Physio-Philosophy of Oken—Horace Binney's Pamphlets.
1862. God and Revelation.

WATTS, ROBERT, is a native of county Down, Ireland; was educated at the Model School, Dublin, for a teacher; emigrated to the United States, and became a student in Lafayette College in 1847–8, and removed with Dr. Junkin to Washington College, Va., where he graduated in 1849. In the same year he entered the Theological Seminary at Princeton, N. J., took the usual three years course, and on the 4th of May, 1853, was ordained and installed pastor of the Westminster church, Philadelphia; a new enterprise, which under his ministry became a flourishing church. About this time he became an occasional contributor to the pages of the *Presbyterian Magazine*, under the signature R. W., and during the sickness of Dr. Van Rensselaer, he assisted him in editing the magazine, and closed the series after his death. He also assisted Dr. Van Rensselaer as Corresponding Secretary of the Board of Education, and upon his resignation in May 1860, Dr. Watts was appointed Assistant Secretary, and held the office till May 1863. The climate of Philadelphia not being favourable to the health of Mrs. Watts, he then resigned his charge of the Westminster church, and was dismissed to the Presbytery of Dublin, Ireland, where he became pastor of a church that had become vacant by the death of the pastor. In 1868 he succeeded Dr. Edgar as Professor of Divinity in the Belfast Theological Seminary, and in 1870 he revisited the United States as delegate from the Presbyterian Church in Ireland to the Presbyterian Churches in America. He is the author of the review in

1859. Barnes on the Atonement.

WEED, HENRY R., was born at Balston, Saratoga county, New York, on July 20, 1787; graduated at Union College, Schenectady, N. Y., in 1812; entered the Theological Seminary at Princeton, N. J., in fall of same year, in the first class of the institution, and finished the course in 1815. He was soon called to the pastorate of the Presbyterian church, Jamaica, L. I., and ordained and installed by the Presbytery of New York, January 4, 1816. In 1822 he became pastor of the First Presbyterian church, Albany, N. Y., and on account of failing health, resigned his charge in 1829 or 1830, and removed to Troy, N. Y., assisting Dr. M. Tucker in the pastorate of the Second Presbyterian church of that city. The health of some members of his family demanding change of climate, he removed to Cincinnati, Ohio, in the spring of 1832, acting as agent for the Board of Education. In the fall of the same year, receiving a call to the First Presbyterian Church, Wheeling, Va., he removed thence, and after labouring as stated supply for some months, was installed pastor. In this pastoral relation he remains until the present time, a period of thirty-eight years, though for several years past, through the infirmities of age, the active duties of the pulpit and pastorate have devolved upon his junior co-pastor, the Rev. D. W. Fisher. Dr. Weed contributed occasionally anonymous articles to the religious periodicals of the Church, including the *Biblical Repertory*, but avoided regular authorship. For the use of his own Bible-class, he published a series of questions on the Confession of Faith, which was afterward published by the Presbyterian Board of Publication.

The only article that we know to be from his pen, is the review of Babington on Education, in the volume for 1832.

WESTERVELT, J. P., was born at Paramus, N. J., November 7, 1816. His parents were at the time members of the Reformed Dutch Church of that place, then, and for

many years, under the pastoral care of the Rev. W. El-
tinge, D. D.   When he was about four years old, his parents
removed to the vicinity of Paterson, N. J., and in the spring
of 1828 he was placed as a clerk in a dry-goods store, in which
capacity he continued for about five years.   During this time
he read many works of romance, adventure, biography, and
history, and during a part of it, took private lessons in English
grammar and in the Latin language.   Early in 1833 he made
a profession of his faith in Christ, and in the spring of the
same year he entered on a course of study of Latin and Greek.

·   In the fall of 1837, he entered Rutgers College, and having
completed his Sophomore year, and being dismissed at his own
request, he took charge, in the autumn of 1838, of the Lafayette Academy at · Hackensack, N. J.   Here he remained six
months, when he resigned and returned again to his father's
house, where he pursued his studies unaided for about six
months.   The next five years of his life were spent in the
cities of New York and Brooklyn, where he gave instruction
in female seminaries and in private families; spending, on an
average, three or four hours a day in teaching, and devoting
the rest of his time to study.

·   In June 1844, he was received under the care of the Classis
of Union of the True Reformed Dutch Church, as a candidate
for the gospel ministry.   His theological studies were pursued
under the direction of the Rev. A. Amerman, of Hackensack, N. J., a graduate of Columbia College, who had taken
a four years course of theological instruction under Dr. John
M. Mason, of New York.   He was licensed June 5, 1845, by
the Classis of Union, and immediately began his labours in Johnstown and Mayfield, N. Y.   He was ordained at Johnstown,
N. Y., on the 22d of October, and installed pastor of the
churches of Johnstown and Mayfield.

In June 1854 a charge was preferred against him before the
Classis for having assisted the Rev. Jeremiah Wood, of Mayfield, in the administration of the Lord's Supper; and for
having read to his own congregation a notice of the dedication
of the Methodist church in Johnstown; and a resolution of
implied censure was passed upon him by the Classis.   Though
dissatisfied, he remained another year at his post, when he
applied for dismission from the body.   A resolution was passed,
allowing him to withdraw on his own responsibility, and
directing the Stated Clerk to furnish him with an attested
copy of said action.   He immediately applied for admission to
the Presbytery of Albany, by which body he was unhesitatingly and cordially received.   Having suffered much from a

bronchial affection, while a pastor, he declined opportunities of immediate settlement, and sought by rest from speaking, and in such other ways as were open to him, to recruit his health. After remaining two years without charge in Johnstown, he accepted an invitation to supply for one year the Reformed Dutch church of Ephratah, a village about eight miles distant from the former place. He removed thither, and supplied said church for two years. In the autumn of 1859, he removed to Princeton, N. J., where he resided till September 1866, when he removed to Paterson, N. J., his present place of residence. Whilst at Princeton, he translated the Life of Van der Palm, and ten of his sermons, which were published in 1865, by Hurd & Houghton, of New York. Since his removal to Paterson, he has written a considerable number of articles for the Cyclopedia edited by Drs. McClintock and Strong. His health being inadequate to a pastoral charge, and being unwilling to turn to any secular employment, he has devoted his time chiefly to linguistic, historical, and theological studies. His occasional preaching has been mainly in the way of relieving his clerical brethren.

His contributions to this periodical consist of the following translations and original articles:

1861. Van der Palm.

1862. Bilderdijk.

1866. Strauss and Schleiermacher—Renan, Strauss, and Schleiermacher.

WHITEHEAD, WILLIAM ADEE, son of William Whitehead, first cashier of the Newark Banking and Insurance Company, was born in Newark, N. J., February 19, 1810. His family removed to Perth Amboy in 1823, and in 1828 he went to Florida, in connection with commercial pursuits. In 1830 he was appointed Collector of the Customs at Key West, which office he filled until 1838. His first published literary efforts were contributions to the newspapers of that place, and a series of "Letters from Cuba," published in the *Newark Daily Advertiser* in 1838, to the columns of which paper he has since been a frequent contributor.

Mr. Whitehead returned to the north in 1838, and entered into active business. For many years he has filled official positions in the New Jersey Railroad Company, and been engaged in advancing the interests of various literary and educational institutions in New Jersey. He is at present President of the Board of Trustees of the State Normal School. He has been associated with the New Jersey Historical Society since its organization in 1845, and its Corresponding Secretary, ånd his published works are mostly of an historical character. "The History of East Jersey under the Proprietary Governments;" "The Papers of Governor Lewis Morris," which he edited; and the "Analytical Index to the Colonial Documents of New Jersey," were published by the Historical Society as Volumes I, IV, and V of its "Collections;" and an address by him, at the bi-centennial celebration of the settlement of Newark, was also published by it, in a supplement to Vol. VI. The "Proceedings" of the society contain several of his minor productions, the most important being a "Review of the Boundary Question between New York and New Jersey," (1867,) and "The Circumstances connected with the settlement of Elizabethtown, N. J.," (1869.) In 1856 he published "Contributions to the early history of Perth Amboy and the surrounding Country." In 1868, "What is the worship of the Protestant Episcopal Church in the United States?" from his pen, was issued as one of the publications of the Evangelical Knowledge Society; and in 1867 he contributed an article on "The alleged Atheism of the Constitution," to the *New Jersey Magazine and Northern Monthly.* In 1845 the honorary degree of A. M. was conferred upon him by the College of New Jeresy.

In 1847 he contributed to this periodical a review of Duer's Life of Lord Stirling.

WIGHT, JOSEPH K., was born in Jewett City, Conn., on February 9, 1824, and graduated from Williams College, Mass., in 1843. After spending a year as a colporteur in Georgia, he entered the Seminary at Columbia, S. C., where he studied theology one session, and then completed a three years course at Princeton. Having devoted himself to foreign missionary work, he sailed for China in October 1848, and was stationed at Ningpo; but in 1850 was sent with Dr. Culbertson to form a new mission at Shanghai. In 1854 he returned to this country in ill health, and after spending a short time, he so far recovered as to be able to return to the mission field, but in the spring of 1857 he found it necessary again to return home. Since that time he has supplied the pulpit of the Second Presbyterian church in Troy, N. Y., for one year, and is now pastor of a church at New Hamburgh, N. Y. His articles in this *Review* are

1855. Huc's Journey through China.
1858. Confucianism.
1859. Budhism in India and China.
40

1860. The Heathen Inexcusable for their Idolatry.
1863. Recent Explorations in Africa.
1864. Modes of Evangelization.

WILSON, JOHN LEIGHTON, was born in Sumter District, South Carolina, on the 9th of March, 1809; graduated at Union College, N. Y., in 1829, and prosecuted his theological studies in the Theological Seminary at Columbia, S. C., in the years 1831, 1832 and 1833, being one of the first class that graduated at that institution. He was ordained, and sailed as a foreign missionary to Africa in 1833, and laboured in that country twenty years, the first eight years at Cape Palmas, and the remainder of the time at the Gaboon. He reduced to writing the Grebo language, spoken at Cape Palmas; and the Mpongwe, spoken at the Gaboon, and published grammars of these languages, and translated portions of the Scriptures, and other books, into both of them. On his return to the United States in 1853, he was appointed one of the Secretaries of the Board of Foreign Missions, and continued in that position till 1861, when he went South, and has since acted as Secretary of Sustentation and Foreign Missions in the Southern Presbyterian Church.

He is the projector of the scheme of Sustentation adopted by the Southern Presbyterian Church, and the author of a volume on Western Africa, and has written several articles in the *Southern Presbyterian Quarterly Review* and the *Bibliotheca Sacra*, and papers for the Transactions of the Ethnological Society of New York.

His articles in this *Review* are,

1855. Ethnographic View of Western Africa—Idolatrous Practices of Northern Guinea.

1858. Missions in Western Africa.

WINCHESTER, SAMUEL GOVER, was born at Rock Run, Harford county, Maryland, on the 17th of February, 1805. From early childhood he discovered a great fondness for oratory, and while at school often contrived to engage his companions in a debate. As the field in which to exercise his talents he chose the law, and was entered as a student of law in the University of Maryland, in January 1825. He had been for several years an attendant at an Episcopal church, but he now occasionally went, in the afternoon, to hear the Rev. William Nevins, of the First Presbyterian church, and after a while joined his Bible-class. In March 1827, an extensive revival took place in Baltimore, of which he was one of the subjects, and on the 6th of May he was admitted to the communion of the First church.

He had now nearly completed his preparatory studies, and the prospect of a successful career at the Bar was not doubtful, but the religious change which had been wrought in him immediately suggested the inquiry, whether it was not his duty to serve God in the ministry of the gospel, and after pondering the question devoutly and earnestly, he was constrained to give it an affirmative answer. Some of his nearest friends, including his father, was opposed to this step, but his convictions of duty would not permit him to yield to their persuasions. He had a small income, sufficient to pay his expenses, left him by his mother, and in November 1827 he entered the Theological Seminary at Princeton. In 1829 he was licensed to preach by the Presbytery of Baltimore, and in the spring of 1830, while still pursuing his studies at Princeton, he was unanimously called to be pastor of the Sixth Presbyterian church in Philadelphia. He accepted the call, and was ordained and installed on the 4th of May, 1830.

He was married to Miss Grace Mactier, of Baltimore, on the 8th of June following, and after a residence in Philadelphia of about seven years, his health became impaired, and he was recommended to visit the Southern States and Cuba. By this tour he gained considerable vigour, and in the spring of 1837 he resigned his charge, and accepted an agency from the Board of Domestic Missions. In the autumn he received a call to the church in Natchez, Miss., and believing that the change of climate would be favorable to his health, he accepted the call, and removed his family to Natchez, where he was able to discharge his duties four years.

In May 1841, he was elected a delegate to the General Assembly, and having leave of absence from his congregation six months, he availed himself of the opportunity to visit Niagara Falls, and made a short tour in Canada. He was evidently very feeble, and when he returned to New York on his homeward way, on the 22d of August he preached in the Reformed Dutch church, in Lafayette Place, an impressive discourse from the text, " Whatsoever a man soweth, that shall he also reap." This was his last sermon. At half-past five o'clock on Tuesday morning, the 31st of August, congestion of the brain took place, and he passed away. His remains were conveyed to Baltimore, and placed in the Mactier vault in Green Mount Cemetery.

" In regard to his personal appearance," says Dr. Engles, "he was above the medium height, finely proportioned, erect and graceful in his carriage, with a face in which dignity and benevolence were happily blended. When animated in conversation, or in public speaking, his eye expressed his emotions, and beamed with light. His countenance in repose was indicative of gentleness, and when the occasion demanded it, could express firm determination and even severity. In the pulpit, or on the floor of a deliberative body, although his appearance was youthful, his person was commanding, his self-possession perfect, his gesticulation easy and graceful, his voice full and well modulated, and his whole manner peculiarly oratorical. The bent of his mind was for argument and discussion, and in deliberative bodies he was often listened to with pleasure, if not surprise, for the happy facility he displayed in developing a point of controversy, particularly when it related to ecclesiastical law. If he was not always right, he was at least always plausible and ingenious. His appearance before the Assembly in 1834 will long be remembered. The subject under discussion related to the grounds of appeal. He was young, he was comparatively unknown to the majority of the members, and nothing unusual was expected of him when he took the floor. The subject was a dry one, and seemingly afforded but little scope for the display of oratorical power; yet it was the kind of subject with which he loved to grapple. In the discussion of it the energy of his mind was fully tasked; his eye kindled, the best points of his naturally oratorical manner were brought forth, and with the self-possession of a practised debater, he reasoned his points with a cogency and fluency which carried conviction to many minds, and held the attention of the house for more than two hours."* The substance of the argument will be found in the volume for

1835. The Doctrine of Appeals and Complaints.
1837. A Course of Legal Study.

WOODBRIDGE, JOHN, was born at Southampton, Massachusetts, on the 2d of December, 1784. All his ancestors, excepting his father, as far back as anything is known of them, were ministers bearing the name of John. Of course we speak only of the male line, though by a maternal ancestor he was descended from the Rev. John Eliot, "the apostle to the Indians." His mother was a woman of remarkable piety, and his father, though a physician, was fond of theological study; hence it is not surprising that their two sons devoted themselves to the ministry, and their only daughter became a minister's wife.

* This article is substantially taken from Sprague's Annals.

The subject of this sketch entered Williams College while in his sixteenth year and graduated in 1804, at which time he delivered a poem which excited considerable notice. He had given great attention to the cultivation of English literature while in college, and the year after leaving college he devoted to the study of law, and writing political articles for the newspapers. Becoming dissatisfied with this life, though not yet a professor of religion, he put himself under the tuition of the Rev. Asahel Hooker of Goshen, Connecticut, to prepare for the ministry. His fellow-students were the Rev. Dr. Humphrey, Dr. Tyler, Rev. Joshua Huntington, and the Rev. Frederick Marsh, of whom all excepting the last are dead. He was licensed to preach in June 1807, and entered upon his work with much ardour, having found Christ in the study of his word, and consecrated himself entirely to his service.

For a time he laboured as a home missionary in the western part of New York; afterwards he preached in the Tabernacle church at Philadelphia, but he declined a call from that people and accepted one from the church at Hadley, Mass., of which he was ordained pastor on the 20th of June, 1810. In 1830 he removed to New York and became pastor of the Bowery Presbyterian church till 1837, when he removed to Bridgeport, Conn., where he only remained two years. At this time the New Haven controversy was at its height, and as he strongly opposed the speculations of Dr. Taylor, both in New York and Bridgeport he met with considerable opposition. From Bridgeport he went to New Hartford, Connecticut, where he found a quiet and pleasant home for three years, when he returned to Hadley, and became pastor of the newly formed Russel church till 1857, when he resigned on account of his increasing infirmities, being then in the seventy-second year of his age. He now resides with his children in Chicago, the gospel which he preached so long being still his consolation, and in the retirement of his chamber blessing the world by his prayers and the example of a holy life.

He was married to Mary Anne Seymour of Hartford, Conn., who became the mother of nine children, seven of whom survive. She died on the 15th of January, 1858.

In 1825 the degree of D. D. was conferred upon him by Williams College. While pastor of the Bowery church he published a work on "Practical Religion," and has written a great many articles in *The Literary and Theological Review, New York Observer, Boston Recorder, New York Evangelist,* and some of the publications of the American Tract Society. His only article for the *Princeton Review* is a review of a work by Dr. Snodgrass. It is entitled, "Perfect Sanctification," is in the volume for 1842, and was reprinted in the Princeton Theological Essays.

YEOMANS, JOHN WILLIAM, was born in Hinsdale, Massachusetts, on the 7th of January, 1800. His parents were in humble circumstances, and when a boy he was apprenticed to a blacksmith, but he had an ardent desire for learning, and had made good use of the opportunities afforded him for acquiring knowledge, and before his apprenticeship was .completed, he bought up the unexpired time, and supported himself by teaching. He entered Williams College in 1824, and was graduated with the second honours of the class. In 1826-7 he was a tutor in the College, after which he studied theology in the Seminary at Andover, and in November 1828 he was ordained and installed pastor over a small congregation in North Adams, Mass., which he had gathered while acting as a tutor in the college. He now collected funds to build for them a house for worship, and continued with them till 1832, when he accepted a call to the First Congregational church in Pittsfield, Mass. At the end of two years he resigned this for the First Presbyterian church in Trenton, N. J., where he became the successor to Dr. James W. Alexander. In 1841 he accepted the presidency of Lafayette College, Easton, Pa., which he resigned in 1844, and after a short residence in Philadelphia became the pastor of the Mahoning church in Danville, Pa., the duties of which he discharged till his death, which took place on the 22d of June, 1863.

He held a high place in the esteem of his brethren in the ministry, and was elected Moderator of the General Assembly in 1860, and had the degree of D. D. conferred upon him simultaneously by three colleges, the College of New Jersey, Williams College, and Miami University.

His desire for knowledge was so powerful that he was never idle. His life was continuous labour, but his aims and his standard of perfection was often too high to be reached. He did not live to complete any of the great works that he had undertaken. He left in an incomplete state Commentaries on the Gospel of John and the Epistle to the Romans. Many of the sermons which he left in manuscript had never been preached by him, probably being laid aside for other strains of thought that had been suggested during their preparation; and some of those preached had been prepared one, two, and three years before they were delivered. He was a good classical scholar, and well acquainted with Mathematics and

the Natural Sciences, but Logic and Metaphysics was the field
in which he delighted to revel, and many of his deductions
were of the most beautiful and satisfactory character.   He
was an eloquent preacher, and in describing and defining the
emotions and affections, his deep study of the human mind
made him peculiarly felicitous.   It is to be hoped that some
of the precious fruits of his industry may yet be published.
The best thoughts in many of his sermons could only be partially apprehended by hearing them from his lips, and deserve
a more permanent form.   The articles he furnished to this
Review are the most valuable of his published works:

1838. Physical Theory of another Life—Baptist Translation
of the Bible.

1839. European Civilization.

1840. Supremacy of Conscience.

1841. Dr. Skinner's Religion of the Bible.

1842. The Pastoral Office—Adaptation of the External
World to the Intellectual Culture of Man.

1845. Bush on the Resurrection.

1846. The Raising of Lazarus—Upham on Spiritual Life—
Forms of Worship.

1847. Public Prayer.

1848. Thoughts on Family Worship—Unity of the Church.

1849. Domestic Missions.

1853. Wines on the Hebrew Laws.

1860. Napoleon and the Papacy.

1861. The Apostolic Benediction—The Kingdom of Christ.

1862. The Presbyterian Historical Society.

1863. The Inspired Theory of Prayer.

YEOMANS, EDWARD DORR, son of the above, was
born at North Adams, Berkshire county, Massachusetts, September 27, 1829, where his father was first settled as pastor.
He was the eldest of six children, four of whom survive him.
In 1841, when in his twelfth year, his father was called to the
Presidency of Lafayette College, at Easton, Pa., and Edward
entered the Freshman class in the College, having been previously prepared, partly in the school of the Rev. Baynard R.
Hall, at Trenton, but mainly by his father's private instructions.   At Easton he finished the Junior year before he had
reached the fifteenth year of his age.   His father then moved
to Philadelphia, and endeavoured to enter him for the Senior
year at the University of Pennsylvania, but the rules of the institution forbidding the graduation of one so young, he pursued his
studies at home, under his father's direction.   He therefore

never took a regular Bachelor's degree, but subsequently received the honorary degree of Master of Arts from Princeton College. While residing in Philadelphia he united with the Penn Square Presbyterian church, then under the care of Dr. Willis Lord.

At the age of fifteen and a half years he began his theological studies, under his father's direction, at Danville. He subsequently spent one year at Princeton Seminary, and was licensed to preach the gospel by the Presbytery of Northumberland, at Muncy, Pa., April 21, 1847, at the early age of seventeen and a half years. After his licensure he remained two or three years in Danville, holding the position of Principal of the Academy, and preaching in the neighbouring churches as occasion offered. During this period he supplied the church of New Columbia, near Danville, every other Sabbath, for a year and a half. About the same time he began the study of the German language with his father, and translated a considerable portion of Dorner's Christology, of which he afterwards wrote a review.

In the fall of 1852, having received proposals from the Rev. Dr. Philip Schaff, then at Mercersburg, for the translation of his History of the Apostolic Church, he removed to Mercersburg, and spent a year in that labour. After the completion of this work, he spent nearly another year supplying vacant churches, when, in September 1854, he received and accepted a call to the Warrior Run church, in the Presbytery of Northumberland.

He was ordained with a view to this settlement, November 29, 1854, by the Presbytery of Northumberland, at the age of twenty-five. Here he remained as pastor four years. In November 1856, he received a call to the Great Island church, Lock Haven, which he declined. In November 1858, he was called to the Fourth church, Trenton, N. J., then organized. Under his pastorate there, the beautiful edifice now occupied by that congregation was erected. Shortly after his settlement in Trenton he was married, January 12, 1859, to Anna Corilla Green, second daughter of George S. Green, Esq., of Trenton. His wife and three children survive him. In May 1863, he was called to St. Peter's church, Rochester, N. Y., where he laboured with zeal and success four years, when he was called, March 1867, to the pastorate of the Central church, Orange, N. J. During his residence in Rochester, in the summer of 1864, the honorary degree of Doctor of Divinity was conferred upon him by Princeton College.

His literary labours, outside of his regular ministerial work, were mainly in the line of German translation. Besides the large volume of Schaff's Apostolic Church already mentioned, he rendered into English soon after, Schaff's Lectures on America, delivered and first published in Berlin, during the author's visit to his native land. He then began the task of translating Schaff's History of the Christian Church, which has thus far reached its third volume. He translated from the author's manuscript, so that the book appears as an original English work. The first volume was published in 1859, the second and third appeared in 1867. For some time before his death he had been engaged upon the translation of John's Gospel, in Lange's Commentary, which is now being issued from the press. He had accomplished one-half of this task, when unmistakable signs of over-taxed powers compelled him to abandon it.

His superior ability in this department of literary labour was freely acknowledged by competent judges. He possessed rare facility in rendering into idiomatic English, German thoughts and forms of speech. A writer in a late number of the *British and Foreign Evangelical Review*, of London, in a notice of the last two volumes of Dr. Schaff's Church History, thus speaks of the style of his translation:—"The Rev. Dr. Yeomans, of Rochester, translated most of it, as he had done the History of the Apostolic Church, into English. In point of style and general structure, there is nothing to indicate that the book is a translation from the German. Indeed, in this respect, it will stand a favourable comparison with the best English classics."

Since his removal to Orange he had also compiled, for the use of his church, a book of "Select Hymns and Tunes," upon which he expended great labour, and for which he was peculiarly fitted by fine musical culture and poetical taste. It was a labour of love for the service of the Lord's house, and for his own church; and he greatly enjoyed the hearty appreciation with which this effort was received by his people. The book is now being used by them with very marked success in the way of promoting congregational singing.

In his habits of study he was remarkably systematic. He wrote sermons without special reference to the time of their delivery. He was always ahead of his work, and was never pushed to complete his preparations for the Sabbath, as he had constantly on hand at least a score of fully and carefully written discourses that he had never used in the pulpit. Scrupulously exact and thorough in everything he undertook, he spared no pains to do well what he attempted to do at all.

41

Over-working of the brain, continued almost from his earliest youth, at length began to tell seriously upon his health. The first indication of disease occurred in February 1868, when he was attacked in the pulpit, as the services were about concluding. While reading the closing hymn,

"From the cross uplifted high,"

a sort of double consciousness came over him; he imagined he heard the voice of the Saviour in the air, just above and before him, echoing the words he read. During the singing of the hymn, he began to misname the words, and as he stepped forward to pronounce the benediction, he could not utter the words at all. In a few moments, however, he revived, rode home, and after remaining a few days under care of his physician, he went to work again.

In May, three months later, he had a second and more severe attack, which decided him to relinquish entirely his labours of translation. He sent off at once all his manuscripts of Lange's Commentary to Dr. Schaff, peremptorily giving up the whole work. For three months after this he suspended entirely all mental labour, and devoted the time to travel and diversion of various kinds. Some of his parishioners generously took him with them upon their summer tours to New England and the sea-shore, and he seemed to be greatly invigorated by his travel. Softening of the brain had been feared by his physician and friends. On Saturday, August 22d, he came home from one of these trips, intending, with the consent of his physician, to resume preaching. On the succeeding Sabbath he attended the services, morning and afternoon, but took no part in conducting them. Tuesday evening he lectured briefly, but with marked earnestness and solemnity at the usual weekly meeting, and after the services remarked that he felt better and brighter than at any time since his first attack. Wednesday morning he had intended going to New York to consult physicians about resuming work, but arose with a headache; and while he was undecided whether to attempt the journey or not, the pain in the back of the head suddenly became very acute, and continued so for about half an hour, when he became unconscious. This was about nine o'clock in the morning. The stupor continued unbroken until half-past three in the afternoon of the 25th of August, 1868, when he died without a struggle.

He had no appetite for mere recreation. Such was his fondness for work; and he would take no rest, though often urged to do so by his loving and indulgent people. With all his severe application, his constant complaint was that his time was running to waste, and he was accomplishing little or nothing. When kindly remonstrated with by members of his session concerning his purpose to resume preaching so early, he replied, "Oh no; I must get to work again. I know it is in the greatest kindness my people urge this delay, but I must go to work—I will die in the harness. I must tell my people soon again of the love of Christ." Such labours, without an originally strong constitution to bear up under them, would, in the nature of the case, soon have run their course; and the sudden attack of apoplexy in which he died, has probably only briefly anticipated an event that was surely at hand.

In concluding this sketch of the life and character of Dr. Yeomans, but little more need be said. His mental faculties were naturally of a high order, and they had been carefully and unremittingly cultivated. His piety was deep and all-controlling, and of the most cheerful type. He was a man of the strictest integrity, discharging religiously every engagement and obligation. He was remarkably genial, and was possessed of the rare faculty of adapting himself to every class in society, and of winning the respect and affection of all. He was a faithful pastor, a wise and loving husband and father, and a true friend. The only article he contributed to this *Review* was in

1860. Dorner's Christology.

YOUNG, DANIEL, was one of the younger members of a large family, the children of John and Elizabeth Young, natives of Nassau, in Germany, who in early life emigrated to the State of New York, where they afterwards married. He was born on his father's farm, in an agricultural district near Scotchtown, a village of Orange county, about twenty miles from Newburgh. His academical education was obtained at Newburgh, and his collegiate education at Union College, Schenectady, where he graduated in 1820. In the same year he entered the Theological Seminary at Princeton, and pursued his studies in the same class with the Rev. Albert Barnes, who was his intimate friend; but ill health obliged him to quit the Seminary before his regular course of study was completed. His most earnest desire was to engage in foreign missionary labour, which his failing health forbade, so leaving the Seminary, he was licensed to preach by the Presbytery of Hudson, N. Y., and commissioned as a domestic missionary to travel in the interior of Virginia, and labour in destitute churches, which he did in 1824 and 1825. After that, an opportunity offering, he went to Europe, spent a year in

Portugal, and was greatly benefitted by travel and the sea-voyages.   On his return he applied himself to the study of the oriental languages, Arabic and Syriac especially.   In 1828 he accepted an appointment in the German Reformed Church, as editor of their magazine at Carlisle, Pa., and the following year was appointed Professor in the Theological Seminary at York.   His sympathy for the church of his forefathers was warm, and he entered zealously upon his work, but one brief year was all he gave to it.   The second year in the Seminary he began his lectures, and being unable to proceed with them, he went to Philadelphia to consult his physician, who advised him to go South without delay, as that only would restore him.   The winter of 1830–31 was spent in a milder climate, but a violent hemorrhage of the lungs terminated his life on the 6th of March, 1831, at Augusta, Georgia.   In the cemetery of that city he lies interred.   He wrote the article in the volume for

1830. Review of Essays and Dissertations on Biblical Literature.

Dr. Culbertson was not known to be the author of the article on the " Revolution in China," when that portion in which his name should have appeared was put to press.

CULBERTSON, MATTHEW SIMPSON, was born in Chambersburgh, Pa., on the 18th of January, 1819; was educated at the Military Academy at West Point, where he served some time as Professor of Mathematics, and on leaving received a commission as Lieutenant of Artillery.   He was much esteemed as an officer, and continued in the service one year after making a Christian profession.   He then resigned his commission, pursued the usual course of study in the Theological Seminary at Princeton, and was ordained as a missionary to China by the Presbytery of Carlisle in 1844.   About this time the Five Ports of China were opened to commerce and Christian missions, and he, with his wife and a small band of fellow-labourers, reached that country in October of that year.   His first station was Ningpo, where he was greatly useful in helping, with others, to lay the foundation of the important and successful mission of the Presbyterian Church at that point.   His training at West Point in engineering, together with his good sense and judgment, made his services in the many practical questions of buying land, building houses and churches, organizing schools, and conducting printing operations, of special value.   He was also a good earnest preacher, and his labours in connection with others were beginning to tell on the strongholds of heathenism in that large city.

In 1850, while on a visit to Shanghai, he was appointed with the Rev. J. K. Wight to the work of commencing a new mission at Shanghai.   His good judgment and ability in practical matters, it was hoped, would be of special service in a new mission, but they were at that time also much needed at Ningpo, so that he was prevented from joining the mission at Shanghai till the following year.

At that time the question in regard to the mode of translating the sacred Scriptures, and the words to be used in rendering *Elohim* and *Theos* into Chinese, had assumed so much importance, and the differences of opinion had diverged so widely, that the translation then in progress, as a joint work of representatives of all the missions, was abandoned.   One version made by Dr. Medhurst and Mr. J. Stronach, represented one phase of that controversy; the other was represented by the translation made by Dr. Bridgman and Mr. Culbertson.   Mr. Culbertson entered with diligence upon the direct work of translating.   He also contributed a pamphlet to the controversy respecting the proper term to be used for God.   Work in connection with the translation occupied the principal portion of his time until his death in 1862.   Besides this he also assisted in the other work of a new mission, and in preaching regularly in Chinese.

Writing to the Board of Foreign Missions, on the 3d of May, 1862, he says, "I have been permitted to bring to its close the great work on which I have been engaged for so many years—the translation of the Bible.   On the 17th of March, 1851, our Committee, consisting of five members, began their work.   On the 27th of March, 1862, I brought it to a close, having been left single-handed by the lamented death of my only remaining colleague, Dr. Bridgman, in November last.   The translation of the New Testament, and of the Old as far as Isaiah, is the joint work of Dr. Bridgman and myself.   From Isaiah to Malachi I translated alone, though most of it was done prior to Dr. Bridgman's death.   I have found it a delightful work, and esteem it a great privilege to have been thus brought into close communion with the word of God, day by day, for so many years.   But the burden of so great a task unfinished, the importance of having it finished, and the uncertainty of being able to accomplish it, has long been a sore trial to the spirit.   My hope now is that I may be spared to see the whole of it printed in a uniform edition.   Such an edition of fifteen hundred copies has been already commenced with the Berlin font.   This will. be a kind of

Family Bible, and when our new fonts of type of small size are completed, we will be able to bring the whole Bible into as small a compass as the medium-sized English Bible."—*Home and Foreign Record.*

These anticipations he did not live to see realized. In August of that year, after having preached all day to the Chinese, in the evening he was seized with cholera, which speedily put an end to his life. We have not been able to ascertain the day of his death, but a portion of a funeral sermon, preached by the Rev. W. A. P. Martin, on the 31st of August, 1862, is printed in the *Home and Foreign Record* for January 1863.

Mr. Culbertson was a man of vigorous constitution, full of energy, methodical in his work, hopeful and buoyant in spirits, uniformly cheerful and agreeable as a companion, considerate and kind in his intercourse with others, seldom giving or taking offence, and ready as a missionary to do his part in any good word or work. He was a man of rare good sense. This was more characteristic of him as a scholar than any brilliancy of intellect or greatness of attainments. He was industrious and persevering. As a Christian he was devout, earnest, reverent, and at the same time cheerful and hopeful. These were the traits which made him successful and honoured as a missionary, and which led his brethren to select him as one of those best fitted to undertake the very arduous and difficult work of translating the Scriptures into Chinese.

In 1856–7, when he visited this country, he prepared a small volume on "The Religions of North China;" and in 1862 the degree of D. D. was conferred upon him by the University of New York.

His only contribution to this *Review* was made in 1854, and was an exposition of the character of the then pending "Revolution in China," or what is now known as the Kwang-se Rebellion, which attracted so much attention during the first stages of its progress by its semi-religious character.

1854. The Revolution in China.

CORRECTIONS.

Page 90, line 39, *erase* "The English Bible."

Page 100, line 11. *for* Jeffersonville, Louisiana, *read* Jeffersonville, Indiana.

Dr. Baird was ordained by the Presbytery of Baltimore, and spent several years in missionary labours in that Presbytery, and in Kentucky and the south-west. Subsequently, after a pastorate of three years in Muscatine, Iowa, he removed to Woodbury, New Jersey.

Page 110, line 15, *for* College *read* Seminary.

Page 171, line 40, *add*, He died at Princeton, N. J., on Wednesday, the 25th of May, 1870.

Page 225, line 17, *for* say a man, *read* say that a man.

Page 256, line 18, *for* friend *read* friends.

PART III.

INDEX TO THE BIBLICAL REPERTORY.

FIRST SERIES—1825-28.

———

NOTE.—As the first series of the Biblical Repertory includes only four volumes, and as their contents consist mainly of translations and select treatises relating to Hermeneutics and Biblical Criticism, it has been deemed best to give an analytical index of the articles in the order in which they stand in each volume, rather than a topical one.

———

VOL. I.—1825.

ART. I.—*Beckii Monogrammata Hermeneutices Nov. Test.; or Outlines of Hermeneutics.*

Hermeneutics, how distinguished from Exegesis, 2; changes in the method of interpretation of Scripture, 3; early Christian interpreters, 5; *Catinæ patrum*—origin and character of, 6; influence of the Reformation on, 7; Homilies and Postills explained, 8; value of Pietist-school of interpreters, 10; nature of the books of the New Testament, 16; their authors the constant companions of Christ, 18; obliged to accommodate themselves to their readers, 19; the Aramæan language, 21; authors who have treated of the purity of New Testament style, 23; the books of the New Testament originally edited as occasion called for them, 24; Canon of New Testament—division of books—authenticity explained, 25; integrity of New Testament, what, 26; credibility, 27; great care taken of the sacred books, 27; autographs early perished, 29; theories as to the method of examining ancient MSS., 30; list of MSS. that have been collated, 32; importance of ancient Versions, 39; list of, 40; oriental, 40; Latin, 41; other western, 42; first editors of New Testament wanted many critical helps, 43; list of early editions, 44; more modern, 45; various readings, criticism of, higher and lower explained, 49; common laws of applicable to profane authors, 50; causes of changes in, 51; higher criticism, common laws of, 52; laws of applicable to New Testament, 53; twofold duty of the interpreter of New Testament, 58; qualifications necessary for, 59; rules for ascertaining the sense of words, 60; *usus loquendi* of Old Testament explained, 62; tropes in New Testament how to be interpreted, 63; *usus loquendi*, in general, meaning of the phrase, 66; rules of applicable to New Testament, 67; allegories and parables, how to be interpreted, 69; proverbs and

caused by the Nile, 169; plague and leprosy, 170; does Egypt yield more corn than Palestine? 172; Niebuhr's account of harvests of Palestine, 173; exposition of Isaiah xxviii. 25, 173; explanation of the Hebrew words rendered *wheat* and *barley*, 176; description of *millet*, 178; in the East *oats* are unknown, 179; *hay* unknown also, 180; Egypt in general not adapted to the culture of the vine, 182; ancient Egyptian notion of the origin of wine, 182; vineyards of Palestine abundant in early times,—many of them destroyed by Mahomet, 183; meaning of the terms Tirosh, new wine, and sweet wine, 185; Egypt has no' oliveyards, while Palestine abounds with them, 187; the olive tree a symbol of fertility, 188; butter abundant in Egypt, but not in Palestine, 189; testimonies of Greek and Latin writers regarding Palestine, 191; Mount Lebanon, and how it contributes to the fertility of Palestine, 437; size of the Jordan, 438; Lebanon called by Samaritans the mountain of snow, 439; Jeremiah xviii. 14 expounded, 440; division of the rains in Palestine, 442; abounds in plants, 443; the palm, 444; sycamore, 445.

ART. IV.—*History of theological knowledge and literature from the beginning of the 18th century to the present time, by Professor Steudlin.*

Great revolution in all branches of theological learning during this period—causes of. 201; the English deists and their influence, 202; influence of Frederick II. on theology and religion, 202; causes of the introduction of deism into theology, 203; influence of Locke and his philosophy and Bayle, 204; of Leibnitz, 205; his opposition to rationalism and naturalism, 206; the system of Wolf, his relations to Spener, 207; Kant, his philosophy, his opposition to Hume, 209; he taught simple deism; French writers, Bayle, Saurin, Beausobre, Lenfant, and others, 211; effects of the growing spirit of toleration, 212; the school of Spener described, 214; I. F. Buddæus, character and influence of his writings, 217; notice of Walch and Roecher, 218; of Mosheim as a theologian, 219; Semler, charged with making piety subordinate to learning, 221; analysis of his work on theology, 222; Herder's Letters on the study of theology, design and character of, 223; change in the course of study for the ministry proposed by Bahrdt and Campe, 224; notice of works of Noesselt, Plank, and Tittmann, 226; theological journals of Germany begun by French emigrants, 229; notices of Gaussen, Heidegger, and Richard Simon, 231; Dupin's Bibliotheca, 232; Cave's Literary History of Ecclesiastical Writers, account of it, 233.

ART. V.—*Knappius De Spiritu Sancto, et Christo Paracletis. On the Divine Paraclete.*

Paraclete, the word used only by St. John, 237; classical usage of παρακαλειν and παρακλησις, 238; usage among Jewish writers, 242; origin of the sense of *teaching* which παρακαλειν has in St. Paul's epistles, 243; reason why the ancient interpreters differ as to the sense of Paraclete, 243; Origen, Jerome, Luther, and Erasmus adopt

42

ART. VIII.—*Morus on the Style of the New Testament.*

VOL. II.—1826.

ART. XI.—*The State of the Protestant Church in Germany; by the Rev. Hugh James Rose, M. A. of Trinity College, and Vicar of Horsham.*

Art. XII.—*Jahn on the Jewish Pentateuch.*

VOL. III.—1827.

ART. I.—*The State of the Protestant Church in Germany; by the Rev. Hugh James Rose, M. A.*

words of Jehovah and those of Elihu, 431; the ancient poetry of nature respecting the earth, which is compared to the erection of a house, 432; the dawn represented as a messenger sent to chase away bands of robbers, 433; exquisite pictures of the heavens and the earth, 434; in the description of inanimate nature, no part is without life, 435; the true poetry of nature defined, 436; every age must make its poetry consistent with its ideas of the system of being, 437; why the simple fables of ancient and unlearned times affect us more than scientific niceties, 438; the beautiful poetry of God's works of creation, 438; poetry that concerns itself with the criminal deeds of men, corrupting, 439; the poetry of Job not intended to teach a system of physics.

VOL. IV.—1828.

ART. I.—*The History of Theology in the Eighteenth Century. By Dr. Augustus Tholuck. Translated from the German, by the Editor.*

How pietism and formal orthodoxy led to scepticism, 14; reasons why the Reformers failed to attain their objects, 15; state of Exegesis and Dogmatic in the Lutheran church, 16; manner of preaching in it very defective, 17; Spener's complaint of the course of study in the Gymnasia, 18; Thomasius' description of a candidate of theology, 19; account of the labours of John Arndt, 20; account of Spener and his labours, 21; his *Pia Desideria*, 23; his pastorate in Dresden, 24; in Berlin, 25; his character, 27; works written against him, 28; effect of his example on others, 29; origin of the term Pietism, notice of pietist societies, 30; their tendency to fanaticism, 31; opposition to them in Mayence, Giessen, Hamburg, and Dresden, 32; internal disputes regarding the Millennium, 33; state of learning and religion at the universities, 34; history of Francke, 35; his labours as professor in the University of Halle, 37; his Paranetic lecture, 40; his Orphan House, 41; the fanaticism connected with this revival, 43; notice of Peterson and his peculiar views, 44; of Arnold, 45; of John Conrad Dippel, and Ernest Hochman, 46; notice of the sect founded by Ursula Maria Butler, 47; of that founded by Elias Eller, the riband weaver, 48; kinds of hypocrisy often found connected with revivals of religion, 49; the threefold aspect of the revival by Spener, 50; its abuses in reference to modes of expression, 51; in reference to means of edification and external conduct, 53; in reference to Christian enterprise, 55; history of the conflict between faith and infidelity, 157; infidelity in its widest sense defined, 158; speculative origin of Pantheism, 159; its logical deductions, 162; distinctive features and history of Deism, 163; two forms of infidelity in the Romish church, represented by John Scotus Erigena, and Simon of Tournay, 166; the infidelity manifested at the time of the Reformation, represented by Servetus, Campanus, and others, 167; infidelity in the Church of England; origin and early history of Protestantism in England, 168; account of the early sects in the Church of England, 171; account of Lord Herbert and his works, 172; of Charles Blount and John Toland, 173; account of Toland's deistical system, 175; account of Thomas Hobbes and his system, 176; account of Lord Shaftesbury and his works, 178; account of Antony Collins and his writings, 180; account of Thomas Wollaston and Thomas Morgan, 182; the bolder form of infidelity as represented by Lord Bolingbroke, 183; notice of Thomas Chubb and Bernard Mandeville, 184; notice of Tindal's Christianity as old as the Creation, 185; he was the first to form a regular system of Deism, 185; popular tendencies to deism of that time, with their causes, 187;

ART. II,— *Preface to the Translation of Hosea, by Bishop Horsely.*

45

ART. XIII.—*Notice of Dr. Castell.*

INDEX TO TOPICS.

NEW SERIES—1829-1869.

A

C

D

Decline of religion, sermon on, by E. M. Johnson, reviewed, xi. 588.

Decorum, in public worship, explained, vi. 190; offences against, 192; in prayer, 193; singing, 195; importance of the duty, 197.

Decrees of God, doctrine of, two essential points in, iii. 161; objections to, and how answered, 169; the ultimate end of, iv. 94; articles of Synod of Dort on, history of, 250; Melanchthon's views of, v. 524; the doctrine of, stated by Samuel Blair, ix. 536; popular objections to the Calvinistic doctrine of, answered, xvii. 574; and free-will reconciled by the Schoolmen, xviii. 210; consistency of with human freedom, by Dr. N. L. Rice, xxiii. 159; Arminian objections to, answered, xxviii. 45; different theories of, explained, xxix. 103; views of John Robinson the Puritan, 174; their relation to second causes, xxx. 319, xxxiv. 279; how Augustine was led to write on the, 423.

Defects of ministers, not cultivating eminent piety, xxvi. 716; not preaching Christ simply, 717; not dealing closely with the conscience, 720; their sermons too much like essays, 721.

Deist, cowardice of, iii. 322.

Deity of Christ, exposition and defence of the Scripture doctrine of, by Flatt, i. 1; testimonies of John and Paul, 18; confirmed by those of Christ himself, 41; objections answered, 159; views of the Polish Unitarians regarding the, v. 182; of the Quakers, 428; relation of to the atonement of, viii. 202; defence of against Dewey, xix. 4; Swedenborg's views of, xx. 338; Bushnell's, xxi. 261; Unitarian cavils against, answered, xxiv. 580; how united to humanity, xxxii. 119, 138, 145.

Delitzsch, F., Exposition of the prophecy of Habakkuk, xxiii. 67; his system of translation discussed, 71; his view of the Song of Solomon, xxvi. 22.

Delta of the Mississippi, time required for its formation, xl. 579; Lyell's characteristic blunder regarding, 579.

Demission of the ministry, overture to the General Assembly regarding, discussed, xxxi. 60.

Demoniacal possession, exhibiting in Africa, xxvii. 608.

Demotic, Grammar of Egypt, xxvii. 649; remains of the character in, 651.

Denominations, religious, reciprocal duties of, xxxvii. 282.

Dens, Peter, on the worship of images, xxvi. 260.

Depravity, human, doctrine of the Reformed church as to its nature and source, iv. 290; its nature and extent, v. 186; Dr. Wood's essays on, reviewed, vii. 546; Dr. Emmons' view of, xiv. 539; native, arguments to prove, xviii. 71; moral and physical, Finney's theory of, refuted, xix. 237; different theories of its origin and nature, xxv. 688; of its nature, xxvi. 101; orthodox view of, 219; of its extent, 227; Unitarian view of, xxix. 568; Edwards' view of, xxx. 592; Dr. N. W. Taylor's, xxxi. 518.

Derbyshire, dialect of, specimen of, xi. 534.

Descartes, his relation to geometry, xiii. 524; his à priori method of investigation, criticised, xv. 233.

49

out of nature and those which depend on circumstances, 119; characteristics of species, 125; Dr. Bachman against Agassiz, 141; the theory of the latter historically as well as zoölogically false, 145; the theories of Dr. Morton on, examined, xxxiv. 435; uncertainty of craniology as bearing on, 440; Dr. Nott's theory refuted, 449; the latest theory of Agassiz, its merits, xxxv. 110; its defects, 118; evidence against his theory from affinity of languages, 333; theory of Prof. Huxley stated, xxxvi. 278; arguments against, 282.

Doane, Bishop, his Reply to Boardman reviewed, xiii. 450.

Dod, Prof. A. B., his character and attainments, xviii. 350.

Docetæ, their doctrine regarding the person of Christ, xxi. 290.

Doctrine, progress of in New Testament, Bampton lectures on, by Bernard, xl. 519; stages of progress, 527.

Doctrines, of the Bible, cautions to be used in showing their accordance with human reason, xx. 209; two great systems of, xxiii. 308; accepted by all real Christians, xxiv. 27; consequences of regarding them as dubious or unsettled, 28; modes of stating and defending them may be improved, 31.

Doctrinal, purity in the church, rival theories regarding, xxiii. 295; Presbyterian view, 296; the true test of, 297; preaching, its characteristics and value, xxviii. 675; knowledge, the same amount of not to be required of private members and of church officers, xl. 176.

Doddridge, Dr. Philip, account of his writings, xxix. 236; his theology, 255; his poetry, 257; account of, and his hymns, xxx. 65.

Dogmatic history, its German origin, xix. 91; works on, 98.

Domestics, hints on their religious instruction, xx. 69.

Domestic missions, how to be conducted, iv. 72, ix. 107; duty to engage in, enforced by the example of Christ, xxi. 310; the offspring of Christian patriotism, 321; bearing of on our country, 325; on the world, 327.

Donatist controversy, its causes and character, xxxiv. 415; account of the sect, xxxvi. 385; the main points of the controversy, 390.

Donegal, Marquis of, notice of, xl. 408.

Doric, temple, architectural character of, xxviii. 480.

Dorner, his account of Schelling's theology, xxviii. 385.

Dort, Synod of, its character, iv. 239; its articles, 240; its members not agreed on all points, 240; causes of its meeting, 245.

Double sense of Old Testament prophecy, poetry, and history, difficulties of the theory, xxvii. 456.

Douglass on the advancement of society, iii. 306.

Dramatic entertainments, why attractive, xxix. 204.

Draper, Dr. J. W., Treatise on forces in the organization of plants, xvii. 345; his views on questions of morals and religion criticised, xxxviii. 145; holds to eternity of matter, 145; denies supernatural agency, 147.

Drawing men to himself, how Christ does it, vii. 367.

Drawing, art of, x. 271; its relation to writing, 272; not a mere

F

1848—xx. 403; notice of the death of Drs. Green and Matthews, 404; right of church members to withdraw from the church, 408.; case of Rev. Dr. John Skinner, 413; overture on Temperance, 424; report on the Finances of the Boards, 432; report on Theological Seminaries, 443.

1849—xxi. 422; church music and a common periodical for the Boards, 423; resolutions on Christian union, 424; on the American Bible Society, 426; case of W. H. Marquis, 441; of J. Leroy Davis, 442; election of Dr. J. W. Alexander as Professor of Church History at Princeton, 447; memorials on slavery, 449; support of aged ministers, 450; overture on examination of ministers, 450; overture for a cheap weekly paper, 451; resolutions on preaching without notes, 453.

1850—xxii. 441; debate on cheap religious papers, 442; proposed modification of Board of Missions, 453; proposed modification of Board of Education, 461; act regarding church members removing without a certificate, 468; complaint of Rev. T. J. Smylie, 471; debate on Western Seminaries, 473; memorial of Presbytery of Ningpo on marriage of Christians with heathen, 476; ordination by only two ministers, 477; rule regarding principal and alternate delegates, 483.

1851—Case of Rev. Dr. Duncan McAuley, xxiii. 521; letter of Rev. Dr. McGill regarding his resignation of his professorship in Allegheny Seminary, 523; report on cheap papers, 526; letter of Dr. J. W. Alexander on cheap papers, 527; division of Synod of New Jersey, 528; missions to Papal lands, 529; Princeton Seminary, resignation of Dr. J. W. Alexander, and transfer of Dr. J. A. Alexander, 536; case of Mr. A. Stone, and appeal of Mr. Perkins from decision of Presbytery of Sangamon, 548; dismission of members to other churches, 550.

1852—xxiv. 462; sermon of Dr. Humphrey, 463; finances of the Assembly, 464; act in regard to Charleston Union Presbytery, 465; overture of Synod of New Jersey in regard to taking testimony, 467; reports of Boards, 468; discussion on cheap newspapers, 480; discussion on Princeton Seminary, 484; decease of Dr. Alexander, 485; election of Dr. Humphrey to that Seminary, 494; overture on reordination of Methodist elders and deacons, and on the rights of conscience, 497.

1853—xxv. 450; irregular commissions of delegates, 451; answer to overture on admission of those to the Lord's Supper who reject the doctrines of the Presbyterian church, 452; on right of sessions to dismiss members to no particular church; new standing committees, 453; address of Dr. Adamson of South Africa, 455; letter to Waldensian church, 459; reports of Boards, 461; reply of Dr. C. C. Jones to objections to the policy of the Domestic Board, 490; discussion on Union Theological Seminary of Virginia, 502; Danville, 506; election of Drs. Breckinridge, Humphrey, Palmer, and Gurley as professors in Danville, 516; of Dr. Boardman to Princeton, 517; Historical Society, 521; church in the city of

New Testament, 41; not composed out of secular documents, 48; the Bible of the patriarchal period, 57.

Geology, history of the science of, xiii. 368 ; sketch of, 370; relation of to the Bible, 384, xxiii. 164; its contributions to Christian evidences, xxiv. 147.

Geometry, analytical, its nature and value. xiii. 524; of the ancients, 526 ; great superiority of the modern, 536 ; the old Greek, excellence of, xxiii. 270 ; science of, objects of, xxxix. 308.

Gerhardt, Paul, notice of his hymns, xxii. 585.

German, philosophy, its aims, iv. 359 ; resemblance to that of the St. Simonians, 360 ; works on the interpretation of Scripture, v. 9 ; periodicals, ix. 103; theological seminaries, 205 ; ministerial qualifications, 210 ; modern philosophers, xi. 43; university education, or the professors and students of Germany, by W. C. Perry, xix. 336; comparison of with those of England, 341; the freedom of, 346 ; the advantages of, 351; Christianity of the last century, threefold conflict in, xxii. 354; theological writers, difference between them and English, 541; hymnology, 575; schools of idealism, xxiv. 261; grammar, how studied in Germany, xxv. 578; university life, curiosities of, xxvi. 33 ; grand elements of, 48 ; philosophy, described, xxviii. 351; consequences of, with reference to theology, 354; Reformed liturgy, account of, xxx. 182.

Germany, religious state of, xviii. 514; hymnology of, history of, xxii. 575 ; church music in Luther's time, 581; theology in, xxv. 430; history of, 434; Semler's influence, 435; the supernaturalists, 436; influence of Hegel and Schelling, 440 ; of De Wette, 442; Schleiermacher and his disciples, 443; Neander, 444; high Lutheran tendency, 446; Pietism, 448; high schools of, education in, xxv. 564; university life in, xxvi. 33.

Gervinus, doctrines of described, xviii. 522.

Gesenius, merits of, as a lexicographer, iv. 273; he does not recognize the inspiration of the Bible, 274; as a philologist, 570; his Hebrew Lexicon, translated by Robinson, ix. 88; personal character of, 89; his Hebrew Grammar, translated by Conant and Stuart, xix. 117·

Ghost-seeing, Swedenborg's law of, xl. 214.

Gibbon, value of his history, xxvii. 65.

Gibson, Bishop, on the instruction of slaves, xv. 25.

Gieseler, his theory of the origin of the Gospels, xx. 598; his Textbook on Church History, reviewed, xxix. 636.

Gilchrist, his scheme of an Indian alphabet described, x. 406.

Gillies, Dr. John, his character as a preacher and pastor, iv. 262.

Gillespie, Rev. Thomas, memoir of, xviii. 27.

Gilfillan, Rev. George, Bards of the Bible, reviewed, xxiv. 53; its exaggerated style, 57.

Gillett, Dr. E. H., Men and times of the Reunion of 1758, reviewed, xl. 608; his mistakes, 624.

Girard college, account of, xii. 245.

Grant, Dr. A., Nestòrians, or the Lost Tribes of Israel, reviewed, xiv. 59.

Grammar, of New Testament dialect, by Prof. Stuart, reviewed, vii. 233; Hebrew, by G. Bush, 341; Latin, laws of, xxiv. 399, 589; Persian, 697.

Graphics, or Manual of Drawing, by R. Peale, reviewed, x. 271.

Great schools of England, account of, xxxviii. 222.

Greece, observations on, by Dr. R. Anderson, iii. 333; history of, xxix. 52; effect of the Macedonian conquest on, 53; relations of the different states of to each other, 57; the rhetoricians and sophists of, in Socrates' time, xxxvi. 228; philosophy the ally of Christianity in, effect of this, 251; relations of with ancient India, xxxviii. 402; intellectual influence of, xxxix. 196.

Greek, and Roman Catholic, their mutual hatred, ii. 572; Christians, how to benefit them, iii. 348; language, its place and character when the New Testament was written, xi. 202; philosophy, notice of, xxiii. 625; geometry, excellence of, 207; mythology, xxiv. 224; language, methods of pronouncing, 583; xxvi. 588; money mentioned in the Bible, xxviii. 242; chevron in architecture, its use vindicated against Ruskin, 476; pediment described, 477; art, its laws, Ruskin's theory of, criticised, 484; prepositions, treatise on, by Prof. Harrison, criticised, xxx. 661; grammar, history of, 662; philosophy, introduction and influence of in Rome, xxxvi. 69; church, present state and government of, xxxix. 100.

Green, Dr. Ashbel, Lectures on Shorter Catechism, reviewed, ii. 297; Address to students in Theological Seminary at Princeton, iii. 350; Address to students on Literary diligence, v. 72; Address to students on Improvements in theology, vii. 529; history of missions, x. 335; notice of his death, xx. 403; memoir of, 404; autobiography of, xxi. 564.

Green River country revival, history of, vi. 337.

Gregory Nazianzen, memoir of, xxxix. 73; his relations to Basil, 84; account of his writings, 87.

Griffin, Dr. Edward D., memoir of, xi. 404; notice of his sermons, 414.

Griffin, George, Gospel its own Advocate, reviewed, xxii 484; his excellent answer to Hume and Gibbon. 485.

Grimm, W. and J., their German Dictionary, notice of, xxvi. 580.

Grindrod, R. B., Bacchus, Essay on Intemperance, reviewed, xiii. 267.

Griscom, Dr., Sanitary condition of the labouring classes in New York, reviewed, xvii. 617.

Grote, History of Greece, reviewed, xxix. 50.

Grotefend, how he decyphered the arrow-headed characters of Nineveh, xxvii. 110.

Guerin de, Eugenie and Maurice, account of, xxxvii. 545.

Guericke's Manual of church history, character of, vi. 412.

Guilt, meaning of the term, ii. 440; imputation of, the several distinct theories of, iii. 410; the word used sometimes in a moral and

53

J

K

source of all progress, 403; the laws of, 411; it has dominion over sin, 416.

King, Lord Chancellor, Constitution of the primitive church, reviewed, xvi. 1.

Kirk of Shotts, great revival at, account of, iv. 434.

Kirkland, Rev. Samuel, account of his labours among the Indians, xxii. 409.

Kirkpatrick, Edward, Historical conception of the University, with special reference to Oxford, reviewed, xxxv. 571.

Kleinert, on the Genuineness of Isaiah, v. 12.

Kliefoth, History of doctrine, xix. 101; divides it into four great periods arising out of the doctrinal problem to be solved, 102.

Knowledge, of God, necessity of in religion and morals, iii. 100; how to be communicated, 102; "is power," how far true, xiv. 223; the order in which the objects of are prepared, 290; and feeling their true relation in matters of religion, xxii. 670; of substance, Mills' theory of, xxviii. 99; reply to it, 101; Faith and Feeling in their mutual relations, xxxiii. 422; terms defined, 425; theories of faith, 430; Hamilton and Mansell's view of it, criticised, 438; the true view, 439; deductions from this view, 445.

Knox, John, the reformation introduced by him into Scotland, x. 362; character of him and his co-labourers, xv. 563; his relations with Calvin, xx. 292.

Knox, Dr. R., Races of men, worthlessness of the book exhibited, xxiii. 168.

Kœppen, The World in the Middle Ages, reviewed, xxvii. 62; causes of the fondness for those times, 63; plan of the author, 67.

Koran, Historical statements of, iv. 195; Sales' version of, 197; its account of the creation, 199; of genii, 200; apostasy of Iblis, 201; Cain and Abel, 202; Abraham, 203; Moses and Pharaoh, 209; John Baptist, 212; Jesus, 220; Tauchnitz edition of, viii. 61.

Kossuth, Louis, notice of, xxiv. 461.

Kurtz, History of the Old Covenant, xxiii. 451; his view of sacred history, 458; his divisions of it, 466; history of the Old Testament, xxviii. 173; design of Israel's residence in Egypt, 175; his theory of the date of it, 191; his account of Balaam, 203.

L

Lachman, Greek Testament, edition of, its character, v. 15; vi. 275.

Laing, Tour in Sweden in 1838, reviewed, xv. 143.

Lambeth, articles of, drawn up by Whitgift, notice of, xx. 391.

Lang, Dr. J. D., View of the origin and migration of Polynesian nations, reviewed, xiii. 54.

Lange, Commentary on Holy Scriptures, reviewed, xxxvi. 653; notice of the author, 655; plan of the work, 656.

Language, how far it is certain, xvii. 420; its lack of fulness and precision, 421; its Divine origin, xxii. 322; is it of human or Divine origin, xxiv. 407; Plato's view, 408; Gebelin's, 411; Rous-

intellect, xxvi. 223; how far it attaches to the affections and desires, xxviii. 510; ground of, Dr. M. Hopkins' view, xxxv. 13; no trace of sense of, in mere animals, 124; imperfect rights and—as related to church discipline, xxxviii. 94; distinction between perfect and imperfect, 97.

Objective properties of style defined, xxxviii. 541.

Obolos, the Greek, its original form and value, xxviii. 239.

Obookiah, of Sandwich islands, account of, xx. 507.

Occum, Samson, account of his labours, xxii. 399.

Octavius, first Roman emperor, notice of, xxxviii. 609.

Odd Fellows, order of, origin of, xxii. 48; its claims, 51.

Odo, the Realist, account of his conversion, xviii. 198.

Œcolampadius, memoir of, xxiii. 218; his relation with Erasmus, 228; his peculiar view of the sacraments, 230. '

Oehler, his view of the Old Testament, xxv. 118.

Offences, what kind cannot be made a bar to communion, xxxviii. 102.

Offor, George, his edition of Bunyan's works commended, xxxi. 232.

Oglethorpe, Governor of Georgia, notice of, xxxiv. 534.

Oken, his Elements of Physico-philosophy reviewed, xxxii. 35; the main dogma of the book, 38; atheistic tendency of his system, 45.

Old Bar of Philadelphia, notice of, xxxii. 642.

Old Dispensation, its relations to the new, xxiii. 635; two extreme views of, 640; a shadow of the new, 646; practical books of, how divided, xxix. 281; criterion of the permanency of its institutions, xxxi. 754.

Old Redstone Presbytery, history of, by Smith, xxx. 280.

Old Testament, genuineness and authenticity of, arguments for, ii. 327; canonical authority of, 334; why quotations in the New, sometimes vary from the original, iii. 11; evils resulting from the neglect of studying, xi. 213; proofs of its inspiration, xvii. 276; its relations to the New, xxiii. 451; rules for determining what parts are Messianic, 455; organic connection of its prophecy and history, 463; Christ the end of the whole of it, 465; its perpetual authority and use, 636, 638; MSS. of, found in China, xxiv. 249; theology of, importance of the systematic exhibition of, xxv. 107; errors of the rationalistic theory of, 111; Hegel's theory of the, 118; Oehler's, 119; three great prophecies pervading the, xxv. 296; contains four great divisions of sacred history, xxvi. 496; unity of, xxxi. 74; classification of the historical books of, xxxv. 500; their anonymous character, 502; their unity, 505; unity of its structure, xxxvii. 161; proofs of its organic structure, 165; method of investigating it, 171; consists of four parts, 177; how preparatory for the coming of Christ, 185.

Olevianus, the reformer, notice of, xxi. 79.

Olney hymns, description of them and of the parish, xxx. 68.

Oman, province of Arabia, account of, x. 183.

features of the age, 514; threefold requirements for, 520; the matter of, 532; the manner of, 541; to sinners, the proper aim of, xxxix. 616.

Predestination, doctrine of, prejudices against, iii. 155; consistent with man's freedom, 158; controversy regarding the doctrine of in the 9th century, account of, xii. 226; and free-will reconciled by the schoolmen, xviii. 210. (See *Decrees.*)

Predicate, quantification of, in logic, explained, xxvii. 591.

Preëstablished harmony of Leibnitz, doctrine of, xxx. 332.

Preëxistence, Dr. E. Beecher's theory of, xxvi. 96; his statement of intuitive truths, 100; his doctrine of depravity, 103; his theory of preëxistence, 109; his argument founded on the silence of Scripture, answered, 117; his intuitive principles criticised, 121; proof that his theory does not solve the great problem of sin, 127; it affords no relief from the difficulties attending the moral government of God, 131; it does not explain the origin of evil, 132.

Prejudice, power of, to resist argument, v. 78.

Prelacy. (See *Episcopacy.*)

Premunire, statute of, account of its origin and design, ix. 8.

Preparatory study for the ministry, necessity of, v. 67.

Presbyterian, ordination, invalidity of, Essay on, by Dr. J. E. Cooke, reviewed, ii. 38; his misrepresentation of Dr. Miller, 39; his theory that Timothy and Titus were diocesan bishops, refuted, 42; his imperfect acquaintance with the fathers, 52; his Letter to the Editors, 310; their reply, 311; government, radical principle of, iv. 28; development of in the primitive church, 30; church, state, and prospects of, vii. 55; how to promote purity and peace in the, 69; policy in regard to learning, 272; church, division of in 1837, account of, ix. 141; its separation from the Congregationalists, x. 244; church case, report of, xii. 92; government, defined, xvi. 276; ordination, validity of, defended, xix. 540; Historical Society, reasons for maintaining it, xxxiv. 584; colleges and high education, plea for, 635, 654; unity, plea and plan for, xxxvii. 53; arguments for, 55; objections to, considered, 62; plan of, 67; proper principles of, 271; reunion, reply to Dr. H. B. Smith's article on, xl. 53.

Presbyterianism, French, history of, xii. 71; in Virginia in the time of Davies, account of, 170; xx. 191, 198; what it is, xxxii. 546; Dr. Thornwell's theory of, 551; peculiarities of his theory, 559; Western, history of, xxxix. 169; its original clements, 173.

Presbyterians, and Independents of England, not the same, viii. 191; and the Congregationalists of the United States, difference between them, xxvii. 246; and Independents under Cromwell, xxxix. 641.

Presbyters, ordination by its validity recognized by the Archbishop of Canterbury, x. 371; how distinguished from ruling elders, xvi. 289; the primitive, exercised the highest offices of the ministry, xix. 540; their succession in Europe and America as certain as that of bishops, 564; primitive, their rank and official powers, xxi. 116;

Q

R

sympathy for the Vaudois, xxiii. 669; how they vindicated their call to the ministry, xxvi. 390; their writings mostly polemic, reasons for it, xxix. 643; their theology, xxxiv. 553; their views of the Sabbath, xxxv. 550.

Regeneration, and the manner of its occurrence, by Dr. S. H. Cox, a sermon, reviewed, ii. 250; he caricatures the doctrines of the old Calvinists, 253; his view of, 255; Charnock's, 256; Owen's, 257; Bates, 258; the divines of Holland and Germany, 259; in what sense old Calvinists held it to be physical, 261; Edwards's view, 268; Bellamy's, 269; Dwight's, 270; Dr. Cox's objections to the true doctrine, stated and answered, 274; Evidences of, vi. 353; sincere love to God as his character is revealed in Scripture, 355; fear of offending Him, 357; a purpose to glorify Him, 358; sincere love of the truth, 359; love of the brethren, 361; trust in God, and a good life, 363; Finney's theory of, vii. 508; his view of the Spirit's work in producing, the same in kind as that of the preacher, 524; practical view of, viii. 477; necessity of, 478; author of, 480; means of, 481; the beginning of, often obscure, 487; views and feelings of the regenerate variously modified, yet essentially the same, 489; Dr. Pusey's view that baptism is, xii. 577; Dr. N. W. Taylor's theory of, xiv. 5; High church theory of, 132; New and Old school views of, 145; President Davies's view of, 154; not a mere change of purpose, 160; Dr. Emmons's theory of, 558; Evidences of as laid down by President Edwards, xviii. 280; Bushnell's theory, 530; baptismal, how the doctrine of originated, xxi. 211; John Robinson's view of, xxix. 183; tests of, by Goodhue and Dr. Kirk, xxxii. 175.

Reichenbach, Baron, his experiments with corpse candles, xl. 301.

Reid, Dr. J. S., History of the Presbyterian church of Ireland, reviewed, xvi. 199.

Reid, Dr. Thomas, his works reviewed, xv. 527; his place among English philosophers, 242; value of his theory of Perception, xxix. 275.

Reign, of the Saints, or Puritans, in England, xvii. 3; of Law, by the Duke of Argyle, reviewed, xxxix. 526.

Rejection, the, of Christ by the Jewish rulers and people, causes of, xxxix. 126; they were a subject people, 131; the three leading sects, 133; their intense pride, 134; their misapprehension of the ceremonial law, 136; John's ministry, 139; they knew that our Lord claimed to be the Messiah, 142.

Rejoinder to the Princeton Review upon the Elohim Revealed, touching the doctrine of Imputation, by S. J. Baird, xxxii. 760.

Relation, the, between Holy Scriptures and geological science, xiii. 368; of religion to diseases of the mind, xxii. 1; of the old to the new dispensation, xxiii. 635; the logical, of religion and natural science, xxxii. 577; the mutual, of knowledge, faith, and feeling, xxxiii. 421; of the church and state, xxxv. 679; of India to Greece and Rome, xxxviii. 394; of the missionary cause to that of science and learning, 611.

Relief church, in Scotland, history of, xviii. 26.

Religion, advancement of society in, iii. 306; self-deception in matters of, 319; revivals of, lectures on, by Sprague, iv. 455; revivals of, importance of, vi. 109; state of in some countries of Europe, viii. 307; difficulties of, letters on, 515; decline of and its causes, by E. M. Johnson, ix. 588; of the Chinese, described, xi. 147; new scheme of in New England described by Pres. Clap, 389; state of among the Dissenters in Virginia, described by Davies, xii. 169; of the Bible, described by Dr. Skinner, xiii. 79; true, the appropriate means of promoting, xiv. 2; includes the body and the soul, 131; spiritual, is compatible with the observance of external forms, 136; authority of tradition in matters of, 598; pure, a national blessing, xv. 110; the Christian, history of by Neander, 604; and insanity, or its supposed connection with partial derangement of the mind, xvi. 352; the Christian, evidence of its truth, 459; in America, by Baird, xvii. 17; true, the spirit of is one, though forms vary, xviii. 275; practical, questions in discussed by Dewey, xix. 1; relation of to diseases of the mind, xxii. 1; object and aim of revealed, 3; of the gospel absorbs the whole man, 7; the world's, as contrasted with genuine Christianity, by Lady Colquhoun, xxiii. 559; of geology and its connected sciences, by Hitchcock, 703; spiritual and ceremonial, of forms, and of the Spirit, contrasted, xxv. 318; the Christian, divine origin and authority of by Dr. Neill, xxvi. 728; the logic of, xxvii. 395; Sidney Smith as a minister of, xxviii. 418; in America, by Baird, 642; in colleges, xxxi. 28; and natural science, their logical relations, xxxii. 577; relations of, to physical science, perplexities of, xxxviii. 345.

Religions, true and false, contrast between, by Dr. Sprague, ix. 524; of the world, in their relation to Christianity, by Maurice, xxvi. 196; of men, their points of diversity and agreement, xxviii. 629; the most opposite have points of analogy, 627; their relation to history, 631; their evidence of culture, 632; not stationary, 633.

Religious, knowledge, how gained, iii. 101; observance of Sabbath, benefits of, 105; prospects of France, 383; condition of Holland, v. 19; obligations of parents, vi. 172; excitement and bodily affections, 336; literature, in some countries of Europe, notice of, viii. 307; state of the country, thoughts on, by Colton, 390; liberty, is Romanism hostile to? ix. 238, 326, 487; instruction of negroes in the United States, by C. C. Jones, xv. 22; insanity, xvi. 352; lectures by Foster, notes of, 478; instruction of negroes, report on at Charleston, xvii. 590; consecration, its relation to holiness, xviii. 300; sentiment, expresses itself in various forms, 487; movement in Germany under Ronge, 514; instruction of negroes, suggestions on, by C. C. Jones, xx. 1; history of Sandwich Islands, 505; insanity, xxii. 1; practices and opinions of the Hindus, two lectures on, xxiii. 94; history of the Slavonic nations, 486; significance of numbers, xxv. 203; endowments, 545; education, two things of almost equal importance, communicating truth, and impressing the

60

S

be criticised like other books, 249; their inspiration, testimony of the Fathers to, xxiii. 387; supreme authority of, in matters of faith and conduct, testimonies of the Fathers to, xxiv. 643; study of, by the preacher, essential importance of, xxvii. 19; evidences of their Divine origin, two classes of, 405; Introduction to, by Horne, a new edition of, by Davidson, criticised, xxix. 375; the plenary inspiration of, by E. Lord, xxx. 180; xxxi. 151; the Divine Human in the, by Tayler Lewis, xxxii 172; historical evidence of the truth of, by G. Rawlinson, xxxii. 378; canon of, examined in the light of history, by Gaussen, xxxv. 171; the organic structure of the proofs of, xxxvii. 161; the inspiration of the, by Dr. Bannerman, 316; evil of the division of the, into chapters and verses, xl 482.

Seals, the apocalyptic, expounded, xix. 143; xxiv. 74; xxvi. 285.

Sears, Dr. Barnas, Classical studies, essays in, reviewed, xv. 369; Life of Luther, reviewed, xxii. 437; fitness of the author for his work, 439.

Sebastianists, a Romish sect in Brazil, account of, xvii. 377.

Seceders, the Scottish, history of their origin, vii 198.

Secession from the Union, the right of, arguments against, xxxiii. 27; the Southern, causes of, 635; history of, 640; the struggle of a false civilization for supremacy, xxxiv. 268; unjustifiable and a great crime, xxxvii. 631.

Second Advent, by the Rev. J. Fry, reviewed, ii. 9; the design and the time of, the only points in controversy, 13; sketch of the millenarian view of, 16; arguments in support of it, 21; arguments against that view, by Dr. D. Brown, xix. 564; bearing of the premillennial scheme of the, on the doctrine of the resurrection. 570; of the general judgment, 573; bearing of the premillennial scheme of the, on foreign missions, xxiii. 186; hostile to the spiritual nature of Christ's kingdom, 194; to the divinely appointed agency for the conversion of sinners, 198; the post-millennial theory advocated, by Waldegrave, xxviii. 537.

Secrecy, the principle of, in relation to man's moral and religious obligations, xxi. 533; what is implied in the love of it, 536; when is it lawful? 539; dangers of, 541.

Secret societies, arguments against, xxii. 42; of the middle ages, account of, 40; of modern times, 45; the earliest, their origin not Christian, but pagan, 57.

Sectarianism, what it is, viii. 501; its nature and the evils of, xii. 465; origin of, xvii. 632.

Sects, argument for the abolition of, by A. Van Dyke, reviewed, viii. 11; spirit of, now more rife than formerly, 36; evils and benefits of, 510; their relation to the church, xix. 303; folly of attempting their organic union on the basis of points on which they now agree, xl. 182.

Secular and spiritual persons, distinction between them as defined by Chrysostom, iv. 11.

Seed of the woman, what is meant by, iii. 274; of the serpent, 277.

U

V

65

W

INDEX TO SHORT NOTICES.

Allibone, Dictionary of English and American authors, xxxi. 167.

Ambassador of God, or the True Spirit of the Christian Ministry, by Rev. John W. Nevin, D. D., xiv. 631.

American Education, its principles and elements, by E D. Mansfield, xxiii. 179.

American Conflict, the. by H. Greeley, xxxviii. 671.

American Biographical Dictionary, by Dr. W. Allen, xxix. 552.

Anabasis of Xenophon, by John J. Owen, xv. 605.

Analogy as a Guide to truth, and an Aid to faith, by Dr. James Buchanan, Edinburgh, xxxix. 154.

Analogy of Religion, Natural and Revealed, by Bishop Butler, xviii. 610.

Analytic Orthography, by Prof. S. S Haldeman, xxxii. 570.

Ancient Church, the, its History for the first three centuries, by Dr. Killen, xxxi. 768.

Ancient Cities and Empires, their prophetic doom read in the light of history and modern research, by E. H. Gillet, xl. 156.

An Earnest Ministry the Want of Our Times, by J. A. James. xx. 496.

Anna Clayton, or the Inquirer after truth, by F. M. Dimmick, on the subject of Baptism, xxxi. 623.

Anglo-Germanism, Address at Marshall College, by Rev. Philip Schaff, xviii. 482.

Anglo-Saxon Language, the, by A. Campbell, xxii. 488.

Annals of the English Bible, by Christopher Anderson, xxii. 338.

Animals, History and Habits of, with special reference to American and those named in Scripture, by Peter Walker, xxxi. 778.

Annual Address before the Philosophical Society of Dickinson College, by Rev. T. V. Moore, xviii. 614.

Anticipations of Man in Nature, by Prof. Dana, Yale College, xxxi. 627.

Antichrist. by J. W. Niven, xx. 627.

Antiquities of the Christian Church, by Rev. Lyman Coleman, xiii. 463.

Apocalypse, the, New Theory of, by Rev. S. S. Ralston, xxxi. 167.

Apologetics of the Christian faith, by Dr. W. M. Hetherington, with an Introduction by Dr. A. Duff, xl. 149.

Apostacy of Mr. Newman, and some traces of Newmanism in New Jersey soil, by a Presbyterian, xviii. 185.

Apostolic Baptism, by C. Taylor, xv. 478.

Apostolic Confirmation. Reasons for discarding the Episcopal, by Rev. James M. Allen, xx. 493.

Apostolical Succession, by James Purviance, xvi. 315.

Apostolical and Primitive Church, Popular in its Government and simple in its worship, by Lyman Coleman, xviii. 465.

Appeal to the Churches on the support of Pastors, by a Hearer of the Word, xxv. 308.

Art, Scenery, and Philosophy in Europe, by H. B. Wallace, Esq., xxvii. 360.

Eloquence of the Pulpit; Oration delivered at Andover, by George
W. Bethune, xv. 173.
Eloquence a Virtue, from the German of Therimin, by Prof. Shedd,
xxxi. 622.
Eloquent Preachers, Sketches of, by Dr. J. B. Waterbury, xxxvii.
160.
Emblems, Divine and Moral, by F. Quarles, xxvi. 726.
Encouragements and Discouragements of the Christian Ministry, by
J. M. Lowrie, xxiv. 337.
Encyclopedia, Protestant, Theological, and Classical, by J. H. A.
Bomberger, xxviii. 593.
English Grammar, with history of the Language, by Prof. W. C.
Fowler, xxx. 394.
English Language in its Elements and Forms, by W. C. Fowler,
xxii. 674.
English Literature and Language, Critical History of, by G. L. Craik,
xxxvi. 186.
English Language, Elements of, by N. G. Clark, Union College,
xxxvi. 186.
English Literature of the Nineteenth Century, by C. D. Cleveland,
xxiii. 699.
Ephesians, Epistle to, Commentary on, by Dr. R. E. Patterson, xxxii.
171.
Episcopal Bishops the Successors of the Apostles, by Bishop Mc-
Crosky. xiv. 526.
Episcopal Doctrine of Apostolical Succession Examined, by William
S. Potts, D. D., xv. 606.
Epoch of Creation. The Scripture Doctrine contrasted with the
Geological Theory, by Eleazar Lord, xxiii. 696.
Errors in Theory, Practice, and Doctrine, a Sermon delivered before
the Synod of Geneva, by John C. Lord, xi. 146.
Errors of Romanism, by R. Whateley, D. D., xvi. 143.
Ethica, an Outline of Moral Science, by J. H. Stinson, xxxii. 782.
Ethical Discourses, by Bishop Butler, xxvii. 707.
Eulogy on the Life and Character of Rev. Dr. F. Rauch, by John
W. Nevin, D. D., xiii. 463.
Evarts, Jeremiah, Tribute to the Memory, by Gardiner Spring, D. D.,
iii. 586; Sermons on the Occasion of his Death, by Leonard
Woods, D. D., iii. 587.
Evenings with Jesus, by Rev. W. Jay, of Bath, xxix. 723.
Evenings with the Doctrines, by Dr. N. Adams, xxxiii. 377.
Evenings with the Prophets. Memoirs and Meditations, by Rev. A.
M. Brown, of Chiltenham, xxvii. 711.
Evidences of the Truth of the Christian Religion, from the literal
fulfilment of Prophecy, by Alexander Keith, D. D., xvi. 459.
Evil tendencies of Corporal Punishment as a means of moral dis-
cipline, Examined and Discussed, by Lyman Cobb, xix. 582.
Exclusive Claims of Prelacy, stated and refuted, by Rev. B. M.
Smith, xvi. 602.

History of Long Island from settlement to 1845, by N. S. Prime, xviii. 180.
History of New London, in Pennsylvania, Sermon by R. P. Dubois, xviii. 182.
History of the American Lutheran Church, by Earnest L. Hazelius, D. D., xix. 288.
History of the Bible, by John Fleetwood, xxvii. 546.
History of the Church of England to the Revolution of 1688, by Bishop Short, xvi. 133.
History of the Jesuits, by Alexander Duff, xviii. 180.
History of the German Reformed Church, Chambersburg, Pa. Also, a Sermon on the Covenant and its Blessings, by Rev. W. Wilson Bonnell, xvi. 603.
History of the Presbyterian Church in Jamaica, L. I., by J. M. Macdonald, xx. 127.
History of the Presbyterian Church in Mercersburg, by Thomas Creigh, xviii. 474.
History of the Reformation of the Sixteenth Century, by J. H. Merle d'Aubigné, xix. 135.
History of the Rise, Progress, Genius, and Character of American Presbyterianism; together with a Review of the Constitutional History of the Presbyterian Church in the United States of America, xii. 297.
History of Western New York and of the Presbyterian Church in that section, by Rev. J. S. Hotchkin, xx. 623.
Holy Bible, with Explanatory Notes and Marginal References, by Thomas Scott, xvi. 605.
Holy Scriptures, (O. T.) translated according to the Massoretic text, after the best Jewish authorities, by I. Leeser, xxvi. 589.
Homer, Iliad of, translated by the Earl of Derby, xxxvii. 518.
Homiletics, a Treatise on, by Dr. D. P. Kidder, xxxvi. 707.
Homilist, the, by E. House, xxxii. 575.
Hopkins, Rev. Mark, Sermon on the Death of Professor Ebenezer Kellog, xix. 132; Miscellaneous Essays and Discourses, xix. 579.
Horæ Solitariæ, by Ambrose Serle, Esq., xiv. 524.
Household Poems, by H. W. Longfellow, xxxvii. 164.
Huntington, Ezra A., Sermon at the dedication of Third Presbyterian Church in Albany, xviii. 183.
Huss, John, Life and Times of, by E. H. Gillett, xxxvi. 181.
Hypatia; or New Foes with an Old Face, by C. Kingsley, Jr., Rector of Eversley, xxvii. 365.

Identity of Judaism and Christianity, by Matthew R. Miller, xxiii. 167.
Igdrasil; or the Tree of Existence, by J. Callen, xxxi. 626.
Impenitent Dead, State of the, by Dr. A. Hovey, xxxi. 373.
Imperial Bible Dictionary, edited by Dr. Patrick Fairbairn, xl. 476.
Importance of Religion to the Legal Profession, by Dr. H. A. Boardman, xxii. 170.

Johnston, J. R., Discourse at opening of the Synod of New York in Brooklyn, xviii. 190.
Journal of Prison Discipline and Philanthropy, xvii. 350.
Junkin, D. X. The Oath a Divine Ordinance, xviii. 176.
Junkin, Dr. George, two Addresses on occasion of his Inauguration as President of Miami University, xiv. 170.
Justification by Faith, by Lyman H. Atwater, xxiii. 706.
Justification by Faith, by Rev. J. F. Stearns, D. D., xxv. 147.
Justification, Sermon by Rev. T. S. Childs, Hartford, xxxiii. 753
Juvenile Songs, by Thomas Hastings, xiv. 175.

Key to the Gospels, for Sunday-school teachers and Bible classes, by I. S. Spencer, iv. 134.
Kings, Book of, Commentary on by Keil, translated by Dr. Murphy, xxx. 395.
Kitto, D.D., John. The Lost Senses; Deafness and Blindness, xxiv.514.

Land, the, and the Book, by Dr. W. M. Thomson, xxxi. 168.
Land of the Forum and the Vatican, by Newman Hall, xxvii. 164.
Last Day of our Lord's Passion, by Dr. W. Hanna, xxxv. 173.
Latin Grammar, Practical, by G. J. Adler, xxx. 578.
Law and Testimony, the, by the author of the "Wide, Wide World," xxv. 687.
Lawfulness of Marrying the sister of a deceased wife, by Rev. Parsons Cooke, xv. 182.
Law of God as contained in the Ten Commandments, explained and enforced, by Dr. W. S. Plumer, xxxvii. 318.
Lectures on Divinity, by George Hill, D. D., xv. 176.
Lectures on Shakespeare, by H. R. Hudson, xx. 501.
Lectures on the Causes, Principles, and Results of the British Reformation, by Bishop Hopkins, xvi. 312.
Lectures on Church Government, by Leonard Woods, D. D., xvi. 462.
Lectures on the Hebrews, by J. A. Seiss, xix. 128.
Lectures on Spiritual Christianity, by Isaac Taylor, xiii. 603.
Lectures upon the History of our Lord, by Rev. H. Blunt, xxii. 601.
Leighton, Bishop, whole Works of, by J. N. Pearson; notice of, xxxi. 382.
Leila Ada, the Jewish Convert, by O. W. T. Heighway, xxvi. 728.
Lessons from the Great Biography, by Dr. J. Hamilton, London, xxix. 724.
Letter to Bishop Potter, in vindication of the principles of Christian Union, xxiii. 167.
Letters and Papers of the late Theodosia, Viscountess Powerscourt, by Rev. R. Daly, D. D., xxii. 675.
Letters by William Romaine, xviii. 468.
Letters on Practical Subjects, to a Daughter, by W. B. Sprague, iii. 588.
Letters on the Early History of the Presbyterian Church in America, to Rev. Robert M. Laird, by Irving Spencer, Esq., x. 322.

Odyssey of Homer, by J. J. Owen, xvii. 344.

Office and Work of the Holy Spirit, by Buchannan, xix. 590.

Old Age; Sermon on the occasion of the death of Joseph Nourse, by Cortlandt Van Rensselaer; Notice of his Life, xiv. 173.

Old and New Theology; or an Exhibition of those differences with regard to Scripture Doctrine which have divided the Presbyterian Church, by James Wood, xi. 145; xxviii. 164.

Old and New; or Changes of Thirty years in the East, xxv. 531.

Old Chest and its Treasures, by Aunt Elizabeth; Anecdotes illustrative of Christian Truth, xxix. 550.

Old Faith, and the Good Way. An Expose of the Doctrine and Discipline of the Presbyterian Church, or the difference between the New and the Old School, by a Committee of the late Caledonia Presbytery, xv. 165.

Old Red Sandstone, by Hugh Miller, xxiii. 349.

Old Sights with New Eyes, by a Yankee, with an Introduction by R. Baird, D. D., xxvi. 201.

"O Mother Dear Jerusalem," History of the Hymn, by W. C. Prime, xxxvii. 318.

On both Sides of the Sea, a Story of the Commonwealth, xl. 156.

One Faith, or Bishop Doane vs. Bishop McIlvaine on Oxford Theology, xv. 472.

Onesimus, or the Apostolic Directions to Christian Masters, in reference to their Slaves, by Evangelicus, xiv. 182.

Our Country, its Trials and Triumphs, by Dr. G. Peck, xxxvii. 663.

Our Friends in Heaven, by Rev. J. M. Killen. xxix. 546.

Our National Preëminence and its True Source; Thanksgiving Sermon, by Willis Lord, D. D., xx. 315.

Outline of the Work of Grace in the Presbyterian Congregation at New Brunswick, N. J., in 1837, by Joseph H. Jones, xi. 451.

Outlines of English Literature, by Thomas B Shaw, xxi. 458.

Owen, Dr., on Temptation and the Mortification of Sin in Believers, xxvii. 708.

Owen Gladden's Wanderings in the Isle of Wight, by Old Humphrey, xviii. 602.

Paley's Evidences of Christianity, by C. M. Nairue, xxvii. 163.

Pantology; or a Systematic Survey of Human Knowledge, by Roswell Park, xiv. 174.

Papal Conspiracy Exposed, by Rev. E. Beecher, D. D., xxvii. 167.

Papism in the XIXth Century, in the United States, by Robert Breckinridge, xiii. 312.

Paradise Lost, by John Milton, with Notes. Edited by Rev. James Boyd, xxiii. 178.

Parish Papers, by Dr. N. McLeod, Glasgow, xxxv. 175.

Parity, the Scriptural Order of the Ministry; a Sermon by the Rev. G. A. Baxter, D. D , xiii. 312.

Particular Providence, in distinction from General, necessary to the fulfilment of the purposes and promises of God, by W. R. Gordon, D. D., xxix. 155.

Party Spirit and Popery, by an American Citizen, xix. 587.

Past, Present and Future, by H. C. Carey, xx. 322.

Warren, D. D., Joseph. Fifteen Years of Missionary Life in Northern India. xxviii. 592.

Waterbury, J. B. A Book for the Sabbath, xviii. 189; Considerations for Young Men—Who are the Happy? xxiv. 341.

Water Drops, by Mrs. Sigourney, xx. 128.

Weygand's Conversations Lexicon, xxiv. 505.

Webster's Edition of the Bible, x. 324.

Western Africa, by Rev. J. L. Wilson, xxviii. 741.

What is Calvinism? by W. D. Smith, D. D., xxvii. 170.

What makes a Church a Bethel? a Sermon by N. Murray, D.D., xv. 166.

White, Rev. Hugh. Reflections on the Second Advent, xv. 478; The Believer, xvi. 136.

William Tell and other Poems, from the German of Schiller, by William Peter, A. M., xii. 605.

Williams, Rev. W. R. Miscellanies by, xxii. 338.

Winchester, Rev. S. G. The Theatre. xiii. 469.

Wines, E. C. Hints on Popular Education, x. 510; How shall I govern my School? x. 510.

Winslow, Octavius. The Inquirer directed, xiii. 156; Personal Declensions and Revivals of Religion in the Soul, xix. 284.

Wolff, Rev. Joseph. Researches and Missionary Labours among Jews, Mohammedans, and other Sects, x. 151.

Woods, Dr. Leonard. The Minister wholly in his work, xii. 166; Works of, xxii. 168.

Works of Thomas Boston, by Rev. A. S. Patterson, xxvii 710.

Works of Joseph Butler, Bishop of Durham, by Samuel Halifax, Bishop of Gloucester, xiv. 528.

Works of Matthew Henry, xxvii. 554.

Works and Life of Mrs. Hooker, xiii. 309.

Works of Rev. H. Scougal; with his Funeral Sermon, by Rev. Dr. Gairden. xviii. 187.

World's Religion, the, as contrasted with genuine Christianity, by Lady Colquhoun, xvii. 353.

Yeomans, John W. Address before the Brainard Evangelical Society, x. 510; Sermon delivered at the Dedication of the Presbyterian Church in Trenton, N. J., xii. 297; Address delivered on occasion of his Inauguration as President of Lafayette College, xiv. 172.

Young Christian's Guide, by Rev. James Eells, xviii. 466.

Young, God's Message to the, by Dr. G. W. Leyburn, xxx. 183.

THE END.